WATFIV:

FORTRAN PROGRAMMING WITH THE WATFIV COMPILER

John B. Moore

RESTON PUBLISHING COMPANY, INC., Reston, Virginia 22090

A Prentice-Hall Company

Library of Congress Cataloging in Publication Data

Moore, John B   1942-
    WATFIV.

    Includes index.
    1. FORTRAN (Computer program language)
2. Compiling (Electronic computers)   I. Title
QA76.73.F25M66   001.6'424   74-28053
ISBN 0-87909-876-7

© 1975 by

RESTON PUBLISHING COMPANY, INC.

A Prentice-Hall Company

Box 547

Reston, Virginia 22090

10 9 8 7 6 5 4 3 2

Printed in the United States of America.

Fortran is a widely used language for writing computer programs. Although it lacks the conciseness and power of some newer programming languages, it has attributes which make it very suitable for solving a wide variety of mathematical and scientific problems. Two Fortran compilers were developed at the University of Waterloo called WATFOR and WATFIV. The features of these compilers make them very suitable for processing large numbers of small Fortran programs. Currently, more than two-hundred educational and commercial organizations are using the WATFIV compiler. In 1974 an extension of WATFIV known as WATFIV-S or structured WATFIV was made available. WATFIV-S contains several language constructs not present in WATFIV.

The purpose of this book is to provide a comprehensive description of the WATFIV language (the Fortran language processed by the WATFIV compiler). Although there are several hundred Fortran texts on the market, I feel this book is the most complete book on the subject yet published.

The book is designed for use both as a text and a reference. It assumes no previous knowledge of computers or computer programming on the part of the reader. Examples and problems in the book are not oriented to any particular academic discipline.

The content is organized into four parts. Part I describes the statements in the language which define and manipulate fixed-point and floating-point values. In Part I, the output device is always a printer, the input device, always a card reader. Unlike most programming texts which present new topics in the sequence: "Here's another statement in the language."; "Here's how it is used."; "Here's some examples.", the approach taken in this book is: "Here's what we are trying to do."; "Here's how we could do it using our existing knowledge."; "Here's an easier way of doing it.". In other words, the approach is to present the language in terms of purpose or function.

Part II describes the use of non-INTEGER, non-REAL values. Chapter 10 presents the concepts. Chapters 11 thru 15 each deal with a specific type of value. Chapter 16 concludes Part II with a summary of the rules for statements which may contain references to more than one type of value.

Part III describes the non-card input, non-printer output features of the language. Separate chapters describe

v

punched output, magnetic tape input-output, direct access input-output, and simulated input-output using CHARACTER variables. Two chapters describing NAMELIST input-output and binary READ-WRITE statements conclude Part III.

Part IV contains ten appendices. Aside from the standard topics usually found in programming texts, there are: hints for program "debugging" and efficiency (Appendix G); a comparison of the Fortran language processed by the WATFIV compiler and that processed by the IBM Fortran compilers (Appendix F). Flowcharting conventions and symbols are described in Appendix B. Flowcharts are not used in the body of the text because of the simple logic required to solve the example problems. Features of WATFIV-S are described in Appendix J.

The text does not contain a description of how computers work. Many suitable books are available to the teacher who wishes to present these topics in parallel with a course on Fortran programming.

Use as a text. Because of the detailed nature of the explanations and example problems, the text can be used in a self-study environment. It is also appropriate for a one or two semester course. At Waterloo, first year students cover the material in Parts I and II in twenty-five lecture hours. They have an additional twenty-five hours of laboratory time during which tutorial help is available for assisting them with their assignments. Topics in Part I which are marked with an asterisk are omitted in this one semester course. The approach taken in lecture periods is to present one or two programming problems, introducing new language features as needed, but leaving the student to learn the details of the new statements on his own. More than five-hundred-and-fifty exercise, drill-type questions are included in the text. These provide the student with the opportunity for intensive practice on specific features of the language.

Use as a reference. Most introductory texts are unsuitable as a reference because the content is organized so that so-called "advanced" topics are presented toward the end of the book or as part of an appendix. This means that information on a particular topic may be found in two or more places thus necessitating much page-flipping and searching to find the required information. The fragmentation of topics is not present in this book.

The text material was prepared, modified and printed using IBM's ATS text editing system. Since I personally prepared and entered the text material, I must accept responsibility for any errors present. My apologies for any inconvenience they may cause.

I would like to acknowledge the contribution of the Department of Applied Analysis and Computer Science at the University of Waterloo -- the developers of the WATFIV compiler. Thanks are also due to Ray Bryars and Ron Clifton, two Engineering students, who programmed the example problems, did all the exercise questions and corrected many errors. The first year students who used earlier drafts of the manuscript are to be congratulated for their patience, thanked for their helpful suggestions, and incidentally, were rewarded financially for each error found.

To you the reader, I hope that you will find this a useful and enjoyable book. I have tried to keep your needs in mind from start to finish.

Waterloo, Ontario, Canada   John B. Moore

TO MY PARENTS

Preface To The Student

This is a book that teaches you how to speak a language -- a language which permits you to use a computer to perform the numerical calculations necessary to solve problems. The language is one member of the Fortran family of languages. It was developed at the University of Waterloo to make using a computer easy for students. Some of you will learn to speak the language well -- others just enough to get by or to solve a specific problem. In either case, I hope you enjoy the learning experience. The more exercises and programming problems you do, the more fluent you will be in the use of the language. Good luck and good programming.

CONTENTS

Contents (continued)

Contents (continued)

Contents (continued)

Contents (continued)

Contents (continued)

Contents (continued)

PART I

THE STATEMENTS
IN THE LANGUAGE

CHAPTER 1   SO YOU WANT TO USE A COMPUTER

Questions Answered In Chapter 1.

   1. What can a computer do?

   2. If that's all it can do, why do we use them?

   3. What steps are necessary to solve a problem
        using a computer?

   4. O.K. - How about an example?

   5. What happens if an error is made?

1.1   What Can A Computer Do?

     Computers are attributed with many remarkable powers.
However, all computers, whether they are the large ones
which control the space flights or ones that look more like
a desk-top calculator, are simply collections of electronic
components which have three basic capabilities.

     First: Every computer has circuits which can do
arithmetic. What kinds of arithmetic can be done? There
are circuits for performing the following five kinds of
arithmetic operations: + - * / **. That is: addition,
subtraction, multipication, division, and exponentiation.
The asterisk or star symbol "*" is used to indicate
multiplication to avoid any confusion with the letter X
which we often like to use as a variable. The "/" symbol
for division should cause no problem since we often write
fractions such a three-sevenths as 3/7. The double
asterisk "**" is used to describe the operation of
exponentiation (raising a number to a power). For example,
two-to-the-fifth is written as 2**5.

     Second: Every computer has a means of communicating with
you and me. After all, if we couldn't put numbers in and
get results back, these machines wouldn't be much use, would
they? The most common method of inputting information is to
use "punched cards". By using a machine called a keypunch
which resembles a big typewriter, we can put holes in a
card. Each different letter or symbol has its own unique
little pattern of holes. Although the keypunch machine
prints a line across the top of the card showing the symbols
corresponding to the holes punched below them, with a little
practice, you can learn to "read the holes". Fortunately
this ability is not necessary to successfully use computers.

The computer's input device, called a card reader, reads the holes punched in the card using a set of wire brushes which close a circuit when a hole is detected.

For outputting information, the most common computer device is a printer. Small hammers push the paper into type slugs which are located on a rapidly rotating chain. This chain contains a large number of slugs, one (or more) for each of the symbols which can be printed.

Third: Computers have circuits which can make decisions. The kinds of decisions which computer circuits can make are not of the type: "Who would win a war between Russia and China?", or "What is the largest city in North America?". Unfortunately, the computer can only decide three things, namely: Is one number less than another; Are two numbers equal; and, Is one number greater than another.

Since all computers have only these three limited capabilities -- simple arithmetic, input-output, and trivial decision-making, it is only natural to ask the following question.

1.2 Why Do We Use Them?

There are perhaps three good reasons why we use these machines in spite of their limited capabilities.

1. Speed. Computers are capable of doing all three things (arithmetic, input-output, decision-making) at tremendous speeds. For example, a very powerful machine can do as many as $20*10**6$ additions per second. By the way, if you thought this value might be 64000000000000 instead of twenty-million, you can look ahead to Section 1 of Chapter 2 to find out why it can only be twenty-million. To gain some appreciation of this speed, it would probably take you or I (working a 40 hour week) about seventeen years to do this many additions. Speeds for doing other types of arithmetic and decision-making are comparable to that for addition. Input and output operations however, involve mechanical motion of cards and paper and hence the speeds for these operations are much slower. On a typical computer system, cards are read at about 1000 cards per minute and lines are printed at an average speed of 1000 lines per minute.

2. Accuracy and Reliability. In spite of newspaper headlines such as "Computer Fails Student", these machines are very accurate and reliable -- especially when you consider the number of operations they can perform every second. Because they are man-made machines they do occasionally break down and have to be repaired. However the mistakes that are made are almost always due to the people who use them, you and I.

4

3. A <u>Big   Problem = A Set Of Little Problems</u>. The most
important reason computers are so widely used today is that
almost all big problems can be solved by solving a bunch of
little problems -- one after the other. Moreover, solutions
to these little problems can be obtained using the very
limited capabilities possessed by all computers.   For
example, the problem of producing the federal civil service
payroll is indeed a big problem. But to solve that problem
we need only do the following kinds of things for each
employee on the payroll. First: Input information about the
employee such as his wage rate, hours worked, tax rate, past
pension deductions, etc. Second: Do some simple arithmetic
and decision making. Third: Output a few printed lines on a
cheque. By repeating this process over and over again   the
payroll will eventually be finished. Since computers can do
all these things accurately and at high speeds, the reason
for using them is obvious.

Having seen what these machines can do and having stated
the reasons for using them, let's find out what steps are
necessary to have them assist us in solving a problem.

1.3   What Steps Are Necessary To Use A Computer To
Solve A Problem?

There are five steps which must be followed before a
computer can be used to solve a problem.

Step 1. Define the problem. Unless the problem is well-
     defined there is no sense in even thinking about using a
     computer to help solve it. The people who get paid the
     highest salaries in the data processing business are
     those who are trying to answer the question: "What,
     precisely, is it that we want to use the computer to
     do?". Glib answers such as "do inventory control" are no
     good. The problem must be well defined.   Before you
     write any program, ask yourself: "Do I know exactly what
     the problem is?".

Step 2. Develop a procedure for solving the problem. A word
     which means "a procedure for solving a problem" is
     algorithm.   The algorithm takes the form of a sequence
     of instructions which, if followed by a moron, will
     solve the problem. There are several different ways of
     describing an algorithm.   One method is called
     flowcharting and is described in Appendix B. This
     second step is the key to using a computer successfully.
     You should closely study the example algorithms
     presented later in the chapter and try to develop
     algorithms for all the problems suggested in the
     exercises. If you can determine a procedure for solving
     a problem, 'programming' is easy.

Step 3. Translate the steps in the algorithm into a language which the computer understands. The set of instructions in the new language is called a computer program. There are literally hundreds of languages which can be "understood" by a computer. The language described in this book is called WATFIV. This language is widely used in North America for describing algorithms which frequently solve problems of a scientific or mathematical nature. Although we may think of the computer as being able to understand WATFIV, all computers actually understand only one language which is made up of long strings of ones and zeros. Some of these strings represent instructions, others represent the data or numbers which are manipulated according to the instructions. The "thing" that performs the translation of the WATFIV language statements into machine language (the ones and zeros), is called a compiler. More will be said about the compiler when we come to Step 5.

Step 4. Keypunch the program. Once the procedure for solving the problem has been written in a language the computer understands, it is necessary to punch this information into cards which will then be input into the computer via the card reader. Information about punched cards and keypunches can be found in Appendix A. Rules for "where things go" on the cards will be given later in this chapter. The set of cards produced is called a source deck . As well as the cards which contain the instructions in the program, two special cards are required -- one at the beginning called the JOB card, and one at the end called the ENTRY card. These cards are used to separate your source deck from other source decks.

Step 5. Run the job. The final step is to have the computer perform the calculations which are necessary to solve the problem. This is accomplished by giving the deck of cards to the computer operator who puts the deck in the card reader and presses a button which causes the cards to be read into the memory of the computer.

Running a job is a two-stage process. As mentioned previously, the instructions and numbers in your program must first be translated into bits (ones and zeros) by a compiler. This compiler is already "inside" the computer at the time your deck is being entered via the card reader. The cards in your deck are read in under the control of the compiler. As each card is read, the information punched in the card is analyzed and translated into the appropriate strings of ones and zeros. As well as producing the required bit strings, the compiler also outputs a line on the printer showing the information punched in the card and messages regarding any errors detected. The interval during which this translation process takes place is called the compile time of the job.

The second stage of running a job is to have the computer actually perform the calculations described in the program. The order and type of calculations performed are those defined by the strings of ones and zeros (the machine language program) produced by the compiler. The interval during which the calculations specified by the program are being done is called the execution time of the job. Any error such as dividing by zero which occurs during the execution time of the job causes the execution to be stopped and an error message to be printed. The two stages which occur when any WATFIV job is run are shown in the following diagram.

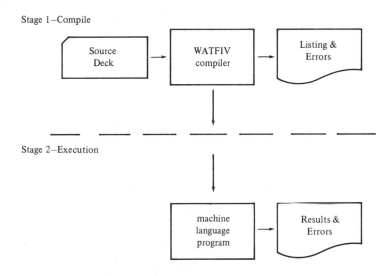

Stage 1—Compile

Source Deck → WATFIV compiler → Listing & Errors

Stage 2—Execution

machine language program → Results & Errors

7

1.4 O.K. -- How About An Example?

Step 1. Problem Definition.

For each value of x=0,1,2,...,9,10, calculate the corresponding value of y using the formula:

$$y = \frac{x^2 - x + 2}{x + 3}$$

Hopefully this is a well-defined problem. We are to take each of the eleven different values of x and produce the eleven corresponding values of y using the given formula.

Step 2. Develop a procedure for solving the problem.

One procedure which would solve the problem is shown below.

Algorithm A

```
 1. Set x = 0
 2. Calculate y using the formula
 3. Write down the values of x and y
 4. Set x = 1
 5. Calculate y using the formula
 6. Write down the values of x and y
 7. Set x = 2
 8. ...
 9. ...
    ...
31. Set x = 10
32. Calculate y using the formula
33. Write down the values of x and y
34. Stop
```

If a robot were to follow this set of instructions, one after the other, the required eleven pairs of values of x and y would be produced. Using this algorithm, each step in the algorithm is executed once. Observe that any algorithm which solves the problem will require a minimum of thirty-four instructions to be executed. Is this a good algorithm? In one sense it is the best because by using this algorithm the minimum number of steps necessary to solve the problem will be executed. Suppose, however, the problem required us to use values of x=0,1,2,...,9999,10000. The algorithm would then contain 30004 instructions! The disadvantage of Algorithm A, then, is due to fact that three instructions must be written down for every value of x used. Furthermore, two of these three instructions are the same regardless of the value of x. Is there any way we could avoid writing the pair of instructions:

Calculate y using the formula
Write down the values of x and y

over and over again? Since instructions 5 and 6 are the
same as 2 and 3, suppose we replace statement 5 with an
instruction to go back to step 2 and carry on from
there. The algorithm would then look like:

    1. Set x = 0
    2. Calculate y using the formula
    3. Write down the values of x and y
    4. Set x = 1
    5. Go to step 2 and carry on

Does this algorithm solve the problem? To find out we
need only act like a robot and follow the instructions.
The successive values taken on by x and y are shown
below.

x	y
0 (step 1)	2/3 (step 2)
1 (step 4)	1/2 (step 2)
1 (step 4)	1/2 (step 2)
1 (step 4)	1/2 (step 2)
.	.
.	.

Clearly this algorithm does not solve the problem since
x never gets larger than one. Because we want each value
of x to be one larger than the previous value, we should
change the 4th instruction to "add 1 to the value of x".
Making this change the algorithm appears as:

    1. Set x = 0
    2. Calculate y using the formula
    3. Write down the values of x and y
    4. Add 1 to the value of x
    5. Go to step 2 and carry on

Does this algorithm solve the problem? If we played
robot again we would soon realize that x will become
indefinitely large. That is, the algorithm is such that
every time we get to step 4, we go back to step 2 and
there is no way of stopping . Since we only want to use
values of x which are less than or equal to ten, we
should make a test to determine if each new value of x
we generate satisfies this requirement. If it does,
then we should calculate y for the value of x and carry
on. If not, then we should stop. The revised algorithm
is therefore:

Algorithm B

1. Set x = 0

2. Calculate y using the formula

3. Write down the values of x and y

4. Add 1 to the value of x

5. If x ≤ 10 go to step 2 and carry on

6. Stop

You should satisfy yourself that this algorithm will indeed solve the problem by performing the instructions in a robot-like manner. While doing this, count the number of times you execute each instruction. By adding these counts you can find the total number of instructions which must be executed to solve the problem using this algorithm. The counts you should obtain are: Step 1 - 1 time; Steps 2 thru 5 - 11 times each; Step 6 - 1 time. This means that a total of 46 instructions must be carried out if Algorithm B is used to solve the problem. Recall that Algorithm A on the other hand only required that 34 instructions be executed to solve the problem. However, to describe Algorithm A we had to write down all 34 instructions, whereas to describe Algorithm B we only had to write down 6 instructions. Looking ahead and realizing that these instructions will be executed by a high-speed computer which can execute hundreds of thousands of instructions every second, the difference in execution times of the two algorithms becomes insignificant, (certainly less than 1/1000th of a second). For this reason and for several others which will become apparent shortly, almost all algorithms are written using the type B approach instead of the "brute force" method of Algorithm A. Algorithms such as B possess a "looping" or "iterative" property. With a little practice , you will find it easy to think "iteratively".

A flowchart is a picture of an algorithm. Different shapes of symbols are used to represent different types of steps in the procedure. A flowchart of the algorithm would look like the following.

Flowchart Of Algorithm B

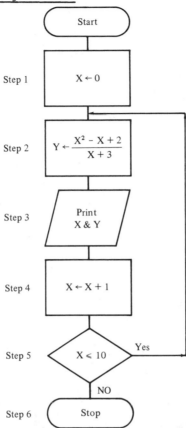

Step 1 $X \leftarrow 0$

Step 2 $Y \leftarrow \dfrac{X^2 - X + 2}{X + 3}$

Step 3   Print X & Y

Step 4 $X \leftarrow X + 1$

Step 5 $X \leqslant 10$

Step 6   Stop

Most of the algorithms you will use to solve problems in the first part of this book are simple enough that the steps in the algorithm can be written using English-like statements as we have done in this example. For algorithms which involve a number of interrelated decisions, a flowchart is often a real help in seeing the solution procedure.

Step 4. Translate the Algorithm Into WATFIV.

Shown below are the steps in the algorithm and the results of translating the steps into WATFIV to produce a WATFIV program. Each line on the right represents what would be punched into a single card.

Algorithm	WATFIV Program

```
                                    $JOB    WATFIV

                                    C   EXAMPLE PROGRAM 1

1. Set x = 0                            X=0.

2. Calculate y using formula        94  Y=(X**2-X+2.)/(X+3.)

3. Print values of x and y              PRINT,X,Y

4. Add 1 to x                           X=X+1.

5. If x≤ 10. go to step 2               IF(X.LE.10.) GO TO 94

6. Stop                                 STOP

                                        END

                                    $ENTRY
```

Let's see how each of the six steps in the algorithm has been translated into WATFIV.

i) The translation of step 1 is straightforward. To assign X a value of zero, we simply write "X=0.".

ii) The translation of step 2 (aside from the "94") shows that arithmetic expressions are written according to the conventional rules of arithmetic.

iii) The translation of step 3 is also straightforward. Note that PRINT,X,Y means print the <u>value</u> <u>of</u> <u>the</u> <u>variables</u> X and Y. It does not mean print the symbol 'X' and the symbol 'Y'.

iv) The translation of step 4 looks a little weird at first. It should be interpreted in the following way. Evaluate the expression on the right hand side of the equal sign and assign that value to the variable on the left hand side of the equal sign. Statements such as these are called "Assignment" statements. An Assignment statement is used to assign a value to a variable. It is the most frequently used type of statement in almost all WATFIV programs. In this example program, three of the first four statements are Assignment statements.

v) The translation of step 5 needs some comment. We are attempting to find out whether x 10 is true or not. In WATFIV, the condition to be tested for truthfulness is enclosed in a pair of brackets.

The symbols ".LE." are the translation of $\leq$ and these symbols indicate the kind of relationship to be tested. There are a total of six types of relationships which can be tested. These are:

.LE. less than or equal to
.LT. less than
.GE. greater than or equal to
.GT. greater than
.EQ. equal to
.NE. not equal to

In the IF statement the word "then" is not translated but is understood to be present following the right bracket. The "go to step 2 and carry on" becomes "GO TO 94". Instead of 94 we could have used any number from 1 thru 99999 provided the same number was put beside the statement which was the translation of step 2 of the algorithm. Thus "GO TO 94" means "get the next instruction at the statement identified by a 94 and carry on".

vi) The meaning of "STOP" in WATFIV is simply to stop executing any more instructions. It is used to indicate the job has been finished.

What of the other four lines in the program which are not translations of any step in the algorithm? These are:

    $JOB   WATFIV
    $ENTRY
    C EXAMPLE PROGRAM 1
    END

i) The "$JOB WATFIV" statement indicates that the program has been written in the WATFIV language instead of some other programming language.

ii) The "$ENTRY" statement follows the last statement of every WATFIV program. The $JOB and $ENTRY cards (they are written here but the information will subsequently be punched into cards), are called job control cards. Both must be present in every WATFIV program you write.

iii) The second line of the program, namely

        C EXAMPLE PROGRAM 1

is called a comment and is identified by a "C" in the first position. Comments can be included anywhere in a program and their purpose is simply to make remarks which can be helpful to understanding or identifying the program. Good programmers generally use a lot of comments, especially in very large programs which may contain thousands of statements.

iv) The "END" statement is also included in every program. Unlike the $ENTRY statement however, there may be more than one END statement in a program. This occurs if programs are written in pieces or segments. In such cases, an END statement is used to end each segment. For the time being however, we will only be writing programs which require one END statement and we should automatically place it ahead of the $ENTRY statement.

A couple of small points about the program. You will have noticed that capital letters have been used when writing the statements in the program. Most keypunches only contain symbols for the capital letters. This is fortunate since using small letters in WATFIV will produce error messages. You must <u>always</u> use upper case letters. The second point concerns whether or not it is necessary to use a decimal point after numbers such as 2, 10, etc. A complete answer will be given in Chapter 2. For the work in this Chapter, no problems will arise if decimal points <u>are</u> used when writing numbers used in a program.

Step 5. Keypunch the program.

Each line in the program is punched on a single card. A punched card contains enough room to punch 80 symbols -- one in each of the eighty columns of the card. The hole pattern for each symbol appears directly underneath it. Shown below are the symbols appearing in each column of the cards in the program.

```
              one        ten       twenty     thirty
               ↓          ↓          ↓          ↓
card        ⎧  0          1          2          3
columns     ⎨  12345678901234567890123456789012345678 9
```

```
        $JOB    WATFIV  acct.# your name
        C EXAMPLE PROGRAM 1
            X=0.
         94 Y=(X**2-X+2.)/(X+3.)
            PRINT,X,Y
            X=X+1.
            IF(X.LE.10.) GO TO 94
            STOP
            END
        $ENTRY
```

14

*************** RULES FOR KEYPUNCHING PROGRAMS ***********

1. Job Control Cards.

Job control cards,(JCL cards -- if you want to sound like a professional), are identified by a $ sign in card column 1. These cards are usually pre-punched and available in the keypunch area. You will require an account number to run your jobs. This account number is used by the computing center to charge the cost of running your job against some budget account. Leave a blank space after the account number and then punch your name. At some computing centers it may be necessary to identify the model of the keypunch used to punch the cards. If so, the JOB card will look like:

$JOB   WATFIV   acct.#,KP=26 your name
                        or
$JOB   WATFIV   acct.#,KP=29 your name

Ask your computer center which model of keypunch (26 or 29) is available.

The $ENTRY card always contains the symbols "$ENTRY" punched in columns 1 to 6.

Other Job Control cards can be used in WATFIV programs. These are described in Appendix E.

2. Comment Cards.

Comment cards are identified by a "C" in column 1. The comment can be punched anywhere in columns 2 thru 72. If the comment is too long for one card, punch a "C" in column 1 of the next card and continue the comment using whatever columns from 2 thru 72 that you wish. There is no limit on the number of comment cards which can appear in a program.

3. WATFIV Statements.

Cards which are not job control cards or comment cards are called Statement cards. The rules for "what goes where"' in statement cards are as follows:

columns 1-5. The statement number. The statement number is optional but, if present, it can be any integer value from 1 thru 99999. The number may be punched anywhere in the first five columns. Statement numbers are only required if it is necessary to reference the statement somewhere else in the program.

15

column 6 . The continuation indicator. Normally this column is left blank. It will contain something other than a zero or a blank only if the information punched in columns 7 to 72 of the card is to be considered a continuation of the statement punched in the previous card. Continuation cards are used whenever a statement is too long to fit on one card. There is no limit to the number of continuation cards which can be used for a single statement. A statement requiring several cards will have a non-zero, non-blank character punched in column 6 of all cards but the first. Columns 1 thru 5 of continuation cards must be blank.

columns 7-72. The statement. When punching WATFIV statements, blanks may be inserted anywhere to improve the readability of the statement. If the statement is such that it would go beyond column 72 then it should be continued on the next card as described above. Columns 7-72 of the continuation card can be considered as being placed on the right of column 72 of the previous card.

columns 73-80. Program identification area. As yet no use has been suggested for the last eight columns of the card. If desired, these columns may be used to identify the program and/or number the cards in the deck. When writing programs which contain several hundred cards, it is a good idea to number your cards sequentially so that if the deck is accidentally dropped, the problem of getting the cards back in their proper order will be easy. The symbols punched in columns 73-80 are ignored by the compiler and are simply available for you to use if you wish.

*4. Multiple Statements In One Card.

WATFIV permits more than one statement to be punched on a single card. The details of this technique can be found in Appendix E. All example programs in the book, however, will be punched according to the rules described above.

**************** END OF KEYPUNCHING RULES *****************

Step 6. Run the job.

As described earlier, running a job is a two stage process -- compilation followed by execution. Shown below is the output produced on the printer during the two stages when the example program is run.

Stage 1. <u>Output Produced By The Compiler</u>.

```
    $JOB    WATFIV D0000UOW JOHN MOORE
    C EXAMPLE PROGRAM 1
1           X=0.
2        94 Y=(X**2-X+2.)/(X+3.)
3           PRINT,X,Y
4           X=X+1.
5           IF(X.LE.10.) GO TO 94
6           STOP
7           END

    $ENTRY
```

Notice that the WATFIV compiler places a number beside each <u>statement</u> in the program. This is done so that any errors can be identified by the statement containing the error.

Stage 2. <u>Output Produced During Execution</u>.

The output below is produced by executing the machine language instructions which the compiler produced when it translated the WATFIV program into strings of ones and zeros. This output begins immediately below the line "$ENTRY" which was printed by the compiler.

```
0.0000000E 00    0.6666666E 00
0.1000000E 01    0.5000000E 00
0.2000000E 01    0.8000000E 00
0.3000000E 01    0.1333333E 01
0.4000000E 01    0.2000000E 01
0.5000000E 01    0.2750000E 01
0.6000000E 01    0.3555555E 01
0.7000000E 01    0.4400000E 01
0.8000000E 01    0.5272727E 01
0.9000000E 01    0.6166666E 01
0.1000000E 02    0.7076922E 01
```

CORE USAGE- (data on amount of memory used by the program)
DIAGNOSTICS- (number of errors and warnings)
COMPILE TIME=...SEC,EXECUTION TIME=...SEC.

There are two points of interest concerning the output produced during the execution time of the job. First. Following job execution, three lines of statistics are printed showing the amount of memory used, information on the number of errors and warnings, and information on the length of time required to compile and execute the program. The second point of

17

interest concerns the way the values of X and Y are printed. All the numbers have the form:

$$0.dddddddE\ ee$$

The symbols "E ee" should be read as "times 10 to the power ee'. For example the the values shown in the third line of output are:

$0.2000000E\ 01$ (a value of $.2 \times 10^1$, or 2.)
and $0.8000000E\ 00$ (a value of $.8 \times 10^0$, or .8)

A number appearing as $-0.23400000E-01$ would mean a value of -0.0234. In a later chapter we shall see how we could have this value printed as -0.0234.

The discussion above has described in some detail the steps which are necessary to solve any problem using a computer. The five steps are:

1. Define the problem
2. Develop a procedure for solving the problem.
3. Translate the algorithm into WATFIV
4. Keypunch the program.
5. Run the job.

Exercise 1.1

1.   Keypunch the example program and run it.

2.   What change or changes would be required in the example algorithm and program if the values of x to be used with the given formula for y were:

   a) 0.,0.5,1.0,1.5,...,9.5,10.0   (1 change required)
   b) 0., 2., 4., 6., ...,20. (2 changes required)
   c) 15.,14.,13.,12.,...,0.   (3 changes required)
       Solve problem (c) by running it on the computer.
   d) For each of the above, decide what changes would be required if you were using the brute-force approach of Algorithm A. By doing this the advantage of the iterative approach of Algorithm B should become more evident.

3.   If x takes on the values 0,-1,-2,-3,...,-10, then at first glance it would appear that the algorithm below would solve the problem.

       1. Set x = 0
       2. Calculate y using the formula
       3. Write down the values of x and y
       4. Subtract 1 from x
       5. If x $\geq$ -10 go to step 2 and carry on
       6. Stop

If this algorithm was translated into WATFIV and the job was run, an execution time error message would be printed. Why? Ask yourself what happens when x has a value equal to -3. Since the denominator is (x+3), its value is zero and the division is undefined. To overcome this problem we must decide what to do when x is -3. One reasonable approach would simply be to ignore the value of -3 and carry on with -4. O.K., how can we change the algorithm so that this will happen? Since we are using a looping technique to generate the successive values of x, this means we must look at each new value and see if it is negative three. If so, we should go to the instruction which will give us the next value of x.

a) Insert an appropriate instruction in the algorithm below to do just this.

1. Set x = 0
2. Calculate y using the formula
3. Write down the values of x and y
4. Subtract 1 from x
5. ....
6. If x $\geqslant$ -10 go to step 2 and carry on
7. Stop

b) For the algorithm above, how many times is each instruction executed in solving the problem?

c) What is the minimum number of instructions which must be executed to solve the problem?

d) Translate the algorithm in (a) into WATFIV and run it on the computer.

4. Use the computer to tabulate (compute and print out) values of the function

$$y = \frac{x^3 - 4x + 1}{3x - 12}$$

for values of x= 2,3,4,...,12.

5. Use the computer to tabulate values of the square and the square root of the first 20 natural numbers. Note that the square root of a number can be obtained by raising the number to a power of .5 .

1.5 What Happens When An Error Is Made?

Let's face it -- we all make mistakes. Errors may occur in the algorithm, in the translation of the algorithm into WATFIV, or in the keypunching of the program. The program below contains at least one obvious error.

```
$JOB    WATFIV  acct.#
C EXAMPLE PROGRAM WITH ERRORS
        X=2.
        Y=X**2-3X
        Z= (Y+X)/ Y+2.)
        PRINT X,Y,Z
        STOP
     $ENTRY
```

Suppose the program was punched as written and run on the computer. The output appearing on the printer is shown below.

```
            $JOB    WATFIV  acct.#
            C EXAMPLE PROGRAM WITH ERRORS
     1          X=2.
     2          Y=X**2-3X
 ***ERROR***    MISSING OPERATOR.UNEXPECTED X
     3          Z= (Y+X)/ Y+2.)
 ***ERROR***    UNMATCHED PARENTHESIS
     4          PRINT X,Y,Z
 ***ERROR***    VARIABLE FORMAT MUST BE AN ARRAY NAME.
                     UNEXPECTED X.
     5          STOP
 **WARNING**    MISSING END STATEMENT. END GENERATED

            $ENTRY

     CORE USAGE (information on memory used by the program)
     DIAGNOSTICS NUMBER OF ERRORS 3,NUMBER OF WARNINGS 1
     COMPILE TIME= ... SEC,EXECUTION TIME= 0.00 SEC.
```

Observe that when an error is detected by the compiler, an error message is printed under the line containing the error.

The first error occurs in the line Y=X**2-3X and the message "MISSING OPERATOR, UNEXPECTED X" indicates that the symbol for some arithmetic operation was expected after the three. Since by "3X" we mean "three times X", we can easily correct the statement by writing it as "Y=X**2-3*X".

The second error, "UNMATCHED PARENTHESIS" is due to our carelessness in omitting the left bracket in the denominator.

20

The third error message, "VARIABLE FORMAT MUST BE AN ARRAY NAME, UNEXPECTED X" is not too meaningful to us at this point. The clue comes from the phrase "UNEXPECTED X". The reason for the error is that we left out the comma after the word PRINT.

Just ahead of the $ENTRY a warning message is printed, indicating that the END statemnt is missing. The compiler assumes you wanted to put an END statement just ahead of the $ENTRY and has inserted one for you. Before running the job again we should punch up an END card and include it in the proper place.

If any errors are detected by the compiler, no attempt is made to execute the job as the print-out shows. (The execution time was 0.). If the only messages are warning messages however, an attempt is made to execute the job. These warning messages should be examined carefully to make sure the reason for the warning does not cause the output to be different from that which was wanted.

There is a third type of message which is sometimes printed by the compiler. It is called an EXTENSION message and is used to indicate statements which are perfectly valid in WATFIV but may not be valid in some members of the Fortran family of languages. Since our purpose is to learn the WATFIV language, the existence and meaning of these messages can be ignored.

Suppose we corrected the errors and added an END statement to the orginal program. The output appearing on the printer when the job is run is:

```
$JOB    WATFIV acct.#
        C EXAMPLE WITH NO COMPILE-TIME ERRORS
1           X=2.
2           Y=X**2-3*X
3           Z=(Y+X)/(Y+2.)
4           PRINT,X,Y,Z
5           STOP
6           END

        $ENTRY
```
ERROR LIMIT EXCEEDED FOR FLOATING POINT DIVISION BY ZERO. PROGRAM WAS EXECUTING LINE 3 WHEN TERMINATION OCCURRED

This example shows that even though there are no compile-time errors in the program, the job could not be executed successfully because an execution time error occured when performing the calculations defined in line 3. The reason for the error is that the denominator has a value of zero in the division described. The meaning of the words "LIMIT EXCEEDED FOR FLOATING POINT DIVISION BY ZERO", will become clear in Chapter 2.

Consider the following program.

```
$JOB
C EXAMPLE OF UNDEFINED VARIABLE
      PRINT,A
      STOP
      END
$ENTRY
```

When this job is run no error messages are printed
either at compile-time or during the execution of the job.
However, the value printed for A will look like
UUUUUUUUUUUUUUUUUUUU. The reason for this is that no value
has been given to the variable A. Its value is undefined and
a string of 'U's is printed to indicate this fact.

A second example program containing an undefined
variable is the following.

```
$JOB
C  EXAMPLE OF AN UNDEFINED VARIABLE
      B=A**2
      A=7.
      PRINT,B
      STOP
      END
$ENTRY
```

In the foregoing example, the job would terminate at
execution time because of the operations specified by the
statement "B=A**2". The error message would be "A
UNDEFINED". Recall that a computer does not have circuits
for doing algebra, only arithmetic. Since no value had been
assigned to A, no value can be assigned to B. This example
further emphasizes the fact that instructions are executed
sequentially. No attempt is made to look ahead and see what
the program is trying to do.

In order to detect undefined values at execution time,
the compiler must generate instructions to see if each
variable used in a statement has previously been assigned a
value. Checking for undefined values slows down the
execution of a job. If a program is known to work, this
checking feature can be bypassed. Details of how this is
done can be found in Appendix E.

One of the reasons the WATFIV language is so widely used
is that its diagnostics (error and warning messages) are
very extensive and thus make the job of correcting
programming mistakes very easy. For this reason you
shouldn't hesitate to try something to see if it will work.
The confidence you have in your ability to write programs
will increase more rapidly if you experiment with different
ways of accomplishing the same thing.

It's sad but true, however, that if you make a mistake in the algorithm, WATFIV can't help you. The ability to correct algorithms is not one of the capabilities of a compiler.

1.6 A Second Example

Step 1. Problem definition. Suppose we are required to find the sum of the first 50 positive integers. That is, the value of the sum 1+2+3+...+50. The total is to be obtained without using any formula.

Step 2. Develop an algorithm. The required total could be obtained by finding successively the totals: 1, 1+2, 1+2+3, 1+2+3+4, ..., and stopping when 50 has been added to the previous total. The initial total would have to be zero and the first number to be added to this total would be one. A brute force algorithm would be:

```
  1. Set Sum = 0
  2. Set Number = 1
  3. Add Number to Sum
  4. Set Number = 2
  5. Add Number to Sum
  6. Set Number = 3
  7. ...
     ...
100. Set Number = 50
101. Add Number to Sum
102. Write down the value of Sum
103. Stop
```

For reasons discussed in the previous example, namely, ease of writing the algorithm, and more important, the flexibility of the algorithm, we should attempt to write the algorithm above using a looping technique. The first three instructions can't be avoided so as a start we have:

```
  1. Set Sum = 0
  2. Set Number = 1
  3. Add Number to Sum
```

Since the number to be added to the total is increasing by one each time, instruction 4 should be "Add 1 to Number". This will cause Number to have a value of 2 which is fine. Looking ahead we realize that Number must always be equal to or less than fifty. To insure this fact the truthfulness of the relation "Number less than or equal to fifty" should be tested. If true, then we should go back and add Number to Sum. If not, then we have completed the calculations and all that remains is to print the value of Sum. Thus a preferable algorithm to the brute force approach is:

1. Set Sum = 0
2. Set Number = 1
3. Add Number to the Sum
4. Add 1 to Number
5. If Number $\leq$ 50 go to step 3 and carry on
6. Write down the value of Sum
7. Stop

Step 3. Translate the algorithm into WATFIV. A translation of the algorithm is shown below.

```
$JOB    WATFIV  acct.# JOHN MOORE
C EXAMPLE PROGRAM 2
C CALCULATE THE SUM OF THE FIRST 50 NATURAL NUMBERS
        SUM = 0.
        NUMBER = 1.
  2864 SUM=SUM + NUMBER
        NUMBER=NUMBER+1.
        IF(NUMBER.LE.50) GO TO 2864
        PRINT,'THE SUM IS',SUM
        STOP
        END
$ENTRY
```

Examine the PRINT statement in the program. It contains the words "THE SUM IS" enclosed in single quotes. It means the phrase "THE SUM IS" is to be printed ahead of the value of SUM. This technique can be used to print any phrases, words or symbols which help to make the output easier to understand.

Step 4. Keypunch the program. The source deck will contain 12 cards, one for each line in the program. The cards should be punched according to the rules given earlier and will appear as shown in the program. In the deck there will be: 2 job control cards; 2 comment cards; and 8 WATFIV statements.

Step 5. Run the job. When the job is run, the compiler will list the information punched in the cards. When the job is executed, the line printed is "THE SUM IS 0.1275000E 04". The answer to our problem is therefore 1275.

Exercise 1.2

1. Modify the algorithm of example 2 to find the sum of $1^2+2^2+3^2+....+50^2$. Write a program and run it to find the answer.

2. Find the sum of $2^3+4^3+6^3+...+20^3$ using the computer.

3. Find the sum of $3^1+3^2+3^3+...+3^8$ using the computer.

4. Find the average of all odd integers from 17 thru 83. Use the computer to obtain the result. A counter should be used to determine how many numbers have been added to the total.

5. Explain the difference between "PRINT,'X'" and "PRINT,X".

1.7 A Third Example.

Step 1. Problem definition. One method of finding the square root of a number is the following. Make an initial estimate of the value of the square root, say one-half the number. Call this initial estimate X_0. If the number is A, we would have $X_0=A/2$. Given this initial estimate, X_1 will be a better estimate of the square root where X_1 is obtained using the formula:

$$X_1 = X_0 - \frac{X^2 - A}{2X_0}$$

An even better estimate, X , can be obtained using the previous estimate X and the same formula. That is:

$$X_2 = X_1 - \frac{X^2 - A}{2X_1}$$

In general, by repeating this process over and over, one can obtain increasingly accurate estimates of the square root of any positive value. Suppose we want to use the computer to find the square root of 79.358. We are to make six improvements to our initial guess.

Step 2. Develop an algorithm.

How can we use a looping technique in our algorithm? To answer this question we must ask the following two questions. "What is it that we are doing over and over again?", and "What is changing each time we do this thing over and over again?". The answer to the first question is , "We are using the same formula six times to get successive improvements of the estimate of the square root.". The answer to the second question is, "We are changing a value in the formula each time.". Thus if we want to execute the formula six times and change the value used in the formula each time, we will need a counter which starts at 1 and goes up to 6. We must also insure the correct value is used in the formula each time. Our algorithm will therefore look like:

```
        1. Set A= 79.358
        2. Set Estimate = A/2
        3. Set Counter = 1
        4. Set Estimate = value obtained using formula
        5. Add 1 to the Counter
        6. If the Counter ≤ 6 go to step 4 and carry on
        7. Write down the value of the Estimate
        8. Stop
```

Step 3. Translate the algorithm into WATFIV. The result is:

```
$JOB    WATFIV   acct# JOHN MOORE
C EXAMPLE PROGRAM 3
C PROGRAM TO FIND THE SQUARE ROOT OF 79.358
        A=79.358
        ESTMAT=A/2.
        COUNT=1.
C OBTAIN IMPROVED ESTIMATE
    55 ESTMAT= ESTMAT-(ESTMAT**2 - A)/(2.*ESTMAT)
        COUNT = COUNT + 1.
        IF(COUNT.LE.6.) GO TO 55
        PRINT,ESTMAT
        STOP
        END
    $ENTRY
```

Step 4. Keypunch the program.

Step 5. Run the job. The value printed as a result of
    executing the program is 0.8908311E 01, that is,
    8.908311 . This result is accurate to the sixth decimal
    place. You should check this out by making ten
    improvements and printing the result.

    The following point is illustrated by this example. In
the example program the names ESTMAT and COUNT are used
instead of ESTIMATE and COUNTER. The reason for this is
that a maximum of six symbols can be used in a name.
Complete details will be given in the next chapter.

Problems and Exercises 1.3

1. Use the computer to find eight improvements to an initial
    estimate of the square root of 4059.26. Print the value
    of each improved estimate.

2. Suppose rather than making a specific number of
    improvements to an initial estimate, it is desired to
    continue making improvements only until the next
    estimate differs from the previous one by less than
    .0001. This means that the decision to improve on an
    estimate will be based on whether or not the change
    (either an increase or decrease) is less than .0001. If
    the improvement is greater than .0001 then we should go

back and get a better estimate. If not, we can print the value of the estimate. To do this it is necessary to "remember" what the previous estimate was in order to compare it with the most recent estimate. This means we will need two variables, OLDEST (the previous estimate), as well as ESTMAT (the current estimate).

a) Using the method of obtaining successively increasingly accurate approximations, develop an algorithm to find the square root of 3.0 until the change in estimates is less than .0001.

b) In WATFIV, the absolute value of the difference of two numbers X and Y say, can be found by writing "ABS(X-Y)". Using this feature of the WATFIV language, translate the algorithm you have developed in (a) into WATFIV and run the job.

3. Examine the following program before answering the questions which follow.

```
$JOB
        J=5
    747 K=J**2
        PRINT,K
        J=J+5
        IF(J.LE.100) GO TO 747
        STOP
        END
$ENTRY
```

a) What is the first value printed
b) How many values are printed?
c) In words, what does the program do?
d) What changes would be necessary in the above program to have it print the values:
   25,36,49,64,81,100,121,144 ?

4. a) Develop a brute-force algorithm to determine which, if any, of the numbers 8,15,22,29,36 divide evenly into a number N. Print only those numbers for which the division is even (leaves no remainder).

    b) How many instructions are executed in solving the problem using this method?

    c) Convert this brute-force algorithm to an iterative algorithm by asking yourself the following questions: (i)What operation is being repeated over and over again?; (ii)What is changing each time the operation is repeated?; (iii)What is the rule for generating the the values which change?; (iv)What is the rule for deciding that no more repetitions are required?

27

d) In the algorithm developed in (c), how many times is
    each step in the algorithm executed in solving the
    problem?   What is the total number of instructions
    which must be executed to solve this problem using
    this algorithm?

e) Although the total found in (d) is somewhat larger
    than that found in (b), why are most algorithms
    executed on a computer written using a looping
    approach?

5. Consider the following algorithm.

        1. Set Number equal to 78.
        2. Set Test equal to 2.
        3. Set Testsq equal to Test times Test.
        4. If Testsq not equal to Number, go to step 7.
        5. Print Test.
        6. Stop.
        7. If Testsq greater than Number, stop
        8. Add one to Test.
        9. Go to step 3.

    a) How many times is each step executed?
    b) What problem is solved by this algorithm?
    c) What advantage is obtained by making the first
       instruction "Set Number = 78" instead of using
       78 each place the word "Number" appears in the
       algorithm?
    d) Why is "Testsq" used instead of "Test" in step 7?

1.8 Summary

    1.   The computer has circuits and components for
         performing simple arithmetic; getting information
         in   and   printing   results out; making simple
         decisions.

    2.   A computer is a valuable aid in solving problems
         because: it is fast; it is accurate and   reliable;
         big problems can be solved by solving a set of
         little problems - one after the other.

    3.   To use the computer to assist in problem solving,
         five steps are necessary.

            1. Define the problem
            2. Develop an algorithm
            3. Translate the algorithm into a
                  programming language
            4. Keypunch the program
            5. Run the job (compilation then execution)

4. Although you can describe a brute force procedure which will solve a problem it is desirable to write algorithms which have a looping or iterative property. The chief reason is that the saving in execution time using a brute force algorithm is more than compensated for by the ease and flexibility of using an iterative approach to solve a problem.

5. Errors may occur during either the compile time of a job or during the execution time of the job. Correcting programming errors is relatively simple: Correcting errors in algorithms may or may not be simple depending on the complexity of the problem.

6. All WATFIV programs will contain a $JOB card, an END card, and a $ENTRY card.

7. Some of the important vocabulary of this chapter: algorithm, keypunch, source deck, program, job, job control cards, WATFIV statements, comments, compiler, compilation, compile time, execution, execution time, machine language, bit string, error message, warning message, iterative algorithm.

CHAPTER 2   NUMBERS, ARITHMETIC AND VARIABLES

Questions Answered In This Chapter.

   1. Why does WATFIV distinguish between numbers
      with, and without decimal points?

   2. What are the rules governing the way in which
      arithmetic expressions are evaluated?

   3. What are variables and how are they defined
      and used?

   4. How can we obtain values of commonly required
      functions such as sines, logarithms, and
      absolute values?

     After completing this chapter you will be able to
translate a large number of algorithms into WATFIV.   You
will have learned about nine of the most frequently used
WATFIV statements.

2.1 INTEGER Values

     In WATFIV, a number which is written without a decimal
point is called an INTEGER constant. Thus -7, 24569, +25, 0
are examples of INTEGER constants. Note that commas are not
used to separate successive groups of digits in the number.
If the number is positive it is not necessary to put a plus
sign in front of the number.

     Since we frequently want to perform operations such as
multiplication and division with pairs of INTEGERS, the
computer must have circuits for performing INTEGER
arithmetic. You will recall that the computer can only
manipulate strings of ones and zeros and that before your
program is executed, the instructions and numbers appearing
in your program are translated into bit strings by the
WATFIV compiler. The bit string produced by the compiler
for INTEGERS represents the value of the number in the base
two instead of the base 10 or decimal number system.
Details of the base two number system can be found in
Appendix C. On the computer systems which process WATFIV
jobs, a total of thirty-two bits (ones and zeros) are used
to represent each INTEGER value. For example, a value of 89
is stored as:

            00000000000000000000000001011001

Because only thirty-two bits are used to store INTEGER values, there is a limit to the size of INTEGER values which can be used in WATFIV. Any INTEGER value used in a WATFIV program must be in the range -2147483648 thru +2147483647 or roughly between plus and minus 2.1 billion.

Operations With INTEGERS.

The five arithmetic operations that can be performed with pairs of INTEGER values are + - * / **. What then are the values of the following expressions?

    i)   3+2*4

   ii)   5+2**3*7

  iii)   -4**2

   iv)   4**2**3

    v)   5/2

   vi)   5/-2

  vii)   3*5/4*2

 viii)   1234**50

We can learn all that is necessary to know about INTEGER arithmetic by studying the eight examples above. In most of the examples it might appear that more than one answer could be given depending on the order in which the operations are performed. To avoid any ambiguity there are rules which define the priorities of each operation. The rules will be summarized following a discussion of each case.

Consider (i). The result must be 11 since multiplication has a higher priority than addition and therefore is done first.

In the second example, the result is 61. Exponentiation is done before any multiplication and therefore the sequence of intermediate results is (5+2**3*7)=(5+8*7)=(5+56)=61.

The value of -4**2 is -16. The rule is that a unary plus or minus (a + or - symbol preceding a value) is treated as though there was a zero in front of the sign. Thus -4**2 is considered to be 0-4**2 and since exponentiation has a higher priority than addition or subtraction, the result -16 is obtained.

The fourth example, namely 4**2**3, is evaluated by doing the rightmost exponentiation first. The expression is therefore equivalent to 4**8 which has a value of 65536.

31

The value of 5/2 is 2. This value is obtained because the result of an arithmetic operation with a pair of INTEGERS must be an INTEGER value. The rule for INTEGER division is to ignore any remainder and use the quotient as the answer.

The sixth example is perhaps a little unfair because this type of expression is not permitted in WATFIV. The reason is that two arithmetic operators cannot appear in succession. If your program included an expression such as 5/-2, the compiler would print an error message below the line containing the expression and you would have to change the expression to 5/(-2) to correct the problem. This points out a further important point -- expressions in brackets are evaluated before any arithmetic operations are done. (The value of 5/(-2) is of course -2.)

The seventh example 3*5/4*2 has a value of 6 since multiplication and division have equal priorities and are performed in the order in which they appear -- left to right.

The last expression, 1234**50, would produce a result which is much larger than the largest INTEGER value allowed in WATFIV. When this happens no error message is printed. You, the programmer, are responsible for avoiding situations where the result of an INTEGER calculation is outside the permitted range. Since the number produced is incorrect, weird results may be obtained if the result is used in subsequent calculations. In some sophisticated problems, a programmer may genuinely desire this "overflow" condition. This is the reason no error message is printed.

The rules for evaluating arithmetic expressions are summarized below.

```
**********************************************************
*                                                        *
*    1. Expressions in brackets, innermost first         *
*    2. Exponentiation, right to left                    *
*    3. Multiplication and division, equal               *
*          priority, left to right                       *
*    4. Addition and subtraction, equal                  *
*          priority, left to right                       *
*                                                        *
**********************************************************
```

Later on, we shall want to add one item to the top of the list and several operations having lower priorities to the bottom of the list.

<u>Exercise 2.1</u>

1. Calculate the value of each of the following INTEGER
   expressions.

   a) 3*5-3   f) 4-2**3/2*2

   b) 3-5*3   g) 4-2**3/(2*2)

   c) 10*5**2   h) -2**4/3

   d) 10**2/5   i) 6/9/(-4)

   e) 3/2**2   j) 3**(1/2)-14*2/30

2. Correct the error in each of the following expressions.

   a) +2*-3
   b) (-16+2/(7-(+6))

3. Rewrite the expression below removing as many pairs of
   brackets as possible. Do not change the value of the
   expression.

   $$((-(5*2)**3)+(14/(2**(-3)))))$$

4. For each of the following write one INTEGER expression
   which has a value of 20 using the operations indicated.

   a) One multiplication and one subtraction operation
   b) Three divisions
   c) One exponentiation, one addition and one division
   d) Two pairs of brackets which are both necessary
   e) Two exponentiations and a division

2.2 <u>REAL Numbers</u> (Numbers with decimal points)

Numbers which have decimal points can be written in many
different but equivalent ways. For example, three different
ways of writing a single number having a value of seven-and-
three-eights are:

   7.375   .007375 x 10^3 737500.0 x 10^{-5}

In mathematics these numbers are frequently called
"floating-point" numbers since the decimal point can "float"
along the line of digits by multiplying by an appropriate
power of ten. In WATFIV, numbers written with decimal
points are called REAL constants. The computer stores REAL
values so that decimal point precedes the first non-zero
digit in the number. Some examples of REAL numbers are:

Value of Number	Value Stored In Computer
7.375	0.7375000×10^{1}
-.00621	$-0.6210000 \times 10^{-2}$
897524.	0.8975240×10^{6}
-0.	-0.0000000×10^{0}

To define REAL numbers in WATFIV the letter "E" is used to indicate "times 10 to the power ...". If the E is omitted, it is understood the number is to be multiplied by ten-to-the-zero which of course is 1. Some examples follow.

Number Appearing In WATFIV Program	Value Stored In Computer
.236	0.2360000E+00
236.74E+02	0.2367400E+05
.0023674E-2	0.2367400E-04
-1234567.	-0.1234567E+07
-123.45E18	-0.1234500E+21
123E02	0.1230000E+05

These examples illustrate the following points when using REAL numbers in WATFIV programs.

    i)   The number can be written with or without an exponent. If an exponent is used, it is indicated by putting an E after the last digit of the number and then writing the value of the exponent.

    ii)   The computer stores the number so that the decimal point precedes the first significant digit. Sufficient zeros are added to the right of the last digit so that seven significant digits are stored for all REAL values.

    iii)   You can be somewhat sloppy in the way the exponent is written. If the exponent is positive, the sign may be omitted. Thus 2.0E2, 2.0E+2, 2.0E+02, and 2.0E02 are equivalent. Similarly, 2.0E-03, and 2.0E-3 are equivalent.

    iv)   If the decimal point is omitted, it is assumed to precede the "E" symbol.

The magnitude of any REAL value used in WATFIV must be in the range $.7237005 \times 10^{76}$ and $.5397605 \times 10^{-78}$. The reason for these peculiar limits is due to the bit pattern scheme used to store REAL values. It is usually sufficient to remember that the limits are roughly ten to the plus or minus seventy-five. If the result of some arithmetic operation lies outside these limits an error message is printed and the job stopped.

Examples of some invalid REAL numbers are:

```
-2,675.3        (comma not permitted)
1.25E           (no exponent value)
10.0E81         (too large)
12345678.       (too many digits, value will be
                 rounded to seven digits)
```

Computers store REAL values using a string of thirty-two bits for each value. The circuits which must be used to perform arithmetic with numbers having decimal points are different from those used for INTEGER operations. For this reason the bit patterns representing the INTEGER value 2 and the REAL value 2.0 are different. Details of the pattern of ones and zeros used to represent REAL values can be found in Appendix C.

Operations With REAL Numbers.

The priorities of the five arithmetic operations are identical to those which apply to arithmetic operations with INTEGERS.

Some examples of simple REAL expressions and their values are shown below.

REAL Expression	Value of the Expression With and Without E Notation	
10./5.+3.46	5.46	0.5460000E 01
6.25-3.**2.	-2.75	-0.2750000E 01
30./8./100.	.0375	0.3750000E-01
-2.**6.	-64.	-0.6400000E 02
2.25/15.*(-.6)	-.09	-0.9000000E-01
3.*(5.**2./8.-1.)	6.375	0.6375000E 01

There are three important points you should be aware of when working with REAL values.

First. Consider the pair of expressions:

```
a) 2.**3
b) 2.**3.
```

As you would expect, the value of both expressions is 8.0. However the values are calculated in different ways. Expression (a), in which the exponent is an INTEGER, is calculated by successive multiplications, namely 2.*2.*2. Expression (b) containing a REAL exponent is evaluated by finding the antilog of 3 times the logarithm of 2. Since this second approach is more complicated, it takes longer to obtain the result. For this reason exponents should be written as INTEGERS in the interest of efficiency.

Consider the expressions:

    c) (-2.)**3
    d) (-2.)**3.

Expression (c) results in a value of -8. as expected but expression (d) causes an error message to be printed½ To see why, we need only remember that (d) will be evaluated by finding the antilog of 3log(-2.). Since logarithms of negative numbers, or zero for that matter, are undefined, the error message is printed. This means you must avoid raising negative REAL numbers to REAL powers.

Second. The computer only stores 7 significant digits for each REAL value. To see what can happen because of this, consider the pair of expressions below.

    a) 5.0E+10 - 5.0E+10 + 1.

    b) 1. + 5.0E+10 -5.0E+10

The value of (a) is 1. and the value of (b) is 0.½ Remember that addition and subtraction have equal priorities and are performed left to right. The steps in the evaluation of each expression are shown below.

```
a)   50000000000.        b)                   1.
    -50000000000.              +50000000000.
    ─────────────              ─────────────
              0.               5000000.E+3
             +1.              -5000000.E+3
    ─────────────              ─────────────
              1.                        0.
```

Third. Numbers inside the computer are stored using the binary number system. It is a fact that many fractions in the decimal number system require an infinite string of decimal digits to represent a value accurately, (for example the value 1./3. = .333333...). The same fact is true in the binary number system. That is, there are many fractional values which would require an infinite string of ones and zeros to accurately represent the number. For example a value of 1./5. in the binary system looks like .001100110011... . Since the computer can only store a finite number of digits for each value, the value stored for some fractional values is really only a very good

36

approximation to the actual number. This means that tiny errors may result when performing REAL arithmetic. For example the value of .2+.2+.2+.2+.2 turns out to be .999999 instead of 1. The point to remember is that if one is performing a large number of calculations with REAL values, the final result may have some small error. REAL values which do not have digits to the right of the decimal point are always stored accurately.

2.3 Operations Combining REAL And INTEGER Values

Expressions such as: 2.+3 , 3./4, 5.**2*10, are called mixed-mode expressions since each expression contains at least one operation which combines a REAL and an INTEGER value. The rule for determining the result of a mixed-mode operation is to perform the calculation as if both values were REAL and to leave the result as a REAL value. The order in which the operations are performed is identical to that for expressions involving values which are all of the same type. Consider the following examples.

    i) 2+3.

   ii) 2/3*4.

  iii) 4.*2/3

   iv) 4.*(2/3)

    v) 123456789 + 1.0E2

   vi) 2.**3

In example (i) the result is 5.0 and the 2 is converted to 2.0 before the addition takes place.

In (ii) the division is done before the multiplication and since the division involves two INTEGERS the remainder is ignored and so the expression reduces to 0*4.. This means the value of the expression is the REAL value 0..

In (iii) the result is 2.666667. The sequence of intermediate results is: 4.*2/3 = 8./3 = 2.666667.

Example (iv) produces a different result from example (iii). Why? Since there are brackets, the INTEGER division is done first and produces a value of 0 which is then multiplied by 4. giving the result 0..

Example (v) is of interest since the INTEGER value 123456789 contains 9 digits. When this number is converted to a REAL value before performing the addition, only 7 decimal digits are stored and so the addition is effectively 1234567.E+2 + 1.0E+2. That is 1234568.E+2.

The last example has already been discussed in some detail. It illustrates the one exception to the rule that INTEGER values are converted to REAL values when combined in an arithmetic operation. If an exponent is an INTEGER it is left as an INTEGER and the calculation is done by successive multiplications.

2.4 Variables.

Thus far we have only considered specific numbers or constants. If we merely wanted to use the computer as a desk calculator, it would not really be necessary to go beyond a discussion of constants. In many problems however we are doing such things as adding to totals, counting inputs, finding increasingly accurate approximations to roots of equations, etc.. In such cases, the value of the total, the count, or the approximation will vary. Quantities whose values may change during the solving of a problem are called variables and names such as TOTAL, COUNT and APPROX can be given to these quantities. If variables are used in a program it is necessary to do three things.

(i) Use a valid name for the variable.

(ii) Tell the compiler the type of value which will be taken on by the variable. (INTEGER or REAL)

(iii) Cause the variable to be assigned or to "take on" the desired value.

Before seeing how each of these things is done we should state the restrictions on the names a variable may have. These rules are easy to learn and are stated below.

```
****************************************************
*                                                  *
*              Valid WATFIV Names                  *
*                                                  *
*    1. A maximum of six symbols may be used in    *
*       a name.                                    *
*                                                  *
*    2. The first symbol must be a letter of the   *
*       alphabet or a $ sign. (The $ sign is       *
*       considered to be an alphabetic character   *
*       in WATFIV.)                                *
*                                                  *
*    3. None of the special symbols such as + -    *
*       ) . ' , ( & = may be used in a name.       *
*                                                  *
*    4. Blanks may be used but are ignored in      *
*       determining if two names are the same.     *
*                                                  *
****************************************************
```

Examples

Valid Names	Invalid Names
MOTHER	9D
IF	A(I
NET PAY	R&D
NETPAY	MOTHERS
$$$$8A	J=I
A9A9$	4YOU
GO TO 8	NET-PAY
DO 10 I	LONG TIME
REAL	INTEGER
PRINT6	$&CENT

Remarks on the Examples.

1. Each of the invalid names violates one or more of the rules stated above. Examine each to determine which rule is being violated.

2. The valid variable names NETPAY and NET PAY are considered identical. (See Rule 4.)

3. Although words like REAL, PRINT and GO TO may be used as variable names, using them for this purpose makes a program harder to understand.

If a variable name has more than six symbols, the compiler prints a warning message and considers the first six non-blank symbols to be the name of the variable. Using variable names containing more than six symbols is unnecessary and should be avoided.

Declaring The Type (REAL or INTEGER) of Variables.

The WATFIV compiler must know whether a variable is to take on REAL or INTEGER values. This is necessary so that the appropriate bit strings and instructions can be generated by the compiler. There are two commonly used ways of providing this information.

    i) Default Typing. In the absence of other information, if the first letter of the variable name is one of I,J,K,L,M,N, the variable is assumed to take on INTEGER values. (Note that the first two letters of the word INTEGER define the range of the letters above.)

    If the first symbol in the name is any one of the remaining letters or a $ sign, the variable is assumed to take on REAL values. That is, in the absence of information to the contrary, a variable

39

name beginning with a letter in the range A thru H,
O thru Z, or a $ will take on REAL values. Thus,
in the examples of variable names given previously,
the variables IF, NET PAY, and NETPAY would be
INTEGER variables and $$$$84, A9A9$, GO TO 8,
PRINT6, DO 10 I, and REAL would take on REAL
values. The phrase "first-letter rule" is a
commonly used synonym for "default typing".

ii) <u>Explicit Declaration of Type</u>. To explicitly declare
certain variables to be of the REAL or INTEGER
type, one simply lists the variable names of each
type at the beginning of the program. The variable
names in the list are preceded by either the word
"REAL" or the word "INTEGER". Consider the program
below.

```
C EXAMPLE OF REAL AND INTEGER STATEMENTS
      REAL N,J96,I,BAF
      INTEGER A,OOPS,PRINT,$$,SUM
      . . .
      . . .
      . . .
      END
```

In this example the variables N, J96, I and BAF will
take on REAL values. The variables A, OOPS, PRINT, $$, SUM
on the other hand have been explicitly declared as being
INTEGER variables. All other variables used in the program
will be typed using the default rule described above. Note
that it was not necessary to include the variable BAF in the
REAL statement -- the first-letter rule would mean that BAF
was of the REAL type anyway. The compiler does not consider
this an error.

The REAL and INTEGER declaration statements are used to
override the first-letter rule. In the absence of either or
both of these statements, variables are typed by default.

Two examples of invalid declaration statements are shown
below.

```
      a) REAL,NUMBER,MAX     (comma after REAL)

      b) INTEGER A,$NEXT
         REAL LOOP,A     (A cannot be both REAL & INTEGER)
```

*2.5 <u>Defining Your Own First-Letter Rule (IMPLICIT)</u>

At the beginning of a program it is possible to define
your own first-letter rule by using an IMPLICIT statement.
The IMPLICIT statement specifies the set of letters which
determine if a variable will take on REAL values or INTEGER
values. A few examples will illustrate its use.

    i)   IMPLICIT REAL(I,J)

   ii)   IMPLICIT INTEGER(A-D,$),REAL(K,L,M)

  iii)   IMPLICIT REAL(A-H,O-Z,$),INTEGER(I-N)

   iv)   IMPLICIT REAL(I,M,N)
         INTEGER IPPSY,M64,M65,NINE

When considering the effect of an IMPLICIT statement, always begin by assuming the default rule is true, then examine the IMPLICIT statement to see what portions of the normal first-letter rule are changed.

In example (i) the first-letter rule applies to all variables except those beginning with the letters I and J. Variables beginning with either of these letters are to be considered as REAL variables.

In example (ii), variables beginning with the letters A thru D or the $ sign will be INTEGER variables and those beginning with K,L or M will be REAL. The first-letter rule will apply to all other variables used in the program.

The IMPLICIT statement of example (iii) defines the normal first-letter-rule and therefore could be ommitted from the program.

Example (iv) shows that the effect of an IMPLICIT statement can be overridden for specific names by using either a REAL or INTEGER declaration statement. In this example, variables other than IPPSY, M64, M65 and NINE which start with one of the letters I,M or N will be REAL. Those four have been specifically declared as being INTEGER variables.

There are two important points to keep in mind when using an IMPLICIT statement in a program.

   i)   Only one IMPLICIT statement can be used and it must be the first non-comment statement in the program.

  ii)   The IMPLICIT statement is used to override any part of or all of the first-letter rule and its effect can be negated for specific variables by using REAL or INTEGER declaration statements for those variables.

2.6 Giving Values To Variables.

Remember that the computer can only do arithmetic and that all variables used in a program must be assigned a value before executing any statement in which they appear.

There are essentially two ways that variables can be assigned values:

a) Using an Assignment statement

b) "Reading-in" the value of the variable

Method 1 -- The Assignment Statement

The general form of an Assignment statement is:

variable name = arithmetic expression

The statement should be interpreted as meaning "The variable on the left side of the equal sign is to be given the value of the arithmetic expression on the right side of the equal sign." Thus

i) A=3.*8./2.**4

ii) JJ=MOM*(3**I)

iii) A=10

iv) LUCKY= 3.7

are examples of Assignment statements. Note that in (ii) it is assumed that the variables MOM and I have been assigned values earlier in the program. If either or both had not, the expression MOM*(3**I) could not be evaluated and the job would terminate with an execution-time error message.

In example (iii) the expression on the right is the INTEGER constant 10 whereas the variable on the left is REAL. Since A must take on a REAL value it is assigned the value 10.0. A similar case is shown in example (iv). LUCKY is an INTEGER variable and cannot be assigned the REAL value 3.7 . When this happens, the fractional part of the REAL value is ignored and so LUCKY takes on a value of 3.

Sometimes one wishes to assign a common value to several variables. This could be accomplished by writing a set of Assignment statements each of which assigned the value to a different variable or an extended Assignment statement could be used. Three examples are shown below.

i) SUM1=SUM2=0.

ii) JJ=NOPE=3.62E+1 +2.

iii) MM=X=I=123456789

When evaluating extended Assignment statements, the assignments are made beginning with the rightmost equal

42

sign. Thus, in example (i), SUM2 is assigned the value 0.
and then SUM1 is assigned the value of SUM2. Therefore both
SUM1 and SUM2 are given a value of 0..

In example (ii) the expression 3.62E+1+2. is evaluated
first, giving a value of 38.2. This REAL value is assigned
to the INTEGER variable NOPE which results in NOPE having a
value of 38 . The variable JJ is assigned the value of NOPE
so both JJ and NOPE have values of 38.

In example (iii) I is given the value 123456789. Since
X is REAL it can only store 7 significant digits and so X
ends up with a value of 1234567.E+02. Since MM is assigned
the value of X, it will have a value of 123456700. The last
two examples illustrate that some caution must be exercised
if you find it convenient to use extended Assignment
statements.

Exercise 2.2

1. For each sequence of WATFIV statements below, determine
    the last value assigned to each variable used. Assume
    that the first-letter rule determines the type of each
    variable unless the variable appears in a type
    declaration statement.

    a) I=4-2*3.5

    b) I=6
       I=I+I

    c) A=3.**2/5
       B=A-A+3.**(2/5)

    d) REAL I,J
       J=2.5
       I=J*J-1

    e) INTEGER X,AA,BOY
       Y=4.1
       I=55.2
       X=I/11
       AA=X*I/5
       BOY=Y*AA

    f) REAL MOO
       INTEGER SUM
       SUM=MOO=1
       SUM=SUM+MOO/(SUM+1)

2. Identify the error in each of the following statements.

    a) REAL,JACK
    b) INTEGER A+10,XXX

43

```
c) REAL JAZZ,LONGNAME
d) XYZ=ABC,PQR=DEF
e) I+10=14
f) H=3.6=G
g) CAR=3*1.62E-99
```

Method 2 -- The READ Statement

Suppose one wishes to assign a value of factorial N to the variable FACTN where N is some positive integer. In other words, FACTN is to have the value of 1x2x3x4....xN. An algorithm which uses a looping technique is:

1. Set FACTN = 1
2. Set Multiplier =1
3. If Multiplier = N go to step 7
4. Multiply FACTN by the Multiplier
5. Add one to the Multiplier
6. Go to step 3
7. Print the value of N and FACTN
8. Stop

You should satisfy yourself that this algorithm will produce a correct result by taking a small value of N and following the procedure above. A program which is a translation of this algorithm is shown below. The program contains an error. What is it?

```
C EXAMPLE PROGRAM 2.2
      INTEGER FACTN
      FACTN=1
      MULPLR=1
   17 IF(MULPLR.GT.N) GO TO 46
      FACTN = FACTN*MULPLR
      MULPLR=MULPLR+1
      GO TO 17
   46 PRINT,N,FACTN
      STOP
      END
$ENTRY
```

If this program is run, an execution time error occurs the first time statement 17 is executed. Why? The reason is simply that no value has been assigned to the variable N. To make the program work for a value of N=5, say, we could put the Assignment statement "N=5" immediately following the INTEGER declaration statement. In other words, we would have to change the program each time a different value of N was to be used. It would be nice if the program could be left unchanged and we could simply punch the desired value of N on a card and then somehow, when the job is executed, cause the desired value to be assigned to N. The following program shows how to do just this.

```
C EXAMPLE 2.3 USE OF A READ STATEMENT
      INTEGER FACTN
      READ,N
      MULPLR=1
      FACTN=1
    8 IF(MULPLR.GT.N) GO TO 841
      FACTN=FACTN*MULPLR
      MULPLR=MULPLR+1
      GO TO 8
  841 PRINT,N,FACTN
      STOP
      END
$ENTRY
   5
```

Observe that the value to be assigned to the variable N appears on a card which follows the $ENTRY card. The instruction which causes N to take on this value is "READ,N". The general form of a READ statement is:

READ,input list

where input list is a set of one or more variable names separated by commas. Examples of valid READ statements are:

READ,X

READ,I,YY,VARNAM,KK

Examples of invalid READ statements are:

READ X   (comma missing)

READ,   (no input list)

READ,10./A   (expression in input list)

The READ statement is used to assign values to variables in the input list. The execution of a READ statement causes a card to be read in at <u>execution time</u> and the values on the card are assigned one-for-one to the variables in the input list. The following points are important.

i) The value(s) punched on the card(s) must be separated by a comma and/or blank columns. All eighty columns of a data card may be used for punching values.

ii) The numbers punched on the data cards should agree in type (REAL or INTEGER) with the variables to which they are being assigned. The data values cannot be expressions, they must be valid constants.

iii) If there are insufficient values on a data card then another card is read in <u>automatically</u> and the values on it are used to continue the assignment operation. This process continues until all variables have been assigned a value.

iv) If a data card contains more values than are necessary to provide a value for each variable in the input list, these extra values are ignored and are not available for use by the next READ statement.

The examples which follow illustrate these rules.

i) One READ statement causing one data card to be read.

```
        READ,X,Y,I
        ...
        ...
$ENTRY
  2.0E4, -7.1    67
```

When executed X=20000., Y=-7.1, I=67

ii) One READ statement causing 2 data cards to be read.

```
        READ,X,Y,I
        ...
        ...
        END
$ENTRY
                  2.0E4
  -7.1,                    67
```

When executed X=20000., Y=-7.1, I=67

iii) Two READ statements, the first causing three cards to be read, the second causing one data card to be read.

```
        READ, X,Y,I
        READ,J
        ...
        ...
        END
$ENTRY
 2.0E4
   -7.1
67,84,     25
   -18  ,   738
```

When executed, X=20000.,Y=-7.1, I=67, J=-18 .
The values 84,25, and 738 are unused.

iv) 'Out of Data' Two variables and only one data value.

```
       READ,I,X
       ...
       ...
       END
$ENTRY
           3
```

When executed, an error message is printed and the job is terminated.

It remains to state the importance of assigning values to variables by using a READ statement. The primary advantage is that programs can be written which are very general in nature and which do not require changes to be made to the program when different numbers are used in the calculations. For example a program can be written to find the values of x which solve the equation:

$$Ax^2 + Bx + C = 0.$$

The required roots can be calculated from the values of A,B and C. The difference in the two approaches (Assignment statements versus a READ statement) is illustrated below.

```
C WITH ASSIGNMENT STATEMENTS   C WITH A READ STATEMENT
       A=...                          READ,A,B,C
       B=...                          (statements to
       C=...                             find the roots)
       (statements to find        END
          the roots)           $ENTRY
       END                        values of A,B,and C
$ENTRY
```

Using the method on the left, three cards must be changed each time a different equation is used. Using the READ statement to assign the values means only the data card needs to be changed. Furthermore, if the program is to be used by someone else, instructions which you would give him describing how to use the method on the right are much simpler than those describing how to use the program on the left.

A second and more significant point is evident if we are required to write a program which would solve several quadratic equations one after the other. In this case using a READ statement is far superior since a loop could be set up which would cause the READ statement to be executed several times. Each time the next set of values of A,B, and C would be read in. Using Assignment statements to assign

47

values to the variables would mean unique variable names would have to be used for each set of coefficients. It would be a messy business.

Exercise 2.3

1. For each of the sequences below, determine what values will be assigned to the variables or the reason an error message will be printed. Assume the variables are typed by default.

    a)   READ,II,JJ
                    ...
        $ENTRY
            2
                        -475

    b)   READ,A,X,M
                    ...
        $ENTRY
        -2.64E+02,   -5.718643
                444   26.2

    c)   READ,ROOT
                    READ,OTHER,$,KLM,ROOT
                    ...
        $ENTRY
            -0.00064E-1, -2.5   3.46E20,10   17
        -0.00064E-1,-2.5   , 10   17.

    d)   READ,A,B,C
                    READ,D,E,F,G
                    READ,H,I,J,K,L
                    ....
        $ENTRY
                1. 2. 3. 4. 5.
        6.
            7.,8.,9., 10.   11.
        12.   13.   14.   15.   16.
        17.

2.7 Built-In Functions

Since the computer can only perform the five kinds of arithmetic operations denoted by the symbols + - * / **, how can commonly required calculations such as obtaining the sine of an angle, or the logarithm of a number or the absolute value be done?

Many function values such as these can be obtained using a formula. For example, the sine of an angle of x radians is given by:

$$\sin x = x - \frac{x^3}{3!} + \frac{x^5}{5!} - \frac{x^7}{7!} + \ldots$$

where the exclamation mark denotes the factorial function. Thus if you require the sine of an angle you could include a sequence of WATFIV statements which would produce the desired result as an intermediate step in the program. Fortunately this is not necessary. The authors of the WATFIV compiler have incorporated into the compiler the ability to recognize such things as SIN(X), ALOG(X), and ABS(X) when these "built-in functions" appear in statements within a source program. When the built-in function is recognized, the compiler automatically generates the necessary machine language instructions to perform the desired calculations. Each of the built-in functions produces a value which is either INTEGER or REAL. The first letter of the function name indicates the type of value produced. The independent variables or "function arguments" may also be either REAL or INTEGER depending on the function being used. The general form of a built-in function is:

$$\text{name (argument1,argument2,....)}$$

where "name" is the name of the function and the arguments are the values of the independent variables. In the table below the variables X,Y,Z,... represent REAL-valued arguments and I,J,K,... represent INTEGER valued arguments. This table describes the commonly used built-in functions available in WATFIV and the number and type of arguments which they use. Examples of the result produced by each of these functions can be found following this information. A complete table of WATFIV built-in functions can be found in Appendix I.

TABLE OF BUILT-IN FUNCTIONS

Purpose	Name And Arguments	Definition	Type of Result
Square Root	SQRT(X)	$\sqrt{X}$	REAL
Trigonometric Functions (angles in radians)	SIN(X) COS(X) TAN(X) COTAN(X)	sine cosine tangent cotangent	REAL REAL REAL REAL
Inverse trig Functions (result in radians)	ARSIN(X) ARCOS(X) ATAN(X) ATAN2(X,Y)	arcsine arccosine arctangent arctan(X/Y)	REAL REAL REAL REAL

Logarithms (X > 0)	ALOG(X) ALOG10(X)	log (base e) log (base 10)	REAL REAL
Exponential	EXP(X)	e^X	REAL
Absolute value	ABS(X) IABS(J)	$\|X\|$ $\|J\|$	REAL INTEGER
Transfer of sign	SIGN(X,Y) ISIGN(I,J)	$\|X\| \times$ sign of Y $\|I\| \times$ sign of J sign= $\begin{cases} +1 \text{ if} \geqslant 0 \\ -1 \text{ if} = 0 \end{cases}$	REAL INTEGER
Truncation	AINT(X) INT(X)	sign of X times largest integer $\leqslant$ abs value of X	REAL INTEGER
Modular arithmetic	AMOD(X,Y)	remainder when X is divided by Y	REAL
	MOD(J,K)	remainder when J is divided by K	INTEGER
Positive difference	DIM(X,Y) IDIM(J,K)	X-min of X & Y J-min of J & K	REAL INTEGER
Largest value	AMAX0(I,J,K...) AMAX1(X,Y,Z...) MAX0(I,J,K...) MAX1(X,Y,Z...)	largest arg. largest arg. largest arg. largest arg.	REAL REAL INTEGER INTEGER
Smallest value	AMIN0(I,J,K...) AMIN1(X,Y,Z...) MIN0(I,J,K...) MIN1(X,Y,Z...)	smallest arg. smallest arg. smallest arg. smallest arg.	REAL REAL INTEGER INTEGER
Type Conversion	FLOAT(I)	value of I as a REAL number	REAL
	IFIX(X)	integer part of X, no round-off	INTEGER

Some examples of the results obtained when these built-in functions are used are shown below.

SIN(.5)= 0.4794255   ARSIN(0.4794255)= .5
COS(.5)= 0.8775826   ARCOS(0.8775826) = .5
TAN(.5)= 0.5463024   ATAN(0.5463024)= .5
COTAN(.5)= 1.830487   ATAN2(0.5463024,1.)=.5

```
ALOG10(100.)= 2.
ALOG(100.)=4.605169        EXP(4.605169)=100.

ABS(-24.3)= 24.3           IABS(-24) =24

SIGN(-2.,24.3)= 2.         ISIGN(-2,24)= 2
SIGN(2.,-24.3)=-2.         ISIGN(2,-24)=-2

AINT(3.5)= 3.              INT(3.5)= 3
AINT(-3.5)=-3.             INT(-3.5)=-3

AMOD( 10., 2.7)= 1.9       MOD( 10, 3)= 1
AMOD( 10.,-2.7)= 1.9       MOD( 10,-3)= 1
AMOD(-10., 2.7)=-1.9       MOD(-10, 3)=-1
AMOD(-10.,-2.7)=-1.9       MOD(-10,-3)=-1

DIM(-3., 5.)=0.0           IDIM( 3,-5)=8
DIM( 4.,-2.)=6.0           IDIM(-4,-1)=0

AMIN0(-2,3,-8)=-8.         MIN0(-2,3,-8)=-8
AMIN1(-2.,3.,-8.)=-8.      MIN1(-2.,3.,-8.)=-8
AMAX0(-2,3,-8)=3.          MAX0(-2,3,-8)=3
AMAX1(-2.,3.,-8.)=3.       MAX1(-2.,3.,-8.)=3

FLOAT(-2)=-2.              IFIX( 2.7)= 2
FLOAT( 2)= 2.             IFIX(-2.7)=-2
```

Some examples of expressions and statements using built-in functions are shown below. These examples illustrate important points which you should know.

    i) AMAX1(SIN(3.),COS(3.),TAN(3.))

   ii) SQRT(EXP(2**ALOG10(ABS(-3.+FLOAT(I)))))

  iii) I=FLOAT(I)

   iv) A=IFIX(A)

    v) L=I+J+K-MIN0(I,J,K)-MAX0(I,J,K)

   vi) I=I+1-2*MOD(I+1,2)

  vii) Y=SQRT(SQRT(X))

 viii) A=X-SIGN(AINT(ABS(X/Y)),1.)*Y

Example (i) produces a value which is the largest of the the sine, the cosine and the tangent of an angle of 3 radians. Note that if the value of 3 had been written without a decimal point, an error would result since the argument of the SIN function must be REAL. This example also shows that the arguments of built-in functions can be expressions which involve built-in functions.

Example (ii) shows that one can evaluate functions of functions. In this example, the functions are nested to a depth of five and the result is obtained by calculating the value of the innermost function first and proceeding outward.

Example (iii) produces no change in the value of I. If I is 2 for instance, FLOAT(I) will have a value of 2.0 and when the assignment is completed I will again have the the INTEGER value 2 .

Example (iv) causes the fractional part of A to be truncated. Suppose A is -3.671, then IFIX(A)=-3 and hence A=-3.0 . The same result could have been obtained by using "A=AINT(A)".

Example (v) shows a single Assignment statement which would produce a result equal to the value of the INTEGER variable which is neither the maximum or minimum of three INTEGER values. For instance if I=-8, J=12, and K=-1, then L=-8 + 12 -1 -MIN0(-8,12,-1) -MAX0(-8,12,-1)=3 - (-8)-12 =-1.

Consider example (vi). Suppose the statement is executed repeatedly. The effect is to increase I by 1 if I is odd and to decrease I by 1 if I is even. Thus the value of I would oscillate between a pair of adjacent INTEGER values. Quite often one can make use of a value such as this which "flip-flops" between a pair of values, say 1 and 2, each time a sequence of statements has been executed. This example shows one way of accomplishing this effect.

Example (vii) shows one way of obtaining the fourth root of a REAL number. (Others, of course, are X**.25, or X**(1./4.), but not X**(1/4).)

Example (viii) shows the steps that are necessary to obtain AMOD(X,Y) and hence could have been written equivalently as A=AMOD(X,Y).

A Word About FLOAT And IFIX

Are the type conversion functions IFIX and FLOAT essential for writing programs in WATFIV? After all, isn't 2.*FLOAT(3) the same as 2.*3? There are two important reasons for having type conversion functions in WATFIV. First, each built-in function must have arguments of a specific type. This means, for example, to obtain the square root of an INTEGER value 25, say, that the expression SQRT(FLOAT(25)) must be used in order to use the built-in function SQRT. Second, many Fortran compilers do not permit

both REAL and INTEGER values to appear in the same
expression. For example, the expression "325.*10" which is
valid in WATFIV would have to be written either as
"IFIX(325.)*10" or as "325.*FLOAT(10)" to be acceptable. In
this book, FLOAT and IFIX are sometimes used in examples
even when the situation does not make their use necessary.


```
************************************************************
*                                                        *
*          Rules For Using Built-In Functions            *
*                                                        *
*    1. The type of function value produced is indicated *
*          by applying the first-letter rule to the name *
*          of the function.                              *
*                                                        *
*    2. The function arguments must be of the required   *
*          type. If not, an error message is produced.   *
*                                                        *
*    3. Functions may be nested to a depth of seven.     *
*                                                        *
*    4. The calculation of function values has the high- *
*          est priority in evaluating arithmetic expressions. *
*          That is, the values of any functions appearing in *
*          arithmetic expressions are calculated before any *
*          other operations are performed.               *
*                                                        *
************************************************************
```


Exercise 2.4

1.   What is the value assigned to each of the variables
     appearing on the left sides of the following sets of
     Assignment statements?

     a) X=AMOD(10.,3.)
        Y=SQRT(49.)
        Z=-SIGN(X,Y)

     b) A=ALOG10(100.)**MOD(7,4)

     c) J=4
        J=SQRT(FLOAT(J))-(SQRT(FLOAT(9))**(-1))

     d) I=J=K=1
        M=MIN0(I+J-2*K,J-K)+MAX0(-MIN0(2,-3),I)

     e) K=IDIM(ISIGN(-2,4),IFIX(FLOAT(MOD(13,-5))))

2. What is the error in each of the following Assignment
   statements?

   a) Y=SIN(3)
   b) ABS(X)=10.
   c) READ,J,MOD(J,2)
   d) Y=IFIX(COS(ABS(X))
   e) R=S+FLOAT(5.)

3. Write a single statement to achieve the same effect as
   Y=ABS(X) using:
                    a) the SQRT function
                    b) the SIGN function
                    c) the AMAX1 function

4.   Write a single statement using the MOD function so that
   an INTEGER variable K which has an initial value of 1
   will take on succesive values of 2,3,4,1,2,3,4,1,2,...
   if the statement is executed over and over again.

2.8 Summary

1. The WATFIV language distinguishes between numbers
    which are written with and without decimal points.

2. The priority of operations in evaluating expressions
    is:
                Functions (right to left)
                Brackets (innermost first)
                Exponentiation (right to left)
                Multiplication and Division (left to right)
                Addition and Subtraction (left to right)

3. Variables may take on REAL values or INTEGER values.
    The type of value is determined:
                1. By default. (the first-letter rule)
               *2. Implicitly. (using the IMPLICIT statement)
                3. Explicitly. (using a REAL or INTEGER
                                   declaration statement)

4. Variables may be given a value in one of two ways.
                1. By using an Assignment (=) statement.
                2. By using a READ statement.

5. WATFIV has a library of built-in functions which are
    handy for obtaining the values of many frequently
    used functions.

2.9 <u>Summary of WATFIV Statements Discussed Thus Far.</u>

The types of statements discussed thus far, and their purposes are:

1. Job Control Statements
   a) $JOB - the first card of any WATFIV job
   b) $ENTRY - separates the source program from the data cards

2. Comments - used to improve a reader's understanding the program

3. WATFIV statements

   a) Non-executable statements - used to provide information for the compiler.

   INTEGER - specifies variables which will have INTEGER values

   REAL - specifies variables which will have REAL values

   *IMPLICIT - defines part or all of a first-letter rule

   END - indicates the end of a program segment

   b) Executable statements - cause something to happen at execution time

   Assignment - assigns a value to a variable

   READ - assigns a value to a variable

   PRINT - displays values on the printer

   GO TO - transfers control to another statement

   IF(...) GO TO - transfers control if a condition is true

   STOP - stops further execution of instructions

Full details of the READ and PRINT statements can be found in Chapters 5 and 6. Details of the GO TO, IF and STOP statements are in the next chapter.

Programming Problems

2.1 Write a program to calculate the value of $12-(6-i)^2$ for values of i of 1, 2, 3, ..., 12. Twelve lines of output should be produced. The first value on each line should be the value of i, the second, the value of the expression.

2.2 Tabulate (calculate and print out) values of x and y given by the formula

$$y = \frac{x^3 - 4x^2 + x - 3}{x + 2}$$

for a) x = 0., .25., .5, .75, ..., 1.75, 2.0
  b) x = -1, -3, -5, ..., -11, -13
  c) x = 10, 9, 8, ..., -9, -10. Note: the value of negative two must be skipped over. To do this test each value of x as it is generated and, if equal to -2, go to the statement which generates the next value of x.

2.3 Write a program which prints the values of integers in the range one thru fifty which divide evenly into one-hundred.

2.4 Read values of X and N. Print the values of X, X/2, X/4, ..., X/2**N.

2.5 The sum of successive powers of the INTEGER values one thru N are given by the following formulae.

  a) Sum of values $\dfrac{N(N+1)}{2}$

  b) Sum of squares $\dfrac{N(N+1)(2N+1)}{6}$

  c) Sum of Cubes $\dfrac{N^2(N+1)^2}{4}$

  d) Sum of Fourth Powers $\dfrac{N(N+1)(2N+1)(3N^2+3N-1)}{30}$

  e) Sum of Fifth Powers $\dfrac{N^2(N+1)^2(2N^2+2N-1)}{12}$

Write a program to calculate the sum of the first, second, third, fourth and fifth powers of the numbers one thru twenty. That is, calculate the value of the five expressions above with N=20.

2.6 Write a program which reads in ten pairs of numbers, each pair representing a distance in feet and inches.

56

After each pair of values is read, convert the distance to an equivalent distance in yards.

2.7   Write a program   which reads in six values, each representing a weight in killograms. After each value is read, convert it to an equivalent weight in grams and milligrams. For example, a weight of 3.56789 kilograms becomes 3567 grams and 890 milligrams. The results of this program will clearly demonstrate the errors which may result when working with fractional REAL values.

2.8   Read twelve values punched one per card each of which represents a number of hours. Express each value as the sum of weeks, days and hours. For example, 193 hours becomes 1 week + 1 day + 1 hour.

2.9   Print those integer values in the range 11 thru 999 which, when divided by the number obtained by leaving off the last digit, give a remainder of zero. For example, 36 is such a number because 3 divides into 36.

2.10   An approximate value of the square root of x for x in the range .1 thru 10 is given by the formula $(1+4x)/(4+x)$. Write a program which calulates the value of the square root of .5, 1., 1.5, ..., 9.5, 10, using both the formula and the SQRT function. Print the value of each result and the percentage error resulting from using the formula.

2.11   For values of x in the range .1 thru 1 an approximate value of the logarithm of x is given by the formula

$$\log x = -.076 + .281x - \frac{.238}{x + .15}$$

Write a program which prints out the values of log x using the formula and the built-in function ALOG. Use values of x of .2, .4, .6, .8, and 1. For each print the absolute value of the difference of the two log values.

2.12   Write a program which reads in values of A, B and C representing the lengths of three sides of a triangle. Calculate the area of the triangle using the formula

$$\text{Area} = \sqrt{S(S-A)(S-B)(S-C)}$$

where S is one-half the perimeter of the triangle. Calculate the radius of the inscribed circle (given by Area/S).

2.13   A series circuit consists of a resistor of R ohms, an inductance of L henries and a capacitor of C farads. If the voltage across the circuit is E volts at F cycles per second, the current in amperes flowing thru the circuit is given by the formula

$$i = \frac{E}{\sqrt{R^2 + \left(\dfrac{2\pi FL - 1}{2\pi FC}\right)^2}}$$

Write a program which reads in values of R, L and C and computes the current thru the circuit at 60 cycles per second for values of E of 100, 200, 300, ..., 900 volts.

2.14 Read a value of N and determine if N is a prime number. To do this, divide each of the numbers 2 thru N/2 into N. If any remainder is zero, print "NOT PRIME" using the statement "PRINT,'NOT PRIME'". Otherwise, print "PRIME".

2.15 Improve the efficiency of the program for question 2.14 by: (a) Testing N for an even value as soon as it is read in; (b) Use only odd-valued test divisors up to the interger value closest to, but below, the square root of N.

2.16 Suppose you borrow $X for a period of N months at a monthly interest rate of i (e.g. .01). The size of your monthly payment is given by the formula

$$iX\left(\frac{(1+i)^N}{(1+i)^N - 1}\right)$$

Write a program which reads values of X, i and N and calculates the size of the monthly payment.

2.17 Tabulate the values of the sine, cosine and tangent of angles of 0 , 5 , 10 , ..., 60 (degrees). Note that the angles must be converted to radians before the built-in functions can be used.

2.18 The greatest common divisor (GCD) of two numbers M and N can be calculated in the following way (Euclid's Algorithm). Divide the larger by the smaller. If the remainder is zero, the GCD is the smaller. If not, divide the smaller by the remainder. If zero, the remainder is the GCD. If not, continue dividing the remainder into the previous remainder until a remainder of zero is obtained. The GCD is the value of the last non-zero remainder. Write a program to find the GCD of any two INTEGER values. Test your program by reading several pairs of data values punched one pair per card. Stop when a pair of zeros is read in.

2.19 You are required to determine the smallest total number of bills required to pay a sum of $1579.00 using

only fifties, tens and one dollar bills. Write a program
to do this.

2.20 Modify the program for question 2.19 so that: the
amount to be paid is read from a card; the values of the
three denominations to be used in paying the bill is
read from a card. Why is the programming problem much
more difficult if you had to read the number of
different types of bills to be used as well as the
denomination of each?

CHAPTER 3   DECISION AND CONTROL

Questions Answered In This Chapter.

    1. How can we control the sequence of instructions
       executed by the computer so that the calculations
       are performed in the desired order?

    2. What is meant by the terms conditional and
       unconditional control?

    3. What are the four types of "if___ then___"
       statements available in WATFIV?

    As we have seen, almost all programs contain a sequence
of one or more instructions which are repeated several times
with a few small changes being made in the numbers used in
the calculations each time the sequence is repeated.
Frequently we do not always want instructions to be executed
in the order in which they are written. To do this we use
instructions to control the order in which statements are
executed. In this chapter we shall examine the different
methods which can be used to control the order of statement
execution.

3.1 Terminating Execution of Instructions.

The STOP Statement

    All the example programs used thus far have included a
STOP statement. This instruction stops any further
execution of instructions and causes the job statistics such
as compile time, execution time and memory used to be
printed. It is permissible to put a number after the word
STOP (eg: STOP 246). This form of the STOP instruction
causes the number to be printed on the computer operator's
typewriter. In most computer centers however, the presence
of a number following the word STOP is ignored by the WATFIV
compiler and hence no number is printed. More than one STOP
instruction may be used in a program but the first one
encountered at execution time terminates the job.

*The PAUSE Statement

    A PAUSE statement causes a temporary halt in the
execution of instructions. It is usually used to permit the
computer operator to perform some special task such as
putting special forms in the printer, or mounting a reel of

tape on a tape drive. When the operator has completed the
required task he presses a start button and processing
resumes. In most installations a PAUSE statement is ignored
by the compiler but in those cases where it is not ignored
it may take one of the following three forms.

PAUSE   - no message or number is printed

PAUSE n - where "n" is a number which is printed
           on the operator's typewriter

PAUSE 'message to operator' - the symbols between
           the quote signs are printed on the
           computer operator's typewriter

3.2 Unconditional Control Statements.

Unconditional control means you can predict with
certainty what the next instruction to be executed will be.
There are two unconditional control statements in WATFIV.

GO TO s

A statement such as "GO TO 27" means "the next
instruction to be executed is the one having a statement
number of 27". The only requirement is that the statement
number following the words GO TO must refer to an executable
statement. Consider the following pair of statements.

        20 REAL JJ
           GO TO 20

The GO TO is invalid since a REAL statement is a
declaration statement and is used to tell the compiler that
JJ is to take on REAL values. The "GO TO s" form of a GO TO
is often called a "simple GO TO" or an "unconditional GO
TO". Since blanks are ignored by the compiler in scanning
the statement it is permissible to write the words GO TO as
the single word GOTO.

CONTINUE

A CONTINUE statement is, in one sense, an instruction
which causes nothing to happen. Consider the following
program.

        C EXAMPLE 3.1 TRIVIAL USE OF A CONTINUE
              A=B=5.
              A=B+SQRT(A)
              CONTINUE
              PRINT,A,B
              STOP
              END

The effect of the CONTINUE statement is simply to say "carry on with the next instruction". You may well wonder why it is included in WATFIV. It is most frequently found teamed up with the DO statement which will be discussed in the next chapter. It is also sometimes handy to use when testing part of a large program. By putting a statement number in front of a CONTINUE and inserting the CONTINUE in front of some statement, you can GO TO the CONTINUE statement to test part of a routine. Once the routine is working, the CONTINUE statement is removed and no re-keypunching of other statements is required.

3.3 Conditional Control

Frequently one wishes to change the normal sequential order of executing instructions provided the variables appearing in the calculations have certain values. In WATFIV there are four types of conditional control statements of the form "If ____ then go to ____". The conditions which are tested in each of the four types of statements may be roughly classified as follows.

Usual Type Of Condition Tested	Statement Name
i) To test the relationship between a pair of arithmetic expressions eg: A.LE.(B+C)	Logical IF
ii) To test an arithmetic expression for being negative, zero, or positive and to go to (usually) different statements depending on the result of the test.	Arithmetic IF
iii) To test an INTEGER variable for a value in the range 1,2,3,...K and to go to (usually) a different statement depending on the result of the test.	Computed GO TO
iv) To test an INTEGER variable for a value equal to one of several statement numbers and to go to the statement number which is the same as the value of the variable.	Assigned GO TO

In many cases it is possible to use two or more of the four types to accomplish the same purpose. Thus the choice of which type of statement to use is matter of personal preference. We shall examine each of the four types in turn.

3.4 The Logical IF Statement

The Logical IF statement has two types of uses. It can be used to transfer control depending on the truthfulness of one or more relationships and to "sneak in" an extra statement. Each of these uses will be discussed in turn.

Used As A Conditional GO TO

When used as a conditional GO TO the Logical IF has the general form:

        IF(this is true) GO TO s

where s is the statement number of some executable statement in the program. Frequently the condition being tested for truthfulness is expressed as the relationship between the values of a pair of arithmetic expressions. Examples are:

   i)   IF(A.LE.B) GO TO 94

   ii)   IF(SIN(X).GT.2.**(-3)) GO TO 8

   iii)   IF(3.EQ.2) GO TO 99999

There are six relationships which can be tested and for review purposes these are: .EQ.,.NE.,.LT., .LE.,.GT.,.GE.. These six sets of symbols are called <u>relational operators</u> and they have lower priority than any of the arithmetic operators. This means the truth of the relationship is tested after the values of any arithmetic expressions have been determined.

If the condition being tested is true, the next statement executed is the one whose statement number follows the words GO TO. If the condition is false, the next statement executed is the one following the IF statement.

Example (iii) above shows a Logical IF statement which is totally unnecessary since the statement following the IF will always be the next one executed.

Because some fractional REAL values are stored with a tiny error (see Chapter 2, Section 4), caution should be exercised when testing two REAL values for equality. Consider the following pair of statements.

        Y=.2+.2+.2+.2+.2
        IF(Y.EQ.1.) GO TO 14

Because a value of .2 in the computer is only a good approximation to a value of one-fifth, the value of Y in the foregoing is not exactly 1. This means control would never transfer to statement 14.

To overcome this difficulty, the following IF statement could be used.

IF(ABS(Y-1.).LE. .000001) GO TO 14

Thus if one is interested in testing two REAL values for equality, it is necessary to compare the absolute value of the difference between them to some very small value. Keep in mind that this is necessary only if the values being compared could have digits to the right of the decimal point.

*Testing Multiple Conditions

Frequently one requires that more than one condition be true before changing the normal sequential order of executing instructions. For example: Suppose you wish to test if the value of a variable X lies in the interval 0.5 to 1.7. If it does, the next instruction to be executed is to be statement 15 and if not, we are to carry on with the next instruction. In WATFIV this can be done using the the following Logical IF statement.

IF((X.GE.0.5).AND.(X.LE.1.7)) GO TO 15
7 ...

In order for the entire condition to be true, both relationships must be true. If either or both are false, statement 7 will be the next one executed. We say that the relationships (X.GE.0.5) and (X.LE.1.7) have been "anded".

If R1,R2,R3 and R4 are relationships which are either true or false then the condition:

(R1.AND.R2.AND.R3.AND.R4)

will be true if and only if all of R1,R2,R3 and R4 are individually true. The same test as made in the previous example could be made using the following pair of Logical IF statements.

IF(X.LT.0.5) GO TO 7
IF(X.LE.1.7) GO TO 15
7 ...

To satisfy yourself that this pair of Logical IF statements is indeed equivalent to the compound IF statement used previously, execute the statements above with values of X of .2, 1.1, and 5.

Suppose statement 15 is to be executed next if X lies outside the interval (.5, 1.7). A sufficient condition is that either X <.5 or X>1.7. This test could be made using the following pair of Logical IF statements.

```
         IF(X.LT.0.5) GO TO 15
         IF(X.GT.1.7) GO TO 15
      7 ...
```

The two conditions could also be tested using the following single Logical IF statement.

```
         IF((X.LT.0.5).OR.(X.GT.1.7)) GO TO 15
      7 ...
```

When a pair of conditions are combined in this manner we say they have been "ored".

In general, if R1,R2,R3, and R4, say, are relationships each of which is either true or false, then the relationship

$$(R1.OR.R2.OR.R3.OR.R4)$$

will be true if one or more of R1,R2,R3,R4 is true.

Occasionally for the sake of clarity or convenience one wishes to test a condition to see if it is not true, that is, false. For example if the relationship (X.LT.1.7) is true then necessarily the relation (X.GE.1.7) must be false. To test the falseness of a condition you can prefix the condition with the operator .NOT.. The pair of statements below are equivalent.

a)   `IF(X.LT.1.7) GO TO 15`
      `7 ...`

b)   `IF(.NOT.(X.GE.1.7)) GO TO 15`
      `7 ...`

To be precise, the use of the operator .NOT. changes the "truth value" of the condition which it precedes. Thus if R is a relationship which is true then .NOT.R is false. If R is false then .NOT.R is true. In the example above suppose X has a value 0. Then (X.GE.1.7) is false and hence .NOT.(X.GE.1.7) is true as is (X.LT.1.7). The expressions .NOT.(X.GE.1.7) and (X.LT.1.7) have the same truth value regardless of the value of X and therefore are equivalent.

Suppose R1,R2,R3, and R4 are four relationships each of which is true or false. How are we to evaluate the truth value of an expression such as:

$$(R1.AND.R2.OR..NOT.R3.AND.R4)$$

As well as rules for evaluating arithmetic expressions, there are rules or priorities for evaluating expressions which contain the operators .AND., .OR., and .NOT. . The operations are performed in the following order.

.NOT.   has the highest priority

.AND.   has the second highest priority

.OR.   has the lowest priority

Processing proceeds left to right in each case and the order in which operations are performed may be modified by using brackets to indicate operations which are to be done first. The example expression is therefore evaluated in the order shown below.

(R1.AND.R2.OR..NOT.R3.AND.R4)

The expression is therefore evaluated as if written with the sets of brackets shown below.

((R1.AND.R2).OR.((.NOT.R3).AND.R4))

Thus if R1 is T (true), R2 is F (false), R3 is F, and R4 is T, then the truth value of the expression is:

T .AND. F .OR. .NOT. F .AND. T =
T .AND. F .OR. T .AND. T = F .OR. T = T

A summary of the priorities of the various operators used in WATFIV is shown in the following table.

```
*****************************************************************
*                                                               *
*              Summary of Operator Priorities                   *
*                                                               *
*   1. Evaluation of functions  (right to left)                 *
*                                                               *
*   2. Brackets (innermost first)                               *
*                                                               *
*   3. Arithmetic Operators                                     *
*          Exponentiation (right to left)                       *
*          Multiplication and Division (left to right)          *
*          Addition and Subtraction (left to right)             *
*                                                               *
*   4. Relational operators (left to right)                     *
*          .LT.  .LE.  .EQ.  .NE.  .GT.  .GE.                    *
*                                                               *
*   5. Logical operators                                        *
*          .NOT. (left to right)                                *
*          .AND. (left to right)                                *
*          .OR. (left to right)                                 *
*                                                               *
*****************************************************************
```

Your decision to use or not to use the logical operators
.AND., .OR. and .NOT. is a matter of personal preference.
However complicated a relationship may look it can always be
written using a sequence of Logical IF statements which do
not use the Logical operators. For example,

```
    IF((A.LT.B).OR..NOT.(C.EQ.D).AND.(E.GE.F))GO TO 15
  7 ......
```

is equivalent to

```
    IF(A.LT.B) GO TO 15
    IF(C.EQ.D) GO TO 7
    IF(E.GE.F) GO TO 15
  7 ........
```

The reasoning which leads us to arrive at the three
statements above is as follows: Let R1, R2, and R3 denote
the three relationships (A.LT.B), (C.EQ.D), and (E.GE.F).
The entire condition will be true if R1 is true. This
accounts for the first IF statement. If R1 is false then
both .NOT.R2 and R3 must be true if the entire condition is
to be true. Now if R2 is true then .NOT.R2 will be false and
the entire condition will be false - thus the second IF
statement. Finally if R1 and R2 are both false then R3 must
be true to make the entire condition true. This accounts for
the third IF statement.

For a further discussion and more examples of Logical
quantities and operators the reader is referred to Chapter
14.

"Sneaking In An Extra Statement"

As well as providing a method of "going to" a particular
statement when a condition being tested is true, the Logical
IF can also be used to "sneak in" an extra statement when a
condition is found to be true. Consider the statement.

```
        IF(A.GT.B) Y=X+ABS(Z)
     24 ...
```

The effect of the IF statement above is: "If A is
greater than B then assign the value of X+ABS(Z) to the
variable Y before executing statement 24, otherwise carry on
with statement 24."

Suppose we wish to assign the variable J a value of 1 if
A equals B and to give J a value 2 if A is not equal to B.
A beginning programmer will often write the following set of
statements to achieve this result.

```
            IF(A.EQ.B) GO TO 6
            J=2
            GO TO 8
          6 J=1
          8 ...
```

A much neater way of achieving the same result is to use the following sequence of statements.

```
            J=2
            IF(A.EQ.B) J=1
          8 ...
```

Using this approach we assume A is not equal to B and set J=2. The value of J is changed only if it is found that A does equal B.

The statement which follows the brackets in a Logical IF statement is called the "trailer". The trailer statement is executed whenever the condition being tested is found to be true. The reader will realize that a GO TO is just a particular type of trailer used to control the sequence in which statements are executed. The trailer can be any executable statement except another Logical IF or a DO statement. (The DO statement is discussed in the next chapter.)

The program below could be used to read in a set of INTEGER values, punched one per card, and calculate the sum of the positive numbers. The program terminates when a value of 99999 is detected.

```
        C EXAMPLE 3.2 FIND THE SUM OF POSITIVE VALUES
              INTEGER TOTAL
              TOTAL=0
            4 READ,J
              IF(J.EQ.99999) GO TO 71
              IF(J.GT.0) TOTAL=TOTAL + J
              GO TO 4
           71 PRINT,TOTAL
              STOP
              END
```

In this program the Logical IF is used in one statement as a conditional control statement and in another to sneak in the statement "TOTAL=TOTAL+J".

The general form of the Logical IF statement is:

```
********************************************************
*                                                      *
*          IF ( e ) s                                  *
*                                                      *
*     where: e is an expression which is either        *
*            true or false, and                        *
*                                                      *
*            s is any executable WATFIV statement       *
*            except another Logical IF or a DO         *
*            statement (Chapter 4 describes the        *
*                 DO statement)                        *
*                                                      *
********************************************************
```

Statement s is called the trailer and is executed whenever e is true. If s does not cause control to be transferred to some other statement, the next statement executed is the one following the Logical IF. If e is false the trailer is ignored and the statement following the Logical IF is the next statement executed.

3.5 The Arithmetic IF

A second type of conditional control statement is called the Arithmetic IF. It automatically compares the value of an arithmetic expression to zero and transfers control to one of (usually) three different statements depending on whether the value being tested is negative, zero, or positive. Example program 3.2 which used two Logical IFs to find the sum of the positive numbers could equally well have been written using a pair of Arithmetic IF statements. The following program shows how.

```
      C EXAMPLE 3.3 FIND THE SUM OF POSITIVE VALUES
      C   STOP WHEN A VALUE OF 99999 IS FOUND
            INTEGER TOTAL
            TOTAL=0
        4 READ, J
            IF(J-99999) 18,71,18
       18 IF(J) 4,4,333
      333 TOTAL =TOTAL+J
            GO TO 4
       71 PRINT,TOTAL
            STOP
            END
```

The operation of an Arithmetic IF is easy to understand. The first IF statement:

              IF (J-99999) 18,71,18

means: i) Determine the value of the expression J-99999.

69

    ii) If this value is negative go to statement 18
   iii) If this value is zero go to statement 71
    iv) If this value is positive go to statement 18

Similarly the second IF statement

$$IF(\ J \ ) \ 4,4,333$$

means transfer control to statement 4 if J is negative or zero and to statement 333 if J is positive.

Suppose EXP is some REAL valued variable and 22, 876, and 3 are statement numbers of executable statements. Then the Arithmetic IF statement shown below on the left is equivalent to the set of statements shown on the right.

Using an Arithmetic IF	Using Logical IFs

IF(EXP)22,876,3	IF(EXP.LT.0.)GO TO 22
	IF(EXP.EQ.0.)GO TO 876
	GO TO 3

Since an arithmetic expression has a value which must be negative, zero or positive (there are no other possibilities), one of the three statement numbers following the expression being tested must necessarily be the number of the next statement to be executed. For this reason the statement following an Arithmetic IF should always be given a statement number if it is to serve any useful purpose in the program. Otherwise there is no way it can ever be executed.

The general form of the Arithmetic IF is:

```
*******************************************************
*                                                     *
*              IF ( e ) s1,s2,s3                       *
*                                                     *
*       where: e is an arithmetic expression, and     *
*              s1,s2,and s3 are numbers of executable *
*              statements appearing elsewhere in      *
*              the program                            *
*                                                     *
*       Control is passed to s1,s2 or s3 depending    *
*          on whether e is negative,zero or positive  *
*                                                     *
*******************************************************
```

Exercise 3.1

1. In each of the following determine which statement will be the next one executed after the statements shown have been executed. State the values of all variables appearing in the sequence at that point

in time. Assume all variables are typed by the
first-letter rule.

a)
```
        I=6
        IF(17.LE.I+8) GO TO 14
    9 ......
```

b)
```
        A=3/2.
        IF(A.NE.1.5) A=A+A
    1 ......
```

c)
```
        A=FLOAT(70/6)
        B=AINT(A/FLOAT(70/6)+2.5)
        IF(A.LT.B) GO TO 4
        IF(-A.GE.-B) A=B
    5 ......
```

d)
```
        I=MOD(MOD(21,17),-3)
        IF(I*I-I) 5,6,7
    8 .......
```

e)
```
        A=2.6
        K=3+IFIX(A)
        IF(IDIM(3-K,8)) 2,18,4
   18 K=2
        GO TO 7
    4 A=2.*K
        STOP
    2 ......
```

f)
```
        Z=A=2.
        IF(Z**2.LE.A+3) IF(A-2.) 6,11,15
    6 ......
```

2. For each of the following Logical IF statements write
   an equivalent Arithmetic IF.

a)
```
        IF(A.LT.B) GO TO 10
    6 ......
```

b)
```
        IF(A.GT.B) GO TO 8
        IF(B.GT.A) GO TO 7
    5 ......
```

3. For each of the following Arithmetic IF statements
   write one or more Logical IF statements to achieve
   the same result.

a)
```
        IF(X-2) 10,20,30
```

b)
```
        IF(10+J+K) 4,7,4
```

4. Explain the error in each of the following.

   a) IF(A=B) GO TO 7
   b) IF(X),5,25,871
   c) IF(A-2) GO TO 17
   d) IF(B-C.GT.14.)10,11,12
   e) IF(10.LT.A) IF(B.GT.C/D) GO TO 5
   f) IF((X.LT.Y)/2.) GO TO 4

5. For each of the three statements below, replace the
   statement with an equivalent unconditional control
   statement.

   a) IF(A-B) 88,88,88
   b) IF(3.EQ.-4) GO TO 5
   c) IF(-6**(-2)) 15,23,8

6. Replace the compound IF statement below with a
   sequence of:
   a) Logical IF statements
   b) Arithmetic IF statements

   IF(A.LE.B.OR..NOT.B.LE.C.AND.D.GT.B)GO TO 70
80 ...

7. Replace each sequence of statements below with
   an equivalent Logical IF statement.

   a)   IF(A.LT.B) GO TO 8
             IF(C.NE.D) GO TO 7
             IF(E.GT.F) GO TO 10
           7 IF(G.GT.H) GO TO 10
           8 ....

   b)   IF(X)1,2,2
           2 IF(Y)3,1,3
           1 IF(Z)4,3,4
           3 ...

3.6 The Computed GO TO

We have seen that the Arithmetic IF provides a
convenient method of branching to (transferring control to)
one of three possible different statements depending on the
value of an arithmetic expression. The Computed GO TO is
another method of branching to one of several statement
numbers depending on the value of an INTEGER variable. As
an example suppose that a set of positive integers is
punched one integer per card and that the value of each
integer is one of 1,2,3 or 4. The problem is to: count the
number of occurrences of each value; print the total number
of each type; stop when a value outside this range is found.
The following program solves the problem.

72

```
C EXAMPLE 3.4 USING A COMPUTED GO TO
C COUNT THE NUMBER OF OCCURRENCES OF 1,2,3 AND 4
C STOP WHEN A VALUE OUTSIDE THE RANGE IS FOUND
      INTEGER COUNT1,COUNT2,COUNT3,COUNT4
      COUNT1=COUNT2=COUNT3=COUNT4=0
    2 READ,NUMBER
      GO TO(14,72,3,86),NUMBER
      PRINT,COUNT1,COUNT2,COUNT3,COUNT4
      STOP
C STATEMENTS TO ADD 1 TO THE APPROPRIATE COUNTER
   14 COUNT1=COUNT1+1
      GO TO 2
   72 COUNT2=COUNT2+1
      GO TO 2
    3 COUNT3-COUNT3+1
      GO TO 2
   86 COUNT4=COUNT4+1
      GO TO 2
      END
$ENTRY
```

In this program, the statement

                GO TO (14,72,3,86), NUMBER

is equivalent to the following set of Logical IF statements.

                IF(NUMBER.EQ.1) GO TO 14

                IF(NUMBER.EQ.2) GO TO 72

                IF(NUMBER.EQ.3) GO TO 3

                IF(NUMBER.EQ.4) GO TO 86

                ...

The dots following the fourth IF statement indicate that
if none of the four relationships tested is true, then the
statement following the last IF is the next one executed.

The Computed GO TO can be used to define conditional
control based on the value of an INTEGER variable which lies
in the range 1,2,3,...,K where K is some positive INTEGER
constant. If the value of the INTEGER variable being tested
lies outside the range 1,2,3,...,K then the statement
immediately following the Computed GO TO is the next one
executed.

The general form of the Computed GO TO is:

```
*******************************************************
*                                                     *
*            GO TO (s1,s2,...,sK),i                   *
*                                                     *
*     where: K represents some positive INTEGER,      *
*                                                     *
*            s1,s2,...,sK are statement numbers       *
*               of executable statements,            *
*                                                     *
*            i is an INTEGER variable                 *
*                                                     *
*******************************************************
```

Two errors frequently made by programmers using Computed GO TOs for the first time are:

i) Forgetting to put the comma ahead of the variable being tested.

ii) Forgetting that the Computed GO TO can only be used to test the value of an INTEGER variable and not an INTEGER expression.

The pair of statements below shows how a Computed GO TO could be used to transfer control to statements 17, 18, or 19 depending on whether the variable IYEAR has a value in the range 1700-1799, 1800-1899, or 1900-1999.

J=(IYEAR-1600)/100

GO TO (17,18,19),J

Observe that one could also replace the Computed GO TO above with an Arithmetic IF as follows.

J=(IYEAR-1500)/100

IF(J-2) 17,18,19

There is one slight difference in the two cases however. To see this we ask "What happens if IYEAR has a value outside the range 1700-1999?". Using the Computed GO TO the next statement executed would be the one following the Computed GO TO. Using the Arithmetic IF however: statement 17 would be the next one executed if IYEAR was less than 1700; statement 19 would be the next one executed if IYEAR was greater than 1999. Thus the choice of which type of conditional control statement to use would be decided on what was to be done if IYEAR was outside the range of interest.

*3.7 ASSIGN and Assigned GO TO

In many programming languages statements in the program
may be given labels. For example statements of the type:

        START READ,N
            ...
            ...
            ...
        GO TO START

can be written. In WATFIV, however, statement numbers and
not labels are used to identify statements. There is a
feature of the WATFIV language however which does permit a
programmer to more or less assign a statement number to an
INTEGER variable and then "go to" the statement number
associated with the INTEGER variable. This feature requires
the use of a pair of statements -- the ASSIGN statement and
the Assigned GO TO statement. The effect shown in the
program structure above could be achieved as follows.

            INTEGER START
        10 READ,N
            ...
        ASSIGN 10 TO START
            ...
        GO TO START,(10)

You will obviously be wondering "Why bother?". Why not
simply replace the ASSIGN and the GO TO above with a plain
and simple GO TO 10. You are absolutely right. The only
reason is that the Assigned GO TO can be used to branch to
one of several statements instead of the one possibility as
shown in the example. For instance if the statement

        GO TO J,(15,10,71,8888)

appears in a program, control will be transferred to the
statement number which matches the value of J provided J had
been ASSIGNed one of the values 15, 10, 71, or 8888
previously in the program. If not, an execution time error
would occur and the job would be terminated.

The ASSIGN statement is used to assign a statement
number to an INTEGER variable for future use in an Assigned
GO TO. The variable which is ASSIGNed a value is often
called a program switch because control switches to one
point or another in the program depending on the value of
the variable. The program below uses a pair of ASSIGN
statements and an Assigned GO TO to read sets of four REAL
values; print them; and terminate when the first of the
group of four has a value zero.

```
C EXAMPLE 3.5 USING ASSIGN AND ASSIGNED GO TO
      INTEGER BACK
      ASSIGN 21 TO BACK
   21 READ,A,B,C,D
      IF(A.EQ.0.) ASSIGN 6 TO BACK
      PRINT,A,B,C,D
      GO TO BACK,(21,6)
    6 STOP
      END
```

The rules and general form of the ASSIGN and Assigned GO
TO statements are as follows.

```
*******************************************************
*                                                     *
*        ASSIGN s TO i                                *
*                                                     *
*        GO TO i , (s1,s2,...,sK)                     *
*                                                     *
*        where: K represents a positive integer,      *
*                                                     *
*               i is an INTEGER variable,             *
*                                                     *
*               s and s1,s2,s3,...,sK are numbers     *
*               of executable statements and s        *
*               is equal to one of s1,s2,...,sK.      *
*                                                     *
*******************************************************
```

With respect to the general form above, the rules of usage
are:
   i) An ASSIGN statement must be used to change the value
      of the variable i.

  ii) The variable i cannot be used in expressions.

          Thus: ASSIGN 17 TO I
                         I=I+6

          is invalid.

 iii) At the time the Assigned GO TO is executed, the value
      of the variable i must match one of the statement
      numbers s1,s2,s3,...,sK or an error occurs.

      There is no need to confuse the ASSIGN statement with
the Assignment (=) statement. The former is only used in
conjunction with the Assigned GO TO and the latter is used
to cause a variable to take on the value of an expression.
An ASSIGN and Assigned GO TO combination can often be used
in place of a Computed GO TO. Which one is used is entirely
up to the programmer.

Exercise 3.2

Assume all variables are typed by default.

1. For each of the following sequences of statements,
   determine which statement will be the next one
   executed.

   a)   I=2
               GO TO (25,7,4,82),I
            82 ......

   b)   JJ=2**3/3-4
               GO TO(6),JJ
            10 ......

   c)   A=-4.7
               K=INT(DIM(ABS(A),6.3))
               GO TO (5,8,12),K
            15 ......

   d)   R=17.
               L=IFIX(R)/5
               IF(R-8..LT.R/3) GO TO(3,6,9),L
            18 ......

   e)   ASSIGN 10 TO LVAR
               IF(2.NE.5/2) ASSIGN 5 TO LVAR
               GO TO LVAR,(10,5,11)
             1 ......

   f)   ASSIGN 4 TO J
               I=3*3/3*3
               IF(I.EQ.1) ASSIGN 16 TO J
               IF(I-2) 1,4,3
             3 GO TO J,(2,4,16)
             1 GO TO (5,12,17),I
            22 ......

2. Explain the error in each of the following.

   a)   GO TO (3,4) I

   b)   ASSIGN 8 TO K
               GO TO K,(1,2,37,88)

   c)   X=1.
               GO TO (3),X

   d)   ASSIGN 1 TO J
               GO TO J,(3.,1.)

   e)   I=4
               GO TO I,(1,4,9)

77

3. Replace each of the following with an equivalent Computed GO TO.

   a) Assume K is 1,2, or 3

       IF(K-2) 1,17,3

   b)   IF (LUMP.EQ.3) GO TO 7
           IF (LUMP.EQ.1) GO TO 7
           IF (LUMP.NE.2) GO TO 19
       7 ......

   c)   IF(I.GT.2) GO TO 12
           IF(I.LT.1) GO TO 12
           IF(I.NE.1) GO TO 8
       7 ......

4. Suppose you wish to transfer to statement 10 if the value of X lies inside the interval -.7 to +1.5 and to statement 82 otherwise. Write a pair of conditional control statements to do this using:

    a) Two Logical IF statements
    b) Two Arithmetic IF statements

5. Assume I has one of the values 1,2,3,97,98,99. Write a sequence of WATFIV control statements which will cause control to be transferred to: statement 333 if I is either 1 or 99; statement 444 if I is either 2 or 98; statement 555 if I is either 3 or 97.
   a) Using 1 Logical IF and 1 Arithmetic IF
   b) Using 1 Logical IF and 1 Computed GO TO
   c) Using 1 Assignment statement and 2 Logical IFs
   d) Using 1 Assignment statement and 1 Arithmetic IF
   e) Using 1 Assignment statement and 1 Computed GO TO

*3.8 A Comprehensive Example.

The example program presented in this section uses the four types of conditional control statements discussed in this chapter: the Logical IF; the Arithmetic ·IF; the Computed GO TO; and the ASSIGN and Assigned GO TO.

The program reads in a sequence of integers punched one per card and determines the longest sequence of increasing values found in the input stream. The program terminates when two successive values are found to be equal.   In the program, the ASSIGN - Assigned GO TO and the Computed GO TO are used as "switches" to indicate the first and last data cards respectively.   That is, the variable being tested in these statements changes after the first and last cards are detected.   During the rest of the program their value

remains the same. The Arithmetic IF is used to obtain a
three-way branch when comparing the most recent value read
with the previous value read. The Logical IF is used to
sneak in an extra statement.

Further comments appear in the program.

```
C EXAMPLE 3.6 USE OF CONDITIONAL CONTROL STATEMENTS
C THE VARIABLES ARE USED FOR THE FOLLOWING PURPOSES
C      N - THE MOST RECENT VALUE READ IN
C      LAST - THE PREVIOUS VALUE READ IN
C      LENGTH - THE LENGTH OF THE CURRENT INCREASING
C               SEQUENCE
C      MAX - THE LENGTH OF THE LONGEST INCREASING
C               SEQUENCE FOUND THUS FAR
C      SWITCH - A VARIABLE WHICH POINTS TO STATEMENT
C               2 UNTIL THE FIRST CARD HAS BEEN PRO-
C               CESSED AND THEN POINTS TO STATEMENT 3
C      ENDCRD - A VARIABLE WHICH HAS A VALUE 1 UNTIL
C               THE LAST CARD HAS BEEN DETECTED AND
C               THEN HAS A VALUE 2
       INTEGER SWITCH,ENDCRD
       LENGTH=MAX=0
       ASSIGN 2 TO SWITCH
       ENDCRD=1
     1 READ,N
       GO TO SWITCH,(2,3)
     2 ASSIGN 3 TO SWITCH
       GO TO 4
C COMPARE CURRENT VALUE TO PREVIOUS VALUE
     3 IF (N-LAST) 7,6,4
     4 LENGTH=LENGTH+1
     5 LAST=N
       GO TO 1
     6 ENDCRD=2
     7 IF(LENGTH.GT.MAX) MAX=LENGTH
       LENGTH=0
       GO TO (4,8),ENDCRD
     8 PRINT,MAX
       STOP
       END
```

The reader should verify that the program will solve the
problem by taking a set of say 10 integers and following the
algorithm described in the program.

3.9 Summary

1. Statements are always executed in the order in which they
   are written unless the statement causes execution of
   further statements to be stopped or causes control to be
   transferred to some other statement in the program.

2. Statements whose purpose is to control the order of execution of statements are called control statements. Control statements are of two types. Unconditional control statements are those in which no test is made on the value of an expression or variable. Conditional control statements on the other hand mean the decision to transfer control to some other statement depends on the result of some test.

Unconditional control statements include STOP, PAUSE, the simple GO TO, and CONTINUE. The conditional control statements are the Logical IF, Arithmetic IF, Computed GO TO, and ASSIGN-Assigned GO TO. The situation in which each of these types of control statements is typically used is described in Section 3 of this chapter.

Programming Problems

3.1 Write a program which reads an INTEGER value and determines the number of non-zero digits in the number. Hint: Divide the number by 10, 100, 1000, etc. and add one to a counter if the quotient is non-zero.

3.2 Read a pair of INTEGER values M and N. Read a value of K. Determine if the last K digits in each number are the same. The output should appear as "LAST __ DIGITS OF __ AND __ ARE EQUAL (UNEQUAL)".

3.3 Read the lengths of the sides of a triangle. Print "0" if the lengths do not form a triangle; "1" if the sides are all unequal; "2" if the triangle is isosceles; "3" if the triangle is equilateral.

3.4 Temperatures in Fahrenheit (F) may be converted to Centigrade (C) and vice-versa using the formulas:

$$F = \frac{9}{5} C + 32 \qquad\qquad C = \frac{5}{9} (F - 32)$$

Write a program which reads ten pairs of values punched one pair per card. The second value of each pair is a temperature in degrees. The first value is a "1" if conversion from Centigrade to Fahrenheit is required, a "2" if conversion from Fahrenheit to Centigrade is required. Print ten lines of the form "__ DEGREES F (C) EQUALS __ DEGREES C (F)".

3.5 The value of the square root of a number may be calculated by starting with two estimates -- one high (H) and one low (L). A better estimate is then (H+L)/2. A check can be made of the new estimate to see if it is high or low. If High, it can be used as the new H value,

80

if low, as the new L value. The process can then be repeated until any desired accuracy is obtained. Write a program which uses 3 and 4 as initial estimates of the square root of 12. Use the procedure above until the estimate differs from the true value (found using the SQRT function) by less than .01. Print the high and low estimates before each new estimate is calculated.

3.6   Read in any four non-negative INTEGER values. Call them I1, I2, I3, and I4. Replace them with the four values $|I1-I2|$, $|I2-I3|$, $|I3-I4|$, and $|I4-I1|$. If they are all equal, print the four values. If at least two of them are different, continue the process using the replacement values as the starting values. Continue until all four differences are equal. Print the values of I1, I2, I3 and I4 at each stage of the calculations.

3.7   The day of the week for any date consisting of a year (Y), a month (M) and day (D) can be found using the following formula.

weekday = MOD(K,7) + 1   where

$$K = D + 2M + \frac{3M+3}{5} + Y + \frac{Y}{4} + \frac{Y}{100} + 1$$

All divisions in the formula are INTEGER divisions. To use the formula, Jan. and Feb. of a year must be considered as months 13 and 14 of the previous year. For example, Jan. 26, 1980 should be considered as the 26th day of the 13th month of 1979. In the formula, a value of 1 for the weekday represents Monday, 2 a Tuesday, etc.. Read several dates including your own birthday and print the day of the week for each. Stop when the year has a negative value.

3.8   Read the X-Y coordinates of three points. Determine if the third point and the origin lie on the same side of the line which goes thru the first two points. Print "YES" if they do and "NO" if they don't. Print the coordinates of the three points.

3.9   Modify programming problem 2.17 in the following way. Read values of X, n, i, and PER where: X is the amount of the loan; n is the number of payments; i is the annual interest rate; PER is the number of months between payments. Calculate the size of the payment made in each period using the given formula. Note that the interest rate for a period is related to the annual interest rate in the following way: (period rate + 1)**m = (annual rate +1) where "m" is the number of periods in a year.

3.10   For any twelve hour period, determine the times to the
nearest minute when the minute hand is as far past six
as the hour hand is away from six.

3.11   Consider any four digit number. Let K1, K2, K3 and K4
be the values of the four digits in the number. Form a
new number by adding the squares of the digit values.
Repeat the process (find the digits, square and add)
each time obtaining a new number. Write a program which
reads in a four digit number and generates new numbers
until either a value of one is found or until a value of
twenty is found for the second time. One of the events
will occur regardless of the number you start with!

3.12   Find the x which produces the largest value of y using
the formula y=Ax+B when x is in the interval beween C
and D. Read the values of A, B, C and D from a card.

3.13   Find the value of x which produces the largest value
of y using the formula $y=Ax^2+Bx+C$ when x is in the
interval between D and E. Read the values of A, B, C, D
and E from a data card. Test your program using at least
the following three sets of values.

        a) A=-1, B=0, C=9, D=-4, E=4
        b) A=+1, B=-4, C=1, D=2, E=8
        c) A=-1, B=6, C=-2, D=-1, E=2

3.14   A rectangular room has a length, width and height of
L, W, and H respectively. The length of the room runs in
an East-West direction. An ant is located on the East
wall a distance AH above the floor and AN North of the
South wall. The ant's food is stuck on the West wall a
distance FB below the ceiling and FS south of the North
wall. Write a program which reads values of L, W, H, AH,
AN, FB and FS and calculates the shortest distance the
ant must travel to reach its food. Hints: The shortest
distance is a straight line which will include travel
along one of the ceiling, floor, South wall or North
wall. (Naturally parts of the East and West walls will
have to be covered as well.) To evaluate the lengths of
the four paths, pretend the room is made of cardboard
and "unfold" it in four different ways to see the four
paths. The length of each path can be calculated easily
using the Pythagorus Theorem.

3.15   A corridor three feet wide and seven feet high makes a
right-angled turn into another corridor having the same
dimensions (The corner is "L" shaped.). A plumber has a
long thin rigid pipe which he wants to take around the
corner. a) What is the longest length of pipe which
will go around the corner? b) What is the narrowest
width of corridor which will permit an eight foot pipe
to go around? c) Do your answers to (a) and (b) change

if the corner is "T" shaped? Write a program to answer
these questions.

3.16   Modify your program for question 3.15 so that it will
        work if the corridors intersect at an angle of x
        degrees.   Assume x is the acute angle at the
        intersection. Answer questions (a) and (b) of the
        previous problem for values of x of 15, 30, 45, 60 and
        75 degrees.

3.17   Brownsville, Jonesville and Smithville are located on
        the same highway. The distances between them are shown
        in the following diagram.

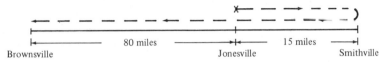

| ├──────────── 80 miles ──────────→|├──── 15 miles ───→| |
| Brownsville | Jonesville | Smithville |

Assume that cars travelling from Smithville to
Brownsville leave Smithville at one minute intervals and
travel at a constant rate of 45 miles per hour. Suppose
you leave Jonesville heading for Smithville just as a
Ford is leaving Smithville heading for Brownsville. When
you reach Smithville, you immediately turn around and
head for Brownsville. a) At what constant rate must you
drive to reach Brownsville at the same time as the Ford?
b) How many cars do you pass on your trip? Include both
the cars you encounter on your trip to Smithville and
the cars you pass on you trip to Brownsville.

3.18   An airline operates planes which have first-class and
        economy seats. If a customer approaches a ticket clerk,
        the clerk asks which type of seat is wanted. If that
        type is available, a ticket is issued for that type. If
        not available, the customer is asked if the alternate
        type of seat would be acceptable (provided one is
        available). If it is acceptable, a ticket of the
        alternate type is issued. If it is not acceptable, no
        ticket is issued. Write a program which will print one
        of the messages "ISSUE FIRST CLASS", "ISSUE ECONOMY", or
        "DONT ISSUE TICKET" based on the rules above. Input to
        the program consists of four INTEGER values punched on a
        card. The variables to which these four values will be
        assigned have (respectively) the following meanings.

WANT = $\begin{cases} 1 \text{ if customer wants first-class} \\ 2 \text{ if customer wants economy} \end{cases}$

ALTNAT = $\begin{cases} 1 \text{ if customer will take alternate type} \\ 0 \text{ if customer won't take alternate type} \end{cases}$

$$\text{FAVAIL} = \begin{cases} 1 & \text{if first-class seat is available} \\ 0 & \text{if first-class seat is not available} \end{cases}$$

$$\text{EAVAIL} = \begin{cases} 1 & \text{if economy seat is available} \\ 0 & \text{if economy seat is not available} \end{cases}$$

For example, a data card containing "2 1 0 1" means: the customer wants an economy seat; he will take the alternate type; no first class seat is available; an economy seat is available. Therefore the message "ISSUE ECONOMY TICKET" should be printed.

Test your program by reading sixteen different data cards -- one for each of the sixteen possible combinations of the four values. Print an appropriate message after each card is read.

CHAPTER 4   LOOPS AND LOOP CONTROL (THE DO STATEMENT)

<u>Questions Answered In This Chapter</u>.

1. What is meant by loops and loop control?

2. What are the three essential activities which are present in every loop?

3. What powerful statement is available in WATFIV for controlling loops in an efficient manner?

4.1 <u>Loops and Loop Control</u>.

In Chapter 1 it was suggested that many algorithms can and should be written so that a single instruction or set of instructions which must be repeated several times is written only once. By doing this a great deal of flexibility is usually added to the algorithm and the time to execute the extra instructions associated with this approach is usually insignificant compared to the saving in programming and keypunching time realized.

A set of steps in an algorithm, (a set of statements in a program), which is repeated several times in succession is commonly called a processing loop.

If we are to use a computer to process more than one job during its working life there must be a way to prevent a set of instructions from being repeated an infinite number of times. The <u>means</u> which is used to accomplish this is called <u>loop control</u>. Loop control may be external to the program or under program control.

External control refers to things such as: the operator hits the "stop button"; the computer equipment breaks down; or a timer reaches a certain limit. The study of this type of loop control is not relevant to our purpose which is to learn to use the WATFIV language. Methods of internal loop control, that is, methods in which the program decides it is time to stop repeating a set of instructions are very important to our purpose.

4.2 <u>Program-Controlled Loops</u>.

Three types of program-controlled loops will be identified. The three types are distinguishable in that the number of executions of the instructions in the loop is:

1. A fixed number

2. A number depending on the result of calculations
   being performed in the loop

3. A combination of 1 and 2.

As will be seen shortly, the WATFIV language has a powerful instruction called the "DO" which is suitable for the first and third types of loop control defined above. The three types can be illustrated using one of the example problems appearing in Chapter 1.

Suppose E is an estimate of the square root of a number X. (The number and the estimate can be any positive values.) Newton developed a formula which said, given X and E, an improved estimate of the square root can be obtained by calculating the value of:

$$E - \frac{E^2 - X}{2E}$$

Furthermore, if one repeats this calculation enough times, the sequence of improved estimates will converge to (become indefinitely close to) the value of the square root of X. If we let X be the number and let our initial estimate E be X/2., then the algorithm below could be used to find 10 improvements to our initial estimate.

1. Set E=X/2.
2. Repeat step 3 ten times
3. Get improved E using the formula
4. Print the estimate
5. Stop

This is an example of the first type of loop control. The instruction loop (namely step 3 in the algorithm) is repeated a fixed number of times.

To illustrate the second type of loop control, suppose that instead of automatically finding ten improvements to the original estimate, improved estimates are calculated until the new estimate results in an improvement (previous estimate minus improved estimate) of less than .0001. A suitable algorithm is:

1. Set E=X/2.
2. Calculate improved estimate
3. Calculate improvement (ie: absolute value
      of the change in the estimate)
4. If the improvement is > .0001 go to step 2
5. Print the estimate
6. Stop

In this example, steps 2, 3, and 4 will be repeated as many times as is necessary to obtain the square root correct to about .0001. That is, the number of repetitions of the three steps in the loop depends on the calculations made in the loop. This is the second type of loop control.

Finally, the two approaches above could be combined by requiring that we obtain as many improvements as are necessary to calculate the square root correct to .0001 but if that degree of accuracy has not been obtained after ten improvements have been made, then stop anyway. The required algorithm is:

1. Set E=X/2.
2. Repeat steps 3,4, and 5 ten times unless told to do differently
3. Calculate improved estimate
4. Calculate amount of improvement
5. If amount of improvement ≤ .0001 go to step 6
6. Print the estimate
7. Stop

This is an example of the third type of loop control. That is, a sequence of instructions are repeated a fixed number of times unless something happens during one of the repetitions which causes the repetitions to stop.

We already have the necessary knowledge to translate the three algorithms into WATFIV. In the first and third cases, a means of determining if a loop has been repeated a fixed number of times is required. The easiest method would be to set up a counter which goes from one to ten in steps of one. Following each execution of the instructions in the loop, one is added to the counter and then the counter is tested for a value equal to or less than ten. If this requirement is met the loop is repeated. The translation of the third algorithm would look like:

```
C EXAMPLE 4.1 THE THIRD TYPE OF LOOP CONTROL
      READ,X
      E=X/2.
      I=1
    1 ENEW=E- (E**2-X)/(2.*E)
      IF(ABS(ENEW-E).LT.0.0001) GO TO 2
      E=ENEW
      I=I+1
      IF(I.LE.10) GO TO 1
    2 PRINT,E
      STOP
      END
$ENTRY
```

In this program, the INTEGER variable "I" plays the role of a counter. Observe that when using a counter to control the number of repetitions of a loop it is <u>always</u> necessary to do the following three things:

   i) Initialize the counter (the statement I=1)

   ii) Add to the counter. (the statement I=I+1)

   iii) Test the counter to see if the loop should be repeated. (the statement IF(I.LE.10)GO TO 1)

Since our purpose in defining the counter was to repeat a set of instructions a fixed number of times, it follows that we could choose any combination of an initial value, an increment to be added, and an upper limit, <u>provided</u> that the combination produces the desired number of repetitions of the the loop. For example, the two counter setups shown below would both cause the set of instructions 23 thru 17 to be repeated ten times.

```
      I=1                          I=4
23 .                        23 .
   .                           .
   .                           .
17 .                        17 .
   I=I+1                        I=I+3
   IF(I.LE.10) GO TO 23         IF(I.LE.31) GO TO 23
```

4.3 The DO Statement.

In WATFIV there is a single statement called the DO statement which is a handy way of controlling the <u>maximum</u> number of repetitions of statements in a loop. The <u>program</u> structures shown below are equivalent. The one on the right shows how the DO statement is used.

```
      I=1                     DO 17 I=1,10,1
23 ...                        ...
   ...                        ...
17 ...                     17 ...
   I=I+1
   IF(I.LE.10) GO TO 23
```

The DO statement contains the five items of information necessary to define and control the number of repetitions of a loop. These are:

   i)   The number of the last statement in the set of instructions to be repeated. This statement is called the <u>object</u> of the DO. In the example above the object of the DO is statement 17. The set of statements which are being repeated is called the <u>range</u> of the DO.

ii) The name of the counter -- called the _index_ of the
     DO. In the example the DO index is the variable I.

iii) The three values which are used to initialize,
      increment and test the counter are called the
      parameters of the DO. The names given to these
      parameters are:

   a) The _initial value_: the starting value of the
                           counter

   b) The _increment_: the value added to the counter
                       after each repetition

   c) The _test value_: the value to which the counter
                        is compared after the addition
                        of the increment

The general form of a DO-loop is shown below.

```
                    DO s index=initial,test,increment
                   (   .
         range    /    .
         of the  {     .
         DO       \    .
                   (   .
                    s ... (object statement)
```

The DO statement defines a simple algorithm which is:

1. Set the index equal to the initial value.

2. Execute all statements up to and including the object
   of the DO.

3. Add the increment to the index.

4. Compare the index to the test value and,
   - if the index is equal to or less than the test
   value go back to step 2;
   - if the index is greater than the test value
   continue executing statements starting with the
   first statement following the object of the DO.

There are several rules about the DO statement and its
use which must be learned. These rules will be illustrated
with examples. A summary of the rules will follow the
examples. Keep in mind that the DO statement is simply a
convenient method of placing, in a single statement, the
five items of information necessary to control a loop using
a counter. Since large programs sometimes contain hundreds
of loops, the DO statement is a feature which is appreciated
by all WATFIV programmers.

4.4 Examples and Rules of DO-loops.

The program below shows how a DO statement could be used in a program to find 10 improvements to an initial estimate of the square root of a number.

```
C EXAMPLE 4.2 USING A DO TO EXECUTE A LOOP 10 TIMES
      READ,X
      E=X/2.
      DO 4 I=1,10,1
    4 E=E-(E**2-X)/(2.*E)
      PRINT,E
      STOP
      END
```

A common way of stating the processing being done under control of the DO statement in this example is:

"Execute statement 4 for values of I starting at 1 and going up to 10 in steps of 1."

If a DO-loop was used in Example 4.1, the program would look like:

```
C EXAMPLE 4.1 (USING A DO-LOOP)
      READ,X
      E=X/2.
      DO 47 JJ=2,65,7
      ENEW=E-(E**2-X)/(2.*E)
      IF(ABS(ENEW-E).LT..0001) GO TO 2
   47 E=ENEW
    2 PRINT,E
      STOP
      END
```

You are probably wondering why the parameters of the DO statement were chosen such that the initial value was 2, the test value was 65, and the increment was 7. Since our objective is to execute the statements in the range a maximum of ten times and since the index JJ will take on the ten values 2,9,16,23,30,37,44,51,58,65 before the "less than or equal to" test fails, these three parameter values will achieve our objective.

What would have happened in this example had we changed the test value to 68? The DO statement would then have been:

DO 47 JJ=2,68,7

With a little thought, you will realize that this change would __not__ affect the number of repetitions of the loop. During the tenth execution of the loop JJ has a value of 65. When 7 is added to the index JJ it is no longer less than or equal to the test value and so the loop will not be repeated and processing will continue with the statement following the object statement. In fact, any test value from 65 thru 71 would cause the loop to be executed a maximum of ten times.

O.K. -- what happens if we have something like the following?

DO 825 K=19,2,5

In this case the initial value is greater than the test value. Remember that when executing a DO-loop, the statements in the range of the loop are executed once before the increment is added and the test made to see if they should be excuted again. This means the index K will have a value of 19 the first time thru the loop and then K becomes 24. This is greater than the test value 2 and so processing will continue with the first statement following the object of the DO. Some other examples are:

DO Statement	Maximum Number Of Executions Of Statements In The Range
DO K=19,9,5	1
DO I=7,16,2	5
DO 283 INDEX=4,4000,4000	1
DO 5 JOHN12=52,64,3	5

Using The Value Of The Index

Sometimes it is handy to use values of the parameters in order to make use of the value of the index within the range. For example, suppose it is required to find the sum of squares of the numbers 4,9,14, 19,...,34,39. A program to do this is:

```
C EXAMPLE 4.3 USING THE VALUE OF THE INDEX
      ISUM=0
      DO 11 N=4,39,5
   11 ISUM=ISUM+N**2
      PRINT,ISUM
      STOP
      END
```

In this example, the program makes use of the fact that the value of N changes each time statement 11 is executed. Since there are 8 numbers whose squares are to be added to the total the program could also have been written in the following awkward way.

```
C EXAMPLE 4.3 AWKWARD WAY
      ISUM=0
      M=-1
      DO 11 N=1,8,1
      M=M+5
   11 ISUM=ISUM+M**2
      PRINT,ISUM
      STOP
      END
```

Using this second approach means two more statements must be written, keypunched and compiled, and eleven more statements must be executed (ten in the loop and one to initialize the value of N). The reason for using the first approach should be clear.

Parameter Values

Suppose we are required to find the average of the integer values between N1 and N2 inclusive where it is assumed that: N1 and N2 are positive; N1 is less than N2; the values of N1 and N2 are unknown at the time the program is written. A suitable program for solving the problem is shown below.

```
C EXAMPLE 4.4 CALCULATION OF AVERAGE
      READ,N1,N2
      ISUM=0
      DO 3 NUMBER=N1,N2,1
    3 ISUM=ISUM+NUMBER
      AVERAG=FLOAT(ISUM)/FLOAT(N2-N1+1)
      PRINT,AVERAG
      STOP
      END
```

Note that the divisor used in obtaining the average is N2-N1+1. The reason for the "+1" is due to the word "inclusive" in the statement of the problem.

In this example, two of the parameters -- the initial value and the test value -- are INTEGER variables whose values have been previously assigned by the READ statement. Any or all of the three parameters of a DO-loop can be INTEGER variables provided they have positive values. This same rule applies when the parameters are constants. That is, the value of each parameter must be greater than zero.

Using A CONTINUE

Suppose we wish to use a DO-loop in a program to tabulate the values of the function:

$$y = (x - 2x + 1)/(x - 3), \text{ for } x = 0, 1, 2, \ldots, 10.$$

A suitable program is the following:

```
C EXAMPLE 4.5 USE OF A CONTINUE STATEMENT
      DO 94 I=1,11
      X=FLOAT(I-1)
      IF(X.EQ.3.) GO TO 94
      Y=(X**2-2.*X+2.)/(X-3)
      PRINT,X,Y
   94 CONTINUE
      STOP
      END
```

There are three important ideas illustrated by this program.

First. The increment parameter does not appear in the DO statement. If the increment is omitted, it is assumed to have a value of 1 and in this example that is the value we wanted anyway.

Second. Since X is to take on values from zero thru ten, why does the index I go from one up to eleven? Recall that the parameters must have <u>positive</u> values. Knowing that the index must be initially greater than zero, the value of X can be easily obtained by subtracting one from the index.

Third. The object of the DO is a CONTINUE statement. Since we have to bypass the calculation of Y when X equals 3, it is necessary to provide a means of increasing the value of the index when this condition is detected. When using DO-loops, the event which triggers the addition of the increment and subsequent test of the index is the execution of the object statement which, in this example, has a statement number of 94. Thus in programs where it is necessary to skip over some of the statements in the range of the DO, a CONTINUE statement should be used as the object of the DO.

There is a second reason for using a CONTINUE statement as the object of a DO. Following each execution of the object statement, the index is incremented and tested. If the "equal to or less than" test fails, the next statement executed is the one following the object statement. This means the object statement cannot be a control statement which might cause a transfer to any statement other than the one which follows it. In other words, the object statement cannot be a: STOP; PAUSE; GO TO of any sort; another DO; or Arithmetic IF. If the program logic is such that one of these statements would be appropriate as the object of a DO, a CONTINUE statement must be used. Some programmers like to use a CONTINUE statement to terminate every DO-loop. They feel it makes a program more readable.

Jumping In And Out Of DO-Loops

Consider the following problem. Read a maximum of 25 INTEGER values punched one per card and find their sum. If, however, a negative value is detected during this process, only the sum of the numbers preceding the negative value is to be printed along with a number indicating how many numbers have been read in. A suitable program would be:

```
C EXAMPLE 4.6 EARLY DO-LOOP EXIT
      ISUM=0
      DO 31 I=1,25
      READ,NUM
      IF(NUM.LT.0) GO TO 3
      ISUM=ISUM+NUM
   31 CONTINUE
      PRINT,ISUM
      STOP
    3 PRINT,I,ISUM
      STOP
      END
```

In this example, the presence of a negative value in the input stream causes control to be transferred outside the range of the loop before 25 executions of the loop have occurred. In WATFIV this is perfectly permissible and when this happens the value of the index variable will be the value it had when control was transferred to a statement outside the loop. This value was used in the statement "PRINT,I,ISUM". However, if control passes from the loop because the required number of repetitions have been completed, we say the DO-loop has been "satisfied" and under these circumstances the value of the index variable is uncertain and should not be used in later processing. For example, if the statement "PRINT,ISUM" in the example was replaced by "PRINT,I,ISUM", the value printed for I could be anything. The reason is that once a DO-loop has been satisfied, no attempt is made to remember the last value of the index.

Suppose that during the processing of a DO-loop, a condition is detected which requires that a few extra instructions be executed which otherwise would have been bypassed. For example, suppose that in the foregoing problem the detection of a negative number meant that there are 25 more values following it in the input stream. We might try to set up the program in the following way.

```
C EXAMPLE 4.7 INVALID TRANSFER OF CONTROL
      NVALS=25
      ISUM=0
      DO 31 I=1,NVALS
      READ,NUM
      IF(NUM.LT.0) GO TO 3
      ISUM=ISUM+NUM
   31 CONTINUE
      PRINT,ISUM
      STOP
    3 NVALS=NVALS+25
      GO TO 31
      END
```

The error in this program is due to the statement "GO TO 31". This statement lies <u>outside</u> the range of the DO-loop and would cause control to be transferred to statement 31 which is <u>inside</u> the range of the loop. The rule is that control can pass to a statement inside the range of a DO-loop only from another statement inside the range or from the DO statement itself. Thus we might try to correct the error in the foregoing problem by changing the value of NVALS inside the range of the loop. This approach would also produce an error since DO-loop parameters cannot be changed while executing statements in the loop. Since the DO statement itself is <u>not</u> in the range of the loop which it defines, the solution to the above difficulties is simply to execute the DO-loop over again when a negative value is detected. A program for solving the problem is therefore:

```
C EXAMPLE 4.8 VALID TRANSFER OF CONTROL
      ISUM=0
    4 DO 31 I=1,25
      READ,NUM
      IF(NUM.LT.0) GO TO 4
      ISUM=ISUM+NUM
   31 CONTINUE
      PRINT,ISUM
      STOP
      END
```

4.5 <u>Summary Of DO-Loop Rules</u>

1. General Form.

$$\text{range of the DO} \left\{ \begin{array}{l} \text{DO s index = initial,test,increment} \\ \cdot \\ \cdot \\ \cdot \\ \text{s object statement} \end{array} \right.$$

   a) "s" must be the number of an executable statement
      which cannot be a DO, simple GO TO, Computed GO TO,

Assigned GO TO, Arithmetic IF, STOP or PAUSE.

b) The index must be a simple INTEGER variable.

c) The parameters must have positive INTEGER values. They can be either constants or simple INTEGER variables.

d) If the increment is omitted it is assumed to be 1.

e) The index and the parameter values cannot be changed by any statement inside the range of the DO.

2. Transfers of Control.

a) Control cannot pass to a statement within the range of the DO from a statement outside the range of the DO except via the DO statement itself.

b) Control may pass from any statement inside the range of the DO to any statement outside the range of the DO. When this happens:

    i) If the transfer is from any statement other than the object statement, the value of the index is known outside the range and equals the value of the index at the time the transfer occurred.

    ii) If the transfer occurs because the specified number of repetitions have been completed, the value of the index is uncertain.

3. Maximum number of Executions of the Object Statement.

a) If the test value is less than the initial value the object statement will be executed once.

b) If the test value is equal or greater than than the initial value the object statement will be executed

$$1 + \frac{test - initial}{increment}$$

times where the division above ignores any remainder.

Exercise 4.1

Assume all variables are typed by default.

1. What are the five items of information present in any DO statement?

2. State in words what is meant by the statement:

```
                DO 89 J=11,45,2
```

3. For loops defined by the following DO statements,
   determine the maximum number of repetitions of the object
   statement.

   a) DO 5 I=2,5
   b) DO 6 J=14,98,14
   c) DO 7 K=9,7,2
   d) DO 8 LOOP=1,1,1
   e) DO 9 MAX0=100,203,50

4. Each of the following statements or sequences contains an
   error. What is it?

   a) DO 10, KK=1,10
   b) DO 12 J=10,1,-1
   c) DO MAX=3,30,2
   d) DO 99999 MINIMUM=12,2
   e) DO 44 N=2,N
   f) DO 585 KLM=6,K*2-1,1
   g) DO 871 X=1,80,90

   h)   8 CONTINUE
            ....
          DO 8 INDEX=4,100,3

   i)   DO 19 NNN=13,26
            ....
            GO TO 5
       12 CONTINUE
            ...
       19 CONTINUE
            ....
        5 GO TO 12

   j)   DO 36 I=1,12,2
               ....
               IF(...) I=I+1
               ...
          36 CONTINUE

   k)   DO 583 MAT=12,143,12
          17 CONTINUE
               ....
         583 GO TO 17

5. In many programs, the requirement that the DO-loop
   parameters have positive INTEGER values means that it is
   necessary to employ a formula which tansforms the index
   value to one of the desired values. For example to
   calculate the sum of the values 2.5,4.5,6.5,...,32.5,
   one could write:

```
      SUM=0.                          SUM=0.
      DO 10 I=2,32,2                   DO 10 I=1,16
      X=FLOAT(I)+.5      or           X=2.*FLOAT(I)+.5
   10 SUM=SUM+X                    10 SUM=SUM+X
```

In each of the following, write one DO statement and an
Assignment statement to convert the successive index
values to those shown.

a) 10., 20., 30.,...,180.
b) .25, .50, .75,..., 2.75, 3.0
c) 10, 9, 8, ..., 1
d) -5,-4,-3,...,3,4,5
e) 5,4,3,...,-3,-4,-5
f) 0,1,2,0,1,2,0,1,2,0,1,2   (Hint: use the MOD function)
g) 1,2,3,4,1,2,3,4,1,2,3,4,1,2,3,4
h) -5,-4,-3,-2,-1,-5,-4,-3,-2,-1
i) 10.,6.,2.,-2.,10.,6.,2.,-2.
j) 101,202,303,404,...,1010

6. In the program below, how many times will the value of K
   be printed?

```
             K=10
             DO 1 I=1,30,2
             PRINT,K
             IF(MOD(I,5).EQ.0) PRINT,K
             IF(I/3*3-I) 4,1,1
           4 PRINT,K
           1 CONTINUE
             STOP
```

7. Can you think of any worthwhile purpose for including
   either of the following in a program?

   a) DO 1 J=1,1,1

   b)   DO 17 LUMP=1,100
      17 CONTINUE

8. What value is printed by the following statements?

```
             NUM=0
           2 DO 5 I=1,100
             NUM=NUM+1
             IF(NUM/20-2) 5,2,4
           5 CONTINUE
           4 PRINT,I
             STOP
```

4.6 Nested Loops.

The program statements below calculate the value of the function

$$z = x^2 - 2xy + y^2 \over (x + 4)(y - 20)$$

when x has a value of three and y takes on values of 4,6,...
26,28,30.

```
          X=3.
          DO 10 J=4,30,2
          IF(J.EQ.20) GO TO 10
          Y=FLOAT(J)
          Z=(X**2-2.*X*Y+Y**2)/((X+4.)*(Y-20.))
          PRINT,X,Y,Z
       10 CONTINUE
```

Now suppose that instead of using just the single value
of X, one is to use the eleven different values of X in the
set 5,4,3,...,-4,-5. For each of these values of X, Y is to
range over the values 4,6,8,...,30. A suitable algorithm
would be:

1. Repeat step 2 for each value of X in the set 5,4,3,
   ...,-4,-5.
2. Repeat steps 3 and 4 for each value of Y in the set
   4,6,...,28,30.
3. Calculate the value of Z using the formula.
4. Print the values of X,Y, and Z
5. Stop.

Before translating this algorithm into WATFIV, the
following points should be noted. Step 1 of the algorithm
is an instruction to repeat step 2 ten times. (A value of
X=-4 is not allowed since the denominator becomes zero.)
Looking ahead, we can anticipate using a DO-loop to control
the value of X. Step 2 which is repeated ten times is an
instruction to repeat steps 3 and 4 fourteen times. Since
we intend to use a DO-loop to control the value of Y, this
means the DO statement will be executed once for each value
of X. In other words, there is a "loop within a loop". A
translation of the algorithm is:

```
       C EXAMPLE 4.8 NESTED LOOPS
             DO 20 I=1,11
             X=FLOAT(6-I)
             IF(X.EQ.-4.) GO TO 20
             DO 10 J=2,30,2
             IF(J.EQ.20) GO TO 10
             Y=FLOAT(J)
             Z=(X**2-2.*X*Y+Y**2)/((X+4.)*(Y-20.))
```

(continued on next page)

```
      PRINT,X,Y,Z
10 CONTINUE
20 CONTINUE
   STOP
   END
```

This example contains a pair of nested DO-loops. The J-loop as defined by "DO 10 J=2,30,2" is called the inner loop and the loop which has I as an index is called the outer loop. The structure of a pair of nested loops is shown below. The purpose of using such an arrangement is to repeat a set of instructions as part of a larger set of instructions which are themselves being repeated under loop control.

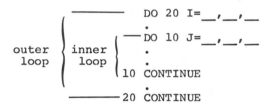

Observe that in example 4.8, the object statements of the I-loop and the J-loop are different CONTINUE statements. Each loop must end in a CONTINUE statement since we wish to bypass the values of X=-4 and Y=20. If the two loops had the same object statement, the statement

IF(X.EQ.-4) GO TO 20

which lies outside the range of the J-loop would transfer control to a statement which lies inside the range of the J-loop. This means the two loops must terminate on different CONTINUE statements. In many cases, however, it is meaningful to terminate two or more loops on the same statement, as the following example shows.

The program prints the sum of each possible combination of I,J, and K where: I has values in the set 1,2,3,...,10; J has values in the set 10,20,30,...,100; and K has values in the set 1000,2000,3000,...,10000.

```
C EXAMPLE 4.9 LOOPS TO A DEPTH OF 3
      DO 4 I=1,10
      DO 4 J=10,100,10
      DO 4 K=1000,10000,1000
      ISUM=I+J+K
    4 PRINT,ISUM
      STOP
      END
```

This example shows loops that are nested to a depth of three. The statement "DO 4 I ..." will be executed one time. The statement "DO 4 J ..." will be executed ten times (once for each value of I). The statement "DO 4 K ..." will be executed a hundred times (once for each combination of I and J values). And the statement "ISUM=..." and "4 PRINT,ISUM" will be executed one-thousand times (once for each combination of I, J, and K values). The order of the first thirty numbers which are printed is shown below.

$$1011,2011,\ldots,10011,1021,2021,\ldots,10021,1031,2031,\ldots,10031$$

| I=1, J=10, | I=1, J=20, | I=1, J=30, |
| K=1000 to 10000 | K=1000 to 10000 | K=1000 to 10000 |

In WATFIV there is no limit to the number of loops which can be nested one within the other except that no program may have more than 255 DO-loops in total.

The rule that transfers must not be made into the range of a DO-loop from outside the loop means that DO-loops cannot be overlapped in the manner shown below.

```
      ┌─────  DO 7 I=__,__,__
      │          .
      │   ┌───  DO 12 J=__,__,__
  {   │   │      .
      │   {   7 CONTINUE
      └   │      .
          └── 12 CONTINUE
```

Such an arrangement would mean that if the program was executed, then following the execution of statement 12 which is outside the I-loop, control would be transferred to a statement inside the range of the I-loop. The compiler checks for invalid overlapping of DO-loops. This same rule can be used to determine if nested DO-loops can end on the same statement. The structure below illustrates this point.

```
        DO 10 I=__,__,__
        ...
        GO TO 10
        ...
        DO 10 J=__,__,__
        ...
     10 CONTINUE
```

In this structure, the statement "GO TO 10" is outside the range of the J-loop and would cause control to be transferred to a statement within the range of the J-loop.

This means a separate CONTINUE statement is required to terminate the I-loop.

Exercise 4.2

Assume all variables are typed by default.

1. For each of the following determine the values which are printed when the program is executed.

a)
```
        X=5.7E-1
        DO 5 I=1,10
        DO 5 J=4,8,2
      5 PRINT,X
```

b)
```
        X=-.0023E04
        DO 6 J=10,100,10
        IF(J.NE.50) GO TO 8
        PRINT,X
      8 DO 6 K=1,3
      6 PRINT,X
```

c)
```
        YZ=AINT(SQRT(2.))
        PRINT,YZ
        DO 11 M1234=1,5
        PRINT,YZ
        DO 2 N1234=1,4
      2 PRINT,YZ
        XZ=FLOAT(M1234)
        PRINT,XZ
     11 CONTINUE
```

d)
```
        DO 5 K=1,4
        N=K+1
        DO 3 L=K,10,N
        PRINT,L
      3 M=K*L+20
      5 PRINT,M
```

2. The sequence of statements below shows an infinite loop. What is the sequence of numbers which will be printed over and over again if the statements are executed?

```
      1 DO 77 I=1,7
        IF(MOD(I,2).EQ.0) GO TO 3
        PRINT,I
      3 DO 77 J=5,25,5
        IF(J.EQ.IFIX(SQRT(FLOAT(J)*I))) GO TO 1
        PRINT,J
     77 CONTINUE
```

3. In the program below suppose that the time between successive executions of statement 15 is .001 seconds.
   a) How long does it take to execute the program?
   b) Why should .001 be regarded as an <u>average</u> time between executions of statement 15?

```
        DO 15 I=1,1000
        DO 15 J=1,60
        DO 15 K=1,60
        DO 15 L=1,24
        DO 15 M=1,365
     15 N=1
```

4. Explain the error in each of the following.

a)
```
        DO 1 I=1,10
        ...
        DO 2 J=3,8
        ...
      1 CONTINUE
      2 CONTINUE
```

b)
```
        DO 3 I=17,12,3
        IF(I.EQ.17) GO TO 3
        DO 3 J=6,24,6
        ...
      3 CONTINUE
```

c)
```
        DO 12 K=1,5
        ...
     10 CONTINUE
        DO 2 J=1,4
        IF(...) GO TO 10
     17 CONTINUE
        ...
      2 IF(A.NE.B) A=B
        ...
        GO TO 17
     12 CONTINUE
```

5. Suppose each of the sequences of values given are required in some program. Write a pair of DO-statements and one or more Assignment statements to print the sequence of values indicated in each case. For example: To print the sequence 2.,4.,6.,8.,2.,4.,6.,8., one could write:

```
        DO 1 I=1,2
        DO 1 J=2,8,2
        X=FLOAT(J)
      1 PRINT,X
```

a) 2,3,4,5,6, 4,5,6,7,8
b) 1,2,3,4,10,20,30,40,100,200,300,400
c) 35,34,33,32,31,15,14,13,12,11,-5,-6,-7,-8,⌐ ⌐
d) 0,-1,-2,0,-1,-2,0,-1,-2,0,-1,-2
e) 1.25,1.50,1.75,3.25,3.50,3.75,5.25,5.50,5.75
f) -.125,-1.375,-2.625,-3.875
g) 1001,101,11,2000,202,22,3000,303,33
h) 1,1,1,0,0,3,3,3,0,0,5,5,5,0,0
i) 1,-30,+500,-7000,+90000,-1100000
j) 1,1,2,1,2,3,1,2,3,4,...,1,2,3,4,5,6,7,8,9,10
k) 10;10,9;10,9,8;...;10,9,8,...3,2,1
l) 1,2,3,4,5,6,7,1,3,5,7,1,4,7
m) 90;81,80;72,71,70;63,62,61,60;...;9,8,7,...,2,1,0

103

4.7 Summary

1. Many algorithms, and hence programs, contain sequences of instructions which must be executed more than once in order to solve the problem. The method used to control the number of repetitions can either be external to the program or under program control.

2. The DO statement is a convenient method of controlling the number of repetitions of a loop when this number is either fixed or has some maximum value.

3. Although there are several rules which a programmer must learn if he is to use the DO statement properly, the added programming power and convenience attained is well worth the effort.

Programming Problems

4.1 Tabulate values of the function $\dfrac{x^2 - x + 7}{x^2 + 2}$

for values of x of:
a) 1, 2, 3, ..., 20
b) 3, 6, 9, ..., 24
c) 0, -1, -2, ..., -8
d) 12, 10, 8, ..., -10

Use a DO statement to generate the x values.

4.2 Tabulate values of the function

$$y = \frac{3\sin^3 x + 4\cos^3 x}{16x^2 + 8x - 3}$$

for x = -1, -3/4, -1/2, ... 3/4, 1. Skip over values of x which make the division undefined.

4.3 If x_0 is an initial estimate of the value of $1/\sqrt{x}$, successively better estimates are given by x_1, x_2, etc. where $x_n = .5x_{n-1}(3 - Xx^2_{n-1})$, n=1,2,... . Use this procedure in a program to calculate the fifth estimate of $1/\sqrt{2}$. Use .4 as your initial estimate. Print each estimate.

4.4 Suppose division could not be done on a computer. One method of obtaining increasingly accurate approximations to a value of $1/A$ is to calculate x_0, x_1, x_2, etc. where x_0 is some initial estimate of the reciprocal and the value $x_n = x_{n-1}(2 - Ax_{n-1})$, n=1,2,3,.... Write a program which calculates the tenth approximation to a value of $1/3$ (i.e: A=3) using the method described above. Use .3 as your initial estimate.

4.5   The sum of cubes of the numbers one thru N is equal to
the square of the sum of the numbers one   thru   N.   For
example, 1^3 $+2^3$ $+3^3$ $=(1+2+3)^2$. Suppose you want to use
this fact to find an approximate   value   of   the   square
root   of   the   number   K.   This   could   be   done in the
following way. Find M such that the sum of cubes of   the
numbers   one   thru M is less than K and the sum of cubes
of the numbers 1 thru (M+1) is greater than   K.   (If   by
chance   the   sum   of   cubes equals K, the square root is
exactly 1+2+3+...+M.) Conclude that the square root of K
lies   somewhere   between   the sum of the values 1 thru M
and the sum of the values 1 thru M+1. Write   a   program
which   reads   a   value   of K and computes an approximate
square root using this method. Accuracy can be   improved
by multiplying   K   by an even power of ten and dividing
the result by   one-half   the   power   of   ten   used.   For
example,   to   find the square root of 12.357, use 123570
as the value of K and divide the result by 100.

4.6   The sequence of numbers 1, 1, 2, 3, 5, 8, 13, ... is
called the Fibonacci sequence. Each term in the sequence
except   the   first   two (which are each equal to one) is
obtained by adding   the   previous   two   terms.   Write   a
program   which reads a value of N and prints the first N
terms of the sequence on separate lines.   Between   each
value   printed,   print   the ratio of the current term to
the previous term. What is apparently true   about   these
ratios as the terms become larger?

4.7   The   probability   that no two people in a group of N
people have the same birthday is given by the formula

$$P_n = P_{n-1} \quad (1-\frac{(N-1)}{365}) \quad \text{where } P_1 = 1$$

Use   this   formula   in   a   program   which determines the
smallest number of people such that the   probability   of
no   matching birthdays is less than one-half. Assume the
result occurs for N less than fifty. Use a DO   statement
in   generating   the values of P_2, P_3, ... Compare each
value to one-half to determine if   it   is   necessary   to
exit from the DO-loop.

4.8   At   a party of N couples, the men pull a lady's name
out of a hat to see who their partners will be   for   the
next   activity.   The chance that no man draws his wife's
name can be obtained from the following relationship.

$$P_n = \frac{n-1}{n} P_{n-1} + \frac{1}{n} P_{n-2} \quad \text{where } P_1 = 0, \text{ and } P_2 = .5$$

Read   a   value of N and calulate the probability that no
man draws his wife's name for groups of people of 1,   2,
3, ..., N.

4.9 A family of functions of x; $F_1(x)$, $F_2(x)$, $F_3(x)$, ... is defined by the following relationships.

$$F_1(x)=1, \quad F_2(x)=x, \quad F(x)= \frac{2n-1}{n} F_{n-1}(x) - \frac{n-1}{n} F_{n-2}(x)$$

where n = 2, 3, 4, ...

Write a program which reads a value of x and calculates the first ten functions of x as defined above.

4.10 Read a value of N. Assume N is ten or less. Print out all triples of positive integer values which add up to N. Print out all triples of non-negative integer values which add up to N.

4.11 Tabulate values of the function

$$z = \frac{x^2 - 2xy + 3y^2}{xy + 3x + 2y + 4}$$

using all pairs of x and y values in the ranges x=1,2,3,...,6; y=1,2,3,4,5. Use a pair of nested DO-loops to generate the x and y values.

4.12 Read a value of K. Assume K is six or less. Print the values of MOD(K,M+N), MOD(K,M*N) and MOD(K,M**N) where M and N can take any values in the set 1,2,3,...,(K-1).

4.13 Suppose computers could only multiply and divide by two. (In fact, this isn't far from the truth!) The product of any two numbers M and N can still be done using the "Russian" method of multiplication. It consists of successively dividing the smaller number by two (ignoring any remainder) and successively multiplying the larger value by two. As this process is being carried out, add to a total only those multiples of the larger value for which the division of the smaller produced an odd quotient. For example, to multiply 37 by 65 the following results would be obtained.

```
37              65
18             130  (not added to total)
 9             260
 4             520  (not added to total)
 2            1040  (not added to total)
 1            2080
              ----
              2405  (the total)
```

If you don't believe it, what is 37 times 65? Write a program which reads a pair of values and calculates their product using the above technique.

CHAPTER 5   INPUT

Questions Answered In This Chapter.

    1. How does a program answer the three questions
        associated with any input operation? These are:

        Where (on what device) are the values recorded?
        What variables are to be assigned values?
        How are the values recorded on the input medium?

    2. What is meant by the terms "format-free input" and
        "formatted input"?

As we already know, there are two ways of assigning
values to variables used in a WATFIV program -- by using an
Assignment statement and by using a READ statement. This
chapter describes a different form of the READ statement
from the one previously discussed. It permits you, the
programmer, to completely control the input values to be
assigned to variables used in a program.

5.1 Input - The Three Questions.

  i) Where are the values recorded?

      The most frequently used medium for recording
values to be assigned to variables is the punched card.
The values are input to the computer memory using a card
reader, a device whose sole function is to send
electrical signals to the memory of the computer which
describe the hole patterns punched in the card. Almost
all computers have other devices which can also be used
to input values to the computer memory. Typewriters,
magnetic tape drives, magnetic disk drives, and "light
pens" are examples of other input devices. In this
chapter, however, we shall always assume the input
device is a card reader and hence the answer to the
question "Where are the values recorded?" is "On punched
cards in the card reader.".

  ii) How are the values recorded on the cards?

      A card has eighty columns and one symbol can be
punched in each column. Since values can be punched
anywhere in a card, it is necessary to know which
columns contain the value to be assigned to each
variable. Furthermore, if the values contain decimal
points and/or exponents as may be the case for REAL

values, it is necessary to provide information as to the position of the decimal point and/or the value of the exponent. As will be seen, this "how" information can either be punched on the card or provided by the program.

iii) What variables are to be assigned values?

The answer to this question depends entirely on the requirements of the program. The READ statement will contain a list of variables to be assigned values.

The purpose of this section is to describe how these questions are answered when programming in the WATFIV language. There are two methods for reading values punched on cards. The methods are called format-free input and formatted input. The essential difference is that when using format-free input, the programmer leaves it up to the WATFIV program to determine how the values have been punched on the cards. In any examples used in the book thus far, the READ statement has been of this type. The WATFIV program has been responsible for deciding what columns were used to punch the values. Under formatted input, the programmer provides this information by using an extra statement called a FORMAT statement to describe how the values have been punched in the cards.

Regardless of which type of method is used, there is the option of:

a) Explicitly naming the input device to be the card reader.

b) Providing the number of a statement in the program to which control will be transferred if you attempt to read a card and there aren't any more.

The available alternatives are as follows.

Forms Of The READ Statement

	Format-Free Input	Formatted Input
Input device assumed to be card reader	READ,input list	READ #,input list # FORMAT(how info)
Input device named as being card reader	READ(5,*) list	READ (5,#) list # FORMAT(how info)
"Out of cards" action specified	READ(5,*,END=n)list	READ(5,#,END=n)list # FORMAT(how info)

The reason for outlining the statement in the upper left hand corner of the table is to indicate that this is the only type of READ statement which has been discussed until now. Before looking at some examples, observe that the thing that is common to all six cases is the input list. An input list is simply a list of variables, separated by commas, which defines the variables to be assigned values by executing the READ statement. Expressions such as I+J are not permitted in an input list since it would not be known how much of the input value is to be assigned to I and how much to J.

5.2 Format-Free Input.

(a) READ,input list

The discussion of this form of the READ statement is essentially a review of the ideas presented in Chapter 2, Section 6. When using this form of the READ statement, the values to be assigned to the variables in the list are punched one or more per card. The values can be separated by commas and/or one or more blank columns. The WATFIV program scans each card looking for numbers punched in the card. As each value is located, it is assigned to the next variable in the input list. The WATFIV program reads as many data cards as is necessary to "satisfy" the input list. Once a data value has been assigned to each variable in the input list, any excess values punched on the last data card read are ignored. The examples below illustrate this and other ideas. Assume all variables are typed by the first-letter rule.

```
i)        READ,I,JOHN,KRUMB
    $ENTRY
       2,    2345
    -17
```

Result: I=2, JOHN=2345, KRUMB=-17

```
ii)       READ,X,Y,LAUGH,Z
    $ENTRY
    245E+04
           -000325.-7
    123456  -81
```

Result: X=2450000, Y=-.0000325, LAUGH=123456, Z=-81.

Observe that when punching REAL values, it is not necessary to punch a decimal point or an "E" (if an exponent is used). The decimal point is assumed to follow the last digit of the number. The exponent value is taken from the digits following the "+" or "-" sign. If you should happen to punch more than seven digits for a REAL value, the number is rounded as well as possible to seven significant digits. If an INTEGER value exceeds the allowed limit or if an exponent is outside the permitted range, an error occurs.

iii)   READ,I,A,B
     $ENTRY
        -17 , -2.0E4
                +6.5,3.1

Result: I=-17, A=-20000., B=6.5, the value 3.1 is unused

One feature of format-free READ statements which is infrequently used permits you to put a repetition factor in front of a data value. The following example illustrates how.

          READ,I,J,A,B,C
     $ENTRY
        2*0,   3*4.96

Result: I=0,J=0, A=4.96, B=4.96, C=4.96

If an INTEGER constant and a "*" appear in front of a data value when is read in using a format-free READ statement, the effect is to repeat the data value the number of times specified by the constant appearing in front of the asterisk. If a large number of variables in an input list are to be assigned the same value, this feature can save some keypunching time.

(b) READ(5,*) list

In this type of format-free READ statement, the number 5 is used to specify the card reader as the input device. The asterisk indicates format-free. In WATFIV, all input-output devices attached to the computer are given a number. In many computer centers the number 5 is used to identify the card reader. If it is different from 5, you simply change the number in the READ statement to its appropriate value. The device number can also be assigned to an INTEGER variable. For example, the pair of statements:

          INPUT=5
          READ(INPUT,*) input list

is equivalent to the single statement:

          READ(5,*) input list

Note that when using this form of the format-free READ statement, there is no comma preceding the first element of the input list. The symbols "(5,*)" replace the comma.

It is only natural to ask why one would want to use this type of READ statement. There are two situations when it may be appropriate. First, you may be testing a program which will eventually use some input device other than the card reader. Once the program has been tested using the card reader for input, the device number can be changed to its appropriate value for the final run. Secondly, perhaps the READ statement will be converted to a formatted READ after the testing phase. To make this change it is simply a matter of replacing the "*" with the number of an appropriate FORMAT statement. (Formatted input is discussed in the next section.)

(c) <u>READ(5,*,END=n) input list</u>

In many programs the number of data values to be read in is not known in advance. Under these circumstances, there are two common ways of providing this information.

i) The first data card contains a value indicating how many data cards or values are to be read.

ii) The last data value is some special number such as -999999. Each value read is compared to this value and when an equal condition is found, no more values are read in.

An alternate way of reading an unknown number of values is simply to keep on reading values until there are no more cards to be read. Suppose we have a set of REAL numbers, punched one per card. We don't know how many there are but we have to calculate the average of all values read. A suitable program is shown below.

```
C EXAMPLE 5.1 USE OF THE END=N IN A READ STATEMENT
      SUM=COUNT=0.
    1 READ(5,*,END=14) X
      SUM=SUM+X
      COUNT=COUNT+1.
      GO TO 1
   14 AVG=SUM/COUNT
      PRINT,AVG
      STOP
      END
```

In this program, the statement GO TO 1 is executed after every data value has been read in and added to SUM. Unless there is an infinite supply of data cards, sooner or later the program will attempt to read a card which isn't there. When this happens, control is transferred to the statement

111

whose number appears after the "END=" parameter of the READ statement. It is important to remember that this transfer of control does not take place until an attempt is made to read a non-existent card. The use of the "END=" parameter in a READ statement is optional. Sometimes it makes programming easier when an unknown number of data values must be processed.

If the "END=" parameter is not included and an attempt is made to read a card when there aren't any more, an error message is printed and the job is terminated.

5.3 Formatted Input - The Concepts

When using any one of the three types of format-free READ statements discussed in the previous section, the WATFIV program is responsible for scanning the data cards and trying to make some sense out of the values punched in them. If however, you, the programmer, know which card columns are used to store the values to be assigned to the variables in the input list, you can make the job of the WATFIV program somewhat easier by describing how the values have been punched in the card. Since you describe usage of the card columns, it is not necessary to separate the data values by commas or blank columns. This means more data values can be recorded on a card. Furthermore, it is possible to omit the decimal point and/or exponent when punching REAL values by including this information in the program.

When the "how" information is contained in the program, a FORMAT statement is used to describe the usage of the card columns. The READ statement is still used to answer the questions "where" and "what". In addition, the READ statement contains a pointer to a FORMAT statement containing the "how" information.

The first type of formatted READ statement has the general form:

        READ fmt#, input list
  fmt# FORMAT(how information)

In this first type of formatted READ statement, the input device is assumed to be the card reader. The "fmt#" is any valid statement number and is a pointer to the FORMAT statement describing how the values have been punched in the card(s). FORMAT statements are non-executable statements and may be placed anywhere in the program. Some programmers prefer to put them all together at the beginning or the end of the program. Different READ statements can point to the same FORMAT statement.

The purpose of a FORMAT statement is to describe where on the card the value for each of the variables in the input list can be found. This is accomplished by providing two items of information for each variable in the list. These two items are represented by the blanks in the following sentence. "Beginning in card column ___, the value for the next variable in the input list is found in the next ___ columns of the card." Let's look at an example.

5.4 Formatted Input of INTEGERS

A simple example is shown below.

        READ 900,JOHN,LOOP

    900 FORMAT(T1,I4,T8,I3)

In this example, the FORMAT statement says: "The value for the first variable in the input list can be found starting in column 1 (T1); is assigned to an INTEGER variable and occupies the next four columns of the card (I4). The value for the second variable in the input list can be found beginning in column 8 (T8), is assigned to an INTEGER variable, and occupies the next 3 columns of the card (I3)." Thus if the symbols punched in the card columns were:

```
              one         ten        twenty
               ↓           ↓            ↓
card      ⎧    0           1            2
columns   ⎨    12345678901234567890
          ⎩
symbols        b-27bbb196bbbbbbbbbb
               ‿‿‿‿   ‿‿‿
                I4      I3
```

then the value assigned to JOHN would be -27, and that assigned to LOOP would be 196. The symbol "b" is used to denote a blank column.

In this example, the "T1" and "T8" are pointers to card columns 1 and 8 respectively. A code of the form "Tp" appearing in a FORMAT statement means: "beginning in column p ...". Since there are 80 columns in a card, the value of "p" must be an INTEGER constant in the range 1 thru 80. Any attempt to reference a column beyond eighty causes an error.

The symbols "I4" and "I3" are examples of "Integer masks". A mask must be provided for each variable in the input list. The word "mask" is appropriate in that the value assigned to a variable is that which is "seen thru the mask". By changing the mask used with a variable, different values may be assigned to the variable. Masks appearing in a FORMAT statement are matched one-for-one with the variables in the input list, beginning from the left. The general form of the Integer mask (I-mask for short) is "Iw" where "w" denotes the number of columns reserved for punching the INTEGER value. The value of w is often called the field width. An I-mask must be provided for each INTEGER variable in the input list.

Operation of the I-mask

For each of the following examples, assume that the symbols punched in the card are those which appear in the card columns covered by the I-mask. The symbol "b" denotes a blank column.

Symbols Appearing In The Card Columns	I-mask	Value Assigned To The Variable
b123	I4	123
b-b99	I5	-99
b-99	I4	-99
+1bbb	I5	1000
-b2b7b	I6	-2070
b1b3b5b7	I8	1030507
9999999999	I10	error (too large)
123.	I4	error (invalid symbol)
12,3456	I7	error (invalid symbol)

These examples show that when using an I-mask:

i) The minus sign can appear anywhere to the left of the first digit.

ii) Blank columns at the beginning, the middle, or the end of the number are treated as zeros.

iii) Error messages result if the data value is outside the permitted range for an INTEGER or if the number is not an INTEGER constant.

iv) The value of "w" must be a positive INTEGER constant.

The link-up between variables in the input list, masks in the FORMAT statement, and values punched on the card is summarized in the following diagram.

114

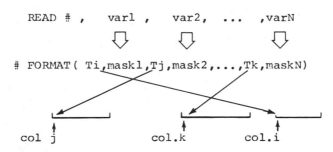

In words, the value which is assigned to the mth variable in the input list is found in the columns covered by the mth mask in the FORMAT statement.

<u>Exercise 5.1</u>

1. For each of the following determine the value assigned to an INTEGER variable if the I-mask shown is used with the data symbols on its left.

Symbols In Columns	Mask	Value
a) b123	I4	
b) +bb45	I5	_____
c) b-3bb	I5	_____
d) -b2b4b	I6	_____
e) +-3456	I6	_____
f) 24.7b	I5	_____

2. Suppose the READ statement

        READ 20,M,N,LUCKY

appears in a program and the data card which is read in by executing the statement contains the values:

    card   ⎧ 0   1   2
    columns   ⎨ 12345678901234567890

        -b147b2589.24b399bbb

What values would be assigned to the variables M,N,and LUCKY using each of the FORMAT statements which follow?

    a) 20 FORMAT(T1,I4,T12,I3,T15,I1)
    b) 20 FORMAT(T1,I2,T12,I6,T4,I4)
    c) 20 FORMAT(T9,I2,T14,I1,T1,I7)
    d) 20 FORMAT(T1,I3,T1,I4,T1,I5)

3. Given the READ statement:

    READ 15,MAX,J12,NO

and a data card containing the values:

card   { 0   1   2
columns { 12345678901234567890123

          123-5b4321-2.+6789bbbbb

Write FORMAT statements which would cause the variables
MAX,J12, and NO to have the following values when the
READ statement is executed.

   a) MAX=23, J12=432, NO=6789
   b) MAX=-2, J12=89000, NO=-5
   c) MAX=504, J12=78, NO=-504
   d) MAX=12, J12=50, NO=-504321
   e) An error message

4. What is the error in each of the following?

   a)   900 FORMAT(T12,I0)
   b)   901 FORMAT(T1,I28,T75,I7)

5.5 Formatted Input of REAL Values (The F-Mask)

    When defining card columns containing values to be
assigned to REAL variables, an F-mask can be used. Consider
the following example.

              READ 825,X,Y
        825 FORMAT(T1,F5.2,T6,F8.3)

    There are two variables in the input list and two masks
in the FORMAT statement, an F-mask of "F5.2" for the
variable X, and an F-mask of "F8.3" for the variable Y.
Furthermore, these masks are positioned to start in columns
1 and 6 respectively. If the first 13 columns of the data
card contain the symbols:

            one   ten   twenty
             ↓   ↓   ↓
card   { 0   1   2
columns { 12345678901234567890

    -b345bbbb2529
         ‿‿
    F5.2   F8.3

the value assigned to X would be -3.45, and the value
assigned to Y would be 2.529. As you might have guessed, the
numbers "w" and "d" in the mask "Fw.d" are such that "w"

116

specifies the number of card columns covered by the mask and
"d" specifies the number of digits to the right of the
decimal.

Operation of an F-mask

The general form of an F-mask is Fw.d where w is the
field width (number of card columns reserved for the value),
and d is the number of digits to the right of the decimal
point. The examples in the following table show the effect
of using different F-masks with various data values.

	Symbols Covered By Mask	Mask	Value Assigned To The Variable
i)	12345	F5.2	123.45
ii)	-b603	F5.4	-.0603
iii)	-b603b	F6.0	-6030.
iv)	987.65	F6.2	987.65
v)	987.65	F6.4	987.65
vi)	bb+2b.b	F7.3	20.0
vii)	12345678	F8.1	1234568.

These examples show that when using an F-mask:

i) Blank columns are treated as being zeros.

ii) If no decimal point is punched in the card, the
value of d in the mask is used to insert a decimal
point such that d digits appear to the right of the
decimal point in the number.

iii) If a decimal point is punched in the card, the
value of d in the mask is ignored.(examples (v) and
(vi)).

iv) If the value punched contains more than 7
significant digits, only 7 significant digits are
stored. The number may or may not be rounded
properly to 7 digits.

v) The only symbols which may appear in card columns
covered by an F-mask are the digits 0 thru 9 and
the symbols + - and . .

*5.6 Formatted Input of REAL Values (The E-mask)

REAL values can also be read using an E-mask. The E-
mask has the general form "Ew.d" where "w" denotes the
number of card columns covered by the mask, and "d" denotes
the number of digits to the right of the decimal point. The
E-mask must be used if a number has been punched with an
exponent. This occurs primarily when the absolute value of
the number being read is either very large, eg: 1.25×10^{25},

or very small, eg: $.2479 \times 10^{-60}$. When indicating the value of the exponent, we can be very sloppy in the way it is punched. For example, to indicate that a number is to be multiplied by ten-to-the-eighth, the exponent can be written in any of the following ways: E+08, E08, E8, E+8, +08, +8. An exponent of -7 can be written as: E-07, E-7, -7, or -07. If the E does not appear in the number, then the sign of the exponent must appear. Some examples follow.

	Symbols Covered By Mask	Mask	Value Assigned To The Variable
i)	+b2.5E+01	E9.1	2.5x10
ii)	-bbb3.41-60	E11.2	-3.41x10
iii)	bb.0045E2b	E10.3	.0045x10
iv)	123	E3.2	1.23
v)	-7766E-3	E8.4	-7.766
vi)	-7766+30	E8.4	-7766.x10
vii)	123456789	E9.2	1234568.
viii)	50.0E2bb	E8.1	error (exponent too large)

These examples illustrate the following points:

   i)   Blanks are treated as zeros.

   ii)   If an exponent is not punched, an exponent of zero is assumed (example(iv)).

   iii)   If a decimal point is punched, the "d" is ignored (exceptions are noted in rule (iv)).

   iv)   If an "E", "+" or "-" appears and no "." is present, the decimal point is assumed to be to the immediate left of the E, + or -. The "d" is ignored.

   v)   If more than 7 significant digits are punched, the number is rounded to 7 digits. Note: the 7th digit may or may not be correctly rounded.

   vi)   If the exponent is outside the permitted range (roughly plus or minus 75) an error occurs.

Example (iv) could of course have been read using an F-mask of F3.2 as well as the E-mask E3.2 and in this sense, E-masks can be used anywhere F-masks can be used. The converse is not true however. If a value of .123E+02 was read under an F-mask, an error would occur since the "E" is considered an invalid character in columns covered by an F-mask.

5.7 Input Containing REAL and INTEGER Values

In the examples of formatted READ statements used thus far, the variables in the input lists have been of the same type. The following examples illustrate formatted input in which the input list contains a mixture of variable types.

i)   READ 50,JACK,EXTRA,FILE,MINMUM
         50 FORMAT(T2,I3,T6,F4.1,T10,F5.3,T16,I1)

If the data card contains the symbols:

```
card       ) 0        1        2
columns    ) 12345678901234567890

          5-36b.0097.388bbbbbb
```

the values assigned to the variables would be: JACK=-36, EXTRA=.009, FILE=7.388, MINMUM=0.

ii)   READ 87,JKL,EEK
          87 FORMAT(T5,I2,T5,F4.1)
         $ENTRY
         bbbb-6.2b

The execution of the READ statement results in JKL having a value of -6 and EEK having a value of -6.2. This illustrates that card columns can be "used twice" by positioning two or more masks so that they overlap.

iii)   READ 555,X,LOST,AA,Z9888
          555 FORMAT(T4,F7.3,T80,I1,T19,I8,T46,F10.5)

Without even knowing what is punched in the card, we can state with certainty that an error message will be produced. To see why, it is simply a matter of matching up the variables in the input list with the masks in the FORMAT statement.

X	LOST	AA	Z9888
F7.3	I1	I8	F10.5

Since AA is a REAL variable and its mask is I8, the message "FORMAT CODE AND DATA TYPE DO NOT MATCH" will be printed. In other words, an I-mask must be used with INTEGER variables and cannot be used with REAL variables. Similarly, F-masks and E-masks can only be used with REAL variables.

119

5.8 A Second Method Of Positioning Masks

Suppose we wish to assign values to the variables DO, N57, and BBB. Assume the values for these three variables are found in columns 1&2, 3 thru 6, and 7&8 respectively. Suppose the appropriate masks are F2.0, I4, and F2.1. We could __explicitly__ position the masks using the FORMAT statement

FORMAT(T1,F2.0,T3,I4,T7,F2.1) .

We could also __implicitly__ position the masks using

FORMAT(F2.0,I4,F2.1) .

The idea here is that if a T-code is not used to position a mask, the mask position is obtained by starting the first mask in column 1 and each successive mask in the column following the last column covered by the previous mask. Thus the mask F2.0 covers the columns 1&2, the mask I4 covers columns 3 thru 6, and the mask F2.1 covers columns 7&8. Implicit positioning of masks can be combined with explicit positioning of masks as the following example shows.

READ 75,K1,K2,K3,K4,K5
75 FORMAT(I6,I3,T80,I1,T14,I2,I2)

This results in the following assignment of variables, masks and card columns.

Variable	Mask	Card Columns Covered	Type Of Positioning
K1	I6	1-6	implicit
K2	I3	7-9	implicit
K3	I1	80	explicit
K4	I2	14-15	explicit
K5	I2	16-17	implicit

5.9 The X-Code.

Another technique for positioning masks to cover the correct card columns is to use an X-code to skip over unused columns. Suppose the value for ICOUNT is punched in columns 3 thru 5 and the value for JHIGH is punched in columns 9 thru 13. When used with the statement

READ 1000, ICOUNT, JHIGH

the following FORMAT statements are equivalent.

```
  i)   1000 FORMAT(2X,I3,3X,I5)
 ii)   1000 FORMAT(2X,I3,T9,I5)
iii)   1000 FORMAT(T3,I3,3X,I5)
 iv)   1000 FORMAT(T3,I3,T9,I5)
```

Each of these four FORMAT statements causes the masks to be positioned as shown below.

```
card      ⎧  0         1          2
columns   ⎨  12345678901234567890
          ⎩    ‿‿‿      ‿‿‿‿‿
               I3       I5
```

A code of "nX" appearing in a FORMAT statement causes the next n columns of the card to be skipped over. The value of n must be a positive INTEGER constant. In the first FORMAT statement for example, the sequence "2X,I3,3X,I5" causes the first two columns to be skipped over, the next 3 are used for the mask I3, then 3 more columns are skipped and the mask I5 covers the next 5 columns.

Is the FORMAT statement

```
        1000 FORMAT(T9,I5,T3,I3)
```

equivalent to the four others? The answer is "no". It does position a mask of I5 to cover columns 9 thru 13 and a mask of I3 to cover columns 3 thru 6. However, when used with the READ statement

```
        READ 1000, ICOUNT, JHIGH
```

the value assigned to ICOUNT would be taken from columns 9 thru 13 and that for JHIGH, from columns 3 thru 6. This is not what was wanted. This example emphasizes the very important point that the mask for each variable, and hence the card columns in which the value is found depend only on the order in which the masks appear in the FORMAT statement.

The following pair of statements show how an X-code could be used to skip all 80 columns of a card.

```
            READ 1
          1 FORMAT(80X)
```

Notice that the input list is empty, it does not contain any variable names. This is quite permissible since our objective was simply to read a card and ignore anything punched in the card. Note that any masks following "80X" would cause an error since they would be positioned beyond the last column available. An easier way of skipping over data cards which aren't needed is described in the following section.

*5.10 The Slash "/" Code

The appearance of a slash symbol in a FORMAT statement causes a new card to be read. Format codes following the "/" apply to the card read in as a result of the slash. The example below illustrates its effect.

READ 50,L,M,N,X

50 FORMAT(I6,/,I3,I7,//,T40,F11.6,///)

When this READ statement is executed, a total of seven data cards will be read. The locations in which the value of each variable in the input list will be found is described in the following table.

Variable	Mask	In Card #	Columns
L	I6	1	1-6
M	I3	2	1-3
N	I7	2	4-10
X	F11.6	4	40-50
		5,6,7	1-80 ignored

Understanding the effect of a slash is simple. There are two points to keep in mind.

i) The left bracket following the word FORMAT causes the first card to be read.

ii) As the FORMAT statement is scanned left to right, each slash encountered causes another card to be read. Masks and other format codes apply to the last card read.

By applying these two ideas to the example given, the results shown in the table should become apparent.

Exercise 5.2

Assume all variables have default typing.

1. For each of the following, fill in the missing item of information.

	Symbols In Card	Mask	Value Assigned
a)	bb.0123	F7.4	_____
b)	b-1.bbb		-1.000
c)	-2345	F5.2	_____
d)	-2377		-237.7
e)	.000002	F7._	.000002
f)	b1b2b3b	____	1020.30

2. Given the pair of statements:

             READ 1,IP,ALPHA,L9,BETA
           1 FORMAT(T5,I6,2X,F7.1,I1,T21,F3.0)

   and a data card containing:

   card   { 0   1   2   3
   columns   { 1234567890123456789012345678 90

           bbb-2473bb77399.568b452.bbbbbb

   Fill in the missing information in the table below.

       Variable   Mask   Mask Positions   Value Assigned

   a)   IP   ___   _____   _____
   b)   ___   ___   13-19   _____
   c)   ___   ___   _____   0
   d)   BETA   ___   _____   _____

3. Write three or more FORMAT statements which are equivalent
   to:
           FORMAT(F17.6,T25,2X,I3,T18,F5.0)

4. Suppose a data card contains the symbols:

   card   { 0   1   2
   columns   { 123456789012345678901 2345

           b-2.46bbb32581.97b43.b2bb

   Suppose the READ statement which causes the data card to
   be read is:
           READ27,A,J,C,M,D

   Write FORMAT statements which will cause the variables in
   the input list to be assigned the values indicated.

	A	J	C	M	D
a)	-2.4	6	32581.	97	43.02
b)	-2.	600	81.97	43	2.0
c)	4.6	-2	1.97	600	3.0
d)	6000.3	581	43.02	0	-2.46
e)	.460	20	.000325	8	70.43
f)	.003	32	32.581	32581	2581.970

5.11 Two Handy Short Cuts.

a) Repeat Factors For A Single Mask

Suppose the answers to a true-false test containing fifty questions are punched in the first 50 columns of a card and a "1" is used to indicate "true", a "0" to indicate "false". To read the answers would mean the input list would contain fifty variable names and its associated FORMAT statement would look like: "FORMAT(I1,I1,I1,...,I1)" where the I1 mask was repeated fifty times. In situations where the same mask is repeated more than once, a repeat factor can be put in front of the mask to indicate the number of times the mask is to be repeated. For the example referred to above, the FORMAT statement could be written as FORMAT(50I1), or FORMAT(31I1,7I1,12I1) or some other combination which would produce the desired 50 repetitions of the mask I1.

A repeat factor can be placed in front of any valid mask. The value of the factor must be a positive INTEGER constant. Thus "2.I1" and "NI1" are invalid. A FORMAT statement such as "FORMAT(F12.3,F12.3,I6)" could be shortened to "FORMAT(2F12.3,I6)".

b) Group Factors For A Set of Codes.

Suppose that in the true-false data referred to above, we were only interested in the answers to questions 5,10,15,...,50. This would mean the READ statement would have ten variables in the input list, and the FORMAT statement could be written as:

FORMAT(4X,I1,4X,I1,4X,I1,...,4X,I1)

where the pair of codes "4X,I1" appears ten times. This can be written in the shorter form:

FORMAT(10(4X,I1))

The inner brackets and their contents are called a group, and the "10" preceding the group is called the group count. Groups and group counts are handy tools for repeating a set of format codes. Groups can be nested just like DO-loops except the maximum depth of nesting is two. That is, we can have a group within a group, but not a group within a group within a group. The following three FORMAT statements are equivalent. Each contains nine masks.

FORMAT(F7.3,I1,2X,I1,2X,F7.3,I1,2X,I1,2X,F7.3,I1,2X,I1,2X)

FORMAT(3(F7.3,I1,2X,I1,2X))

FORMAT(3(F7.3,2(I1,2X)))

In the third case, "(F7.3,2(I1,2X))" is called the outer group and (I1,2X) is called the inner group. As always, when interpreting expressions involving brackets, proceed from the innermost brackets outwards. One further point. Are the FORMAT statements below equivalent?

FORMAT(10F6.3)   FORMAT((10F6.3))   FORMAT(10(F6.3))

Technically, the answer is "No, they are all different.". In the first and second cases, the 10 is a repeat factor. In the third, it is a group count. Furthermore, the second contains a group with an assumed group count of one. The first does not contain a group. In this example, it doesn't matter which one is used. In more complex FORMAT statements, it _may_ matter. This point will be clarified in the following section.

5.12 Two Unanswered Questions.

In each of the examples discussed thus far, the number of masks in the FORMAT statement has been the same as the number of variables in the input list. It is only natural to ask the following two questions.

i) What happens if there are more masks than variables?

ii) What happens if there are fewer masks than variables?

Question 1 (More Masks Than Variables)

The first question is easy to answer. If there are more masks than variables, only those format codes preceding the first unnecessary mask are processed. One example should suffice. Consider the statements:

```
        READ 27,J,K,A
   27 FORMAT(2(I3,1X),F7.2,10X,I8)
```

The variables J and K each have a mask of I3. The variable A has a mask of F7.2. The code 10X is processed and the mask I8 is ignored. The reason for pointing out that the 10X is processed is to emphasize that codes up to the first unnecessary mask are processed. In this example, the 10X has no effect but had slash codes preceded the mask I8, they would have been processed.

Question 2 (Fewer Masks Than Variables)

When there are fewer masks than variables in the input list, the question "What happens?" is easy to answer provided there are no groups. Consider the following example.

```
      READ 14, X, Y, Z
   14 FORMAT(F6.0)
```

The execution of the READ statement causes a card to be read
and the value of X is found in columns 1-6 of the first
card. Since there are no more masks and since there are no
groups, the FORMAT statement is repeated. The left bracket
following the word FORMAT can be viewed as causing the next
card to be read. Thus the value for Y is found in columns
1-6 of the second card. Since no mask has yet been found for
Z, the process is repeated again and hence the value for Z
is found in columns 1-6 of the third data card. Thus the
pair of statements above is equivalent to the following set
of four statements.

```
      READ 14,X
      READ 14,Y
      READ 14,Z
   14 FORMAT(F6.0)
```

Provided that there are no groups in the FORMAT
statement, the rule is that if there are fewer masks than
variables, the format codes are used once and then the
FORMAT statement is repeated. During this recycling process,
the left bracket following the word FORMAT causes the next
data card to be read. The recycling process is repeated
until a mask has been found for each variable in the input
list.

A word of caution. The statements

```
      READ 10,N,X,Y
   10 FORMAT(I6,F11.3)
```

will cause an error. The reason is that the mask for Y is
found by recycling the FORMAT statement. This means an
attempt is made to associate the I-mask I6 with the REAL
variable Y, hence the message "FORMAT CODE AND DATA TYPE DO
NOT MATCH".

When there are groups present in the FORMAT statement,
the part of the FORMAT statement that is recycled over and
over until a mask has been found for each variable in the
input list can be described as "beginning with the group
count of the group whose right bracket is nearest the right
hand end of the FORMAT statement". This probably sounds
complicated but the examples below should make the idea
clear. The arrow in each case shows the portion of the set
of format codes which are recycled.

```
      FORMAT(...10(...)...)
              ↑_____
```

126

```
FORMAT(...2(...)...(...)...)
         ↑_____
FORMAT(...3(...4(...)...6(...)...)...)
         ↑_____
```

5.13 Other Forms of the Formatted READ Statement.

For each type of format-free READ statement, there is an equivalent formatted READ statement. The three types are:

    READ fmt#, input list

    READ(5,fmt#) input list

    READ(5,fmt#,END=n) input list

All examples so far have used the first type in which the input device is assumed to be the card reader and in which no statement number was provided to which control would be transferred if an attempt was made to read a non-existent data card.

Recall that the "5" is used to specify the card reader as the input device and that the device number of the card reader can be stored in an INTEGER variable.

When the "END=" parameter is included in the READ statement, control will be transferred to the statement number following the "=" sign if the READ statement is executed and there are no more data cards.

The program below could be used to read in an unknown number of data cards each of which contains from one to three REAL values. The number of data values punched in each card is recorded in column 80 of the card. The values are punched according to a mask F5.0 and appear in columns 1-5, 6-10, and 11-15. The program prints the total number of values read and the average of their squares.

```
C EXAMPLE 5.2 AVG OF SUM OF SQUARES
      SUMSQ=0.
      NVALS=0
    1 READ(5,302,END=16) N,A,B,C
  302 FORMAT(T80,I1,T1,3F5.0)
      SUMSQ=SUMSQ+A*A+B*B+C*C
      NVALS=NVALS+N
      GO TO 1
   16 AVG=SUMSQ/FLOAT(NVALS)
      PRINT,NVALS,AVG
      STOP
      END
```

Note that if there are only two values in a card, columns 11 thru 15 will be blank and therefore the variable C will have a value of zero. Thus the addition of C*C will not affect the total SUMSQ. What would happen if it was necessary to use a format-free READ statement because we were unsure of how many columns had been used to punch each of the (possibly) three values? With our present knowledge we could not solve the problem. Techniques for solving this problem are described in Chapters 15 and 20.

Exercise 5.3

Assume all variables are typed by default.

1.   For each of the FORMAT statements below:
     a) How many masks are there in the statement?
     b) What part of the FORMAT statement would be recycled
        if there were more variables than masks?
     c) How many cards would be read if the input list
        contained twenty variables?
     d) On what card, and in what columns of that card is the
        value assigned to the 12th variable in the list?
     e) If the eighth variable is REAL, would an error occur?

       i) FORMAT(2I6,3X,F7.2)
      ii) FORMAT(T5,8F1.0,2X,I5)
     iii) FORMAT(2I12,3I3,F6.1)
      iv) FORMAT(1X,2(I18,3F2.2),2X,3(I4))
       v) FORMAT(2I1,2(2X,F7.4,2(3X,I2)))

2.   Suppose two data cards are such that the first contains the symbols "1234567890" in columns one thru ten and the second contains the symbols "0987654321" in columns one thru ten. Assume both cards have blanks in columns eleven thru eighty. Given the statement,

         READ 44,X,M,Y,N

     write a single FORMAT statement containing no slashes which will result in the assignment of values to variables indicated in the table below.

	X	M	Y	N
a)	12.34	5	678.	900
b)	12345.6	89	9876.5	32
c)	678.90	12	543.21	9
d)	4.5	78	90.	76
e)	34.56	78	9.87	65
f)	67.8	90	9.8	21

5.14 A Word About Commas.

Each format code used in the examples has been separated from those preceding or following it by a comma. It is not necessary to use commas if their ommission would not cause any ambiguity in the meaning of the FORMAT statement. As an example, the pair of codes "3X,F6.3" could be written as "3XF6.3" without an error message being produced. On the other hand, we could not write "T5,2I1" as "T52I1" since this could also mean "T52,I1". As a general rule, use commas to separate format codes. It can't hurt and it makes the FORMAT statement more readable.

*5.15 Literals In Input FORMAT Statements

This section describes a type of format code which is almost never used in input operations. A "literal" is simply a string of symbols. Literals can be defined in two ways. Depending on which method is used to define the literal, it is called a "Quote-type" literal or an "H-type" literal. Examples of each appear in the following table.

Symbol String	As A Quote-Type Literal	As An H-Type Literal
ABCDE	'ABCDE'	5HABCDE
PAYROLL REPORT	'PAYROLL REPORT'	14HPAYROLL REPORT
JAN. 1,1980	'JAN. 1,1980'	11HJAN. 1,1980

As can be seen from the foregoing examples, Quote-type literals are defined by enclosing a string of symbols in single quotes. H-type literals (sometimes called Hollerith strings or Hollerith constants) are defined by prefixing the symbol string with "nH" where n represents the number of symbols in the string, including blanks. H-type literals are the only literals recognized by many Fortran compilers. Either type is acceptable in WATFIV.

If a literal is present in a FORMAT statement used in a READ operation, the symbols punched in the card columns covered by the literal replace the symbols of the literal in the FORMAT statement when the READ statement is executed. Literals are positioned in precisely the same way as masks are positioned (implicitly or explicitly).

Consider the following two examples.

a)   READ 900,K
        900 FORMAT('WIPED OUT',I4)
            ...
     $ENTRY
     WITH THIS1234

       Result: K has a value of 1234 and the FORMAT
           statement has become "FORMAT('WITH THIS',I4)"

b)   READ 900
        900 FORMAT(T2,5HXXXXX)
            ...
     $ENTRY
     HELLO

       Result: The FORMAT statement is changed to
         FORMAT(T2,5HHELLO)

In both of these examples, the symbols of the literal in the FORMAT statement are changed to the symbols appearing in the card columns covered by the literal.

What is the purpose of having literals in FORMAT statements? There are two reasons. First, it provides a means of changing a FORMAT statement. Much better techniques exist however and are described in Chapters 15 and 20. Second, literals do serve a valuable function in FORMAT statements used for output. Use of this technique may mean the same FORMAT statement can be used for both input and output (formatted output is discussed in the next chapter). In spite of these reasons, the inclusion of literals in FORMAT statements used for input is of very little practical value.

*5.16 <u>The G-Mask.</u>

The G-mask is a general purpose mask which can be used to read both REAL and INTEGER values under control of a FORMAT statement. Its general form is "Gw.d" where "w" denotes the number of card columns covered by the mask and "d" denotes the number of digits to the right of the decimal point. The value of d is ignored (and in fact ".d" may be omitted) when a G-mask is used with an INTEGER variable. The examples which follow show that the effect of the mask Gw.d is the same as that of the mask Iw, if used for an INTEGER variable; and the same as the mask Ew.d, if used for a REAL variable. The G-mask is used primarily to save time writing FORMAT statements. Its use may also mean that input lists can be altered with no change required in the associated FORMAT statement.

Type Of Variable	Symbols In Cols. Covered by Mask	G-Mask	Value Assigned To Variable
INTEGER	12345	G5	12345
INTEGER	-1234b	G6.3	-12340
REAL	12345	G5.2	123.45
REAL	12.345	G6.2	12.345
REAL	.024E-2	G7.3	.00024
REAL	24E-2	G5.1	.24

*5.17 F-Mask Modification - The P-Code.

Numbers punched in card columns covered by an F-mask can be multiplied by a power of ten before the value is assigned to a variable. This operation, often called decimal scaling, is done by prefixing an F-mask with a P-code of the form "sP" where "s" denotes the power of ten to be used.

The table below shows the effect produced for several combinations of data values and modified F-masks.

Symbols In Columns Covered by Mask(s)	Mask(s)	Value(s) Assigned To Variable(s)
12345	F5.2	123.45
12345	2PF5.2	1.2345
12345	0PF5.2	123.45
12345	-3PF5.2	123450.
876.5	2PF5.3	8.765
8.765	-1PF5.3	87.65
12345678	-1P2F4.0	12340. & 56780.
12345678	-1PF4.0,F4.0	12340. & 56780.
12345678	-1PF4.0,0PF4.0	12340. & 5678.

The general form of the P-code is "sP" where "s" is an INTEGER constant. The rules of usage as illustrated by the foregoing examples are:

a)   Using only the F-mask, determine the value in the card columns covered by the mask. Assign 10**(-s) times this value to the input variable.

b)   If a repeat factor is used, the format code is "sPrFw.d" where "r" is the repeat factor. See the third last example.

131

c)   Any P-code encounted applies to all subsequent F-masks used in the FORMAT statement <u>unless</u> its effect is negated by another P-code. (See the last two examples.)

Most people have difficulty remembering whether a positive "s" in a code "sP" means multiply by ten to the s or ten to the minus s. Well, the German word for "one" is "eins" and eins way to remember the rule is:

$$\underline{E}xternal\ value = \underline{IN}ternal\ value\quad 10^{\underline{s}}$$

⇧   ⇧   ⇧

on the card   in the computer   in the code
"sP"

Note that the underlined letters spell "EINS".

Why use P-codes? Their most important use is in converting REAL numbers with fractional values to whole numbers. Recall that many exact decimal values (5.21 for example) are stored with a small error in a computer because their representation in the base two number system has a non-terminating fractional value. Whole numbers are stored exactly. Therefore, to improve accuracy in critical computations such as payroll calculations, it may be desirable to convert a REAL input value such as a wage rate to a whole number prior to performing any arithmetic with the value. After calculations have been completed, division by an appropriate power of ten can be done to obtain the final result.

Another use of decimal scaling is simply to drop or add zeros to a value. For example, values in the range zero thru nine could be instantaneously be made into millions using the code -6PF1.0.

A final question. Why do the two sets of statements below cause X to have slightly different values? If you know why, you know why P-codes are sometimes used.

```
        READ 900,X                  READ 901,X
    900 FORMAT(-2PF4.2)         901 FORMAT(F4.2)
        ...                         X=X*100.
        ...                         ...
$ENTRY                      $ENTRY
5.21                        5.21
```

132

*5.18 The ERR=m Parameter

The READ statement in WATFIV can include the sequence of symbols "ERR=m" as a parameter. If present, "m" is the number of an executable statement in the program to which control will be transferred if a machine or hardware error occurs during the transmission of the data from the input device to the computer memory. It may appear with or without the END=n parameter in both formatted and format-free READ statements as shown in the following table.

Format-Free   READ(device,*,ERR=m) list

                     or

            READ(device,*,END=n,ERR=m) list

Formatted   READ(device,fmt,ERR=m) list

                     or

            READ(device,fmt,END=n,ERR=m) list

In the foregoing table, the order of the "END=" and "ERR=" parameters doesn't matter.

When should the "ERR=" parameter be used? When using WATFIV, a portion of the WATFIV program remains in memory during the execution of a program and acts somewhat like a "mother hen". If a transmission error occurs, the mother hen feature intercepts the error and prints an appropriate error message before the job is terminated. For this reason it is not necessary to use the ERR=m parameter when running under WATFIV. If, however, you wish to attempt further execution of the program or print your own error message, the ERR=m parameter could be included in a READ statement.

A second reason for its inclusion would be that you intend to compile your source program using one of the many Fortran compilers available. In most of these, the mother hen feature is not present and hence you are responsible for handling transmission errors to your satisfaction.

5.19 Summary

1. There are three questions which must be answered in any input operation. These are:
   a) What variables are to be assigned values?
   b) On what device are the values recorded?
   c) How are the values recorded on the input medium?

2. The programmer answers question (a) by defining an

133

input list of variables.

The programmer answers question (b) by writing the READ statement either as:

READ,list   or READ(5,...) list .

The programmer may or not answer question (c). If he does not, the input operation is said to be format-free. With format-free input, WATFIV is resposible for determining how the values have been recorded on the input medium. If the programmer provides the "how" information, the operation is said to be formatted. In this case, a FORMAT statement is used to describe the usage of the card columns.

3. When using formatted input, a mask must be provided for each variable in the input list. The following points are significant.
      i) Masks are assigned to variables in the input list in a left to right fashion.
     ii) An I-mask is used for INTEGER variables.
    iii) An F-mask or E-mask is used for REAL variables.

4. Masks may be positioned:
      i) Explicitly (using a T-code)
     ii) Implicity (card columns are used sequentially)
    iii) A combination of (i) and (ii)

5. An X-code may be used to skip over unused columns.

6. A slash code may be used to read in another card.

7. Repeat factors and group counts can be used to reduce the effort of writing long strings of format codes.

8. Repeat factors, group counts, and values of p, n, w, and d in the codes Tp, nX, Iw, Fw.d, Ew.d must be positive INTEGER constants.

Programming Problems

In each of the following problems use formatted input statements unless specifically requested to use format-free input.

5.1   The input to the program consists of payroll data. Each of ten different employee's data is punched on a single card according to the following rules.

card cols.	mask	item
1-3	I3	employee number
4-6	F3.2	regular wage rate
7-9	F3.1	regular hours worked
10-12	F3.2	overtime wage rate
13-15	F3.1	overtime hours worked

Read the cards one at a time and calculate the gross pay for each employee. Print the total number of regular hours, overtime hours, regular pay, overtime pay and total pay for the ten employees. For each of the ten employees print a line of the form "GROSS PAY FOR EMPLOYEE ___ IS $ 0.dddddddEee".

5.2   If an equation can be written in the form $x-F(x)=0$, then, subject to certain conditions, a root of the equation can be found by obtaining increasingly accurate approximations of the root. If x_0 is some initial estimate of the root, then x_1, x_2, ... will be better estimates where $x_n=F(x_{n-1})$. Suppose $F(x)$ has the form $A/(x+B)$ and the initial estimate is called C. Write a program which reads values of A, B and C each of which is punched using a mask of F4.2. Calculate increasingly accurate estimates of the root until the change in two estimates is less than .0001. Print every tenth estimate as well as the final estimate. Test your program using first: A=12.3, B=5.4, C=2.0; secondly, A=3.99, B=-4. C=2.0.

5.3   Write a program to solve two equations in two unknowns of the form

$$Ax + By = C$$
$$Dx + Ey = F$$

Read values of A, B and C from one data card and the values of D, E and F from a second data card. Use the "END=" parameter in the first read statement and test your program on an unknown number of pairs of equations.

5.4   Read an unknown number of INTEGER values punched one value per card. Print the largest and smallest value of those that are read as well as each value which is read.

5.5   A fraction of the form

$$\cfrac{a}{b + \cfrac{a}{b + \cfrac{a}{b + \ldots}}}$$

is called a continued fraction. Its value may be approximated to any desired accuracy by evaluating

135

A_0/B_0 , A_1/B_1 , A_2/B_2 , etc. where

$A_0=0$, $A_1= a$, and $A_n= aA_{n-2} + bA_{n-1}$ for n=2, 3, ...

$B_0=1$, $B_1= b$, and $B_n= aB_{n-2} + bB_{n-1}$ for n=2, 3, ...

Write a program which reads several pairs of values of values of "a" and "b" and for each, calculates A_{10}/B_{10} . Test your program on at least the following two cases. (i) a=1, b=1; (ii) a=1, b=2.

CHAPTER 6

Questions Answered In This Chapter.

   1. How do we answer the three questions associated with
      any output operation, namely:

        - Where (on what device) are the values to be dis-
          played?
        - What values are to be displayed?
        - How are the values to be displayed?

   2. What do the terms "format-free" and "formatted" mean
      when applied to output operations?

   In   the   examples   used thus far, the results of
computations have been printed using a PRINT statement. The
values   appearing   on   the   page were spaced out across
successive lines according to rules which are incorporated
into the WATFIV program. The purpose of this chapter is to
describe how you, the programmer, can control the appearance
and placement of printed values.

6.1 Output - The Three Questions.

   i) Where are the values recorded?

        The most frequently used medium for displaying the
     results of calculations done during the execution of a
     program is the printed page. Most large computer
     systems have one or more high speed printers, one or
     more typewriters, and possibly several TV-type display
     devices. A typewriter prints characters at a typical
     rate of fifteen characters per second. A high speed
     printer can print at a rate of a thousand or more lines
     per minute. Video display devices are even faster but do
     not produce a permanent record which can be kept for
     later reference. In this chapter we shall assume the
     answer to the question "Where are the values recorded?"
     is "On a high speed printer.".

        In   WATFIV   there   are two verbs which cause
     information stored in the computer memory to be
     transmitted to a printer. These are the verbs "PRINT"
     and "WRITE". When using the PRINT statement it is not
     necessary to identify the printer as being the output
     device. When using the WRITE statement, it is.   The
     differences between PRINT and WRITE statements are
     discussed at the end of this section.

ii) What values are to be printed?

Output statements normally contain an output list. The elements of the list are the variables, constants or expressions whose values are to be printed. The elements of the list must be separated by commas. Examples of valid output lists are:

    i) X,I

    ii) 333,ABC,-6.0E+24/BB

    iii) +(X+Y)/(X-Y)

These output lists contain two, three, and one element respectively. An important point which is sometimes forgotten is illustrated in example (iii). That is that expressions appearing in output lists cannot start with a left bracket. If a bracket is necessary, as in this example, a plus or minus sign must appear in front of the left bracket. The reason is to avoid having the expression interpreted as a special type of element which will be discussed in the next chapter.

iii) How are the values to be printed?

When sending values to the printer by using either a PRINT statement or a WRITE statement, you have a choice. You can either let WATFIV decide where the values will appear on the page or you can control the placement of values. When WATFIV assumes the responsibility of positioning the output, the term format-free is used. When you are in control, the term formatted is used to describe the operation. When using formatted output, a FORMAT statement is used in conjunction with either the PRINT or WRITE statement. The FORMAT statement supplies the "how" information. The four types of output statements are shown in the following table.

Forms Of Output Statements

	Format-Free Output	Formatted Output
Output device assumed to be the printer	PRINT,output list	PRINT #,output list # FORMAT(how info)
Printer named as the output device	WRITE(6,*) list	WRITE(6,#) list # FORMAT(how info)

The double line around "PRINT,output list" in the foregoing table indicates the only type of output statement considered previously.

6.2 Three Facts About Printed Output.

The following facts are true for both format-free output and formatted output.

1. a) A line of printing contains 10 symbols per inch.
   Note: A blank is considered to be a symbol.

   b) There are six lines of printing in each vertical inch. This means that 66 lines can be printed on the normal page of eleven inches.

2. Each line of printing has 133 print positions. One symbol can be stored in each position. Only the symbols stored in positions 2 thru 133 are printed. The symbol stored in position 1 is used to control the vertical spacing and is not printed. The number 133 applies to the most commonly used printer. You should check with your computing center to find out the "width" of the print line.

3. After each line is printed, blanks are put in all 133 print positions. This means you automatically start with a clean slate before sending any symbols you want printed to the printer.

For reasons which will become apparent in Section 6.17, the topic of formatted output will be discussed first.

6.3 Formatted Output - The Concepts.

The two types of formatted output statements are:

```
    PRINT #, output list
    # FORMAT( format codes )
```

and

```
    WRITE(6,#) output list
    # FORMAT( format codes )
```

The only difference in the two forms of output statements is that when using the WRITE statement, the printer is named as being the output device. In most computing centers, the number 6 is used to identify the high-speed printer. If it is different, the appropriate value should be used in the WRITE statement. For convenience, the PRINT command will be used in the examples of this chapter. The WRITE statement may be preferable if

the output which is being sent to the printer will
eventually be sent to some other output device such as a
card punch or magnetic tape drive. In such cases, it is a
simple matter to change the device number to the desired
value. In addition, most of the programming languages in
the Fortran family of languages do not accept the PRINT
statement as being valid. Thus if your program will be run
using a non-WATFIV compiler, you should use the WRITE
statement to produce your printed output. The number of the
ouput device can be stored in an INTEGER variable. Thus the
statement pair

IPRINT=6
WRITE(IPRINT,#) output list

is equivalent to the statement "WRITE(6,#) output list".

When using formatted ouput, the programmer must control:

a) The horizontal position of the symbols being printed.
   i.e: the position of the item along the print line.

b) The vertical position of the symbols being printed.
   That is, how many lines below the last line printed.

c) The appearance of REAL values including:
      i) whether or not an exponent is to be printed,
     ii) how many digits are to appear to the right of
         decimal point.

These three types of information are included in a
FORMAT statement which is linked to a PRINT or WRITE
statement by its statement number. FORMAT statements can
appear anywhere in a program. Some programmers prefer to put
them all together at the beginning or end of the program.
Several PRINT or WRITE statements can refer to the same
FORMAT statement.

The principles of horizontal control, vertical control,
and appearance of printed items can be illustrated by
considering the output of INTEGER values. Once these
techniques are understood, they can be easily extended to
the printing of REAL values and literals.

6.4 Formatted INTEGER output

INTEGER values in WATFIV range from -2147483648 to
+2147483647. This means that, including a possible negative
sign, an INTEGER value could occupy as many as eleven print
positions (one position per symbol). Most INTEGER values
used in a program do not contain ten digits and therefore
fewer than eleven print positons are necessary to display
the value.

140

To print an INTEGER value in WATFIV you must specify
which print positions are to be reserved for displaying the
value. This is done by telling the compiler two things --
the first (leftmost) print position reserved and secondly,
how many print positions to reserve. Consider the following
example.

```
      PRINT 900, -85
  900 FORMAT(T2,I3)
```

The PRINT statement indicates that a value of negative
eighty-five is to be printed and that the positions in which
it is to be printed are described in the FORMAT statement
having the statement number 900. In the FORMAT statement
the code "T2" points to print position two. The "I" in the
code "I3" says that an INTEGER value is to be printed and
the "3" means three print positions are to be reserved for
displaying the value. Therefore the effect of the sequence
"T2,I3" is to reserve print positions two, three and four
for displaying an INTEGER value. This means that when the
PRINT statement is executed, the symbols "-85" appear in the
second, third and fourth print positions.

Consider the following pair of statements.

```
      PRINT 901, 7294, -38
  901 FORMAT(T3,I4,T8,I3)
```

Result: A line is printed in which the following symbols
appear in the print positions shown.

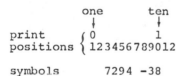

```
             one        ten
              ↓          ↓
print        ( 0         1
positions    { 123456789012

symbols        7294 -38
```

In this example the "T3" and "T8" are examples of "T-codes".
A code of the form "Tp" where "p" is some integer value in
the range 1 thru 133 means "beginning in print position p
...". The "I4" and "I3" are examples of "Integer masks" (I-
masks). An I-mask is used for each INTEGER value in an
output list. The word "mask" is appropriate because the
appearance of the value printed is that which is "seen" thru
the mask. By changing the mask, the appearance of the
printed line can be changed. The general form of an I-mask
is "Iw" where "w" specifies how many print positions are to
be reserved.

You are no doubt wondering what will happen if more (or
fewer) print positions are reserved than are necessary to
display a value. The following table contains several
examples which illustrate how an INTEGER value appears

within the positions reserved by its I-mask. In the table the symbol "b" denotes a blank.

	Value Being Printed	Mask	Symbols Stored In Reserved Positions
i)	12345	I5	12345
ii)	12345	I6	b12345
iii)	12345	I3	***
iv)	0	I2	b0
v)	-0	I3	b-0
vi)	-12345	I6	-12345
vii)	-12345	I8	bb-12345
viii)	-12345	I5	*****

These examples illustrate the following points regarding the use of an I-mask.

i) If the number is positive, the plus sign is not printed. See examples (i) thru (iv).

ii) If the number is negative, the negative sign appears to the left of the leftmost digit. See examples (v) thru (viii).

iii) If more print positions are reserved than are necessary to print the value, blanks are added to the left of the value to fill out the excess print positions. To be precise, the surplus positions to the left of the value are unchanged by the insertion of the value in the rightmost positions. Since the print positions are all initially blank before processing of the format codes begins, this normally means that the excess positions contain blanks.

iv) If fewer positions are reserved than are necessary to store the value, the print positions reserved by the mask are filled with asterisks. It is not necessary to reserve a position for the sign of a postive or zero value.

To summarize. INTEGER values (constants, variables and expressions) appearing in an output list can be positioned anywhere across a print line. This is done by providing an I-mask for each INTEGER value in the output list. The first position covered by the mask is determined by the T-code which precedes the mask. At execution time, the codes in the FORMAT statement are scanned left to right. As each T-code – I-mask combination is encountered, the next item in the output list is picked up and its value is stored in the print positions covered by the mask.

Two additional points. In the codes "Tp" and "Iw", the "p" and "w" must be unsigned positive integer values. Any position referred to by a T-code or covered by an I-mask must be in the range 1 thru 133. For example, the following FORMAT statement causes the message "BUFFER LENGTH EXCEDED" to be printed. The reason is that the mask "I6" extendes beyond position 133.

FORMAT(T130,I6)

Exercise 6.1

1. What T-code must precede a mask so that it will start in position 100?

2. If the T-code "T75" precedes the mask I8, what is the last position reserved by the mask?

3. Write a sequence of T-codes and I-masks to reserve the print positions 16-24, 25, and 80-90 for three INTEGER items appearing in an output list.

4. a) Write a FORMAT statement which, when used with the statement:
   PRINT 82,-123,4567,89
   will cause the symbols -123456789 to appear in print positions 8 thru 17.

   b) For the same PRINT statement as used in (a), write a FORMAT statement which will cause the symbols 4567b89bb-123b to appear in print positions 2 thru 15. Check the correctness of your FORMAT statements by using the computer to print the results.

5. Predict the output obtained by executing the statements:

   PRINT 99,333,22,1
   99 FORMAT(T10,I3,T10,I2,T10,I1)

   Check your prediction using the computer.

6. Explain the difference between:

   PRINT,100,200   and PRINT 100,200

6.5 Vertical Control.

The preceding section described one method of positioning values along a print line. In order to control the vertical positioning of printed items, we make use of print position number 1. The symbol stored in position 1 is called the Vertical Control Character, or VCC for short. The VCC is not printed but all symbols stored in the remaining

132 positions are. The different symbols and the effect of using each is shown in the following table.

Vertical Control Character	Action	Meaning: "The line is printed ...."
1	new page	at the top of the next page
+	no space	on the same line as the last line printed
blank	single space	on the line below the last line printed
0	double space	on the line two lines below the last line printed
-	triple space	on the line three lines below the last line printed

Any Vertical Control Character other than one of the five in the table has the same effect as a blank.

To cause the desired VCC to be put in print position one is simply a matter of enclosing the VCC in a pair of single quotes and putting the code T1 ahead of it. For example, the sequence "T1,'0'" causes a zero to be stored in position one and therefore the line will be printed on the second line following the last line printed. The program below prints the number 1 at the top of a page; the number 2 underneath it; and the number 3 after two blank lines have been left.

```
      C EXAMPLE 6.3 EXAMPLE OF VERTICAL SPACING CONTROL
            PRINT 100,1
            PRINT 200,2
            PRINT 300,3
            STOP
      100 FORMAT(T1,'1',T2,I5)
      200 FORMAT(T1,' ',T2,I5)
      300 FORMAT(T1,'-',T2,I5)
            END
```

The output produced is:

```
print      ⎰
positions  ⎱1234567890

           1    (at the top of a page)
           2
           b ⎱  two blank
           b ⎰     lines
           3
```

6.6 A Second Method Of Horizontal Control.

When the VCC or a mask is positioned along the print
line by putting a T-code in front of the element, the format
element is said to have been positioned _explicitly_. If a T-
code does not precede a format element, the VCC or mask is
said to be positioned _implicitly_. When implicit positioning
is used, print positions are assigned consecutively to the
format elements beginning with print position one. Some
examples will illustrate this second method of horizontal
control. The seven FORMAT statements which follow each put:
a "0" in position one; the mask I6 in positions 2-7; and the
mask I5 in positions 8-12.

   i) FORMAT('0',I6,I5)

  ii) FORMAT('0',T2,I6,I5)

 iii) FORMAT('0',I6,T8,I5)

  iv) FORMAT(T1,'0',I6,T8,I5)

   v) FORMAT(T1,'0',T2,I6,I5)

  vi) FORMAT(T1,'0',T2,I6,T8,I5)

 vii) FORMAT(T2,I6,T8,I5,T1,'0')

In example (i), there is no T-code preceding the VCC and
therefore the zero is stored in the first available print
position, namely, position 1. Since no T-code precedes the
mask I6, the next 6 print positions are used for the mask
I6. Similarly, since no T-code precedes the mask I5, it is
positioned implicitly in positions 8-12. In example (ii),
the T-code "T2" is unnecessary since the mask I6 would be
positioned in positions 2 thru 7 anyway. Examples (ii) thru
(v) and (vii) show that a combination of implicit and
explicit positioning of format elements may be used. Note
that in these seven examples, the mask I6 always precedes
the mask I5 in the list of format elements. This is
necessary if we are to claim that the seven examples are
equivalent. Keep in mind that regardless of where a mask is
positioned on the print line, the first mask in the format
elements is used with the first item in the output list; the
second with the second, etc. Thus the FORMAT statement

FORMAT('0',T8,I5,T2,I6)

is not equivalent to any of the seven since the order in which the masks I6 and I5 appear is different.

6.7 The X-Code.

When positioning masks along a print line, an X-code can be used to skip over consecutive print positions. The X-code has the form "nX" where "n" is the number of positions to be skipped. The value of "n" must be an unsigned positive INTEGER constant. The output produced by the pair of statements below illustrates the effect of an X-code.

                    PRINT 3,-1234567
                  3 FORMAT(' ',4X,I10)

Since there are no T-codes, all items in the FORMAT statement are positioned implicitly. Thus the VCC is stored in position 1, the next four print positions are skipped because of the code 4X, and the next ten positions are used for printing the value of -1234567 according to the mask I10. If a T-code precedes an X-code, it specifies the first print position to be skipped. The sequence "T91,5X" for example, causes positions 91 thru 95 to be skipped.

The following example emphasizes the facts that: the print positions are initially all blank; the elements in a FORMAT statement are processed left to right; only those positions which contains symbols after the operation of an I-mask are changed by the operation of the mask. The output produced by the statements:

                  PRINT 900, 111111, 2222, 33
              900 FORMAT(T2,I6,T2,2X,I4,T2,I6)

is

    print   {
    positions { 1234567

               112233

The sequence of events leading to this result is

    print   {
    positions { 1234567

                  bbbbbbb   (initially all blank)
                  b111111   (after the codes "T2,I6")
                  b112222   (after the codes "T2,2X,I4")
                  b112233   (after the codes "T2,I6")

146

6.8 "Hiding" The VCC.

In previous examples, the vertical control character was stored in print position one either implicitly or explicitly. Since an X-code of "1X" also leaves a print position unchanged, the FORMAT statement FORMAT(1X,...) is equivalent to FORMAT(' ',...). Another way of putting a VCC in position one is to let the first position reserved by a mask do the job. The FORMAT statements below are equivalent.

      i) FORMAT(' ',I14,...)
     ii) FORMAT(1X,I14,...)
    iii) FORMAT(I15,...)

Each causes position one to have a blank. We must be a little careful however in permitting the first position of a mask to be used as the VCC. What is the output of the following pair of statements?

              PRINT 300,1475
          300 FORMAT(I4)

The result is that a value of 475 will be printed at the top of a page! This happens because the mask I4 is positioned implicitly in positions 1 thru 4. When the value in the output list is used with the mask I4, a 1 is stored in the first print position. A VCC of 1 of course, causes a skip to the top of a page and since the VCC is never printed, only the digits 475 appear.

Exercise 6.2

1. For each of the following FORMAT statements, write at least two other FORMAT statements which are equivalent.

    a)   FORMAT('+',T5,I12)
    b)   FORMAT(I14,T20,I3)
    c)   FORMAT(I12,T1,'0',20X,I3)

2. Predict the output of the following sets of statements. Check your predictions using the computer.

    a)   PRINT 2,1,2,3
       2 FORMAT('1',I2,2X,I4,2X,I3)

    b)   PRINT 5,1,2,3
       5 FORMAT('0',I2,T14,I1,T6,I4)

    c)   PRINT 8, -1,-2
       8 FORMAT(I2,T1,I2)

    d)   N=17
         PRINT 14, N,MOD(18,N),MOD(N,18),N/3
      14 FORMAT(I10,2X,I3,T1,'0',20X,I4,1X,I2)

147

    e)   PRINT 16,1234567,IFIX(SQRT(10000.))
       16 FORMAT(' ',I6,T4,I3)

6.9 Printing REAL Values.

In order to print the values of expressions and variables appearing in the output list which are REAL values, it is simply a matter of using an F-mask or E-mask instead of an I-mask. The E-mask is used when the number is to be printed with an exponent. The E-mask should be used for printing values which are either very large, for example $5.\times10^{20}$, or very small, for example $5.\times10^{-20}$. It is also a good idea to use an E-mask if you are uncertain as to the value being printed. The F-mask is usually used for values which are somewhere in the range between .0000001 and one million. When using either of these masks, you must specify the number of print positions reserved for displaying the value and the number of digits to be printed to the right of the decimal point. The effect of using F-masks and E-masks is shown in the examples which follow.

Operation of the F-mask

General form: Fw.d where w is the number of print
                    reserved, and d is the number of
                    digits to the right of the decimal.

	Value of Number	F-mask	Symbols Stored In The Print Positions
i)	123.45	F7.2	b123.45
ii)	123.45	F10.4	bb123.4500
iii)	123.45	F6.0	bb123.
iv)	123.45	F6.1	b123.5
v)	123.45	F4.3	****
vi)	-123.45	F7.2	-123.45
vii)	-123.45	F9.3	b-123.450
viii)	-123.45	F5.0	-123.
ix)	-123.45	F4.0	****
x)	0.0	F2.0	0.
xi)	10.**20	F8.0	********
xii)	10.**(-9)	F8.6	b.000000
xiii)	.5	F3.1	0.5
xiv)	.5	F2.1	**
xv)	-.5	F4.1	-0.5

These examples illustrate the following points when using F-masks to display REAL values.

   i) The sign is not printed unless the value is
      negative. In this case the sign appears immediately
      to the left of the value.

ii) If more positions are reserved than are necessary to display the value, the print positions not used for the negative sign, digits or decimal point are left unchanged. The value occupies the rightmost positions reserved by the mask. If the absolute value of the number being printed is less than 1.0 a zero is printed to the left of the decimal point. This means that when using the mask Fw.d, that w must be at least two larger than d for positive values and at least three larger than d for displaying negative values.

iii) If fewer positions are reserved than are necessary to display the value, asterisks are stored in the positions reserved by the mask.

iv) The value printed never contains an exponent. This means that numbers less than .0000001 in absolute value will be shown as a zero since only seven significant digits are stored for REAL values. Numbers which have a large absolute value will appear correctly (to seven significant digits), provided a sufficient number of positions are reserved for displaying the value.

v) If significant digits are dropped because of the value of d in the mask, the number is rounded to d decimal places. Rounding in the sixth decimal place or the digit in the seventh place may be inaccurate because of the internal representation of the number.

Operation of the E-mask

General form: Ew.d where w is the number of positions reserved, and d is the number of digits appearing to the right of the decimal point.

Numbers printed using an E-mask have the general form:

s0.dddddddEsee

where: the first "s" denotes the sign of the number; the second "s" denotes the sign of the exponent; and each "d" represents a digit in the number. The number of digits appearing between the decimal point and the "E" is determined by the value of "d" in the mask Ew.d. The following examples illustrate the effect of an E-mask.

Value of Number	E-mask	Symbols Stored In The Print Positions
i) 123.45	E12.5	b0.12345Eb03
ii) 123.45	E15.7	bb0.1234500Eb03
iii) 123.45	E13.7	0.1234500Eb03
iv) 123.45	E12.7	************
v) -123.45	E14.5	bb-0.12345Eb03
vi) -123.45	E13.7	*************
vii) 0.0	E10.3	b0.000Eb00
viii) 9876.543	E12.4	bb0.9877Eb04
ix) -.00067890	E10.2	b-0.68E-03

These examples illustrate the following points regarding the use of E-masks.

i) The sign of the number and the exponent are not printed unless these values are negative.

ii) If more positions are reserved than are required to display the number, the print positions not used for a negative sign (if the number is negative), the leading zero, the decimal point, the digits in the number, the E, the sign of the exponent, the value of the exponent, are unchanged when the number is stored in the reserved positions. The number is stored in the rightmost positions reserved by the mask.

iii) If fewer positions are reserved than are necessary to display the value, asterisks are stored in the positions reserved by the mask. Note that there are seven positions of overhead if a number is negative and six positions of overhead if the number is positive or zero. This means that the value of w in the mask Ew.d must be at least seven larger than d when printing negative values, and at least six larger than d when printing positive values. The overhead positions are for the sign of the number, the leading zero and decimal point, and the four positions required by the exponent.

iv) If significant digits are dropped because of the value of d in the mask, the number is rounded to d digits. Rounding in the sixth decimal place or in fact, the digit appearing in the seventh decimal place may be inaccurate because the internal representation of REAL values does not use the decimal number system.

The program sequence below shows that E-masks and F-masks are positioned in precisely the same way as I-masks.

```
C EXAMPLE 6.4 POSITIONING REAL MASKS
      A=-.0064
      B=5.273E2
      C=-0.
      PRINT 50,A,B,C
   50 FORMAT('0',T13,F8.4,2X,F7.1,T2,E11.3)
```

Result:

```
          one       ten       twenty
           ↓         ↓          ↓
print     ⌠ 0         1          2
positions ⌡ 12345678901234567890123456789

          0bb0.000Eb00bb-.0064bbbb527.3
          ‿‿‿ ‿‿‿‿‿‿‿ ‿‿‿‿‿‿‿ ‿‿ ‿‿‿‿‿
          '0'  E11.3    F8.4   2X   F7.1
               (C)      (A)         (B)
```

When the print list contains a mixture of INTEGER and REAL items, the FORMAT statement must contain a set of I-masks and E or F masks so that INTEGER items are used with I-masks and REAL items are used with either an E or F mask. For example, without knowing any other details of the FORMAT statement, we can state with certainty that an error occurs when the following pair of statements is executed.

```
      PRINT 75,-(17/3+4),SIN(X),3.6E2,1
   75 FORMAT(...I12,...E16.3,...F7.2,...F8.4,...)
```

The reason that the message "FORMAT CODE AND DATA TYPE DO NOT MATCH" will be printed is that the fourth item in the output list is INTEGER valued and the fourth mask in the FORMAT statement is an F-mask which can only be used with REAL values.

*6.10 The General Mask - The G-Mask

A G-mask can be used in place of any mask. Because of this, it can sometimes make the writing of FORMAT statements easy for a beginning programmer. Its general form is "Gw.d" where "w" denotes the number of print positions to be reserved and "d" denotes (for REAL values) the number of significant digits to be printed.

When used with INTEGER values, the mask "Gw.d" is equivalent to the mask "Iw". The symbols ".d" can be omitted.

151

When used with REAL values, the mask "Gw.d" is equivalent to either

      Ew.d   or   F(w-4).d , 4X

Which one of the above is used depends on the value being printed. If an output value X, say, is in the range defined by $.1 \le X < 10**d$, then the F-form is used. If it is outside this range, the E-form is used. The following examples illustrate this distinction.

Value To Be Printed	G-Mask	Symbols In The Mask Positions	Equivalent Code(s)
12345	G5	12345	I5
12345	G5.3	12345	I5
.01	G9.2	b0.10E-01	E9.2
.1	G9.2	b0.10bbbb	F5.2,4X
99.	G9.2	99.00bbbb	F5.2,4X
100.	G9.2	b0.10Eb03	E9.2

If the magnitude of REAL values which are printed with G-masks are not known at the time the program is written, it is wise to make "w" at least seven larger than "d" so that sufficient positions are available should the E-form be used.

*6.11 Mask Modification - The P-Code

A P-code can be used to change the appearance of REAL values printed using an E-mask and to change the value of REAL values printed using an F-mask. In either case the P-code has the form "sP" where "s" is called the scale factor.

Use With E-Masks

When used with an E-mask, the P-code controls the position of the first significant digit relative to the decimal point. For example, a value of .2345E+03 can be displayed as 23.45E+01 by putting the code "2P" in front of the mask E9.2. In general, the format code "sPEw.d" causes: "w" print positions to be reserved for displaying a value; "s" digits to be printed to the left of the decimal point; "d" digits to be printed to the right of the decimal point. The value of "s" can be positive, negative or zero. Other examples are shown in the following table.

Value Of Number	Mask	Symbols In Reserved Positions
7.123	E12.4	bb0.7123Eb01
7.123	0PE12.4	bb0.7123Eb01
7.123	2PE12.4	b71.2300E-01
7.123	-3PE12.4	bb0.0007Eb04

These examples illustrate the following points.

   i) A scale factor of zero is ignored.

   ii) The "d" in the code "sPEw.d" determines the number of digits appearing to the right of the decimal point and not the number of significant digits printed.

   iii) If "s" is positive, the decimal point appears s positions to the right relative to the output produced with no scale factor. The exponent value is modified to reflect the change.

   iv) When "s" is negative, s zeros are placed ahead of the the first significant digit and the exponent value is adjusted to reflect the change.

Use With F-Masks

When a scale factor of "sP" is placed in front of an F-mask, the value of the number is multiplied by 10**s before the number is printed according to the F-mask. Some examples follow.

Value Of Number	Mask	Symbols In Reserved Positions
123.	0PF8.1	bbb123.0
123.	2PF8.1	b12300.0
123.	-2PF8.1	bbbbb1.2

Why would one want to change the value of a REAL number before printing it? The reason is primarily to obtain increased accuracy when working with fractional values. Recall that many fractional values are stored as good approximations to the actual value. The following two sequences show how P-codes can be used to improve accuracy. Each sequence finds the sum of five values of one-fifth.

```
X=.2                        X=2.
Z=X+X+X+X+X                 Z=X+X+X+X+X
PRINT 8,Z                   PRINT 8,Z
8 FORMAT(E15.7)            8 FORMAT(-1PF4.1)
```

Result: the symbols printed   Result: bl.0 is printed
are bb0.9999999E 00

In the left hand sequence, X has a value of .2. The tiny
error associated with the internal representation of this
value when compounded five times in an addition operation
results in a value very close to 1 but not exactly 1. In
the right hand sequence however, X is given an integer
value. And, since integer values are stored accurately, the
value of Z is ten. Then when the scale factor of -1 is
applied when printing the value of Z, the result is the
correct value of one. If writing programs in which extreme
accuracy is important, it may be necessary to convert
fractional values to integer values. Then, at output time,
division by an appropriate power of ten can be performed
using P-codes.

There are three additional points concerning the use of
P-codes. First, a P-code appears in front of any repetition
factor which might be used with a mask. For example, to
modify the four masks defined by "4E15.3" using a scale
factor of three, the code should be written as "3P4E15.3".
Second, any scale factor present in a a FORMAT statement
applies to all masks which follow it unless subsequently
modified by another P-code. This may mean a zero scale
factor may be required to erase the effect of an earlier P-
code. For example, the two FORMAT statements below <u>are</u>
equivalent.

FORMAT(-1PE16.5, F7.2)

FORMAT(-1PE16.5, -1PF7.2)

Third, if a P-code is used as a scale factor for a G-mask
(G-masks are discussed in the previous section.) the effect
of the P-code depends on whether or not the G-mask takes on
the E-form or the F-form (assuming REAL output items). This
means that you should be extremely careful when using scale
factors with G-masks because, depending on the value of the
output item, the scale factor may only cause a change in
appearance or it may cause a change in value.

6.12 <u>Literals</u>.

A literal is a string of symbols. Literals are used to
explain the output, print report headings or as we have
already seen, define the VCC. Examples of literals are:
'1','DAILY REPORT', 'X=', etc.. A literal then, is simply a
string of characters enclosed by a pair of single quotes.

154

The number of print positions occupied by a literal is simply the number of symbols between the quotes. Literals can be included in FORMAT statements and are positioned in the same way that masks are positioned. Thus a T-code can be used to specify the print position to be occupied by the first symbol in the literal. A literal can also be positioned implicitly in which case the first position reserved for the literal is the one immediately following the last position reserved by the preceding element in the the FORMAT statement. The effect of executing the statements:

```
      Y=-2.6573
      PRINT 1,Y
    1 FORMAT('1','THE VALUE OF Y=',F8.4)
```

is to print the line

    THE VALUE OF Y= -2.6573

at the top of the page. Since no T-code precedes the literal "THE VALUE OF Y=", its symbols will occupy positions 2 thru 16 of the print line. This FORMAT statement contains two literals. The VCC can be the first symbol in a longer literal. For example, the two literals in the foregoing example could have been combined in the following equivalent way.

    1 FORMAT('1THE VALUE OF Y=',F8.4)

What is the effect of the following pair of statements?

```
      PRINT 2
    2 FORMAT('0PROGRAMMING IS DIFFICULT',T17,'EASY')
```

The symbols printed are,

        PROGRAMMING IS EASYICULT

Since the FORMAT statement is processed left to right, the sequence "T17,'EASY'" causes print positions 17-20 to contain the symbols "EASY". Since the positions 17 thru 25 previously contained the word DIFFICULT, only the first four letters of DIFFICULT are affected by the symbols in the literal 'EASY'. This explains the output produced.

One further point. Suppose you would like to print the word "IT'S". If it is necessary to have a quote as one of the symbols in the literal, then two consecutive quotes must be used. The literal "IT'S" for example is defined as 'IT''S' but still would occupy four print positions which would contain the symbols IT'S. Similarly, a literal containing six consecutive apostrophes (''''''), defines a literal consisting of the symbols ''.

*H-type Literals

An H-code is an alternate means of defining a literal. Its general form is "nHsss...s" where each "s" denotes a symbol and "n" is the number of symbols in the literal. Examples of H-type literals are "7HTUESDAY", "1H*", and "10HTIME TABLE". H-type literals are positioned in precisely the same way as quote-type literals. For example, the statements below are equivalent.

```
FORMAT('0',T20,'ONE',T10,'TWO')

FORMAT(1H0,T20,3HONE,T10,3HTWO)
```

Most programmers prefer using quote-type literals to H-type literals. The reason is simply that the number of symbols in an H-type literal must be counted if an H-type literal is used. Some Fortran compliers do not permit quote-type literals and therefore H-type literals must be used.

6.13 The Slash "/" Code -- A Second Type Of Vertical Control

As has been described previously, the symbol stored in the first print position controls the vertical spacing of printed output. A second method of causing the paper to move forward one or more lines is to use a slash code in the FORMAT statement. When the "/" symbol is encountered in a FORMAT statement, three things happen.

i) A line is printed made up of the symbols stored in the print positions by the action of the format elements processed before the slash was encountered.

ii) All print positions are set to blanks.

iii) The format codes following the slash are processed as if they were the first codes in another FORMAT statement.

Note that the slash symbol itself is not stored in any print position. It merely triggers the printing of a line which displays the current contents of the print positions.

The following pair of examples illustrates the effect of the slash code.

```
Example (i)    JKL=4000
               YY=-2.34E-06
               PRINT 8,JKL,YY
             8 FORMAT('1JKL=',I5,/,' YY=',E10.3)
```

Result: Two lines are printed at the top of a page and appear as:

```
          JKL= 4000
          YY= -0.234E-07
```

In this example, note that the VCC for the second line printed is hidden in the literal ' YY='. This blank which begins the literal causes the line to appear on the line immediately following the first line printed.

```
Example (ii)    JKL=4000
                YY=-2.34E-06
                PRINT 2,JKL/1000,YY*10.E+4
              2 FORMAT(///,' JKL/1000=',I3//,'0YY*10000=',
                *F9.5,//)
```

When executed, the output consists of:

```
a blank line    (due to first slash)
a blank line    (due to second slash)
a blank line    (due to third slash)
JKL/1000=  4    (due to slash following the mask I3)
a blank line    (due to second slash after the mask I3)
a blank line    (due to VCC of 0 in the literal '0YY...'
YY*10000=  -0.02340 (due to first slash after F9.5)
a blank line    (due to second slash after F9.5)
a blank line    (due to  reaching the end of format codes)
```

This second example illustrates the following points.

    i) It is not necessary to use commas to separate slash codes from each other or from other elements in the FORMAT statement. eg: "I3//'0YY*10000='".

    ii) Frequently when using slashes, the list of format elements is lengthy and it is necessary to use a continuation card to continue the set of format elements. Recall that this is done by punching a non-zero, non-blank character in column six of the continuation card and viewing columns 7 thru 72 of this card as being appended to the right of column 72 of the previous card.

    iii) Regardless of whether or not there are slash codes in the FORMAT statement, a line is printed when the right bracket at the end of the FORMAT statement is encountered.

Although a slash code can be used to produce blank lines, its actual function is to cause a line to be printed before the end of the FORMAT statement is reached.

6.14 Two Short Cuts.

(a) Repetition Factors.

If there are five INTEGER elements in an output list and each is to be displayed using a mask I8, the five masks can either be written as "I8,I8,I8,I8,I8" or more conveniently as "5I8". In other words, a positive INTEGER constant put in front of any mask has the effect of repeating the mask the number of times defined by the constant. The FORMAT statement below contains five masks.

FORMAT('0',2F5.1,2X,3I6)

It is equivalent to the statement,

FORMAT('0',F5.1,F5.1,2X,I6,I6,I6) .

Repetition factors must be positive INTEGER constants. Examples of invalid repetition factors are NI17 and 3.F12.1.

(b) Groups and Group Counts.

If you wish to repeat a set of format codes instead of just a single mask, it is simply a matter of enclosing the group of codes to be repeated within brackets and putting a group count in front of the left bracket. For example, the two FORMAT statements below are equivalent.

FORMAT('0',2(I3,1X,E17.5))
FORMAT('0',I3,1X,E17.5,I3,1X,E17.5)

In the first FORMAT statement, the number 2 is a group count which causes the group (I3,1X,E17.5) to be repeated twice. If a group count is omitted, it is assumed to be 1.

It is permissible to have groups within a group but one cannot have a group within a group within a group. That is, groups can only be nested to a depth of two. A FORMAT statement containing nested groups is:

FORMAT('1',2(2X,3(I3,F7.2),I5))

In this FORMAT statement, there are 14 masks. The order in which they appear is: I3,F7.2, I3,F7.2, I3,F7.2, I5, I3,F7.2, I3,F7.2 I3,F7.2,I5. Sometimes when using groups, one forgets how many print positions are being "chewed up" by the format codes. For example, the FORMAT statement above reserves a total of 75 print positions. Suppose the mask I3 had been changed to I15. In this case, the set of format elements would span 147 print positions. Since there are only 133 available, an error would result and the job would be terminated.

Are the following statements equivalent?

        i)   FORMAT(2I5)
       ii)   FORMAT((2I5))
      iii)   FORMAT(2(I5))

The answer is "That depends.". Technically, the "2" in (i)
and (ii) is a repetition factor whereas in (iii), it is a
group count. Furthermore, (ii) contains a group and (i) does
not. If the PRINT or WRITE statement which used one of these
FORMAT statements contained either one or two elements in
its output list, they would all produce the same result. If
not, the output produced by (iii) would be different. The
reasons for this difference are explained in the next
section.

Exercise 6.3

1. Fill in the third column of the table below indicating
   the symbols stored in the positions reserved by the mask.

Item In Output List	Mask	Symbols In Mask Positions
a) -12345	I7	
b) -12345	I5	
c) 12345.	F8.2	
d) -123.45	F7.1	
e) .00024E-02	F9.4	
f) -.00025	E10.2	
g) 2.0006	E12.5	
h) 10.E5	F8.0	
i) 10.E-10	F9.7	
j) 2.64	I4	
k) 3	F4.0	

2. For each of the following, state the positions reserved
   by each mask and/or literal in the FORMAT statement.

   a) FORMAT('0',T5,I8,T2,I3)
   b) FORMAT(F12.7,3X,T20,F8.0,T17,'X=')
   c) FORMAT('1X(I)= '/E20.6,F17.4)
   d) FORMAT(T5,I8,2X,E15.6,T1,'12345')

3. Consider the FORMAT statement:

   FORMAT('0',2(3I2,3X),3F6.2,3(2X,F8.0))

   With respect to this statement,

   a) How many groups are there?
   b) How many masks are there?
   c) What is the 5th mask?
   d) What positions are reserved by the first F8.0 mask?

e) Which mask reserves positions 13 and 14?
f) What positions are reserved by the third F6.2 mask?
g) If the fifth item in the output list was REAL, would an error occur?
h) If the eighth item in the output list had a value of 12345.67, what symbols would be printed in the pprint positions reserved by its mask?

4. Predict the output of the following PRINT statements. Check your predictions using the computer.

a)
```
              X=+49.
              I=-25
              PRINT 3,X**(1./2.),I
            3 FORMAT('1',F3.0,T1,I4)
```

b)
```
              PRINT 1,2.,3.,4,5,6,7.,8.,9,10,11
            1 FORMAT('1',2(3X,2F4.1,I4,2I5))
```

6.15 Two Unanswered Questions.

In all the examples of formatted output appearing previously, the number of masks in the FORMAT statement has been the same as the number of items in the output list. It is only natural to ask:

> i) What happens if there are fewer items in the output list than there are masks in the FORMAT statement?

> ii) What happens if there are more items in the output list than there are masks in the FORMAT statement?

Question 1. (Fewer items than masks)

The set of format elements is processed left to right. When a mask is detected, the next item in the output list is picked up and put in the print positions reserved by the mask. This means that if there is a surplus of masks in a FORMAT statement, sooner or later a mask will be found for which there is no element in the output list. When this happens, the first excess mask and all format codes which follow it are ignored and the line is printed using the symbols stored in the print positions up to that point. One example should suffice. When the statements:

```
              X=2.34
              Y=5.
              PRINT 999,X
            999 FORMAT('1 X=',F5.2,/,'   Y=',F5.2)
```

are executed, the symbols:

```
X= 2.34
Y=
```

appear on two lines at the top of the next page. Note that the slash and the second literal are processed since they precede the first unnecessary mask. Had there been other format elements after the second F5.2 mask, they would have been ignored.

Question 2. (More items than masks)

When there are more items in the output list than there are masks in the FORMAT statement, the answer to the question "What happens?" is "That depends.". It depends on whether or not there is a group in the FORMAT statement. However, regardless of whether or not there are groups, we can state with certainty that more than one line will be printed. The reason for this fact is that each time the end of the FORMAT statement is reached, a line is printed which displays the contents of the print positions. Furthermore, a mask must be found for each item in the output list. Thus the lack of sufficient masks can be viewed as a third method of vertical control. Let's look at a simple example.

```
        PRINT 10,1,2,3
    10 FORMAT(' ',I3)
```

When executed, three lines will be printed. Clearly the first element in the output list will be used with the mask I3. Then the end of the FORMAT statement is encounted and so a line is printed with a 1 appearing in print position four. Then all print positions are set to blanks. However, there are two more elements in the output list. In order to find a mask for the second element in the output list, the FORMAT statement is recycled beginning from the left bracket which defines the set of format codes. This means that the value 2 is stored in print position four. Again we reach the end of the FORMAT statement and so a second line in printed with the value 2 appearing directly below the value 1. Since a mask has not yet been found for the third item in the output list, this recycling process is repeated and the value 3 is printed below the value 2.

The rule illustrated by this example is:

"Provided there are no groups in the FORMAT statement, a line is printed each time the end of the FORMAT statement is reached. The set of format codes are repeated over and over again until a mask has been found for each item in the output list."

Naturally, during this recycling process, an I-mask must be the first one encountered for each INTEGER item, and an

161

E-mask or F-mask must be the first one encountered for each REAL item.

When there are one or more groups present in the FORMAT statement, the only difference is that the groups determine the part of the FORMAT statement which is recycled. Consider the following example.

```
        PRINT 777,1,2,3
777 FORMAT(' ',(I3))
```

The only difference between this example and the previous one is that the FORMAT statement now contains the group "(I3)" with an assumed group count of 1. When the PRINT statement is executed, the output appears as:

print ⎰
positions ⎱ 1234567

```
bbb1
bb2
bb3
```

This result is obtained in the following way. The VCC for the first line is a blank and the item 1 is therefore stored in position four using the mask I3. A line is printed because the end of the FORMAT statement has been reached. The mask for the second item is found by recycling to the group count of the group appearing in the FORMAT statement. Since, in this example, the group count is one by default, the value 2 is stored using the mask I3 which spans the first three print positions. The VCC for this second line then, is the symbol in the first position reserved by the mask I3. Again the end of the FORMAT statement is reached causing a line to be printed and the 2 appears in position three. This process is repeated in order to find a mask for the third item and so the 3 appears underneath the 2.

If it was desired to have the three values appear underneath each other, then either the group could be left out as was done previously, or the FORMAT statement below could have been used.

```
FORMAT(' ',(T2,I3))
```

If there is more than one group in a FORMAT statement, the format elements which are recycled may be stated as:

"Beginning with the group count of the group whose rightmost bracket is nearest the end of the FORMAT statement".

The arrows in the following three cases indicate the point at which the set of format elements are recycled.

162

```
FORMAT (...3 (...)...)
        ↑_____

FORMAT (...2 (...)...5 (...)...)
                    ↑_____

FORMAT (... (...)...4 (...3 (...)...)...)
                    ↑_____
```

One further example is:

```
            X1=19.7
            X2=179.3
            X3=-6.
            X4=8.2E-1
            PRINT 666,1,X1,2,X2,3,X3,4,X4
        666 FORMAT('1',2(' X',I1,'=',F7.2,2X))
```

The output produced appears as:

```
print      ⌠ 0         1         2
positions  ⌡ 123456789012345678901 2345

           1bX1=bb19.70bbbX2=b179.30
           bX3=bb-6.00bbbX4=bbb.82
```

In this example there are eight items in the output list and four masks in the FORMAT statement, all of which are part of the group. When the format codes are recycled beginning with the group count the VCC for the second line is obtained from the first character of the literal ' X'. This is the reason the symbols on the second line are shifted one position to the left.

Exercise 6.4

1. How many lines of output are produced in each of the following if the PRINT statement is PRINT 1,100,200,300 ?

a)   1 FORMAT(' ',I4)
b)   1 FORMAT(3I5)
c)   1 FORMAT(' ',2I5)
d)   1 FORMAT(' ',2(3X,I4))

2. Predict the output of each of the following. Check your predictions by using the computer.

a)   PRINT 70, -(3.**4),-2**5,0.
       70 FORMAT('1THREE**4=',E11.2,T21,I4)

b)   PRINT 80
       80 FORMAT(' ',6('OVER AND OVER '))

163

c)   PRINT 90,11,2
     90 FORMAT(I2)

d)   PRINT 100,3.5,4.5
    100 FORMAT(' ',T10,'ITEM1=',F4.1,T2,'ITEM2=')

e)   PRINT 110,123,123,123
    110 FORMAT(' ',3X,2('123',I3))

3. With respect to the FORMAT statement,

FORMAT(' LINE',5I1,3(1X,2I3,2X,3I2))

a) How many masks are there? (Don't forget repetition
   factors and group counts.)
b) How many positions are reserved by the X-codes?
c) If the output list contains 16 INTEGER items, how many
   times is the word "LINE" printed?
d) If the output list contains the values 0,1,2,...,98,99,
   then,
        i) How many lines are printed?
       ii) What values are printed on the 2nd line, the
           6th line, the last line?
      iii) In what print positions do the values 2, 16,
           48 and 99 appear?
       iv) On how many lines does print position 11
           contain a blank?

6.16 A Word About Commas.

In each of the example FORMAT statements, commas have
been used to separate adjacent format elements. This
practice is recommended since it improves the readability of
the FORMAT statement. Commas can be omitted if their
omission would not cause any ambiguity. The pair of FORMAT
statements below are equivalent.

FORMAT(T5,'LITERAL',2I1,T15,'END')
FORMAT(T5'LITERAL'2I1T15'END')

If a sequence such as "T11,I11,1X" appears in a FORMAT
statement, both commas are necessary since their omission
would permit the codes to be interpreted as "T1,1I1,11X" for
example. As a general rule, it is a good idea to use commas
to separate format codes.

6.17 Format-Free Output.

When a programmer chooses to use one of the two
statements available for producing format-free output of
printed values, he is primarily interested in seeing the
results of computations performed in the program and is not
particularly concerned with the precise positioning of

values on the page. The two forms of the format-free output statement are:

PRINT,output list

WRITE(6,*) output list

The "6" in the WRITE statement is the device number usually associated with the high speed printer. It may be different which means you would change it to its appropriate value. The device number can also be assigned to an INTEGER variable and the variable name used in place of the "6" in the WRITE statement. The reasons for using the WRITE instead of the PRINT are similar to those suggested in the case of formatted output.

When an unformatted output statement is used,

    i) A mask of I12 is used for each INTEGER item in the output list.

    ii) A mask of E16.7 is used for each REAL item in the output list.

This means the outputs produced by the following are identical.

    i)   PRINT,1234567,.1234567

    ii)   WRITE(6,*) 1234567,.1234567

    iv)   PRINT 99,1234567,.1234567
        99 FORMAT(I12,E16.7)

    iv)   WRITE(6,99) 1234567,.1234567
        99 FORMAT(I12,E16.7)

One further point. When using format-free output, if the total number of print positions reserved by the default masks I12 and E16.7 exceeds the number of available print positions, then extra lines are printed using the same technique until all output items have been printed.

6.18 Summary

1. When printing items which are stored in the computer memory, the following three questions must be answered.

    i) Where (on what device) are the items to be printed?

    ii) What values or symbols are to be displayed?

    iii) How are the values to appear on the output device?

165

In WATFIV, the programmer answers the "What" question by defining an output list of items to be displayed. He answers the "Where" question by either using the word PRINT or by using the WRITE statement with a pointer to the high speed printer. If the appearance of items on the page is controlled by the programmer, the output is formatted. If WATFIV looks after the placement of the items, the output is unformatted, or format-free.

2. Formatted Output.

With formatted output, the appearance of the printed output is controlled by a set of codes which are included in a FORMAT statement. The FORMAT statement is linked to the PRINT or WRITE statement by its statement number.

The position along the print line at which an item is printed depends on the positions spanned by the mask associated with the output item. Masks are matched one for one, beginning from the left, with items in the output list. An I-mask must be used for each INTEGER item and an E-mask or F-mask must be used for each REAL item. Masks may be positioned either explicitly or implicitly.

There are three techniques for controlling the line on which an item is printed. These are:

    i) By the vertical control character stored in print
       position one.

    ii) By the use of one or more slash codes.

    iii) By having fewer masks in the FORMAT statement than
         there are items in the output list.

Literals can be included in the FORMAT statement and they are positioned in the same way as masks.

The format codes discussed in this chapter are:

    Iw - the mask for INTEGER items

    Fw.d - a mask for REAL items

    Ew.d - a mask for REAL items

    Tp - a code to explicitly position an item

    nX - a code to skip over print positions

    / - a code to cause a line to be printed

    ' ' - used to define literals

r - used to repeat a mask r times

g - used to repeat a set of codes g times

g(...) - used to repeat a group of format elements

In the above, the lower case letters must be positive INTEGER constants.

3. After any line is printed, blanks are stored in all print positions.

Programming Problems

6.1   Punch ten data cards, each containing a different person's height H (in inches) and weight W (in pounds). Write a program which reads the cards one at a time and prints a table of the form shown below.

HEIGHT	WEIGHT	CHARACTERISTIC
XXX	XXX	XXXXXX
XXX	XXX	XXXXXX
etc.	etc.	etc.

Use a mask of I3 to print the height and weight. For the characteristic print: "SKINNY" if $W < 3.8H - 118$; "FAT" if $W > 4.2H - 132$; "NORMAL" otherwise. Note that three different FORMAT statements, each containing a different literal, will be required.

6.2   Add to the program for the previous question calculations to determine the average height and average weight of the ten people. In addition, print a count of the number of skinny, fat and normal people. Print the three additional items of information as shown below.

```
AVERAGE HEIGHT IS XXX.X INCHES
AVERAGE WEIGHT IS XXX.X POUNDS
NUMBER OF SKINNY PEOPLE IS XX
NUMBER OF FAT PEOPLE IS XX
NUMBER OF NORMAL PEOPLE IS XX
```

6.3   Two ladders of lengths twenty feet and thirty feet respectively are positioned across a laneway between two buildings as shown in the following diagram. They cross at a point eight feet above the ground. How wide is the laneway?

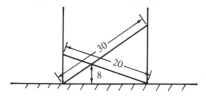

167

Print your answer as "THE LANE IS XX.XXX FEET WIDE". Obtain your answer by starting with two estimates -- one high say 21, and one low, say 3. Use the average of the high and low estimates as a better estimate. Calculate where the ladders would cross if the lane had a width equal to the new estimate. Based on this result, use the new estimate to replace either the previous high estimate or the previous low estimate. Repeat the procedure. Continue repetitions until the difference in two successive estimates is less than .001. Can you find an equation which, when solved, would give the exact value of the width? (This is not an easy equation to find.)

6.4   Check balancing. A deck of cards contains a deposit-withdrawal code in column one and a dollar amount of the form XXX.XX in columns three thru eight. A "1" in column one indicates a deposit and a "2" indicates a withdrawal. The dollar amount indicates the size of the deposit or withdrawal. Write a program which reads an unknown number of cards and for each prints either

$XXX.XX DEPOSIT, BALANCE IS NOW $XXXX.XX
or
$XXX.XX WITHDRAWAL, BALANCE IS NOW $XXX.XX

Assume the starting balance is zero. If the attempted withdrawal is larger than the balance, print the line "WITHDRAWAL OF $XXX.XX WOULD EXCEDE BALANCE, NOT PROCESSED".

6.5   The product of $(x-a)(x-b)(x-c)(x-d)$ is a fourth degree polynomial of the form $px^4+qx^3+rx^2+sx+t$. Write a program which reads values of "a", "b", "c", and "d" and calculates the values of p, q, r, s, t. Print a line of the following form.

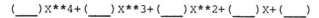

where the dashes represent the values calculated.

6.6   Read an unknown number of data cards each of which contains two INTEGER values. Each of the values is either a 1, a 2, or a 3. Count the total number of ones, twos and threes and print a line of the form "MORE 2'S THAN 1'S OR 3'S" based on the counts obtained. Use only one FORMAT statement in your program.

CHAPTER 7   SETS OF VARIABLES

Questions Answered In This Chapter.

    1. Why are some seemingly easy problems awkward to
       program using our present knowledge?

    2. How can we define and use sets of variables which
       will make the programming of these problems easy?

    3. What is compile time initialization?

7.1 It Looks Easy But ...

    Suppose we are to write a program to solve the following
simple problem.

        1. Read a value of N. (assume N is 5 or less)
        2. Read N more values.
        3. Print the N values read during step 2 in the
           reverse order to which they were read. Print
           only one value per line.

    Before looking at the program below, spend a couple of
minutes trying to set up a program which will solve the
problem.

    One method which could be used to solve the problem is
the following.

```
C EXAMPLE 7.1 PRINT N VALUES IN REVERSE ORDER
C ASSUME N IS 5 OR LESS
        READ,N
        IF(N.GE.1) READ,X1
        IF(N.GE.2) READ,X2
        IF(N.GE.3) READ,X3
        IF(N.GE.4) READ,X4
        IF(N.GE.5) READ,X5
        IF(N.GE.5) PRINT,X5
        IF(N.GE.4) PRINT,X4
        IF(N.GE.3) PRINT,X3
        IF(N.GE.2) PRINT,X2
        IF(N.GE.1) PRINT,X1
        STOP
        END
```

There are three important observations we should make.

i) Since the values must be printed in reverse order, we must read all N values before any lines can be printed.

ii) Since there may be as many as five values to be read, there must be five variables in the program to store the five possible values. Furthermore, a separate READ statement containing a single variable in the input list must be used to assign values to the variables since it is not known at the time the program is written how many variables are to be assigned a value.

iii) If the value of N was permitted to be very large, the program would be ridiculously long since we cannot use a looping technique. In order to use a looping technique, we would have to be able to change the name of the variable in the READ statement.

To summarize, the awkwardness arises from the facts that we don't know how many values are to be read until the program is executed and we have no way of changing the name of a variable in a WATFIV statement and thus cannot use a looping technique.

What we would like to do would be to set up a program of the following type. The program contains several errors but we are simply trying to develop the idea.

```
        READ,N
        DO 49 i=1,N
    49  READ, Xi
        DO 17 i=N,1,-1
    17  PRINT,Xi
        STOP
```

Observe that the name of the variable in the READ list and PRINT list is dynamic. The variable name changes as the value of i changes. In all programs thus far, the name of any variable appearing in a WATFIV statement has been fixed. The primary purpose of this chapter is to describe how we can change the name of a variable which is used in a statement.

In WATFIV, the REAL and INTEGER statements are used to specify the type of value to be taken on by a variable. In particular, they have been used to override the first letter rule. The REAL and INTEGER statements can also be used to define sets of variables. For example, a set of variables could be defined for use in the foregoing problem using the statement:

REAL X(5)

This declaration statement:

    i) Defines a set of variables called X. There are five elements in the set.

    ii) The names of the variables in the set X are: $X(1)$, $X(2)$, $X(3)$, $X(4)$, and $X(5)$. Each of these five variables takes on REAL values.

The set X is called a one-dimensional array of variables. The variables $X(1),X(2),X(3),X(4)$, and $X(5)$ are called singly subscripted variables. For each of these variables, the number inside the brackets is called the subscript. Thus the subscript of the variable $X(3)$ is 3. The program below shows how we could use the set X to make the programming of our original problem much easier.

```
C EXAMPLE 7.2 USING SUBSCRIPTED VARIABLES
      REAL X(5)
      READ,N
      DO 49 I=1,N
   49 READ,X(I)
      DO 17 I=1,N
      J=N+1-I
   17 PRINT,X(J)
      STOP
      END
```

In this program, the statement "READ,X(I)" will be executed N times. Each time it is executed, the value of I changes and so the name of the variable in the input list, namely $X(I)$, changes. Similarly, the name of the variable in the output list of the PRINT statement changes as the value of J changes. The purpose of the statement "J=N+1-I" is simply to create a subscript value which will go from N down to 1 as I increases from 1 up to N. (Recall that the parameters of a DO statement must be positive.)

When using a REAL or INTEGER statement to define sets of variables, an INTEGER constant is put in brackets following the set name. The value of this constant defines the number of elements in the set. Both of the statements below violate the rule that the number of elements in a set must be defined by a positive INTEGER.

```
      INTEGER ABC(M)
      REAL S1923(6.0)
```

If it is not known at the time the program is written how many variables might be needed, the set should be defined to have the maximum number of variables that might possibly be required.

The statement

REAL LUCKY(20),JACK,BOOK(1000)

defines a total of 1021 REAL variables for use in a program. Twenty of these belong to the set LUCKY and their names are LUCKY(1),LUCKY(2),LUCKY(3),...,LUCKY(20). JACK is called a simple (or scalar or non-subscripted) REAL variable and is included in the declaration statement simply to override the first-letter rule. BOOK is the name of a set of 1000 REAL variables whose elements are BOOK(1), BOOK(2), BOOK(3), ... ,BOOK(1000).

Any valid WATFIV name can be used as a set name. For example, DADDY9, GOTO, J12345 are valid set names whereas OHNO+, 9POT, and ABCDEFG are invalid.

In this book, the words "set" and "array" are synonyms. Each refers to a collection of variables. Variables in the same set or array differ only by the value of their subscripts.

7.2 A Second Example Using Subscripted Variables.

One of the more famous sequences of numbers is called the Fibonacci sequence. The first few numbers in the sequence are 1,1,2,3,5,8,13,21,... . Each number in the sequence, except for the first two, is obtained by adding the previous two values. Suppose we wish to write a program to print the first twenty numbers in the sequence all on the same line. We will require 20 variables in the output list of the PRINT statement and if we wish to calculate the values of these twenty variables using a looping technique, we will need variable names which can be changed "on the go". A suitable program is shown below.

```
C EXAMPLE 7.3 FIBONACCI NUMBERS
      INTEGER F(20)
      F(1)=1
      F(2)=1
      DO 6 I=3,20
    6 F(I)=F(I-1)+F(I-2)
      PRINT 900,F
  900 FORMAT('1',20I6)
      STOP
      END
```

There are two new ideas in this program. The first is that the statement "PRINT 900,F" is used to print the values. The output list of this statement contains the name of a set of variables which is used to create an output list consisting of the variables in the set. Using a set name in an output list is a short form way of putting all the variables in the set in the output list. We should consider this output list as having twenty items. Secondly, the variables F(I-1) and F(I-2) are used in the statement which calculates the successive values in the sequence. This is perfectly permissible in WATFIV and in fact, any arithmetic expression can be used to specify a subscript value. With reference to the set F used in the program, it would be permissible to include variables such as the following in the program.

i) F(20-I**J/K)

ii) F(1.5)

iii) F(ABS(SIN(3.*ALOG(6.))-.0001))

iv) F(32*3)

v) F(-2)

vi) F(F(4))

vii) F(F(F(6)-2)-3))

Since the names of the variables in the set are F(1), F(2), F(3),...,F(20), each of the above must reduce to one of these variable names or an error will result since we would be attempting to reference a variable which was not an element of the set F. In each of the seven examples given, the subscript value is either a REAL or INTEGER expression.

In example (i), the expression "20-I**J/K" must have a value in the range 1 to 20. If not, an error would occur.

In example (ii), the subscript has the REAL value 1.5 . If a subscript is REAL valued, the fractional part of the REAL number is truncated and thus the variable F(1.5) is equivalent to the variable F(1).

In example (iii) we know the value of the SIN function will be between +1 and -1, and so the value of the subscript will be a fraction in the range 0 to something less than 1. When the fraction is truncated, the variable being named is F(0) and since this variable is not an element of the set F, an error will occur.

Examples (iv) and (v) also produce errors since the variables F(96) and F(-2) are not in the set F.

Example (vi) is interesting in that the subscript expression is the name of a variable in the same set. F(4) has the value of the fourth number in the sequence, namely 3. This means that F(F(4)) is the same as F(3) and hence the value of F(F(4)) is 2. Note that F(F(9)) would cause an error since F(9) has a value 21 and F(21) is not in the set.

173

Example (vii) is an extension of the idea presented in example (vi). Thus the evaluation of example (vii) proceeds as follows: F(F(F(6)-2)-3)=F(F(8-2)-3)= F(8-3)=F(5)=5.

7.3 Valid and Invalid Uses of Subscripted Variables.

Suppose you and I have calculated the values of the first twenty Fibonacci numbers independently of one another and have stored the results in the sets YOURF and MYF respectively. The sets have been defined by the statement:

INTEGER MYF(20),YOURF(20)

If we wanted to compare the two sets of results, we might write a statement such as:

IF (MYF.NE.YOURF) GO TO 999

Unfortunately, this type of statement is not permitted. All arithmetic expressions, logical expressions, and Assignment statements which reference values in a set must refer to a specific element of the set. This means that a statement such as "MYF=YOURF", or an expression such as "MYF-YOURF" is invalid. Thus in order to compare the two sets of values, we should set up a DO-loop such as the following.

```
        DO 3 I=1,20
        IF(MYF(I).NE.YOURF(I)) GO TO 999
      3 CONTINUE
```

Errors will result for each of the statements shown below because a subscripted variable is used.

    i)   GO TO(2,76,843,1),F(I)   - in Computed GO TOs

    ii) a) ASSIGN 6 TO F(I)   }- in ASSIGN statements and
        b) GO TO F(I),(4,8,6,23)   Assigned GO TOs

    iii) a) DO 10 JJ=F(I),100
         b) DO 10 JJ=1,F(I)   in any DO
         c) DO 10 JJ= 1,100,F(I)   statement
         d) DO 10 F(I)=1,10

Exercise 7.1

1. Consider the program below.

```
        REAL A(4)
        DO 8 I=1,4
        A(I)=FLOAT(I)*2.+3.
      8 PRINT,A(I)
        STOP
```

a) Is each variable in the set assigned a value? Why?

b) How many values printed are prime numbers?
c) Why doesn't an error message result since the values assigned to variables in the set A are outside the range one to four?

2. Consider the statements:

```
INTEGER BAC(5)
    DO 1 JKL=1,5
1 BAC(6-JKL) = JKL
```

a) What is the value assigned to BAC(4)?
b) What variable has the value 4?
c) What is the value of:
    i) BAC(2)*3/BAC(3)
    ii) MOD(BAC(4),3)+MOD(3,BAC(4))
   iii) BAC(4)**BAC(3)**BAC(4)
    iv) (BAC(3)-BAC(2).LT.BAC(1)/4)   (true or false?)
    v) BAC(BAC(BAC(BAC(1))))

3. What is the error in each of the following. Assume the sets A and HAPPY have been defined by:

```
INTEGER A(2)
REAL HAPPY(3)
```

a) A(2)=HAPPY(4)
b) X=HAPPY

c) I=3
    A(1)=I
    HAPPY(1)=IDIM(I,A(I))

d) J=IFIX(A(1))
e) A=AMOD(3.,2.5)

4. Define a set of INTEGER variables called SET. Write a DO statement and one other statement to assign the values below to successive elements of SET.

a)   2,5,8,11,14,17
b)   -5,-4,-3,-2,-1
c)   -5,-7,-9,-11,-13
d)   1,3,7,15,31,63
e)   1,0,1,0,1
f)   1,0,-1,1,0,-1

7.4 Input-Output of Subscripted Variables.

Input

Suppose an array X has been defined using the statement "REAL X(6)". Values are to be assigned to the six variables in the set X by reading the values from data cards. Four different ways of doing this are:

    i)   READ,X(1),X(2),X(3),X(4),X(5),X(6)

    ii)   READ,X

    iii)   DO 99 I=1,6
         99 READ,X(I)

    iv)   READ,(X(I),I=1,6)

In (i), the input list contains six elements. In (ii), only the set name appears following the comma. This is equivalent to defining an input list which contains all the variables in the set and hence is equivalent in every way to method (i). Thus in method (ii), there are really six elements in the input list and using the set name is just a short form way of creating the desired list.

In method (iii), the READ statement contains only one element and is executed six times.

Method (iv) is completely equivalent to methods (i) and (ii). The symbols "(X(I),I=1,6)" are called an _implied DO-loop_. The purpose of an implied DO is to create an input list of variables using a DO-loop. In this example, the implied DO defines a set of six variable names which are the elements X(I) as I goes from 1 to 6 in steps of 1. In other words, the input list defined by the implied DO is X(1), X(2), X(3), X(4), X(5), X(6). The rules for writing implied DO-loops are similar to those for the DO statement except that the word "DO" does not appear and the loop is defined by enclosing the information in brackets. Implied DOs are handy tools for creating input or output lists as later examples will show.

The general form of an implied DO-loop is

       (list, index = initial, test, increment)

The "list" contains one or more variables, expressions and/or array names. (Expressions such as "I+J" are not allowed if the implied DO-loop is an element of the input list of a READ statement.) The terms "index", "initial", "test" and "increment" serve the same purposes as when present in a DO statement. The list is repeated once for each value of the index specified by the parameters.

176

Are the four methods equivalent? The answer is a qualified "yes". Methods (i), (ii) and (iv) are definitely equivalent in that each of these uses only one READ statement and the input lists in each case are identical even though they are created in different ways. Method (iii) on the other hand, requires that the READ statement be executed six times, and therefore a minimum of six data cards will be read using method (iii). This means that if the data values were punched on separate cards, the four methods would be equivalent. If more than one value appeared on any card, method (iii) could not be used.

Output Of Subscripted Variables

Suppose a set of 400 INTEGER variables has been defined by the statement "INTEGER N(400)" and suppose that values have been assigned to each of the variables in the set. We are required to print the 400 values so that eight are printed on each line. The mask I10 is to be used for each value printed. Four methods of achieving this result are:

```
i)       PRINT 900, N
     900 FORMAT(' ',8I10)

ii)      PRINT 900,(N(J),J=1,400)
     900 FORMAT(' ',8I10)

iii)     DO 6 I=1,393,8
       6 PRINT 900,(N(I+J-1),J=1,8)
     900 FORMAT(' ',8I10)

iv)      DO 7 I=1,50
       7 PRINT 900,(N((I-1)*8+J),J=1,8)
     900 FORMAT(' ',8I10)
```

In example (i), the set name is used to create an output list of 400 items. The order of the elements in the set is of course $N(1),N(2),N(3),...,N(400)$. Since the FORMAT statement contains only eight masks: the values of $N(1)$ thru $N(8)$ will be printed on the first line. The FORMAT statement will be recycled and the next 8 values will appear on line 2. This process will be repeated until 50 lines have been printed.

In (ii), an implied DO-loop is used to create the same ouput list as in method (i). Method (ii) is therefore equivalent in every way to method (i).

In method (iii), the PRINT statement will be executed for values of I of $1,9,17,25,...,393$. The output list of the PRINT statement contains 8 variables created by the implied DO. When I is 1, the variables are $N(1),N(2),...,N(8)$. When I is 9, the variables are $I(9)$ thru $I(17)$, and so on until when I is 393, the output list is $I(393),I(394),...,I(400)$.

Thus the required fifty lines will be printed. In this example, the value of I specifies the value of the subscript of the first variable printed in each line.

In example (iv), the value of I is the line number. If we know the line number, we can determine the eight variables whose values are to be printed on that line. An implied DO is used to create a list of the eight variables which are to appear on line I. For example, when I is two, the eight variables in the list are N(9),N(10),...,N(16).

Suppose that we wanted to print the 400 values in the set N in four columns so that the values of N(1) thru N(100) appeared in column 1, those of N(101) thru N(200) in column 2, etc. That is, the values are to be positioned as shown below.

```
N(1)      N(101)    N(201)    N(301)
N(2)      N(102)    N(202)    N(302)
N(3)      N(103)    N(203)    N(303)
 .         .         .         .
 .         .         .         .
 .         .         .         .
N(100)    N(200)    N(300)    N(400)
```

Four different methods of achieving this result are:

```
  i)     DO 4 I=1,100
       4 PRINT 54,N(I),N(I+100),N(I+200),N(I+300)
      54 FORMAT(' ',4I8)

 ii)     DO 5 I=1,100
       5 PRINT 54,(N(I+J-100),J=100,400,100)
      54 FORMAT(' ',4I8)

iii)     PRINT 54,(N(I),N(I+100),N(I+200),N(I+300),
       * I=1,100)
      54 FORMAT(' ',4I8)

 iv)     PRINT 54,((N(I+J-100),J=100,400,100),I=1,100)
      54 FORMAT(' ',4I8)
```

In examples (i) and (ii), the PRINT statement is executed 100 times, once for each value of I. In both of these cases the ouput list contains four elements, the only difference being that an implied DO is used to create the output list in example (ii).

In examples (iii) and (iv), the output list contains 400 elements but of course only 100 lines will be printed since the FORMAT statement contains four masks. In example (iii), there are four items preceding the definition of the implied DO-loop. This means that the output list is created by

repeating this set of four variables, once for each value of
I. In other words, the first few variables in the output
list of example (iii) are: N(1),N(101),N(201),N(301),
N(2),N(102),N(202),N(302),... . Since four values are
printed on each line, the required output will be produced.

In example (iv), an inner implied DO is used to create
the same four variable names which appeared in the implied
DO of example (iii). This inner implied DO consisting of:

$$(N(I+J-100),J=100,400,100)$$

defines the variables N(I),N(I+100),N(I+200),N(I+300) and
this list is repeated for each value of I. Thus (iii) and
(iv) are equivalent. This fourth example shows that implied
DOs can be nested in the same way that ordinary DO-loops are
nested. In this example, the J-loop is the innermost and
therefore the value of J will range over its permitted set
of values before the value of I is changed.

A word of caution. The commas shown in these examples
of implied DO-loops are necessary and cannot be omitted.
Note that a comma must precede the index of each loop and
that if implied DOs are nested, a comma follows the right
bracket of each inner loop.

With respect to the foregoing example, how could you
cause the first printed line to appear at the top of a page
and the remaining 99 lines to be single spaced? To do this
using the technique of examples (i) and (ii) would require
two PRINT statements each using a different FORMAT
statement. The first would be used to print the first line
and the second would be used for the other 99 lines. Using
the method of example (iii) or (iv) however, the following
FORMAT statement could be used.

54 FORMAT('1',1(T1,4I8))

The reason why it works is the masks for elements printed on
the second and subsequent lines are positioned implicitly
beginning with the group count instead of the beginning of
the FORMAT statement. This example assumes of course, that
the values assigned to elements of the set require seven or
fewer print positions including a negative sign.

One could use an implied DO to print a line of 132 zeros
across the top of a page as follows:

    PRINT 21,(0,K=1,132)
 21 FORMAT('1',132I1)

What would be printed using the following pair of
statements?

```
      PRINT 571,((J-1,J=1,10),I=1,12)
  571 FORMAT('1',120I1)
```

The output list contains 120 INTEGER constants. They are generated by calculating values of J-1 as J goes from 1 to 10 for each value of I as I goes from 1 to 12. Thus the digits 0 thru 9 are repeated 12 times across the first line on a page.

Exercise 7.2

1. Suppose a set of 12 variables has been defined by:

```
      INTEGER S(12)
```

Suppose the first four data cards contain the symbols, beginning in column 1,

```
      -27bb30bbb4
      bb5b627bbb3
      b89bbb1b109
      b15637bb88b1
```

What values are assigned to variables in S using the following READ statements?

```
  a)          READ 6,S
            6 FORMAT(3I4)

  b)          DO 2 J=1,10,3
            2 READ 8,S(J),S(J+1),S(J+2)
            8 FORMAT(3I4)

  c)          DO 3 K=1,4
              L=(5-K)*3
            3 READ 5,S(L),S(L-1),S(L-2)
            5 FORMAT(I2,I5,I3)

  d)          READ 7,(S(M),S(M+1),M=1,11,2)
            7 FORMAT(2I2,1X,I2)

  e)          READ,S
```

2. Suppose the sets D and T are defined by:

```
      REAL D(16),T(16)
```

For each of the following, state the number and order of the variables appearing in the output list.

```
  a)    PRINT,T,D
  b)    PRINT,(T(I),D(I),I=1,16)
  c)    PRINT,(T(I-1),T(I),I=2,16,2)
  d)    PRINT,((D(I+J-1),J=1,4),I=1,13,4)
```

180

e)   PRINT,((T(I+J-1),J=1,13,4),I=1,4)

3. Consider the statements:

```
     INTEGER WEE(5)
     WEE(3)=1
     DO 7 N=1,2
     WEE(N+3)=3-N
   7 WEE(3-N)=3+N
```

a) What are the values assigned to the elements of WEE?

b) For each of the following, describe the output.

    i)   PRINT 1,WEE
         1 FORMAT(' ',I3)

   ii)   PRINT 2,(J,WEE(J),J=1,5)
         2 FORMAT(' WEE(',I1,')=',I2)

  iii)   PRINT 3,WEE(5)
           PRINT3,(WEE(6-K),K=2,5,1)
         3 FORMAT(' ',2(I3,2X,I2))

4.   Write a pair of statements to cause a line containing
100 symbols to be printed across the top of a page. The
required symbols are ten zeros followed by ten ones
followed by ten twos etc.. Use a pair of implied DOs to
create the output list. How could this be done without
using an implied DO? Why can't it be done using only
one implied DO?

7.5 Tables Of Variables

Frequently our understanding of a problem is made easier
if we picture a set of numbers as being stored in a table.
For example, suppose we made a door-to-door survey of six
houses on a street with the idea of finding for each house,
the number of pre-school children, public school children,
high school children, and adults. We might record the
results as shown below.

	PRE-SCHOOL	PUBLIC	HIGH SCHOOL	ADULTS
House 1	0	1	2	2
House 2	2	0	0	2
House 3	0	0	0	1
House 4	1	2	0	2
House 5	1	0	1	2
House 6	0	2	3	2

In this table of numbers there are six horizontal rows,
one for each house, and four vertical columns, one for each

type of information collected. A rectangular array of numbers such as this is often called a matrix. We can refer to any position in a matrix by specifying a row number and column number. For example, the number in position (5,2) of the table above refers to the number in row 5 and column 2, that is, the number of public school children in the fifth house. Similarly, the sum of the numbers in positions (2,1), (2,2), (2,3) and (2,4) represents the total of the numbers in row 2 of the table, that is, the total number of people in the second house. The sum of the numbers in positions (3,3), (4,3), (5,3) and (6,3) represents the total number of high school children in houses three thru six.

If we want to use the information in the table to answer questions such as: "Which houses have no pre-school children?"; "How many adults are there in the six houses?"; or, "Which house has the fewest children?", then we must be able to give a name to each of the 24 items of information in the table. In order to write programs to answer questions such as those above, a set of twenty-four variables must be defined. Furthermore, it would be very helpful if the name given to each of the variables referred to one of the positions in the table.

In WATFIV, an appropriate set of variables could be defined using the statement

INTEGER S(6,4)

This statement defines a set of 24 INTEGER variables. The names of these variables are:

```
S(1,1)  S(1,2)  S(1,3)  S(1,4)
S(2,1)  S(2,2)  S(2,3)  S(2,4)
S(3,1)  S(3,2)  S(3,3)  S(3,4)
S(4,1)  S(4,2)  S(4,3)  S(4,4)
S(5,1)  S(5,2)  S(5,3)  S(5,4)
S(6,1)  S(6,2)  S(6,3)  S(6,4)
```

The set S is called a two-dimensional array (or matrix or table) of variables. Any variable in the set S such as S(3,2) is called a doubly subscripted variable. When using doubly subscripted variables, the first subscript always refers to the row number and the second subscript always refers to the column number. The two subscripts are always separated by a comma.

The general structure of a table of values is shown in the following diagram.

182

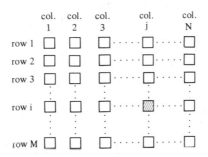

In the diagram above, the shaded box is the (i,j)th element of the table since it is in row i and column j.

The following program reads the twenty-four values to be assigned to the elements of S. Four numbers are punched on each of six cards. The four numbers correspond to the four items of information obtained about each house. The output of the program is the total number of public school children in the six houses.

```
C EXAMPLE 7.4 SURVEY ANALYSIS 1
      INTEGER S(6,4),PUBSUM
C READ IN THE 24 ITEMS OF DATA, ONE ROW AT A TIME
      DO 8 I=1,6
    8 READ,(S(I,J),J=1,4)
C FIND THE TOTAL NUMBER OF PUBLIC SCHOOL CHILDREN
      PUBSUM=0
      DO 11 I=1,6
   11 PUBSUM=PUBSUM+S(I,2)
      PRINT 80, PUBSUM
   80 FORMAT('0','TOTAL IN PUBLIC SCHOOL IS',I3)
      STOP
      END
```

In this program, the READ statement is executed once for each value of I as I goes from 1 to 6 in steps of 1. The implied DO in the READ statement is used to create an input list of the four variables S(I,1),S(I,2),S(I,3) and S(I,4). This means that the four values punched on the Ith data card are assigned to the variables in row I of the table.

The statement "PUBSUM=PUBSUM+S(I,2)" is executed once for each value of I in the range 1 thru 6. This means that the six values added to PUBSUM are those in column 2 of the matrix.

The same set of rules which apply to singly subscripted variables also apply to doubly subscripted variables.

The program below could be used to find out which house has the most people. To do this we must find the total number of people in each house. As each total is obtained, the total is compared to the highest total found previously. In this program the variable BIGHSE is used to identify the house with the most people.

```
C EXAMPLE 7.5 SURVEY ANALYSIS 2
      INTEGER S(6,4),HOUSE,BIGHSE
      READ,((S(I,J),J=1,4),I=1,6)
      MOST=0
      DO 12 HOUSE=1,6
C FIND THE NUMBER OF PEOPLE IN HOUSE
      NPEEPL =0
      DO 4 J=1,4
    4 NPEEPL=NPEEPL+S(HOUSE,J)
C SEE IF THIS IS LESS THAN LARGEST FOUND SO FAR
      IF(NPEEPL.LT.MOST) GO TO 12
      MOST=NPEEPL
      BIGHSE=HOUSE
   12 CONTINUE
      PRINT 777,BIGHSE,MOST
  777 FORMAT('1HOUSE ',I2,' CONTAINS',I2,' PEOPLE')
      STOP
      END
```

In this example, a pair of nested implied DOs was used in the READ statement to create an input list of 24 variables. J, being the second subscript, refers to the column and since the J-loop is inside the I-loop, the 24 variables are named row-by-row, that is: row 1 followed by row 2 followed by row 3 etc.. Note also the statement "DO 12 HOUSE=1,6". It is permissible to use HOUSE as a DO-loop index since it was declared as being an INTEGER variable in the declaration statement which was also used to define the set S.

Suppose we wanted to print the twenty-four values in the table so that the six numbers in column 1 of the table were printed on the first line, the six in column 2 on the second line, those in columns three and four on the third and fourth lines respectively. Three equivalent methods of doing this are shown below.

```
i)        DO 15 J=1,4
      15 PRINT 27,(S(I,J),I=1,6)
      27 FORMAT(' ',6I3)

ii)       PRINT 27,((S(I,J),I=1,6),J=1,4)
      27 FORMAT(' ',6I3)
```

iii)   PRINT 27,S
         27 FORMAT(' ',6I3)

In method (i), the output list contains six elements which are the six variables in column 1 of the table. The PRINT statement is executed once for each column in the table.

In method (ii), the pair of nested implied DOs create an output list of twenty-four variables such that the set of six variables in columns 1,2,3 and 4 follow each other.

In method (iii), only the set name appears in the PRINT list. It is important to remember that this creates a list in which the variables are named column-by-column. This same idea applies in creating an input list for a READ statement. For example, suppose we had written the statement:

                READ,S

in programs 7.4 or 7.5. Since this would create an input list in which the variables appeared column by column, it would mean the four values which should be stored in row 1 would actually be assigned to the first four variables in column 1. The next four would be assigned to the last two variables in column 1 and the first two variables in column 2. This process of filling up the columns one after the other would continue until the entire table was filled. In fact, the only variables which would necessarily have the correct values would be $S(1,1)$ and $S(6,4)$ since they are the first and last elements in the list regardless of whether or not the variables are named row-by-row or column-by-column. Further examples are provided in the exercises.

The reason why a set name creates an output list in which variables appear in column by column order is discussed in detail in Chapter 9. Until then, this is one fact which you must remember.

Exercise 7.3

1 Consider the following table of numbers.

         2   5   -7   3
         4   8   22   7
         5   9   -8   3

   a) How many rows and columns are there?
   b) What is the element in position $(3,2)$?
   c) What are the positions of the prime numbers?
   d) What is the sum of the elements in the second row?, the third column?

2. Suppose A and B are two set of 6 INTEGER variables each.

The variables in A are arranged into two rows and three columns. B has three rows and two columns.

a) Define the sets.
b) What subscript values appear in A but not in B?
c) Suppose the value assigned to A(I,J) is I+J for all elements in A and the value of B(I,J) is I-J for all elements in B. Then:

    i) What pairs of I and J values are such that
       B(I,J)+A(I,J)=2*I ?
   ii) What pairs of I and J values are such that
       B(I,J)-A(I,J)=-2*J ?
  iii) What is the value of,
       A(1,1)*B(1,1)+A(1,2)*B(2,1)+A(1,3)*B(3,1) ?

   iv) What is the output of:

```
1.    PRINT 5,((A(I,J),J=1,3),I=1,1)
    5 FORMAT(3I2)

2.    J=2
      PRINT 4,(A(J,K)*B(K,J),K=3,5,4)
    4 FORMAT(I6)

3.    DO 6 I=1,3
    6 PRINT 8,MOD(A(2,I),A(1,I))
    8 FORMAT(3I3)
```

    v) What is the value of:

```
1. A(B(2,1),A(1,2)) ?
2. B(A(2,B(3,1))-1,B(A(1,B(3,1)),1)) ?
```

3. In what order do the variables appear in the output lists in the PRINT statements below? Assume Q has been defined by:

```
      REAL Q(4,2)
```

a) PRINT,Q
b) PRINT,(Q(J,1),Q(J,2),J=1,4)
c) PRINT,((Q(K,NUM),Q(K+2,NUM),K=1,2),NUM=1,2)
d) PRINT,(Q(5-J,2),Q(5-J,1),J=1,4)

4. What is the output of the following:

```
       PRINT 10,(((I+J+K-2,K=1,3),J=1,6,5),I=1,4,3)
    10 FORMAT(' ',6I3)
```

5. Suppose the sets X and Y have been defined by:

```
      REAL X(5,2),Y(2,5)
```

Write three statements (2 DOs and an Assignment statement) which will transfer the values in X to those in Y such that Y(I,J) is given the value of X(J,I).

*7.6 Higher Dimensioned Arrays.

Suppose the house survey referred to in the preceding section was taken in two different years for the same six houses. This would mean we would have two tables of data, each of which contained 24 data items organized into six rows and four columns. A set of 48 variables could be defined by the statement:

INTEGER S(6,4,2)

In this case, the set S is called a three-dimensional array and variables in the set S are triply-subscripted variables. Our interpretation of the variable S(I,J,K) is that I denotes the house number, J the type of information, and K, the year in which the survey was done. In WATFIV, it is permissible to define sets of variables having as many as seven dimensions.

When working with sets having three or more dimensions, the appearance of the set name in an input or output list defines a list of variables such that the rightmost subscript is varied the least rapidly, and the leftmost subscript is varied the most rapidly. This is the same rule which applies to two dimensional sets except that it is much easier to state the rule in this case as "the variables are ordered column-by-column". As an example, in order to print the 48 items of information obtained in the two surveys so that one number is printed on each line, then the following five methods are equivalent. In each case the FORMAT statement is "20 FORMAT(I3)".

```
i)      PRINT 20,S

ii)     PRINT 20,(((S(I,J,K),I=1,6),J=1,4),K=1,2)

iii)    DO 9 K=1,2
      9 PRINT 20,((S(I,J,K),I=1,6),J=1,4)

iv)     DO 17 K=1,2
        DO 17 J=1,4
     17 PRINT 20,(S(I,J,K),I=1,6)

v)      PRINT 20,((S(I,J,1),I=1,6),J=1,4),((S(I,J,2),
      * I=1,6),J=1,4)
```

The reason they are all equivalent is simply that the order in which the variables are named is the same in all cases. Although there are different numbers of elements in the output lists, the fact that there is but a single mask

187

in the FORMAT statement will cause the results to be the same.

7.7 Assignment of Values at Compile Time.

In Chapter 2 it was stated that there are two ways to give a value to a variable. The first is to use an Assignment statement such as "A=3.2". The second is to use a READ statement such as "READ,A". There is a third way which differs from these two methods in that the assignment of the value to the variable is made at compile time rather than execution time. (The Assignment statement and the READ statement are executable statements which mean that the action specified by them occurs during the execution of the program and not during the translation of the program into machine language.) Sometimes it is convenient to give a value to a variable during the compilation of a program so that when the program starts executing, the variable will already have an appropriate value. How to do this is the topic of this section. Keep in mind that compile time assignment of values is a matter of convenience and not of necessity.

To calculate the sum of the first fifty natural numbers, we might write the program:

```
C EXAMPLE 7.6 ASSIGNMENT AT EXECUTION TIME
      INTEGER SUM
      SUM=0
      DO 4 I=1,50
    4 SUM=SUM+I
      PRINT,SUM
      STOP
      END
```

In this program, the variable SUM must be set to zero before the total can be calculated and this has been done using the Assignment statement "SUM=0". To assign a value of zero to SUM at compile time, the program would look like:

```
C EXAMPLE 7.7 ASSIGNMENT AT COMPILE TIME
      INTEGER SUM/0/
      DO 4 I=1,50
    4 SUM=SUM+I
      PRINT,SUM
      STOP
      END
```

The statement "INTEGER SUM/0/" declares SUM as being an INTEGER variable and also causes the compiler to assign SUM an initial value of zero. Some other examples of compile time initialization of variables are:

i) REAL X/3.2E04/,JACK/2./,LOOP

ii) INTEGER A,B/5000/, C/0/

iii) INTEGER F(3)/1,2,3/

iv) REAL ZZ(4)/4*0./,B(2)/0.,0./

v) INTEGER COUNT(10)/2,5*0,4*1/

vi) REAL T(3,4)/12*0./

vii) REAL A(3,2)/3*0.,3*8./

In example (i), the variable X is given an initial value of 32000., the value of JACK is initialized to 2., and LOOP is simply declared as being a REAL variable.

In (ii), the variables A,B, and C are declared as INTEGER variables and B and C are initialized to 5000 and 0 respectively.

In example (iii), the three variables in the set F are given values such that F(1) is 1, F(2) is 2 and F(3) is 3.

In (iv), the four variables in the one-dimensional array ZZ are all initialized to zero. The "4*" indicates that the constant which follows is to be used 4 times. The two elements of B are both set equal to zero and this pair of initializing values could also have been written as "/2*0./" instead of as shown.

In example (v) the variable COUNT(1) is initialized to 2; the variables COUNT(2) thru COUNT(6) are each set equal to zero; and the remaining four variables in the set are given an initial value of 1.

In example (vi), the matrix of twelve variables in the set T are all initialized to zero.

In example (vii), the variables A(1,1),A(2,1) and A(3,1) are set to zero, and those in column 2 namely, A(1,2), A(2,2), and A(3,2) are given a value of 8. In other words the order in which the constants appearing between the slashes are assigned to elements in a matrix is column-by-column. This of course is the same order in which variables appear in an input or output list created by the use of the set name.

Five common errors occur when using REAL or INTEGER statements to initialize variables. Each of the example statements below will produce an error message.

i) REAL A/2/ Reason: The constant must be of the same
          type as the variable being initialized.

ii) REAL X(2)/ALOG(10.),SIN(.3)/ ,Reason: The initial-
          izing value(s) must be constants.

iii) INTEGER OK(2)/0,0,0/ ,Reason: There are fewer var-
          iables than initializing constants.

iv) REAL NOP(3)/2*0./ Reason: There are more variables
          than initializing constants.

v) REAL X/1./ Y/2./ Reason: Comma missing before Y.

*7.8 The DATA Statement

In some non-WATFIV versions of Fortran, initial values
cannot be specified using a type declaration statement.
Instead, they must be specified by a DATA statement. The
pair of statements below is equivalent to the single
statement "REAL M/1./".

```
REAL M
DATA M/1./
```

The rules for DATA statement usage are similar to those
discussed in the previous section. A summary can be found at
the end of this section.

The DATA statement has three advantages. First,
variables of different types can be initialized in the same
DATA statement. For example, the single statement

```
DATA I/4/, A/3./
```

is equivalent to the pair of statements

```
INTEGER I/4/
REAL A/3./
```

Secondly, the variables to be given initial values can be
defined by an implied DO-loop. For example, the statements
below define X to be a table of REAL variables having two
rows and seven columns. Variables in row one are given a
value of ten and those in row two a value of twenty.

```
REAL X(2,7)
DATA (X(1,I),I=1,7)/7*10./,(X(2,I),I=1,7)/7*20./
```

A pair of nested DO-loops could have been used instead of
the two single loops shown. Note that to achieve the same
effect without using implied DO-loops would require a
statement such as the following.

```
REAL X(2,7)/10.,20.,10.,20.,10.,20.,10.,20.,10.,20.,
* 10.,20.,10.,20./
```

The reason for the long string of initializing constants is
that the initial values are assigned column-by-column. This
means "/7*10.,7*20./" would not produce the correct result.

Third, in a very few exceptional cases the DATA statement
must be used. These cases concern the ordering of statements
within a program and are discussed in Chapter 16.

The rules of the DATA statement are as follows.

   i) Any variable whose type is not specified by the
      first-letter rule must have the type declared by a
      statement which precedes the DATA statement in
      which the variable appears. Shown below are valid
      and invalid ordering of statements.

   Valid   Invalid
   ____   _____
         INTEGER X   DATA X/2/
         DATA X/2/   INTEGER X

  ii) Specification of an array must precede any DATA
      statement used to initialize variables in the
      array. For example,

   Valid   Invalid
   ____   _____
         REAL A(3)   DATA A/3*0./
         DATA A/3*0./   REAL A(3)

 iii) Specific variables in an array can be initialized.
      The variables can, if desired, be defined by an
      implied DO-loop. The DO parameters must be
      constants. For example,

             INTEGER S(100)
             DATA S(74)/463/, (S(I),I=1,99,2)/50*1/

      Nested loops may be used.

  iv) The initializing values do not need to immediately
      follow the variable being initialized. That is, a
      list of variables can be followed by a list of
      initial values as illustrated in the following
      example.

             REAL X(2)
             DATA X(1),K,A,X(2)/0.,999,-8.,0./

   v) The number of initial values in a list must be the
      same as the number of variables preceding the list.
```
```

A constant must have the same type of value as the variable which it initializes.

*7.9 The DIMENSION Statement

A DIMENSION statement can be used to define sets or arrays of variables. However, elements in arrays which are defined by a DIMENSION statement are typed by the first-letter rule unless the set name appears in a type declaration statement. Furthermore, the DIMENSION statement cannot be used to specify initial values for elements in an array.

The statement which follows defines X to be a set of ten REAL variables and KSET to be a set of six INTEGER variables.

                    DIMENSION X(10), KSET(6)

To override the first-letter rule, the set name should appear in a type declaration statement. For example, either pair of the following statements define P to be an array of twelve INTEGER variables having four rows and three columns.

                INTEGER P   DIMENSION P(4,3)
                DIMENSION P(4,3)   INTEGER P

Two methods are available for performing compile time initialization of elements of arrays defined by a DIMENSION statement. First, a REAL or INTEGER statement can be used as shown in the following example.

                    DIMENSION A(3),K(4,5)
                    REAL A/2.,17.,-5./
                    INTEGER K/20*0/

Second, a DATA statement can be used. For example, the three statements above could be replaced by the following pair.

                    DIMENSION A(3), K(4,5)
                    DATA A/2.,17., -5./, K/20*0/

Note that when using either method, only the set name appears in a statement used to specify initial values.

The primary advantage of a DIMENSION statement is that it permits arrays having different types of variables to be defined in the same statement. Furthermore, in some versions of Fortran, it is the only statement which can be used to define sets of variables. In WATFIV, its use is only a necessity in very special cases. These cases are discussed in Chapter 16 (See "Ordering of Statements".).

7.10 A Third Example Using Subscripted Variables.

Suppose values of the function $(x^2-2x+3)/(3x^3-2x^2+5)$ are to be calculated for various values of x. The values of x to be used are obtained in the following way. On the first data card a value of N is punched which indicates the number of _ranges_ of values of x to be used. Assume N is twenty-five or less. Beginning on the same card which contained the value of N, N pairs of numbers are punched. The first number in each pair denotes the lowest value in the range of integer values to be used. The second number in the pair denotes the highest value in the range. For example, if there were two pairs of numbers say 2,5 and 11,15, the values of x to be used would be 2,3,4,5 and 11,12,13,14,15. The following program prints the value of each x used and the corresponding value of the function. The message "UNDEFINED" is printed if the denominator has a value of zero.

```
    C EXAMPLE 7.8 TABULATE FUNCTION FOR SEVERAL RANGES
          INTEGER X,DOLIM(25,2),START,END
          REAL NUMER
          READ,N,(DOLIM(I,1),DOLIM(I,2),I=1,N)
          PRINT 721
      721 FORMAT('1',T20,'X',10X,'FUNCTION VALUE',///)
          DO 555 K=1,N
    C FOR EACH PAIR SET INITIAL VALUE AND TEST VALUE OF
    C   A DO LOOP TO VALUES REFLECTING THE RANGE LIMITS
          START=DOLIM(K,1)
          END=DOLIM(K,2)
          DO 444 X=START,END
          DENOM=3*X**3-2*X**2+5
          IF(DENOM.EQ.0.) GO TO 71
          NUMER=X**2-2*X+3
          FUNC=NUMER/DENOM
          PRINT 8,X,FUNC
        8 FORMAT(' ',T18,I4,10X,E14.6)
          GO TO 444
       71 PRINT 9,X
        9 FORMAT(' ',T18,I4,10X,'UNDEFINED')
      444 CONTINUE
      555 CONTINUE
          STOP
          END
```

In this program, a table called DOLIM having 25 rows and 2 columns is used to store the pairs of numbers defining the ranges of x-values to be used. Note that in the READ statement, the limit of the implied DO index is N, a variable which appears as the first element of the input list. For each of the N pairs of values a DO-loop is constructed having appropriate intitial and test values which are obtained from the elements of the table DOLIM. The X-loop is used to perform the calculations for a given range of values. Note also that this program works only for ranges which are defined by pairs of positive INTEGERS. Modifications are necessary to have the program work for ranges in which one or both limits could be negative or zero.

7.11 Summary

1. Frequently we must write programs in which we do not know at the time the program is written:

   a) How many variables are required,
   b) Which variables will have values needed for some special purpose.

2. This problem can be overcome in WATFIV by defining a set of variables using a REAL or INTEGER declaration statement which specifies not only the set name but also the number of variables which might be needed. Variables which are elements of sets have dynamic variable names. That is, the name of the variable can be changed by changing the value of the subscript(s). This introduces a great deal of flexibility into programs because it permits the use of an iterative approach which otherwise could not be used.

3. For convenience, sets of variables may be thought of as being in a simple list (a vector), or organized in a rectangular array (a matrix).

4. Implied DO-loops are handy tools for creating input and output lists.

5. It is permissible and sometimes convenient to initialize variables at compile time. The REAL and INTEGER statements can be used for this purpose.

Programming Problems

7.1   Read five INTEGER values from a single card and store them in a set of variables called K. On four successive lines print the values; the subscripts of the variables which have positive values, negative values, and zero values.

7.2   Read a set of ten INTEGER values punched on a single card. Print all pairs of values from the set which add up to twelve.

7.3   Read a set of ten INTEGER values each of which represents some person's age. Determine which two persons are: closest in age; farthest apart in age.

7.4 Suppose A and B are sets of eight INTEGER values each. Read the two sets of values using implied DO-loops. Print those values which are in: both A and B; either A or B or both; A but not B; B but not A; either A or B but not both. Test your program using the following sets of values. A=(2, 5, 8, 4, 7, 1, 6, 10). B=(9, 8, 4, 10, 3, 5, 12, 11).

7.5 Read four cards each of which contains seven REAL values representing daily temperatures (one card per week). For each week, calculate the average temperature and the maximum and minimum temperatures. Calculate the average, high and low temperatures for the four week period. Display your results as shown below.

```
                 TEMPERATURES
         M    T    W    TH   F    S    S    AVG    HI   LO
WEEK 1   XX   XX   XX   XX   XX   XX   XX   XX.X   XX   XX
WEEK 2   XX   XX   XX   XX   XX   XX   XX   XX.X   XX   XX
WEEK 3   XX   XX   XX   XX   XX   XX   XX   XX.X   XX   XX
WEEK 4   XX   XX   XX   XX   XX   XX   XX   XX.X   XX   XX
                                            ----   --   --
         FOUR WEEK STATISTICS               XX.X   XX   XX
```

7.6 Add additional statements to the program for the previous problem so that the average, high and low temperatures for each day of the week are calculated. Display the additional information using appropriate FORMAT statements.

7.7 Most credit cards have an account number in which the last digit is called the "check digit". Its value depends on the values of the other digits. When the account number is read from a card, the last digit is compared with what it should be based on the other digits in the number. Suppose an account number has ten digits (including the check digit). One method of calculating the check digit is as follows. Find the sum of the 2nd, 4th, 6th and 8th digits (begining from the left). Call this total SUM1. Form a number consisting of the first, 3rd, 5th, 7th and 9th digits. Multiply this value by two and add the digits in the result. Call this total SUM2. Add SUM1 and SUM2 and subtract the last digit from ten to obtain the check digit. For example, to see if the number 2520764263 is valid: we have SUM1=5+0+6+2=13; now 2*22746 = 45492 and therefore SUM2=4+5+4+9+2 = 24; thus SUM1 + SUM2 = 37 and so the check digit should be 10-7=3. Thus the account number is valid. Write a program which reads an unknown number of ten digit account numbers and determines which are valid (the check digit agrees with that calculated according to the rules above). When testing your program use at least two valid account numbers. Note that to obtain SUM2 you will need to extract the individual digits in a number. This can be done by repeatedly dividing the number by ten and using the remainder as the value of the next digit.

7.8   Start with any four digit INTEGER value in which at least two of the digits have different values. Form the largest and smallest possible numbers from the digits. Subtract them to give a new number. Compare the number to 6174. If equal, stop. If not, repeat the entire process until the number 6174 is obtained. (It will show up in at most seven steps regardless of the number you start with!) For example, if you start with 1998 you get successively: 8082 (from 9981 - 1899); 8532 (from 8820 - 0288); 6174 (from 8532 - 2358). Print your starting value and each number obtained during the procedure.

7.9   Write a program which reads an INTEGER value and finds all of its divisors. For example, the divisors of 6 are 1, 2, 3, and 6. Store the divisors in a vector called VEC. For each element of VEC, determine how many divisors it has. (For the example, these would be 1, 2, 2, and 4. Store these values in a vector called NDIVS. Find the sum of cubes of the elements of NDIVS and compare this with the square of the sum of the elements of NDIVS. They will be equal! This is a general procedure for finding sets of numbers having this property. Write a program which reads several values and generates the set of values associated with each input number according to the rules above.

7.10   Read an unknown number (less than fifty) of INTEGER values one at a time. Stop when any value occurs for the second time. Print the message "THE VALUE XX WAS THE XX AND XX VALUE IN THE SEQUENCE".

7.11   Write a program which reads in three pairs of X-Y values representing the coordinates of the vertices of a triangle. Read the coordinates of a fourth point. Determine if the fourth point lies inside, on the edge of, or outside the triangle defined by the first three points. Print the coordinates of all four points along with an appropriate message.

7.12   Modify example program 7.8 so that the DO-loop ranges can have negative or zero values.

7.13   Modify example program 7.8 so that all three parameter values (initial, test and increment) are read from a card. Assume the data values are REAL numbers.

7.14   Write a program which reads in the house survey data shown in the table at the begining of section 7.5. Punch the data for each house on a separate card. Answer the following questions. Which house has the most

children? Which houses have more than one child in high
school? What is the ratio of children to adults in each
house? In the houses containing no children in public
school or at least one pre-school child, what is the
average number of high-school children?

7.15 A data card contains twenty INTEGER values each of
which is zero or some positive value. Read the values
and store them in a vector called DATA. Print the values
in DATA. Create a new set of values called DENSE from
the elements of DATA as follows. If there are N
consecutive zero values in DATA, store a value of -N in
the next element of DENSE. If an element of DATA is
positive, store its value in the next element of DENSE.
(See example below.) Print the values in DENSE. Finally
use the elements of DENSE to generate the original set
of values by reversing the logic used to create DENSE.
Store the re-created set of values in COPY and print its
values. For example,

    DATA 2 3 0 0 0 0 1 5 7 0 0 8 4 0 9 6 0 0 3 0

    DENSE 2 3 -4 1 5 7 -2 8 4 0 9 6 -2 3 0

    COPY 2 3 0 0 0 0 1 5 7 0 0 8 4 0 9 6 0 0 3 0

7.16 Read ten INTEGER values and store them in the first
row of a table having two rows and ten columns. Find
the smallest value and store its column number in a
variable called BEGIN. Find the second smallest value
and store its column number in row two of the column
containing the smallest value. Continue to find
successively larger values and store their column
numbers in row two of the column containing the
previously found value. Finally, in row two of the
column containing the largest value, store a zero. (See
the example below.) Having done this use the value of
BEGIN and the row two values to print the original set
of values in order of smallest to largest. For example,

column 1	2	3	4	5	6	7	8	9	10
Row 1 15	-10	12	-19	8	45	-11	66	30	-2
Row 2 9	10	1	7	3	8	2	0	6	5

and BEGIN = 4 (points to column 4)

Write the program in such a way that it will work for
any ten INTEGER values.

7.17 The Ackermann function ACK(i,j) is defined as follows.
ACK(0,j)=j+1; ACK(i,0)=ACK(i-1,0); ACK(i,j) = ACK(i-1,
ACK(i,j-1)). Write a program which stores the values of

197

ACK(0,0) thru ACK(9,9) in a ten-by-ten table. The element in the ith row and jth column should be the value of ACK(i-1,j-1).

7.18   Here is a game you can try with a friend. Each player writes down three non-negative integer numbers which add up to five. Examples are (0 0 5), (1 3 1), (2 2 1), etc.. Compare your numbers with those of your opponent. The person who has the higher first number gets seven points (no points if a tie). The higher second number is worth five points and the higher third number is worth four points. Play ten times. The winner is the one with the highest total number of points. Write a program which generates all possible triples of numbers which can be used in the game. Use these to identify the rows and columns of a matrix. In the (i,j)th element of the matrix, store the point value which would be obtained by someone who chose the triple associated with row i if his opponent chose the triple associated with column j. Print the values in the matrix with appropriate row and column headings.

7.19   Suppose that a function f(x) is given and that the values of f(a), f(a+h), f(a+2h), etc. are calculated. The difference between two successive values of f(x) where the x values differ by an amount h (i.e: f(x+h) − f(x)) is called the first difference of the function for an interval of differencing h. Since f(x+h) − f(x) is itself a function of x the operation of differencing can be repeated to obtain the second difference of f(x). That is, if we define $\Delta f(x)=f(x+h)-f(x)$, then the second difference is defined as $\Delta(\Delta f(x)) = \Delta f(x+h) - \Delta f(x)$. In general the nth difference of f(x) is defined by $\Delta^n f(x)$ $= \Delta^{n-1}f(x+h) - \Delta^{n-1}f(x)$. For example, let $f(x) = x^3-3x^2+ 5x +7$. Let "a" = 0 and let h = 2. The differences for several values of the function are shown in the following table.

x	f(x)	$\Delta f(x)$	$\Delta^2 f(x)$	$\Delta^3 f(x)$	$\Delta^4 f(x)$
0	7				
		6			
2	13		24		
		30		48	
4	43		72		0
		102		48	
6	145		120		
		222			
8	367				

Using the above example for checking purposes, write a program which reads in the (n+1) coefficients of an nth degree polynomial. The value of n should be read first. Assume the polynomial has the form

198

$$c_n x^n + c_{n-1} x^{n-1} + c_{n-2} x^{n-2} + \ldots + c_1 x + c_0$$

Read values of "a" and "h". Calculate and display a difference table of the form shown in the example for the first $(n+1)$ differences of $f(x)$ for $x = a$, $a+h$, $a+2h$, ... , $a+(n+1)h$. Calculate the value of $c_n n! h$ and check that this value is the same as $\Delta^n f(x)$. (In the example $\Delta^4 f(x) = 1*3!2 = 48$.) Difference tables and other operations associated with them are useful in solving some interesting problems in mathematics. See for example "Numerical Methods For Science And Engineering" by R. E. Stanton, Prentice-Hall (Pub.).

CHAPTER 8   SUBPROGRAMS -- THE BASICS

Questions Answered In This Chapter

  1. Using our present knowledge, how can a sequence of
     instructions which is required at several points
     in a program be written only once?

  2. What factors make this approach awkward?

  3. What are the features available in WATFIV which
     overcome these disadvantages and limitations?

     In this chapter, the concept of writing a program in
pieces or segments is introduced. There are many reasons
for writing a program in segments. Some are:

  - The same segment can be used in different programs
     with no changes required in the statements of the
     segment.

  - The segments can be tested independently of one
     another to make sure each segment works before
     linking them together.

  - A library of segments can be built up which can be
     linked together in different ways to solve a wide
     range of problems.

  - Different programmers can write and test segments
     which will be linked together to solve a problem
     and the programmers needn't be concerned about the
     variable names or statement numbers used by other
     programmers.

     In this chapter we shall begin by writing a routine to
calculate factorial N. Next we shall describe the steps
necessary to use this routine at different points in the
same program using our present knowledge. After discussing
the awkwardness of this approach, it will be shown that by
making the routine a "subprogram", that the awkwardness is
removed.   The routine will be converted to two different
types of subprograms, a SUBROUTINE subprogram and a FUNCTION
subprogram.   Subprograms are one of the most powerful tools
available to WATFIV programmers. Knowledge of their purpose
and rules of use will greatly increase your programming
competence.

8.1 A Problem Requiring Factorials.

Suppose we wanted to find the value of an expression such as:

$$\frac{L!}{M!K!}$$

where L,M, and K are three non-negative INTEGER values. Recall that L!=1x2x3...x(L-1)xL and that 0! equals 1. An algorithm for evaluating the expression is:

```
1. Assign values to L,M, and K
2. Set FACTL = factorial L
3. Set FACTM = factorial M
4. Set FACTK = factorial K
5. Set ANSWER=FACTL/(FACTM*FACTK)
6. Print the value of ANSWER
7. Stop
```

Before writing a program, a procedure for calculating the value of a factorial must be developed. For example, to calculate $N\frac{1}{2}$, the following algorithm could be used.

```
1. Set FACTN = 1
2. If N ≤ 1 go to step 5
3. For values of i going from 2 up to N, repeat
      step 4.
4. Multiply FACTN by i
5. Stop.
```

If this method is used to obtain the value of a factorial, a program to solve the problem would be:

```
C EXAMPLE 8.1 FACTORIAL PROBLEM
      READ,L,M,K
C CALCULATE FACTL
      FACTL=1.
      IF(L.LE.1) GO TO 4
      DO 3 I=2,L
    3 FACTL=FACTL*FLOAT(I)
C CALCULATE FACTM
    4 FACTM=1.
      IF(M.LE.1) GO TO 6
      DO 5 I=2,M
    5 FACTM=FACTM*FLOAT(I)
C CALCULATE FACTK
    6 FACTK=1.
      IF(K.LE.1) GO TO 8
      DO 7 I=2,K
    7 FACTK=FACTK*FLOAT(I)
    8 ANSWER=FACTL/(FACTM*FACTK)
      PRINT,ANSWER
      STOP
      END
```

Observe that when writing this program, the set of statements to calculate a factorial was written three times, once for each variable whose factorial was required. In each of these three sets of statements, different variable names were used for the factorial value and the number whose factorial was being calculated. This may be O.K. if only a few factorial values are required, but if there were, say, fifty factorial values required, we would like some way of writing the factorial routine only once. Suppose we wrote the statements:

```
1 FACTN=1
  IF(N.LE.1) GO TO 3
  DO 2 I=2,N
2 FACTN=FACTN*FLOAT(I)
3 GO TO ____
```

where the statement number in the GO TO of the last statement is temporarily left blank. This set of statements could be used to calculate each factorial required provided:

   i)   Each value for which the factorial was required was assigned to the variable N before control was passed to statement 1.

  ii)   After control was returned from the routine, the value of FACTN was assigned to an appropriate variable.

 iii)   We devise some way of returning to the correct statement each time the factorial routine is completed. To do this conveniently we could use either a Computed GO TO or an Assigned GO TO.

A program in which the factorial routine appears only once is shown below. In this program, a Computed GO TO is used to return control to the appropriate point.

```
C EXAMPLE 8.2 THE FACTORIAL PROBLEM USING A
C  FACTORIAL ROUTINE WHICH APPEARS ONLY ONCE
      INTEGER BACK
      READ,L,M,K
C CALCULATE FACTORIAL L
      N=L
      BACK=1
C GO TO ROUTINE
      GO TO 1
   10 FACTL=FACTN
C CALCULATE FACTORIAL M
      N=M
      BACK=2
      GO TO 1
   20 FACTM=FACTN
```

```
C CALCULATE FACTORIAL K
      N=K
      BACK=3
      GO TO 1
   30 FACTK=FACTN
      ANSWER = FACTL/(FACTM*FACTK)
      PRINT,ANSWER
      STOP
C
C FACTORIAL ROUTINE
    1 FACTN=1.
      IF(N.LE.1) GO TO 3
      DO 2 I=2,N
    2 FACTN=FACTN*FLOAT(I)
    3 GO TO (10,20,30), BACK
      END
```

What has been achieved using this approach?

1. The routine to calculate a factorial has been written only once.

2. We are able to transfer control back to the appropriate statement by using a Computed GO TO.

The general method of using a routine in this fashion is:

```
C 'MAINLINE' PROGRAM
      .
      .
      =...)    assign values to
      =... }   variables used in
      =...)        the routine

  var = ...     (set up the return point)

  GO TO  ...    (transfer control to the routine)

      =...)    assign values calculated
      =... }   to variables used in the
      =...)        mainline
```

To emphasize: The four things which must be done in order to use a routine from different points in the same program are:

1. Assign values to variables used in the routine.
2. Set up the proper return point.
3. Transfer control to the routine.
4. Store the values calculated by the routine after control returns from the routine.

In spite of having to do these four things each time the routine is required, this approach is still advantageous if the routine has a fairly large number of statements. The

reason is that the routine is written only once and
therefore there is a:

- saving in keypunching time
- saving in compile time
- saving in memory space required for the
  instructions in the program.

Suppose now that several programs must be written each
of which requires us to calculate one or more factorials. If
we were to take the factorial routine and "drop it" into
another program, what difficulties, if any, might there be?

For one thing, since our factorial routine uses
statement numbers 1, 2, and 3, no program which made use of
the routine could use these statement numbers elsewhere in
the program. Also, since the factorial routine uses the
variable names N, FACTN, I, and BACK, errors could result if
these variables were used indiscriminately for other
purposes elsewhere in the program. Then there is the
problem of returning control to the right statement after
the factorial routine has been executed. In the routine we
used the statement:

GO TO (10,20,30), BACK

for this purpose. This would imply that control could return
to at most three different statements and the numbers of
these statements would have to be 10,20 and 30. This means
the statement in the routine which returns control to the
"mainline" program might have to be changed.

Another point is that the routine could not be accessed
from any point inside a DO-loop since on the return, control
would be passed from a point outside the range of the loop
to a statement inside the range of the loop.

Then there is the nuisance of having to assign values to
variables used in the routine before control is transferred
to the routine and to save the values calculated in the
routine after control is returned to the mainline.

If this weren't bad enough, suppose we had several
prewritten routines which we planned to use in different
programs. For example, one might write a routine to find
the roots of a quadratic equation, find the largest or
smallest value in a set, calculate the average of a set of
numbers, etc.. If each of these had to have their own set
of variable names, statement numbers and return points, it
would soon be a messy business to make profitable use of
these pre-written routines.

Fortunately, in WATFIV all of these disadvantages are overcome by making the routine a subprogram. In other words, when a subprogram is used:

i) The variable names and statement numbers used in the subprogram can also be used in the mainline program or in other subprograms and no confusion or ambiguity is introduced.

ii) The problem of returning to the proper point after the statements in the subprogram have been executed is taken care of by WATFIV and is therefore "automatic".

iii) The assignment of values to variables used in the subprogram before it is executed and assignment to mainline variables of values calculated or changed by executing the subprogram is also automatic (taken care of by machine language instructions generated by WATFIV at compile time).

There are two commonly used types of subprograms. They are called FUNCTION subprograms and SUBROUTINE subprograms. The similarities of the two types far outweigh the differences. Each type is easy to use. We shall begin with SUBROUTINE subprograms.

8.2 SUBROUTINE Subprograms.

A First Example

The first task is to see how the factorial routine is converted to a SUBROUTINE subprogram. After completing this description, we will show how the SUBROUTINE is used in the solution of our original problem.

When the factorial routine is written as a SUBROUTINE, it appears as:

```
      SUBROUTINE CALFAC(N,FACTN)
      FACTN=1.
      IF(N.LE.1) GO TO 3
      DO 2 I=2,N
    2 FACTN=FACTN*FLOAT(I)
    3 RETURN
      END
```

Remarks:

1. The first statement of the the SUBROUTINE contains three types of information. These are:

type of the subprogram	name of the subprogram	parameters of the subprogram
⇩	⇩	⇩
SUBROUTINE	CALFAC	(N , FACTN)

2. A "RETURN" statement is used to transfer control back to the appropriate statement in the mainline.

3. An "END" statement is used to define the end of the statements in the subprogram.

It remains to see how to use the SUBROUTINE CALFAC in solving our original problem which was to calculate the value of $L!/(M!K!)$. A suitable mainline program is the following.

```
C EXAMPLE MAINLINE USING CALFAC SUBROUTINE
      READ,L,M,K
      CALL CALFAC(L,FACTL)
      CALL CALFAC(M,FACTM)
      CALL CALFAC(K,FACTK)
      ANSWER=FACTL/(FACTM*FACTK)
      PRINT,ANSWER
      STOP
      END
```

Remarks:

1. The statement which calls the SUBROUTINE into action is a "CALL" statement. A CALL statement contains:

name of the SUBROUTINE being called	arguments
⇩	⇩
CALL CALFAC	(L , FACTL)

2. The name of the SUBROUTINE is CALFAC. Any valid WATFIV name can be used.

3. The arguments are simply values or variables which are used by the SUBROUTINE or which are to be assigned a value by the execution of the SUBROUTINE subprogram.

4. When the CALL statement is executed, the values of L and FACTL are assigned to the corresponding

parameters N and FACTN. Control then passes to the
SUBROUTINE.   When   the   RETURN   statement   in   the
SUBROUTINE is executed, the reverse process occurs.
That is, the values of the parameters N and FACTN
are assigned to the variables L and FACTL.   Control
then   transfers   to   the   statement   immediately
following   the   CALL   statement.   It doesn't matter
that FACTL did not have   a   value   assigned   to   it
before   the CALL statement is executed.   After all,
that was the purpose of calling the   SUBROUTINE   --
to obtain a value for FACTL.   Similarly, it doesn't
matter when returning from the SUBROUTINE that   the
value of N is assigned to L since the SUBROUTINE
did not change this value during its execution.   If
the   value   of N had been changed in the SUBROUTINE
however, the values   of   L   before   and   after   the
execution of the SUBROUTINE would be different.

The   mainline and the subprogram are placed between the $JOB
and $ENTRY cards in any order.   Most programmers prefer to
put   the   mainline segment ahead of any subprograms used but
this is not necessary. The organization of the card deck for
a job containing a single SUBROUTINE subprogram is shown
below.

```
        $JOB
        C MAINLINE PROGRAM
            ...
            ...
            ...
            END

            SUBROUTINE name (parameter list)
            ...
            ...
            ...
            END
        $ENTRY
```

    In   all the programs considered thus far, there has only
been a mainline segment. Regardless of how many   subprograms
are   included   in   a   job,   there   must   be one and only one
mainline segment. The compiler can tell   which   segment   is
the   mainline   since all subprograms have a unique statement
as the first one of the subprogram. The   first   statement
executed in any job is always the first executable statement
in the mainline. What happens   after   that   depends   on   the
program.   Subprograms   can   use   any   of   the   executable
statements available in the language.   This means that
subprograms can have READ, PRINT or STOP statements, for
example, if they are appropriate to the purpose of the
subprogram.

One further point. Each program segment must have an END statement. This lets the compiler know that this is the end of the segment. The $ENTRY statement follows the last segment and is used as a signal to stop compilation and begin execution.

Before looking at a second example, it would be wise to summarize the ideas developed this far. These can be illustrated by examining the program structure below.

```
C MAINLINE PROGRAM              SUBROUTINE name(p1,p2,...,pN)
    .                               .
    .                               .
    CALL name(a1,a2,...aN)          .
    .                           RETURN
    .                               .
    END                         END
```

When the CALL statement is executed, the sequence of events is as follows:

1. The values of the <u>arguments</u> a1,a2,...,aN are assigned to the <u>parameters</u> p1,p2,...,pN.

2. Control is passed to the first executable statement in the SUBROUTINE.

When a RETURN statement is executed (there may be several),

1. The values of the parameters p1,p2,...pN, are assigned to the arguments a1,a2,...,aN.

2. Control is passed to the statement following the CALL statement. (If a CALL statement is the object of a DO, the effect is the same as if a CONTINUE statement had followed the CALL.)

Naturally there must be the same number of elements in the argument and parameter lists and furthermore the corresponding elements in each list must be of the same type (either REAL or INTEGER).

A Second Example

Suppose we need to solve a series of equations of the form,

$$ax^2 + bx + c = 0.$$

The values of x which satisfy this equation can be calculated from the values of the coefficients "a", "b", and "c" using the well-known formulae:

208

$$\text{root } 1 = \frac{-b + \sqrt{b^2 - 4ac}}{2a}$$

$$\text{root } 2 = \frac{-b - \sqrt{b^2 - 4ac}}{2a}$$

A program which reads values of the coefficients and prints the roots of the equation is shown below. In this program, it is assumed that (b^2-4ac) is non-negative. If "a" has a value of zero, the job is terminated.

```
C EXAMPLE 8.3 ROOTS OF EQUATION
      1 READ,A,B,C
        IF(A.EQ.0.) STOP
        CALL QUAD(A,B,C,ROOT1,ROOT2)
        PRINT 70,ROOT1,ROOT2
     70 FORMAT(' ROOT1=',E20.6,',ROOT2=',E20.6)
        GO TO 1
        END

        SUBROUTINE QUAD(X,Y,Z,ONE,TWO)
        PRINT 70,X,Y,Z
     70 FORMAT('0EQUATION (',F9.4,')X**2+(',F9.4,
       *')*X+(',F9.4,')=0.')
        D=SQRT(Y*Y-4.*X*Z)
        ONE=(-Y+D)/(2.*X)
        TWO=(-Y-D)/(2.*X)
        RETURN
        END
$ENTRY
2., 5., 3.
0., 0., 0.
```

When the program is executed with the data cards shown, the output appears as:

```
EQUATION (   2.0000)X**2+(   5.0000)X+(  -3.0000)=0.

ROOT1=        -0.1000000E 01,ROOT2=        -0.1500000E 01
```

In this example, the argument and parameter lists each contain five variables. When the CALL statement is executed, the SUBROUTINE parameters X, Y, Z, ONE, TWO are assigned the values of A, B, C, ROOT1, ROOT2 respectively. It doesn't matter that ROOT1 and ROOT2 have not been assigned a value in the mainline since they will be assigned the values of the parameters ONE and TWO when the RETURN is executed. The execution of the RETURN statement also causes A, B and C to be assigned the values of X,Y, and Z. Since these latter three variables were not assigned new values in the SUBROUTINE, the values of A, B and C will be unchanged by executing the SUBROUTINE. To further illustrate this point, consider the following example.

209

```
C EXAMPLE 8.4
      X=Y=1.
      DO 10 I=1,5           SUBROUTINE SUB(A,B)
      CALL SUB(X,Y)         A=A+B
   10 PRINT,X               RETURN
      STOP                  END
      END
```

In the SUBROUTINE, the value of the parameter A is changed.
This means that each time the RETURN is executed, the value
of the argument X will be different from the value preceding
the execution of the SUBROUTINE. The parameter B, on the
other hand, is not changed by executing "SUB" and so the
five lines printed will display the values 2., 3., 4., 5.,
and 6.

A Third Example

Suppose we are required to write a SUBROUTINE which
scans an array of ten INTEGER values and determines the
position of the element in the set having the smallest
value. The "input" to the SUBROUTINE will be the set of ten
values and the "output" will be the value of the subscript
of the element having the smallest magnitude. The algorithm
used in the subprogram which follows is simply to assume
initially that the first element of the set is the smallest
and then examine each of the remaining nine values in the
set to see if it is smaller than the smallest found so far.

```
        SUBROUTINE FIND(SET,LOC)
C A SUBROUTINE TO DETERMINE THE POSITION OF THE
C SMALLEST VALUE IN A SET OF 10 INTEGER VALUES
        INTEGER SET(10),SMALL
        LOC=1
        SMALL=SET(1)
        DO 6 I=2,10
        IF(SET(I).GE.SMALL) GO TO 6
        SMALL=SET(I)
        LOC=I
      6 CONTINUE
        RETURN
        END
```

This SUBROUTINE could be used in the following way.
Suppose a set of 10 INTEGER values is read and the values
are to be printed in order of increasing magnitude. A
brute-force algorithm for solving this problem is:

1. Read in the set of 10 values.
2. Find the position of the smallest and
   print the value in that position.
3. Find the position of the smallest, excluding
   that found in step 2, and print the value in
   that position.

4. Find the position of the smallest, excluding
   those found in steps 2 and 3, and print the
   value in that position.
5. ...
6. ...
   .
   .
11. Find the position of the smallest, excluding
    those found in steps 2 thru 10, and print the value
    in that position.
12. Stop

In order to use an iterative approach, a method of
"excluding those found in steps 2 thru ..." must be found.
An easy way of achieving this result is to replace the
smallest value found each time by some very large number.
By doing this, the position of the smallest value will
change each time because the very large value, say, 999999,
will not be the smallest in the set. Thus an algorithm for
the mainline would be.

1. Read in the set of 10 values
2. Repeat steps 3 and 4 ten times.
3. Find the position of the smallest
   element and print the value in
   that position.
4. Replace the value by 999999.
5. Stop.

A translation of this algorithm is:

```
C EXAMPLE 8.5 SORTING 10 INTEGERS
      INTEGER NUM(10),POS
      READ,NUM
      DO 6 I=1,10
      CALL FIND(NUM,POS)
      PRINT,NUM(POS)
    6 NUM(POS)=999999
      STOP
      END
```

In this mainline segment, the set name "NUM" has been used
to create a set of ten arguments. These ten, plus the
variable "POS", correspond one-to-one with the parameters
defined by "(SET,LOC)" in the SUBROUTINE FIND. Note that
when a set is passed back and forth between program
segments, that

i) Only the set name appears in the argument and
   parameter lists.

ii) The array must be defined in each segment.

iii) The arrays defined in the two segments must be of

211

the same type and have the same number of elements.

Before summarizing the rules of SUBROUTINE usage, it should be pointed out that SUBROUTINES can call other SUBROUTINES. This idea is illustrated in the program structure below.

```
C MAINLINE                    SUBROUTINE SUBA(...)
     .                             .
     .                        CALL SUBB(...)
  CALL SUBA(...)                  .
     .                        CALL SUBC(...)
     .                             .
  END                        END
```

In this program structure, SUBB could not contain a CALL to SUBA since this amounts to a subprogram calling itself. If this was permitted, it would mean the values assigned to the parameters of SUBA as a result of the mainline CALL would be wiped out and it would also wipe out the means of returning to the mainline. For these reasons, an error results if a subprogram attempts to call itself either directly or indirectly.

8.3 Basic Rules of SUBROUTINE Usage.

1. The general form of a CALL statement is:

   CALL name (a1,a2,a3,...,aN)

   where,
   a) "name" is the name of a SUBROUTINE subprogram. The name can be any valid WATFIV name.
   b) "(a1,a2,a3,...,aN)" is the argument list. An argument can be: a variable name, a set name, or an arithmetic expression or constant.

2. A SUBROUTINE statement must be the first statement in any SUBROUTINE subprogram. Its general form is:

   SUBROUTINE name(p1,p2,p3,...,pN), where

   a) "name" is the name of the SUBROUTINE.
   b) "(p1,p2,p3,...pN)" is the parameter list. A parameter can be either a non-subscripted variable or a set name.

3. a) The number of arguments must equal the number of parameters.

   b) The type (REAL or INTEGER) of each argument must be the same as the type of the corresponding parameter.

   c) If an argument is a set name, the corresponding parameter must be a set having the same dimensions.

4. The execution of a RETURN statement (there can be any number in a subprogram) causes control to be transferred to the first statement following the CALL.

5. The value of each argument is assigned to the corresponding parameter before control passes to the SUBROUTINE. The value of each parameter is assigned to the corresponding argument before control returns to the calling segment.

6. Initialization of subprogram parameters at compile time is not allowed.

7. A SUBROUTINE may transfer control to another subprogram provided that any chain of subprogram transfers does not form a loop.

8. If an argument is a constant, an expression, a DO-loop index, or a DO-loop parameter, the value of the corresponding parameter in the subprogram cannot be changed. If the value of the parameter is changed during the execution of the subprogram, an error message will be printed and the job terminated <u>after</u> control returns to the calling segment.

9. If the same element appears more than once in an argument list, no change should be made in the value of any of the corresponding parameters during the execution of the subprogram since this would mean the argument would not have a unique value when control returned to the mainline.

Exercise 8.1

1. For each of the following, describe the output.

   a)
   ```
   I=2                    SUBROUTINE FCN(K,L)
   CALL FCN(I,J)          L=K**2-3*K+5
   PRINT,I,J              RETURN
   STOP                   END
   END
   ```

213

b)
```
     REAL AB(10)/10*1./      SUBROUTINE ADD(TAB)
     DO 3 N=1,4              REAL TAB(10)
   3 CALL ADD(AB)            DO 6 I=2,10,2
     PRINT 14,AB             TAB(I-1)=TAB(I-1)-1
  14 FORMAT(' ',5F4.0)     6 TAB(I)=TAB(I)+1
     STOP                    RETURN
     END                     END
```

c)
```
     M=0                     SUBROUTINE R(J,N)
     DO 1 J=1,4              DO 2 K=1,J
   1 CALL R(J,M)           2 N=N+K
     PRINT,M                 RETURN
     STOP                    END
     END
```

d)
```
     READ,X                  SUBROUTINE IN(Z)
     CALL IN(Y)              READ,Z
     PRINT,X,Y               RETURN
     READ,P                  END
     CALL IN(Q)      $ENTRY
     PRINT,P,Q          -2.
     STOP               -3.,    -4.
     END                 5.,     6
                         7.
```

e) Take your time on this one.

```
     INTEGER L/1/,K/2/       SUBROUTINE HELP(K,L)
     CALL HELP(L,K)          INTEGER KL/5/
     CALL HELP(K,L)          KL=KL*K/L
     PRINT,L,K               K=KL*L
     STOP                    RETURN
     END                     END
```

Hint: The second time HELP is called, the value of KL will not be 5. It will be the value it had after the SUBROUTINE finished executing the first time.

f)
```
     KA=1                    SUBROUTINE SUB
   3 CALL SUB                INTEGER N/1/
     PRINT,KA                IF(N.GT.10) STOP
     KA=KA+1                 N=N+1
     GO TO 3                 RETURN
     END                     END
```

2. Determine the error in each of the following.

a) CALL SUB(X,Y)   SUBROUTINE SUB(Z)

b) CALL AB(I,3.**2-5)   SUBROUTINE AB(J,NA$)

```
c)  INTEGER MAX(1)             SUBROUTINE T6666(J,R)
    CALL T6666(MAX,R)

d)  REAL A(10),JO              SUBROUTINE ADD(B,ZY)
    CALL ADD(JO,A)            REAL B(100)

e)  CALL EVERY(3)              SUBROUTINE EVERY(OH)

f)  CALL (A,B,C,D,E)           SUBROUTINE (W,X,Y,Z,E)

g)  CALL TROOP(MAT(10),F)      SUBROUTINE TROOP(MAT(10),F)

h)  CALL OOPS(5.3)             SUBROUTINE OOPS(S)
                              REAL S(1)

i)  X=SUB(Y)                   SUBROUTINE SUB(Y)

j)  CALL WRONG(A)              SUBROUTINE WRONG(1.375)

k)  ABC=5.                     SUBROUTINE OOPS(RST,XYZ)
    CALL OOPS(ABC,DEF)        RST=RST+XYZ
    STOP                      RETURN
    END                      END

l)  X=Y=2.                     SUBROUTINE POWER(X,Y,Z)
    CALL POWER(X,Y,X)        Z=X**Y
    STOP                      RETURN
    END                      END
```

8.4 FUNCTION Subprograms.

The other type of frequently used subprogram is called a
FUNCTION subprogram. The differences between FUNCTION
subprograms and SUBROUTINE subprograms are few. The choice
of which type to use in a given situation is largely a
matter of personal preference.

To illustrate some aspects of FUNCTION subprograms, the
routine to calculate factorial N will be converted to a
FUNCTION subprogram called FACTN.

```
    C FUNCTION SUBPROGRAM TO CALCULATE FACTORIAL N
          FUNCTION FACTN(N)
          FACTN=1.
          IF(N.LE.1) RETURN
          DO 2 I=2,N
        2 FACTN=FACTN*I
          RETURN
          END
```

Some remarks.

1. The first statement of the FUNCTION subprogram contains three types of information.

> type of   name of   parameter
> subprogram subprogram   list
>
> ⇩   ⇩   ⇩
>
> FUNCTION   FACTN   (N)

2. Within the subprogram, the FUNCTION name is used as a simple variable. It appears on both the left and right sides of an Assignment statement. Since there is no information to the contrary, the value of FACTN is REAL.

   This illustrates one of the important differences between FUNCTION subprograms and SUBROUTINE subprograms. The FUNCTION name is assigned a value in a FUNCTION subprogram. A SUBROUTINE name is simply used to identify the routine.

3. As with SUBROUTINES, a RETURN statement is used to transfer control back to the segment which activated the subprogram.

The FUNCTION subprogram FACTN could be used to help solve the original problem which was to calculate $L!/(M!K!)$. A mainline segment which "calls" the FUNCTION subprogram to obtain the factorial values is shown below.

```
C MAINLINE SEGMENT USING THE FUNCTION FACTN
      READ,L,M,K
      FACTL=FACTN(L)
      FACTM=FACTN(M)
      FACTK=FACTN(K)
      ANSWER=FACTL/(FACTM*FACTK)
      PRINT,ANSWER
      STOP
      END
```

Notice that the FUNCTION subprogram is "called" by using the FUNCTION name with an argument list in an expression. This is the second major difference between the two types of subprograms. That is, a CALL statement is used to activate a SUBROUTINE whereas the appearance of the FUNCTION name with an argument list "calls" a FUNCTION subprogram.

The word "calls" will be used for both SUBROUTINE and FUNCTION subprograms. The terms "calling segment" and "called segment" refer, respectively, to the segment from which and to which control passes regardless of the type of subprogram.

The general form of a program containing a mainline segment and a single FUNCTION subprogram is:

```
C MAINLINE SEGMENT              FUNCTION name(p1,p2,...pN)
     .                               .
     .                          name=.......
     =...name(a1,a2,...aN)           .
     .                               .
     .                          RETURN
     END                        END
```

Some remarks.

1. A FUNCTION subprogram is called when the FUNCTION name followed by an argument list appears on the right hand side of an Assignment statement or as part of an expression.

2. When a FUNCTION subprogram is called,

    a) The values of the arguments are assigned to the corresponding parameters.
    b) Control is transferred to the first executable statement of the FUNCTION subprogram.

3. During the execution of the subprogram a value must be assigned to the FUNCTION name. The type of value taken on is based on the first-letter rule. (An example will be given shortly which shows how to explicitly type the FUNCTION value.)

4. When a RETURN statement is executed,

    a) The values of the parameters are assigned to the corresponding arguments.

    b) The value assigned to the FUNCTION name in the subprogram is assigned to the element in the expression which activated the FUNCTION.

    c) Execution continues from the point immediately following the appearance of the FUNCTION in the calling expression.

Three important differences between FUNCTION subprograms and SUBROUTINE subprograms are:

    i) A CALL statement is used to call a SUBROUTINE. The appearance of the FUNCTION name and argument list calls a FUNCTION subprogram.

    ii) With a SUBROUTINE, control returns to the statement following the CALL. In the case of a FUNCTION subprogram, execution continues from a point following the appearance of the FUNCTION name.

iii) The assignment of argument values to parameter values and parameter values to argument values occurs for both SUBROUTINE and FUNCTION subprograms. However, with FUNCTION subprograms, an additional assignment is made when the RETURN statement is executed, namely, the value assigned to the FUNCTION name in the subprogram is taken on by the element in the expression which called the subprogram.

This third point indicates the kind of situation when one would normally use a FUNCTION subprogram instead of a SUBROUTINE subprogram. That is, when the purpose of the subprogram is to calculate a single value. Since the purpose of the factorial routine used as an example was just that, to calculate a single value, most programmmers would choose to make the routine a FUNCTION subprogram and not a SUBROUTINE subprogram.

Because of the point to which control returns, a FUNCTION subprogram can be activated several times within the same statement. For example, the mainline to solve the original problem could be shortened to the following four statements.

```
READ,L,M,K
PRINT,FACTN(L)/(FACTN(M)*FACTN(K))
STOP
END
```

If a SUBROUTINE were used, a minimum of three additional statements would have to be written. These would be required for the three CALLs to obtain the values of the factorials.

Before summarizing the rules of subprogram usage, a second example of a FUNCTION subprogram will be discussed. The program could be used to sort a set of ten INTEGER values. The purpose of the subprogram POINT is to produce a pointer to the element in the set having the smallest value. You will recall this same problem was solved previously using a SUBROUTINE subprogram. (See Example Program 8.5.)

```
C EXAMPLE 8.6
      INTEGER NUM(10),POINT          INTEGER FUNCTION POINT(S)
      READ,NUM                       INTEGER S(10)
      DO 6 J=1,10                    POINT=1
      K=POINT(NUM)                   DO 6 I=1,10
      PRINT,NUM(K)                   IF(S(I).LT.S(POINT))POINT=I
    6 NUM(K)=999999                6 CONTINUE
      STOP                           RETURN
      END                            END
```

This example shows how to override the first-letter rule applied to a FUNCTION name. In the example, the name of the FUNCTION is POINT which, by the first-letter rule, would normally be REAL-valued. Since POINT is used as a subscript in the mainline, it should be INTEGER valued. This means POINT must be declared as having INTEGER values in <u>both</u> the the mainline <u>and</u> the FUNCTION subprogram. In the <u>mainline</u>, this is done by using an INTEGER statement to inform the compiler that POINT is to take on INTEGER values. In the FUNCTION subprogram, this is accomplished by preceding the word "FUNCTION" with the word "INTEGER".

Thus to cause a FUNCTION to have a type of value different from that assigned by the first-letter rule the FUNCTION name must appear in a declaration statement in the calling segment, and the word REAL or INTEGER must precede the word FUNCTION in the first statement of the FUNCTION subprogram. With SUBROUTINES this is never necessary since the SUBROUTINE name is only the name of the routine and no value is assigned to the name.

Note that when using the built-in functions in the WATFIV library, it is not necessary to put the FUNCTION name in a declaration statement since the name of each built-in function is appropriate to the type of value taken on by the function.

The chart on the following page summarizes the rules for SUBROUTINE and FUNCTION subprograms and describes the important differences and similarities.

8.5 <u>Subprograms -- Basic Rules</u>

The chart on the following page summarizes the basic rules of SUBROUTINE and FUNCTION subprogram usage. Additional features and uses of these two types of subprograms are found in Chapter 9.

```
****************************************************************************
*                          *                                              *
*        SUBROUTINEs       *                 FUNCTIONs                     *
*                          *                                              *
****************************************************************************
*                          *          FUNCTION name(p1,p2,...pN)          *
*                          *                     or                        *
* Definition   SUBROUTINE name(p1,p2,...pN) * REAL FUNCTION name(p1,p2,...pN) *
*                          *                     or                        *
*                          * INTEGER FUNCTION name(p1,p2,...pN) *
****************************************************************************
*                          * Appearance of "name(a1,a2,...aN)" *
* Activated by  CALL name(a1,a2,...,aN) * in an expression in the calling *
*                          * segment.                                     *
****************************************************************************
* Return point  statement following the CALL * point in the statement following *
*                          statement.        * the appearance of the function *
****************************************************************************
* Permitted type of  set names, simple or subscripted variables, constants, *
* arguments for                    and expressions                         *
****************************************************************************
* Permitted type of                set names, simple variables             *
* parameters                                                               *
****************************************************************************
* Agreement of  * There must be the same number of elements in each list. Sets must *
* arguments and * be defined as having the same number of elements in both segments. *
* parameters    * Coressponding elements must be of the same type.          *
****************************************************************************
*              1. If an argument is a constant, expression, DO-loop index, or DO-loop*
*                 parameter, the corresponding parameter cannot be changed while *
*                 executing the subprogram.                                *
* Four Errors  2. Subprogram parameters cannot be given values at compile time. *
*              3. If the same item appears more than once in an argument list, the *
*                 value of each of the corresponding parameters must not be changed *
*                 during the execution of the subprogram.                  *
*              4. A chain of subprogram linkages cannot form a loop.        *
****************************************************************************
```

Exercise 8.2

Assume all variables are typed by default unless declared otherwise.

1. For each of the following, describe the output produced.

a)
```
I=4                        FUNCTION MN(K)
J=MN(I)                    MN=1
PRINT,J**2                 L=K*2*K
STOP                       IF(L.EQ.K) MN=2
END                        RETURN
                           END
```

b)
```
REAL JAY,A/5./,B/3./       REAL FUNCTION JAY(I)
C=AMOD(A,B)*JAY(A-B)       REAL I
PRINT,A,B,C                JAY=I+SIGN(I,-I)
STOP                       RETURN
END                        END
```

c)
```
INTEGER I/1/,J/2/,K/3/     FUNCTION F1(L)
PRINT,F1(I)*F2(J,K)        F1=F2(L,L/2)
STOP                       RETURN
END                        END
        FUNCTION F2(M,N)
        F2=M*(M+N)*(M-N)
        RETURN
        END
```

d)
```
REAL X/1./                 FUNCTION KELLY(Z)
DO 3 I=1,4                 KELLY=Z*Z/Z*Z
X=KELLY(X)                 RETURN
3 PRINT,X                  END
END
```

e)
```
INTEGER BETA/10/,GREG,F  SUBROUTINE NEXT(A,B)
CALL NEXT(GREG(BETA),F)  INTEGER A,B,C/2/
CALL NEXT(GREG(BETA),F)  C=C+2
PRINT,GREG(BETA),F       B=A+C
STOP                     RETURN
END                      END

        INTEGER FUNCTION GREG(MINI)
        INTEGER ALPHA/1/
        GREG=MINI-2*ALPHA
        RETURN
        END
```

f)
```
REAL LUMP,HUMP(4)/4*2./    REAL FUNCTION LUMP(BUMP,A)
Z=LUMP(HUMP,HUMP(3))       REAL BUMP(4)
PRINT,Z,HUMP(3)            BUMP(IFIX(A-1.))=DIM(-A,A)
STOP                       LUMP=BUMP(1)
END                        RETURN
                           END
```

221

2. Determine the error in each of the following.

a) Y=FUNCTION ADD(3.)   FUNCTION ADD(X)

b) PRINT,ZZ(5)   INTEGER FUNCTION ZZ(J)

c) T=INTO(FLOAT(3))   FUNCTION INTO(LUCKY)

d) REAL A(3)/3*0./   REAL FUNCTION AA(B(1),B)
    M=AA(A(1),A)   REAL B(3)

e) M=2.5   FUNCTION AFTER(JASPER)
    CALL AFTER(2*M)

f) TITLE=6*FACT(3)   FUNCTION FACT(K)
                                FACT=1
                                IF(K.GT.1)FACT=FACT(K-1)
                                RETURN
                                END

g) (three errors)

    A=B=5.5E-01   SUBROUTINE LOCATE(X,Y)
    CALL LOCATE(A,B)   Y=FIND(X,Y)
    STOP   RETURN
    END   END
            FUNTION FIND(A,B)
            B=A/B
            CALL LOCATE(B,A)
            RETURN
            END

h) MAX=MAX(2)   FUNCTION MAX(I)
                                MAX=I*FLOAT(I)
                                RETURN
                                END

i) GAMMA=FCN(2,4,6)   FUNCTION (K,L,M)

j) TEST=ARAN(6.0,B)   FUNCTION ARAN(A,B)
                                REAL B/5./,ARAN/1./
                                ARAN=A+B+ARAN
                                RETURN
                                END

8.6 Statement Functions

Occasionally the same formula is required at several points within a single program segment. Provided the formula value can be calculated in a single statement, the formula may be defined as a Statement Function. Once a Statement Function has been defined, it is used in the same way as any FUNCTION subprogram or built-in function. Using Statement Functions may make a program easier to understand and may also reduce the programming and keypunching time required to solve a problem.

Suppose the formula

$$distance = velocity \times time + \frac{1}{2} accel. \times time^2$$

is required in a problem. A program which makes the formula into a Statement Function and subsequently uses it, is the following.

```
$JOB
C EXAMPLE 8.7 STATEMENT FUNCTIONS
C STATEMENT FUNCTION DEFINITION
      DIST(VEL,TIME,ACC)=VEL*TIME+.5*ACC*TIME**2
      READ,A,B,C
C STATEMENT FUNCTION USAGE
      D=DIST(A,B,C)
      PRINT 900,A,B,C,D
  900 FORMAT(' VEL=',F6.2,' TIME=',F6.2,' ACC=',
     * F6.2,' DISTANCE=',F6.2)
      STOP
      END
```

Note that the formula definition appears before the first executable statement of the program. The formula is used by including the name and an argument list in an expression. That is, a Statement Function is called in precisely the same way that a built-in function is called.

The general structure of a segment containing a Statement Function is shown below. Rules of usage follow.

```
$JOB   WATFIV
       .
       name(parameter list)=expression
       .
C BEGINNING OF EXECUTABLE STATEMENTS
       .
       ...=...name(argument list)...
       .
       END
```

Rules For Statement Functions

1. The name of a Statement Function can be any valid
   WATFIV name. The parameter list contains one or
   more non-subscripted variables separated by commas.
   Elements in the parameter list are typed by the
   first-letter rule unless they have been typed by a
   previous statement. The expression can be any valid
   WATFIV expression involving the parameters and
   (optionally) other non-parameter variables,
   constants, built-in functions and other previously
   defined Statement Functions.

2. The function is activated by the appearance of

   name (argument list)

   in an expression. The arguments may be constants,
   variables and expressions. Arguments should agree
   in number and type with the corresponding
   parameters.

3. All Statement Function definitions must be placed
   ahead of the first executable statement in a
   segment.

4. Statement Functions can only be used within the
   program segment in which they are defined.

5. Variable names used as parameters in Statement
   Function definitions can be used as names of simple
   variables for other purposes in the segment.

Exercise 8.3 (Statement Functions)

1. For each of the following, state the values printed.

   a)   F(X)=X*X-1.
               PRINT,F(3.)

   b)   INTEGER A,B,MAT(2)/-3,4/
               A(B,C)=IABS(B*IFIX(C))
               G=7.94
               D=A(MAT(1),G)
               F=A(MAT(2),D)
               PRINT,F,D

   c)   REAL B(2)/1.,2.5/
               OOPS(I,J)=3-B(I)+I/J
               AHA(K,L)=3-OOPS(K,L)*I/J
               I=J=3
               PRINT,OOPS(2,I),AHA(IFIX(B(2)),J)

2. What is the error in each of the following?

    a)
```
          I=2
          B(K)=SQRT(K*100.)
          PRINT,B(I)
```

    b) Two errors
```
          INTEGER Y/3/,Z,K(2)
          X(Y,M)=M*FLOAT(Y)+K(1)
          Z=X(3,17)
          PRINT,Z,SQRT(Y)
```

    c)
```
          F(A)=2*A**2-G(B)
          G(X)=X*(-1/3.)
          B=8.
          PRINT,F(5.)
```

3. a) Can a Statement Function have no parameters? Why?

    b) How can the compiler tell whether a statement which begins "FUN(I)=..." is a Statement Function definition or an Assignment statement?

8.7 Summary

  1. Routines which solve a set of equations, multiply matrices, sort a set of numbers, etc., are often required at different points in the same program, or in several different programs. The programmer has the choice of making the routine part of the mainline or making the routine a SUBROUTINE or FUNCTION subprogram. A comparison of the two approaches is shown below.

	Routine Is Part of the Mainline	Routine Is A Subprogram
Variable names used in the routine can be used indiscriminently outside the routine.	no	yes
Statement numbers used in the routine can be used indiscriminently outside the routine.	no	yes
Routine can be accessed from inside a DO-loop.	no	yes

225

Assignment of values to variables used in the routine is done by ...	statements written by the programmer	WATFIV
Assignment of values calculated in the routine to variables used in the mainline is taken care of by ...	statements written by the programmer	WATFIV
Can the routine be used easily in different programs?	no	yes

2. The use of Statement Functions may reduce programming time in cases where the same formula is required at several points in the same segment.

Programming Problems

If a problem requests that only a subprogram be written, write a simple mainline to test the subprogram.

8.1   Write a SUBROUTINE subprogram called TRIAIR to calculate the area of a triangle from the length of the base and the altitude. The subprogram will have three parameters -- BASE, ALTUDE and AREA. The first two values are supplied by the calling segment. The value of AREA is calculated in the subprogram. Write a mainline segment which reads in five pairs of REAL values punched one pair per card. The values in each pair are the lengths of the base and altitude respectively. The mainline should print the input values and the area for each of the five triangles using appropriate FORMAT statements.

8.2   Make the subprogram TRIAIR in problem 1 a FUNCTION subprogram. Note that it will then have only two parameters, BASE and ALTUDE.

8.3   Write a SUBROUTINE subprogram in which the parameter is a vector of ten INTEGER values. The subprogram should reverse the order of the ten values before returning control to the calling segment.

8.4   Write a FUNCTION subprogram called DET which calculates the value of the determinant of a two-by-two matrix. The subprogram will have a single parameter, the name of the two-by-two matrix of REAL values.

8.5   Write a SUBROUTINE subprogram to solve a system of two
equations in two unknowns. The SUBROUTINE should have
the parameters COEFF, RS, ROOTS and IFLAG where: COEFF
is a 2-by-2 matrix of the coefficients in the equations;
RS is a vector of the right hand side values of the
equations; ROOTS is a vector of the pair of values which
solve the equations; IFLAG is calculated by the
subprogram and has a value of zero if the equations have
no solution, 1 if there is one solution, and 2 if there
are an infinite number of solutions. For example, to
solve

$$2x + 3y = 12$$
$$-4x + 8y = 4$$

The values passed to the SUBROUTINE would be

$$COEFF = \begin{pmatrix} 2. & 3. \\ -4. & 8. \end{pmatrix} \qquad RS = \begin{pmatrix} 10. \\ 4. \end{pmatrix}$$

The values calculated by the SUBROUTINE would be

$$ROOTS = (3., 2.) \qquad IFLAG = 1$$

8.6   Write a SUBROUTINE called RANDI to generate a set of
100 "random" INTEGER numbers R(1), R(2), R(3),... in
the range J thru K. Use the following method. Set R(1)
equal to any odd positive INTEGER value. For N=2, 3,
..., 100, set R(N)=MOD(65539*R(N-1),2147483648). This
will generate 100 random numbers in the range zero thru
roughly 2.1 billion. To reduce the range to that of J
thru K, replace R(I) by

$$R(I) - R(I)*.4656613E-09*(K-J+1) + J$$

The parameters of the SUBROUTINE will be R, J, and K.
Test your subprogram by writing a mainline segment which
prints out the one hundred numbers generated by RANDI on
ten lines of ten values each.

8.7   Use the SUBROUTINE RANDI written for the previous
problem in this problem. Generate two hundred random
INTEGER values in the range one thru six. Use these
numbers to represent the outcome on one hundred throws
of a pair of dice. That is, if the values of R(1) and
R(2) were 3 and 6 respectively, this would mean the dice
on the first throw showed 3 and 6. Write a program which
answers the following questions about the hundred thows
of the dice. How many times did each of the 36 possible
results occur? Print the data in a table having six
rows and six columns where the row indicates the value
on the first die. The column indicates the value on the
second die. What percentage of the time did each of the
eleven possible totals 2, 3, 4, ..., 12 occur in the

227

hundred throws? Print suitable headings followed by eleven lines of statistics.

8.8   Write a SUBROUTINE which has two parameters -- K, a set of twenty INTEGER values, and INSERT. Values in K and the value of INSERT are passed to the subprogram. The SUBROUTINE should insert the value of INSERT into the set K so that values in K are non-decreasing (increasing order of magnitude except for ties) and then return control to the calling segment. Write a mainline segment which initializes a set of twenty INTEGER values called NSET to zero and then reads one INTEGER value from each of twenty cards. After each value is read, use the SUBROUTINE to insert the value in the proper position in NSET. After the twenty values have been read, print the values in NSET and verify that they have been stored in order of increasing magnitude.

8.9   Write a FUNCTION subprogram called ANG which, for the triangle shown below, calculates the size of angle A in degrees.

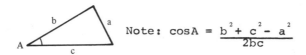

Note: $\cos A = \dfrac{b^2 + c^2 - a^2}{2bc}$

The lengths of the sides "a", "b" and "c" are passed to the subprogram. Test your subprogram by writing a mainline segment which reads in the lengths of the sides and uses ANG to calculate the sizes of the three angles in the triangle.

8.10   The area of a regular polygon of N sides in which each side has a length "s" is equal to $Ns^2 \cot(180/N)/4$. Write a FUNCTION subprogram called POLAIR having parameters N and s to calculate the area. Test POLAIR by writing a mainline segment which uses the subprogram to calculate the areas of regular polygons of <u>perimeter</u> one having 3, 4, 5, ..., 20 sides.

8.11   Write three Statement Functions called SIND, COSD and TAND to produce the sine, cosine and tangent values of an angle in degrees. Use the Statement Functions in a program which prints the cosecant, secant and cotangent of angles of 10, 20, 30, ..., 80 degrees.

8.12   Write a Statement Function which will round off any REAL value greater than 0.1 correct to N decimal places. Assume N is positive. Note that this can be done by: adding $5.*10.**(-N)$ to the value; multiplying by $10**N$; using the function AINT; dividing by $10**N$. All of this can be done in one statement. Test your function by rounding the value of 12.73469 correct to 1, 2, 3, and 4 decimal places.

8.13   Write   a   Statement   Function   called LOGB having two parameters X and B. The value of   the   Function   is   the logarithm of X using base B. Note that

$$\log X_B = \log_A X / \log_A B$$

Use   the Statement Function to print a table of the logs of the values one thru ten using bases 2, 4, 6,   8,   and 10.

8.14   Write   a Statement Function called KRON which has two INTEGER parameters M and N. The value of KRON should   be zero   if M and N are unequal and one if M equals N.   You may find the   IDIM   built-in   function   useful   in   your function   definition.   Make up your own program to test the Statement Function.

CHAPTER 9   SUBPROGRAMS -- THE DETAILS

Questions Answered In This Chapter.

1. How are numbers stored and organized in the computer?

2. When subprogram parameters take on values of the corresponding arguments, they can be "called by value" or "called by location". What is meant by these terms?

3. Variables used in a subprogram can automatically be given the values of variables used in other program segments by putting all such variables in a "common" area of memory. How is this done?

4. What is meant by execution time dimensioning of arrays? Why and how is this feature used?

5. If a subprogram must be written which requires the use of some other unknown subprogram, how is the compiler informed of this fact?

6. How can a subprogram be entered at some statement other than the first executable statement in the subprogram?

7. How can a SUBROUTINE return to a statement other than the one immediately following the "CALL" statment?

In the last chapter, the basic features of SUBROUTINE and FUNCTION subprograms were described. This knowledge may be sufficient to write and use all subprograms you will ever need. This chapter describes other "advanced" features of subprograms which, when used properly, may: (i) reduce the programming effort required; (ii) reduce the amount of memory used for instructions and data.

In order to use the features of the WATFIV language described in this chapter to best advantage, it is necessary to understand some of the basic concepts of how the memory is used by the compiler in translating a WATFIV program into machine language. Keep in mind that these topics are presented as concepts. The details of how these concepts have been implemented may be found in the WATFOR/WATFIV Implementation Guide available from the Computing Center at the University of Waterloo.

9.1 "Memory" Concepts

The memory (sometimes called storage) of a computer has thousands and often millions of memory cells or "bits". Each bit of the memory has a value of one or zero. In many computers, a memory cell is a little iron donut about an eighth of an inch in diameter, with several wires going thru the hole. By changing the quantity and direction of the current in the wires, the iron ring can be magnetized in either a clockwise or counter-clockwise direction. These two directions of magnetization represent the values of one and zero. One and zero are the two symbols used in the binary (base two) number system and the word "bit" is a contraction of the words "Binary digIT".

Bits are grouped together in sets of eight. A group of eight consecutive bits is called a byte. In order to be able to reference the contents (the bit pattern) of each byte, a unique number is associated with each byte of the computer memory. The number is called the address of the byte. Byte addresses start at zero and go up by one to the total number of bytes in the computer memory. These byte addresses are used in the machine language instructions generated by the compiler.

A group of thirty-two consecutive bits is called a word. The terms half-word and double word mean groups of sixteen and sixty-four consecutive bits respectively. The address of a half-word, full word, or double word is the address of its leftmost byte. The symbol "K" means 1024 bytes. For example, a computer having a 32K memory is one in which there are 32,768 bytes of memory. The diagram below shows the relationship between the sizes of the different quantities of memory. In the case of half-words, full words and double words, the asterisk denotes the byte used for addressing the storage locations.

Units Of Memory

Bytes	*	*	*	*	*	*	*	*
Half-Words	*		*		*		*	
Words	*				*			
Double Word	*							

Each program segment is compiled separately. Recall that program segments each have an END card to separate the segment from any which may follow. After the last segment has been compiled, and before execution begins, the segments are linked together and the memory used by the program is organized as shown on the following page.

Execution-Time Layout Of Memory

| Instructions for mainline segment

Constants and simple variables used
in the mainline |
| Instructions for subprogram 1

Constants and simple variables used
in subprogram 1 |
| Instructions for subprogram 2

Constants and simple variables used
in subprogram 2 |

| Array area for entire program |

Remarks.

1. One full word of memory is reserved for each REAL or INTEGER constant. One full word of memory is reserved for each REAL or INTEGER variable.

2. The compiler creates one or more machine language instructions for each executable WATFIV statement in a program. Machine language instructions have the general form:

| operation | address 1 | address 2 |

For example, when the statement "A=2.5" appears in a program, the compiler:

i) Creates a bit string of 32 ones and zeros which represents the REAL constant 2.5; reserves a word of memory for this bit pattern and remembers its address.

ii) Reserves a word of memory for storing the value of A and remembers its address.

iii) Creates a machine language instruction which essentially says, "Replace the bit pattern of the word at the address of 'A' with the bit pattern of the word at the address of '2.5'".

3. In the array area, a word of memory is reserved for each element in a REAL or INTEGER set of variables. For example, the statement:

    INTEGER DATA(10)/10*0/

would cause ten consecutive words of memory to be reserved and the compiler would also store the bit pattern for the INTEGER value zero in each of the ten words. Similarly, a set defined by:

    REAL X(3,2)

causes six words of memory to be reserved. The correspondence between the elements of the set and the six reserved words is shown below.

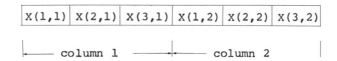

Note that elements in the set are assigned to words of memory "column-by-column". This is one reason why the use of a set name in an input or output list creates a list of variables which are such that the rightmost subscript varies least rapidly. (In the case of a matrix, this is the same as saying that the variables are named column-by-column.) By knowing the address of the word of memory reserved for the first element in a set and the number of rows and columns (or more precisely, the maximum value of each subscript), it is a simple matter to calculate the address of the word used to store any particular element of the set. This calculation is always done at execution time.

Note that the storage reserved for arrays follows the memory used by the constants and simple variables of the last program segment. The reason for putting the arrays in a common area is discussed in the next section.

If you look at the statistics printed following the execution of a WATFIV program, you will observe that the first line contains the information:

    OBJECT CODE=xxxxx BYTES,ARRAY AREA=yyyyy BYTES,

    TOTAL AREA AVAILABLE=zzzzz BYTES

The number of bytes of object code is the number of bytes of memory used by the machine language instructions, constants and simple variables used by all the program segments. The array area is the number of bytes reserved for the arrays. Since there are four bytes to a word, this value is four times the number of words, and hence four times the total number of subscripted variables, used in the program. The total area available is simply the number of bytes made available to your program. This number will vary from one computing center to another and is decided upon by the computing center administration. Knowing the total number of bytes available means that you can determine the maximum size of an array or arrays which could be used in a particular program.

Exercise 9.1

1. What two values can a "bit" of memory have?

2. How many bits in a byte?, bytes in a word?, bits in a double word?, half-words in 8K?

3. How many unique bit patterns can a byte have?

4. Since a REAL or INTEGER value occupies a word of memory, what is an upper limit on the total number of REAL or INTEGER values which can be stored in a word?

5. For each of the following, determine the number of bytes of memory used by the elements in each statement.

       a) REAL JASPER,N
       b) INTEGER T67(5),GAMMA
       c) INTEGER ALPHIE(2,7),AGGIE(10,10,10)
       d) REAL B(1)/2./,A(15,3)

6. Suppose a set has been defined by "REAL G(6)" and that the address of the first word of memory reserved for G is 2036. What is the address of G(2)? What is the the address of the last word of memory used by the the set G?

7. Suppose a set has been defined by "INTEGER S(4,6)". If the element S(2,3) is stored in a word whose address is 5048, what are the addresses of the following elements: S(1,1),S(4,6),S(3,3),S(2,5).

8. Suppose that an average of three machine language instructions are produced for each executable WATFIV statement and that a machine language instruction has an average length of four bytes. Consider the following program.

```
      REAL A(20)/10*1.,10*0./
      INTEGER B(5)/1,2,3,4,5/,I/1/
    3 J=I+5
      A(I+10)=A(I)+B(I)
      A(J+10)=A(J)+B(I)
      PRINT,A(J)
      I=I+1
      IF(I.LE.5) GO TO 3
      STOP
      END
```

a) How many bytes of object code are required?
b) What is the size of the array area?
c) If the total number of available bytes was 20,000,
   what is the maximum number of elements which the
   set A could have?

9.2 Transfer of Values at "Call" and "Return" Times.

The FUNCTION subprogram below illustrates three
different methods of assigning a value to a simple variable
used in a subprogram.

```
      FUNCTION FUNC(A)
      REAL B/0.6/
      READ,C
      FUNC=A*B*C
      RETURN
      END
```

As you would expect, the compiler reserves a word of
memory to store the value of FUNC as well as reserving a
word for each of A, B, and C. When the FUNCTION is
activated, the value for A is obtained by copying the bit
pattern stored in the word reserved by the argument of the
subprogram into the word reserved for the parameter A. The
question we would like to answer is, "Since the value we
want to use for A in the subprogram is already stored in
some word of the computer's memory, why not have the
subprogram instructions which reference A, refer to the word
of memory in which the value is stored instead of working
with a copy of the value? After all, wouldn't this save an
extra word of memory and also mean that it would be
unnecessary to execute a copy instruction?". The answer is,
"Sure, Why not?". To do this, it is simply a matter of
enclosing the parameter A in slashes. The label given to
this method of assigning a value to a parameter is "call by
location". The normal method is labelled "call by value".
The difference in the two approaches is indicated in the
program structures below.

235

Call By Value	Call By Location
FUNCTION FUNC(A)	FUNCTION FUNC(/A/)
.	.
.	.
FUNC=A*B*C	FUNC=A*B*C
.	.
END	END

The differences are:

i) If a parameter is called by location, no storage is reserved for the parameter in the area of memory occupied by the subprogram. Instead, those instructions in the subprogram which reference the parameter, refer to the memory locations occupied by the corresponding argument. This means that no copying operation is necessary either preceding or following execution of the subprogram.

ii) If a parameter is called by value, storage is reserved for the variable in the subprogram. The subprogram actually works with a copy of the argument value during the execution of the subprogram. When the RETURN is executed, the final value of the parameter is copied into the storage locations reserved for the argument.

Two other examples of parameter lists in which one or more of the parameters are called by location are:

INTEGER FUNCTION SOME(/IJK/,ART,/NETPAY/)

SUBROUTINE BYEACH(A,B,/CYEAR/,/DYEAR/)

Note that parameters of SUBROUTINE subprograms can also be called by location. The examples below, however, will produce error messages.

FUNCTION AHA(/R,S/) SUBROUTINE MID(/T/)
                     REAL T(4,10)
Reason: Slashes must enclose
each parameter.   Reason: Only simple variables
                     can be called by location.

Sets cannot be called by location because this process is automatic in WATFIV. To further illustrate this idea, consider the following program.

236

```
C EXAMPLE 9.1                        SUBROUTINE VECSUM(X,TOTAL)
      REAL VEC(1000)                 REAL X(1000)
      READ,VEC                       TOTAL=0.
      CALL VECSUM(VEC,SUM)           DO 1 I=1,1000
      PRINT,SUM                    1 TOTAL=TOTAL+X(I)
      STOP                           RETURN
      END                            END
```

In this example, the parameter X is a set having 1000 elements. If X were called by value, it would mean that 1000 words of storage would be reserved for each of the sets VEC and X. It would also mean that a thousand copy operations would be necessary at the beginning and end of executing the subprogram. To avoid this waste of memory and execution time, arrays are automatically called by location. You can easily verify this fact by running the above program and observing that the array area is 4000 bytes, that is, a total of 1000 words.

When a parameter is a set of variables, the two items of information necessary to have the machine language instructions of the subprogram reference the correct word of memory for any variable in the set are the address of the word reserved for the first element in the set and secondly, the dimensions of the set. The first item of information (the address) is passed to the subprogram when it is called. The second, the dimensions of the set, are obtained from the statement which defines the set in the subprogram.

9.3 Execution Time Dimensioning of Arrays.

In examples used previously, all parameter arrays were defined as having precisely the same dimensions as the corresponding argument array. If this requirement had to be followed without exception, it would mean that the statement defining the parameter array would have to be changed each time the subprogram was used with argument arrays having different dimensions. It also might mean that a program would require several versions of the same subprogram in order to work with sets of different sizes.

In WATFIV, the dimensions of a parameter array can be supplied at execution time. In other words, at execution time, the calling segment can pass the dimensions of a set to the called segment. The two factors which make this feature possible are: One, parameter arrays are called by location and hence no storage is reserved for the set in the subprogram; Two, the calculation of the address of the memory locations reserved for any element in a set occurs at execution time and not at compile time. Consider the following example.

237

```
C MAINLINE                        SUBROUTINE SUB(A,N)
      REAL X(20)                        REAL A(N)
      .                                 .
      .                                 .
      CALL SUB(X,20)                    DO ___ I=1,N
      .                                 .
      .                                 .
      END                               END
```

In the program structure above, the number of elements
in the set X is passed to the subprogram as an argument. At
execution time, the subprogram parameter N will have a value
of twenty before execution of the subprogram begins. More
precisely, the value of N is used to determine the number of
words in the set X which can be used by the subprogram SUB.

In the program structure below, the subprogram is used
to read the values to be stored a set VALUE. At the time the
program is written, it is not known how many values are to
be read.

```
C MAINLINE                        SUBROUTINE READ(SET,SIZ)
      INTEGER VALUE(1000)               INTEGER SIZ, SET(SIZ)
      READ,NVALS                        READ,SET
      CALL READ(VALUE,NVALS)            RETURN
      .                                 END
      .
      END
```

There are several points illustrated by this example.

    i) Since storage must be provided for the maximum
number of values which might be read, the set VALUE
has been defined in the mainline to reserve a
thousand words of memory. The number of words
actually used will, of course, depend on the value
of NVALS.

    ii) The number of elements in the parameter SET is
passed to the subprogram via the parameter SIZ.
Since the dimension of any set of variables must be
an INTEGER constant or an INTEGER variable, the
first-letter rule has been overridden by declaring
the variable SIZ to be INTEGER.

    iii) The set name is used in the READ statement of the
subprogram to create the input list. The list will
have SIZ items. Incidentally, this is the most
efficient way to read in a variable number of
elements. That is, use a subprogram in which the
set dimensions are supplied at execution time and
in which the set name is used to create the input
list in the READ statement. A further discussion of
this point can be found in Appendix G.

The following example should be studied closely. The FUNCTION subprogram NTOT is used to calculate the sum of the elements of an M by N matrix. The mainline program reads in the values of M and N and then reads in MN more values before calling the subprogram. It is assumed that M and N are both four or less and so the set A in the mainline has been defined as having four rows and four columns. The question is, "What value is printed, and why?".

```
C EXAMPLE 9.2                        FUNCTION NTOT(X,M,N)
      INTEGER A(4,4)/16*0/           INTEGER X(M,N)
      READ,M,N                       NTOT=0
      READ,((A(I,J),J=1,N),I=1,M)    DO 8 I=1,M
      NSUM=NTOT(A,M,N)               DO 8 J=1,N
      PRINT,NSUM                   8 NTOT=NTOT+X(I,J)
      STOP                           RETURN
      END                            END
$ENTRY
 3,3
 1,1,1,1,1,1,1,1,1
```

When the program is executed, the value printed is 7 and not 9! Here's why.

i)   When the mainline is compiled, sixteen words of memory are reserved for the set A since it has four rows and four columns. The first four are reserved for column 1, the next four for column 2, etc.. Initially, all sixteen words contain a value of zero.

ii) When the program is executed, the values of M and N are both 3. This means that the nine data values read by the mainline are stored in words 1 to 3, 5 to 7, and 9 to 11 of the sixteen reserved for A. (See the diagram below.)

iii) When the function NTOT is called, the address of the first word of A is passed to the subprogram. Since the parameters M and N are both equal to three, the subprogram assumes the array X(M,N) requires nine words of memory. (It has no reason to assume anything else.) Thus, when the elements of the parameter set X are summed, the total is obtained by adding the contents of the first nine words of memory reserved for A. The diagram below should make these ideas clear.

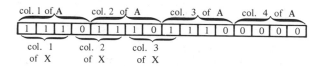

239

In order to obtain the desired answer of 9, the instructions in the subprogram must reference the correct words of memory. To cause this to happen, it is simply a matter of passing the overall dimensions of the set A, as well the part of A actually used, to the subprogram. The revised version would then be:

```
C EXAMPLE 9.3                      FUNCTION NTOT(X,K,L,M,N)
      INTEGER A(4,4)/16*0/         INTEGER X(K,L)
      READ,M,N                     NTOT=0
      READ,((A(I,J),J=1,N),I=1,M)  DO 8 I=1,M
      NSUM=NTOT(A,4,4,M,N)         DO 8 J=1,N
      PRINT,NSUM                 8 NTOT=NTOT+X(I,J)
      STOP                         RETURN
      END                          END
```

The foregoing program will cause proper correspondences between the elements of the argument array A and the parameter array X. In general, the rule is that if a parameter array is dimensioned at execution time and if the parameter array is a subset of the corresponding argument array, then the subprogram must be provided with the overall dimensions of the argument array as well as the portion of the array actually being processed if proper correspondence of elements is to be obtained. This extra information is not required in the case of one dimensional arrays because storage locations are assigned to variables in order of increasing subcript values.

The following example illustrates a somewhat different use of execution time dimensioning of arrays. In the program, the mainline segment reads in 100 REAL values and stores them in a set called VAL. The SUBROUTINE AVG is used to obtain ninety-nine different averages of elements in VAL. These are the averages of: all the values, all values except the first, all values except the first two, all values except the first three, etc.. The reader will realize that the algorithm used is by no means the most efficient but our purpose is to illustrate another use of execution time dimensioning of sets.

```
C EXAMPLE 9.4 MOVING AVERAGES      SUBROUTINE AVG(RESLT,Z,N)
      REAL VAL(100)                REAL Z(N)
      READ,VAL                     RESLT=0.
      DO 1 I=1,99                  DO 2 J=1,N
      CALL AVG(R,VAL(I),100-I)   2 RESLT=RESLT+Z(J)
    1 PRINT,R                      RESLT=RESLT/FLOAT(N)
      STOP                         RETURN
      END                          END
```

In the example, note that the second argument is the Ith element of the set VAL. The corresponding parameter is a set

240

having a number of elements equal to the value of the third argument. At execution time, the address of VAL(I) is passed to the subprogram and this address is used as the address of the first element in the parameter set Z. As the value of I increases by one each time the subprogram is called, the number of elements in the set Z decreases by one. Furthermore, since the first element in the set Z is the Ith element in the set VAL, the SUBROUTINE will process the desired set of values.

This example illustrates a case where an argument is an element of a set and the corresponding parameter is a set. This situation is permissible provided the storage occupied by the parameter set does not extend beyond the storage reserved by the argument set. In the example, an error would occur for instance, if the third argument had a value of 102-I because the last element of Z would correspond to the 101rst element of VAL. Since the compiler only reserves a hundred words of memory for VAL, the error results.

A slightly different use of the principle described in the foregoing example is illustrated by the program below. In this program, the FUNCTION subprogram COLSUM is used to obtain the sum of values in a column of a matrix.

```
C EXAMPLE 9.5 COLUMN SUMS
      REAL MATRIX(100,100)
      READ,NROWS,NCOLS
      READ,((MATRIX(I,J),J=1,NCOLS),I=1,NROWS)
      DO 1 J=1,NCOLS
    1 PRINT 50, J ,COLSUM(MATRIX(1,J),NROWS)
   50 FORMAT(' COLUMN',I3,' SUM=',F10.4)
      STOP
      END

      FUNCTION COLSUM(X,NROWS)
      REAL X(NROWS)
      COLSUM=0.
      DO 2 I=1,NROWS
    2 COLSUM=COLSUM+X(I)
      RETURN
      END
```

In this example, the mainline defines a matrix of 100 rows and 100 columns. Data values are read into the first NROWS and NCOLS as shown below.

241

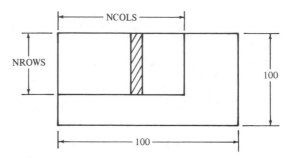

Only two arguments are passed to the subprogram. The address of the first word of storage reserved for the Jth column of MATRIX, and the number of elements in the column which contain values. Since storage is reserved column by column, the words of memory referenced in the parameter set X correspond to the the first NROWS of memory reserved for column J of the mainline set MATRIX. This example also illustrates that corresponding sets in the argument and parameter list need not have the same number of subscripts. One further point. If a parameter is a set, no check is made to see that the argument and parameter are of the same type. The allowed correspondences between arguments and parameters are summarized by the following three rules.

Rules of Argument/Parameter Correspondence

1.   If a parameter is a simple variable, its type must be the same as the corresponding argument value(s). The argument can be a constant, expression, simple variable, subscripted variable or set. If the argument is a set, the value taken on by the parameter variable is that found in the first storage locations used by the set.

2.   If a parameter is a set, there is no restriction on the type of value of the corresponding argument. Furthermore, the argument may be a constant, expression, simple variable, subscripted variable, or set. The one requirement is that the storage locations required by the parameter set must not exceed those used to store the argument value(s). (Recall that when a parameter is a set, it is always called by location.) If the argument is a subscripted variable, the parameter set must not require more storage locations than used to store all variables in the argument set beginning with those used to store the subscripted variable which is the argument. (Example program 9.4 illustrates this idea.)

3.   Under no circustances can a parameter be a constant, expression or subscripted variable.

242

9.4 Communication Between Segments Via A Common Block.

Communication between program segments can be achieved using argument and parameter lists. This two-way communication results from either having the parameter variable occupy the same storage locations as the argument (call by location), or by putting a copy of the argument value in the location reserved for the parameter (call by value). Another method is available to the WATFIV programmer. This second technique consists of:

i) Asking the compiler to reserve a block of storage which will be accessible from all program segments. (If desired, a shared block of memory can be accessed only from specific program segments.)

ii) Assigning variables used in a program segment to storage locations within the block in such a way that communicating variables share the same storage locations.

Consider the program structure below.

```
C MAINLINE                  SUBROUTINE NEW(....)
      COMMON X,Y                COMMON A,B
      .                         .
      CALL NEW(...)             .
      .                         .
      END                       END
```

In the foregoing program structure, the programmer has asked the compiler to reserve a block of memory which is to be common to (shared by) the program segments. A COMMON statement is used to make the request. The variables in the Common list are assigned sequentially to the storage locations of the "Common Block" of memory. Because of the statement "COMMON X,Y" in the mainline, the Common Block consists of two words of memory. The first word is used to store the value of X, and the second, the value of Y. In the subprogram, the compiler is told that values of A and B are located in the Common Block. Instructions in which A and B appear will reference the first two words of memory in the Block. Put another way, the addresses of X and A are the same and those of Y and B are the same. This of course means that changes in X are changes in A and that changes in Y are changes in B. The following diagram illustrates these ideas.

```
mainline variables        X         Y
                          ↓         ↓
Common Block           ┌────────┬────────┐
                       │ word 1 │ word 2 │
                       └────────┴────────┘
                          ↑         ↑
subprogram variables      A         B
```

The following program computes the average of N REAL
values and also determines the largest and smallest values
in the set. The important features of COMMON statements are
illustrated by this example.

```
C EXAMPLE 9.6 USING A COMMON BLOCK
      COMMON N,SMALL
      COMMON BIG
      REAL X(1000),SMALL/10.E70/,BIG/10.E-70/
      READ,N,(X(I),I=1,N)
      PRINT,AVG(X),SMALL,BIG
      STOP
      END

      FUNCTION AVG(X)
      COMMON M,HILOW(2)
      REAL X(M),SUM/0./
      DO 1 I=1,M
      SUM=SUM+X(I)
      IF(X(I).LT.HILOW(1))HILOW(1)=X(I)
    1 IF(X(I).GT.HILOW(2))HILOW(2)=X(I)
      AVG=SUM/FLOAT(M)
      RETURN
      END
```

Remarks.

  i) Variables appearing in COMMON statements which
      follow the first COMMON statement of a segment are
      appended to the end of the Common list and thus
      increase the length of the Common Block. For
      example, the pair of statements

```
      COMMON A,B,C
      COMMON I,J,K
```

      is equivalent to the single statement

```
      COMMON A,B,C,I,J,K
```

  ii) If a variable in a Common Block is initialized at
      compile time, the COMMON statement in which the
      variable appears must precede the statement which
      defines the initializing value. For example,

```
REAL BIG/10.E-70/
COMMON BIG
```

is invalid, whereas

```
COMMON BIG
REAL BIG/10.E-70/
```

is acceptable.

The reason is that the compiler must know the
address of the variable being initialized in order
to store the initial value.

iii) Sets of variables can be put in a Common Block. A
COMMON statement can be used to define the set or,
the set can be defined in a REAL or INTEGER
statement and the set name put in the Common list.
The set dimensions however, cannot be defined in
both a COMMON statement and a type declaration
statement. In the foregoing example, the statement
"COMMON M,HILOW(2)" is used to define the set
HILOW. The statement pair:

```
REAL HILOW(2)
COMMON M,HILOW
```

achieves the same result. The pair:

```
REAL HILOW(2)
COMMON M,HILOW(2)
```

would produce an error message since the set
dimensions are defined in two different statements.
When a COMMON statement is used to define a set of
variables, the first-letter rule determines the
type of variables in the set unless the set name
appears in a type declaration statement. For
example, the sequence

```
INTEGER HILOW
COMMON HILOW(2)
```

specifies that HILOW is a set of two INTEGER
variables.

iv) A set of variables which is dimensioned at
execution time cannot be in a Common Block. The
set must be included in the parameter list. The
values specifying the dimensions, however, may be
stored in a Common Block. (In the example, the
subprogram set X is dimensioned at execution time
and the dimension of the set, namely M, was stored
in the Common Block.) The following program

structure would produce an error message because
the array SET whose dimensions are supplied at
execution time is in a Common Block.

```
C MAINLINE                      SUBROUTINE INSET
      REAL X(1000)                  REAL SET(N)
      COMMON N,X                    COMMON N,SET
      READ,N                        .
      .                             .
      CALL INSET                    .
      ..                            .
      END                           END
```

v) The elements in the Common lists of different
program segments need not agree in number, type or
length. In the example program, for instance, the
Common list in the mainline has the items "N,SMALL,
and BIG". The Common list in the subprogram is
"M,HILOW". The correspondence between variables and
storage locations is shown below.

mainline variables   N   SMALL   BIG

                  ↓   ↓   ↓

Common Block | word 1 word 2 word 3 |

                  ↑   ↑   ↑

subprogram variables   M HILOW(1) HILOW(2)

No error message would result if a third segment
included a statement such as "COMMON K(3)" even
though K(1), K(2) and K(3) are INTEGER variables.
It should be noted, however, that there are <u>very</u>
few circumstances where a programmer wants to use
the same storage locations for variables of
different types.

The length of Common Block is the total number of
bytes of memory reserved by elements in the Common
list. Since REAL and INTEGER variables occupy four
bytes of memory, the length of the Common Blocks
defined in the mainline and the subprogram of the
example are twelve bytes. If the length of the
Common Block defined in two different segments is
not the same, a warning message is printed at
compile time.

There are two other rules which are included here for
the sake of completeness. The two error conditions described
below result from attempting to store a value in two
different storage locations. First, a subprogram variable
or set cannot appear in both a parameter list and a Common
list. The statement pair below, for example, is invalid.

```
SUBROUTINE SOLVE(X,A)
COMMON X
```

Second, an element of a Common list may also be an argument provided a subprogram does not assign a value to the corresponding parameter. The example structure below illustrates this type of error.

```
C MAINLINE                    SUBROUTINE NAME(Y)
      COMMON X                 COMMON Z
    .                          Z=...
    .                            .
      CALL NAME(X)             Y=....
    .                            .
      END                      END
```

The use of a Common Block should be viewed as one method of providing communication between program segments. All subprogram variables stored in a Common Block are, in effect, called by location. Since elements of different Common lists need not agree in number, type, or length, added flexibility is achieved.

9.5 Multiple Common Blocks

If a program contains a large number of segments, some of which share a great deal of data in common and others very little, it may be desirable to define several Common Blocks -- each with a unique name, to make the programming task easier. In addition, the use of several Common Blocks permits a certain degree of privacy in programs of a confidential nature such as payroll. Even if there is more than one Common Block, one block may be unlabelled. This no-name or unlabelled block is the type discussed in the previous section.

There are really only two differences between labelled (named) Common Blocks and the unlabelled ("blank") Common Block. These are:

    i) The labelled blocks have a name.

    ii) A special program segment called a BLOCK DATA subprogram must be used to perform compile-time initialization of variables located in a labelled Common Block.

Definition of Labelled Blocks

A COMMON statement is used to define a labelled block. Several blocks may be defined in the same statement. Previously defined blocks may be "added to" by other COMMON statements.

Example (i)

        COMMON /AREA1/ A,B,C

This statement defines a Common Block called AREA1. Assuming A,B and C are simple REAL variables, the length of the block is twelve bytes (three words). When defining labelled blocks, the block name is enclosed in slashes.

Example (ii)

        COMMON P,Q,R/NAME1/I,Z(20)/NAME2/R,S,T,U

This single statement defines three Common Blocks. Since no name precedes the elements P, Q and R, the storage locations for these variables are in the unlabelled Common Block. The items I and Z are in a block called "NAME1". R,S,T,U are in a "NAME2" block. The single statment above is equivalent to the following three statements.

        COMMON P,Q,R
        COMMON /NAME1/I,Z(20)
        COMMON /NAME2/R,S,T,U

Example (iii)

        COMMON /BLK1/X,P//A,S,T/BLK2/M
        COMMON U,V/BLK1/R/BLK2/Z

In this example, three Common Blocks are defined in the first COMMON statement. They are: BLK1 with elements X and P; the no-name (unlabelled) block (indicated by a pair of consecutive slashes with no name between them). The elements A, S and T are in the unlabelled block; BLK2 has the single element M. The second COMMON statement specifies that additional variables are to be stored in each of the three blocks. Since no block name precedes the elements U and V, they are added to the end of the unlabelled block. The elements R and Z are added to the end of BLK1 and BLK2 respectively. The pair of COMMON statements in this example has the same effect as the single statement

        COMMON A,S,T,U,V /BLK1/X,P,R /BLK2/M,Z

COMMON Statement Rules

The general form of a COMMON statement is:

COMMON x1,x2,x3,...

i) Each x item consists of a list of variables, array names or array names followed by dimension information. Optionally, each list may be preceded by a name enclosed in slashes or a two consecutive slashes. Note that no commas precede or follow a slash. The double slash indicates that elements of the list are to be put in the unlabelled Common Block. If no slash follows the word COMMON, list elements preceding the first slash belong to the unlabelled Common Block. Those which follow a "/name/" belong to a block of the indicated name.

ii) If dimension information for an array is present in a COMMON statement, no other statement can contain the dimension information. The array type, however, may be specified by an explicit type declaration statement.

iii) Variables or arrays cannot be put in more than one Common Block.

iv) Sets which are dimensioned at execution time cannot be put in a Common Block.

v) Storage locations in a labelled block may only be initilized by means of a BLOCK DATA subprogram. Unlabelled Common Block storage locations can be initialized by a type declaration statement or DATA statement which follows the COMMON statement.

vi) Blocks need not have the same length in different program segments. A warning message is printed at compile time.

9.6 BLOCK DATA Subprograms

A BLOCK DATA subprogram has one purpose -- to assign initial values to storage locations in Common Blocks. It is the only method available for initializing storage locations in labelled Common Blocks but may also be used, at the programmer's discretion, to specify initial values for storage locations in the unlabelled Common Block.

The general form of a BLOCK DATA subprogram is as follows.

```
BLOCK DATA
    .
    .
    .
END
```

The statements between the BLOCK DATA statement (which must be the first statement) and the END statement (which must be the last statement) are used to:

a) Define the structure of the Common Blocks containing storage locations to be given initial values.

b) Specify the initial values.

Example (i)

```
BLOCK DATA
COMMON /BLK1/I,A,S(12)
INTEGER I/2/
REAL S/12*0./
END
```

In this example, values are assigned at compile time to storage locations in the Common Block called BLK1. An INTEGER value of 2 is stored in the first word of memory of the block. The second word (used to store the value of the variable A) is left unchanged and the remaining twelve words in the block are given a bit pattern representing the REAL value zero.

Example (ii)

```
BLOCK DATA
IMPLICIT INTEGER(A-D),REAL(I,N)
REAL E(4)
COMMON B,C /BBLK/E,F
COMMON /ABLK/INS(3,2)//R
REAL B,E/4*10./
DATA B,C/2.,3/,((INS(I,J),J=1,2),I=1,3)
*  /2*1.,2*2.,2*3./
INTEGER R/999/,F/0/
END
```

The effect of the BLOCK DATA subprogram is to initialize storage locations as shown below.

Unlabelled Block	2.	3	999		

ABLK Block	1.	2.	3.	1.	2.	3.

BBLK Block	10.	10.	10.	10.	10.	0

Rules For BLOCK DATA Subprograms

i) A BLOCK DATA statement must be the first statement. An END statement must be the last statement.

ii) A BLOCK DATA subprogram cannot contain any executable statements. (Its purpose is strictly to define initial values.) The only types of statements permitted are: IMPLICIT, type declaration statements, COMMON, DIMENSION and DATA.

iii) An IMPLICIT statement, if used, must immediately follow the BLOCK DATA statement.

iv) All initializing values of a Common Block must be located in the same BLOCK DATA subprogram.

v) The standard rules for ordering statements must be followed. These are as follows.

    a) DATA statements must follow any DIMENSION, COMMON or type declaration statement which references the variable or array.

    b) If a type declaration statement is used to provide initial values for a simple variable, it must follow any COMMON statement which references the variable.

    c) If a type declaration statement is used to define initial values for an array, it must follow the COMMON or DIMENSION statement which defines the dimensions of the array.

9.7 EQUIVALENCE (Sharing Storage Within The Same Segment)

The topic of this section does not rightfully belong in this chapter -- it has nothing to do with subprograms. However, the concepts necessary to understand the material of this section were not presented until the beginning of this chapter. This is the reason for its inclusion here.

Recall that COMMON statements are used as means of causing variables in different program segments to share the same storage locations. The EQUIVALENCE statement on the other hand is used to cause variables in the same program segment to share the same storage locations. For example, if the variables I and J are Equivalenced using the statement

EQUIVALENCE (I,J)

then any change in the value of I is automatically a change in the value of J and vice-versa.

The two programs below illustrate the effect of Equivalencing a pair of variables. In the program on the left, two INTEGER variables are Equvivalenced and in the one on the right, an INTEGER and a REAL variable are Equivalenced.

```
EQUIVALENCE (I,J)          EQUIVALENCE(I,A)
INTEGER I/1/               INTEGER I/1/
PRINT,J                    PRINT,A
STOP                       STOP
END                        END
```

Result: A value of 1 is   Result: A value of
        printed.   0.0000051E-79 is printed.

The reason for having different values printed in the two cases is not difficult to understand. In the program on the left, the variables I and J (both INTEGER) are Equivalenced. This means they are synonyms and are stored in the same word of memory. That is, the bit pattern for I and the bit pattern for J is the same. When the statement "PRINT,J" is encountered, the bit pattern stored in the word of memory is treated as that of an INTEGER value and therefore has a value of one. In the program on the right, the same bit pattern is present in the word of memory whose contents will be printed. This time, however, the print statement is "PRINT,A" and therefore the bit pattern is interpreted as being that of a REAL value. Put another way, the bit patterns for an INTEGER value of one and a REAL value of .0000051E-79 are identical.

Why use the EQUIVALENCE statement? One reason is to permit different programmers who are writing parts of the same program to use variable names which are meaningful to them. When the parts are put together to form the program segment, EQUIVALENCE statements are added to tell the compiler that different variable names are really synonyms for each other and are to refer to the same storage locations. Even if a program is written by one person, he may inadvertently mispell a variable name in one or more program segments. By using an EQUIVALENCE statement, all spellings can be made equivalent. A second reason involves Equivalencing a simple variable with an element of a set in order to use a simple variable name in a statement where a subcripted variable is not permitted. By doing so, a number of Assignment statements can be eliminated. For example, suppose a series of DO statement parameters are to be read in from cards. The three parameters are to be stored in a set called PARAM. Somewhere -- later in the program -- the values are to be used in a DO statement. Since DO parameters cannot be subscripted variables, the problem could be overcome without using any Assignment statements as shown in the following program.

```
      C EXAMPLE 9.7 EQUIVALENCE OF DO PARAMETERS
            INTEGER PARAM(3)
            EQUIVALENCE (PARAM(1),ISTART),(PARAM(2),IEND)
            EQUIVALENCE (PARAM(3),IBUMP)
          1 READ,PARAM
            .
            .
            DO 2 I=ISTART,IEND,IBUMP
            .
            .
          2 CONTINUE
            .
```

Note that in the foregoing program structure, no Assignment statements were required to assign the values in PARAM to the DO parameter variables.

The third and perhaps most important reason for Equivalencing variables is to save memory. Suppose X and NUM are two arrays having 300 and 450 variables respectively. Provided the values of X and NUM are used at different times in the same program, memory could be saved by Equivalencing the two sets. The program structure would be of the following type.

```
                  REAL X(300)
                  INTEGER NUM(450)
                  EQUIVALENCE (X(1),NUM(1))
                  READ,X
  statements to   ⎧  .
  process the X   ⎨  .
    values        ⎩  .
                  READ,NUM
  statements to   ⎧  .
  process the     ⎨  .
  NUM values      ⎩  .
                     .
```

Without the EQUIVALENCE statement in the foregoing example, the array area for the program would be 300 words larger. In situations where memory space is at a premium, this technique may be valuable. In the foregoing example, either or both of the set names "X" and "NUM" could have been used instead of "X(1)" and "NUM(1)". Use of a set name in an EQUIVALENCE statement is effectively the same as using the name of the subscripted variable which occupies the first storage locations used to store the values in the set.

Rules For EQUIVALENCE

The EQUIVALENCE statement is used to inform the compiler that two or more variables within a segment are to share the same storage locations. This means that Equivalenced variables have the same address in the computer memory and also that they have the same bit pattern.

1. The EQUIVALENCE statement has the general form

         EQUIVALENCE (listl), (list2), (list3), ...

    where each list is a sequence of variable names and/or array names separated by commas. If a list element is an array name, it implies that the first variable in the array (each subscript value is one) shares the same storage locations as other variables in the list. Regardless of the number of dimensions of an array, an array name may (optionally) be followed by a single subscript value. If the subscript has a value of "K", it means the variable in the Kth word of memory used to store the variables in the array is to be Equivalenced. In the following example, the variable MAT(3,2) is Equivalenced to the variable A. Recall that variables are stored column-by-column.

         REAL MAT(4,2)
         EQUIVALENCE (MAT(7),A)

    This is the one exception to the rule that a subscripted variable must have the same number of subscripts as there are dimensions in the array.

2. Any assignment of initial values to Equivalenced variables must be done by a statement which follows the EQUIVALENCE statement. The sequence

         REAL X/2./
         EQUIVALENCE (X,B)

    is invalid whereas

         EQUIVALENCE (X,B)
         REAL X/2./

    is valid.

3. Subprogram parameters and variables used in ASSIGN statements cannot be Equivalenced. Each of the following pairs of statements would cause an error.

       SUBROUTINE WR(X)   EQUIVALENCE (J,K)
       EQUIVALENCE (X,Z)   ASSIGN 12 TO J

4. An EQUIVALENCE statement cannot imply that a variable is stored in two different locations. Consider the following example.

          INTEGER A(10),B(10)
          EQUIVALENCE (A(1),B(1)), A(2),B(5))

The error occurs since if A(1) and B(1) are made Equivalent then A(2) and B(2) must of necessity also be equivalent. The list "(A(2),B(5))" attempts to contradict this fact.

5. There are three rules with respect to Equivalencing variables in a Common Block.

a) In any list in an EQUIVALENCE statement, at most one element of the list can be in a Common Block.

b) If an array is Equivalenced to a variable in a Common Block, it may cause the Block to be "extended to the right". This is not an error but may cause unexpected results since other variables in the Common Block may unintentionally be Equivalenced to elements of the array. Consider the following example.

          REAL X(4)
          COMMON A
          EQUIVALENCE (A,X)
          COMMON B

The preceding four statements result in a Common Block having a length of 16 bytes. The variable B occupies the same storage locations as the variable X(2).

c) An EQUIVALENCE statement cannot be used to extend a Common Block to the left. That is, an EQUIVALENCE statement cannot cause the first variable in a Common Block to be Equivalenced to any array variable other than the first one in the array. The statement sequence below illustrates this type of error.

```
          REAL X(5)
          COMMON A
          EQUIVALENCE (A,X(3))
```

The foregoing statements are attempting to force the alignment indicated in the following diagram.

↓ boundary of Common Block

		A		
X(1)	X(2)	X(3)	X(4)	X(5)

Exercise 9.2

1. For each of the following, state the values printed and the last value assigned to each variable.

```
a)    COMMON A(3)              SUBROUTINE ZIP
      REAL A/1.,2*2./          COMMON X,Y,Z
      CALL ZIP                 Z=AMAX1(X/Y,Y/Z)
      STOP                     RETURN
      END                      END

b)    COMMON J,K,L             FUNCTION KNOTS(M)
      INTEGER J/2/,K/10/,L/3/  COMMON N,NN,NNN
      M=0                      KNOTS=M+N*NN/NNN
      DO 1 I=J,K,L             IF(KNOTS.GT.30) STOP
      M=M+I*J/K                RETURN
    1 PRINT,KNOTS(M)           END
      END

c)    COMMON X/TWO/Y           SUBROUTINE NUTS
      COMMON /TWO/Z//W         COMMON /TWO/A,B//C,D
      REAL X/2./,W/3./         B=AMIN1(C,D)
      CALL NUTS                A=AMAX1(B,C,D)
      PRINT,W,X,Y,Z            RETURN
      STOP                     END
      END

d)    EQUIVALENCE(X,Y)
      REAL X(2,3)/3*1.,3*2./
      REAL Y(6)
      PRINT,(Y(J),J=2,6,2)
      STOP
      END
e)    EQUIVALENCE (A,X,I,J)
      REAL A/2./,B/3./
      IF(X.NE.B) I=6
      PRINT,J
      STOP
      END
```

256

2. Describe the error in each of the following.

a) REAL X(3)/3*0./
    COMMON A(3)/3*0./

b) COMMON /ONE/A//B
    REAL A/2./,B/4./

c) REAL B(5,2),C(10)
    COMMON B,C
    EQUIVALENCE (B(4),C(1))

d) REAL B(5,2),C(10)
    COMMON B
    EQUIVALENCE(B(1),C(3))

e) SUBROUTINE ANDON(X,Y,Z)
    REAL X(10)
    COMMON Y
    RETURN
    END

f) COMMON A   SUBROUTINE NEXT(X,Y)
    REAL A/40./   COMMON Z
    CALL NEXT(A,B)   X=Z+Y
    PRINT,B   RETURN
    STOP   END
    END

3. Consider the following sequence of statements.

```
      INTEGER ARRAY(3,4,5),MAT1(6,5)
      INTEGER MAT2(6,5),VEC(20,3),STRING(60)
      EQUIVALENCE (ARRAY,MAT1,VEC)
      EQUIVALENCE (ARRAY(31),MAT2,STRING(31))
      DO 1 I=1,60
    1 STRING(I)=I
```

a) What is the value of each of the following variables?
   STRING(4), VEC(1,8), MAT1(3,4), ARRAY(2,2,2)

b) For each of the following, name three other variables
   which share the same storage locations.
   STRING(2), VEC(2,13), ARRAY(2,4,1), MAT2(3,4)

c) Describe the output produced by the formatted PRINT
   statements which follow.

```
      PRINT 900,MAT1
  900 FORMAT('0',6I5)

      PRINT 901,(VEC(K,2),K=1,20)
  901 FORMAT('0',2I10)

      PRINT 902,((MAT2(K,L),L=1,5),K=1,6)
  902 FORMAT('0',5I6)

      PRINT 903,(((ARRAY(I,J,K),J=1,4),K=1,5),I=1,3)
  904 FORMAT('0',1(T2,5(4I3,2X)))
```

9.8 Multiple Entries To Subprograms.

When a subprogram is called, control normally passes to the first executable statement in the subprogram. This section describes a means of entering a subprogram at a statement other than the first executable statement in the subprogram. The method involves the use of ENTRY statements at those points in the subprogram where entry is permitted. The general form of the ENTRY statement is shown below.

ENTRY name (parameter list)

Note that an ENTRY statement does not contain either the word FUNCTION or the word SUBROUTINE. The name which follows the word ENTRY in an ENTRY statement can be any valid WATFIV name. The parameter list has the same purpose as it does when used in a FUNCTION or SUBROUTINE statement.

To illustrate the use of an ENTRY statement, recall that whenever a part of a matrix is used in a subprogram, the overall dimensions of the matrix (as defined in the calling segment), as well as the dimensions of the part to be used in the subprogram, must be passed to the subprogram. Now suppose a program is required to read ten different matrices and calulate the row sums of each. The following program could be used. Study it carefully as it illustrates most of the important features of ENTRY statement usage.

```
C EXAMPLE 9.8 MAINLINE
      REAL MATRIX(100,100)
      CALL DIMENS(MATRIX,100,100)
      DO 1 I=1,10
      READ,MROWS,NCOLS
      CALL READ(MROWS,NCOLS)
      CALL SUMALL(SUM)
    1 PRINT,SUM
      STOP
      END

      SUBROUTINE DIMENS(X,KROWS,LCOLS)
      REAL X(KROWS,LCOLS)
      RETURN
      ENTRY READ(M,N)
      DO 1 I=1,M
    1 READ,(X(I,J),J=1,N)
      RETURN
      ENTRY SUMALL(TOTAL)
      TOTAL=0.
      DO 2 I=1,M
      DO 2 J=1,N
    2 TOTAL=TOTAL+X(I,J)
      RETURN
      END
```

In the example subprogram, there are, in effect, three different SUBROUTINES. DIMENS is simply used to obtain the overall dimensions of the matrix. DIMENS is only called once by the mainline. The statement "ENTRY READ(M,N)" defines the beginning of a sequence of statements which read and store data values in the first M rows and N columns of X. Note that is not necessary to include either X or the overall dimensions of X in the parameter list of the ENTRY point called READ. This information had been previously passed to the subprogram with the call to DIMENS. The routine with the ENTRY point SUMALL needs only one parameter. The other information has been previously passed to the subprogram using calls to DIMENS and READ.

The rules of ENTRY statement usage are as follows:

   i)   Any number of ENTRY statements may be used in a subprogram. Each has the general form:

         ENTRY name (parameter list)

         where "name" is any valid WATFIV name and the parameters must agree with the arguments as described previously at the end of Section 9.3.

  ii)   Within a SUBROUTINE, each ENTRY statement defines an ENTRY point of a SUBROUTINE. In a FUNCTION subprogram, each must be the ENTRY point of a FUNCTION.

 iii)   All declaration statements, Statement Functions, etc. which are required in any part of the subprogram must be placed at the beginning of the entire subprogram.

  iv)   Variables appearing in a parameter list need not agree in number type or oder with those of other parameter lists used in the subprogram. However, if the same variable appears in more than one parameter list it must always be called the same way (by location or by value). For example, the following structure is not permitted.

         FUNCTION name1(X)
         ...
         ...
         ENTRY name2(/X/)
         ...
         ...
         END

   v)   An ENTRY statement cannot be placed within the range of a DO-loop.

vi)   ENTRY statements are not executed. At execution
time, their existence is ignored if they fall
within the range of a sequence of statements which
is being executed.

vii)   When control passes to an ENTRY point, the value
of any non-parameter variable used in the
subprogram is the value most recently assigned to
it.

The use of ENTRY points is often a convenience when:
two subprograms are very similar; only a part of a
subprogram is required; if initial values must be passed to
a subprogram. Keep in mind that multiple entries to
subprograms are almost never a necessity, simply a
convenience.

9.9 Multiple Returns From SUBROUTINES

The first RETURN encountered in a SUBROUTINE normally
causes control to be transferred to the first statement
following the CALL. In some circumstances, it may be that
the processing done in the SUBROUTINE requires that control
should be returned to some other statement. For example, an
error condition detected in the SUBROUTINE may require that
control be passed to an error routine in the mainline. To
provide alternate return points from a SUBROUTINE (It makes
little sense in the case of FUNCTION subprograms since they
are typically used to calculate a single value.) the calling
segment supplies the SUBROUTINE with a list of the statement
numbers to which control can be returned.

In the following program, a normal RETURN is executed if
all elements of a set X are positive; to statement 74 if all
elements have negative values and to statement 12 otherwise.

```
C EXAMPLE 9.9                    SUBROUTINE TESTX(X,*,*)
      REAL X(10)                 REAL X(10)
      READ,X                     IF(X(1).EQ.0.)RETURN 2
      CALL TESTX(X,&74,&12)      POSNEG=X(1)/ABS(X(1))
      PRINT,'X POSITIVE'         DO 1 I=2,10
      STOP                       IF(POSNEG*X(I))3,3,1
   74 PRINT,'X NEGATIVE'       1 CONTINUE
      STOP                       RETURN 1
   12 PRINT,'X MIXED'          3 RETURN 2
      STOP                       END
      END
```

The foregoing program illustrates the important points concerning the use of the multiple RETURN feature. These are:

   i)   In the calling segment, the argument list has the general form

$$(\ldots,\&s1,\ldots,\&s2,\ldots,\&s3,\ldots)$$

where "s1", "s2", etc. are statement numbers of executable statements to which control is permitted to return . Each such statement number is preceded by an "&" symbol.

   ii)   In the SUBROUTINE, an asterisk appears in the parameter list in those positions which correspond to the return points defined in the argument list. To return to the statement following the CALL, a simple RETURN statement is used. To return to the statement whose number is the nth return point in the argument list, the statement "RETURN n" is used in the subprogram. The value of "n" in "RETURN n" is usually an INTEGER constant but its value can also be assigned to an INTEGER variable. For example,

        NEXT=4
        RETURN NEXT

is permissible provided at least four return points have been specified in the argument list.

9.10 EXTERNAL Subprograms

Suppose a subprogram is required which will find the maximum and minimum values of any function f(x). Suppose f(x) is defined for values of x of 1,2,3,...,100. O.K., so what's the problem? Well, if our routine is called MAXMIN, say, then we require some means of telling MAXMIN the name of the function "f" to be used in any particular instance. In other words, one of the arguments in any call to MAXMIN must be the name of the desired function. The corresponding parameter will "take on" this name at execution time. An EXTERNAL statement is used in the calling segment to specify that a particular argument is to be treated as the name of a built-in function or subprogram.

Suppose the largest and smallest values of the following two functions are required.

261

$$FA(i) = (50-i)^2/i^2 \quad \text{for } i=1,2,\ldots,100$$

$$FB(i) = 120 - (i-60)^2 \quad \text{for } i=1,2,\ldots,100$$

The following program could be used.

```
C MAINLINE                          FUNCTION FA(J)
      EXTERNAL FA,FB                 FA=(50.-J)**2/J**2
      CALL MAXMIN(BIG,SMALL,FA)      RETURN
      PRINT,'FA MAX AND MIN',        END
    * BIG,SMALL
      CALL MAXMIN(BIG,SMALL,FB)      FUNCTION FB(K)
      PRINT,'FB MAX AND MIN',        FB=120-(K-60)**2
    * BIG,SMALL                      RETURN
      STOP                           END
      END


      SUBROUTINE MAXMIN(BIG,SMALL,FUN)
      BIG=SMALL=FUN(1)
      DO 1 I=1,100
      X=FUN(I)
      IF(X.GT.BIG) BIG=X
    1 IF(X.LT.SMALL) SMALL=X
      RETURN
      END
```

In this program, the SUBROUTINE MAXMIN is called twice. Each time it is called, the last element in the argument list is the name of the function to be used by MAXMIN during its execution. In the mainline, the statement

EXTERNAL FA , FB

informs the compiler that FA and FB are the names of two subprograms. It means that if either or both of FA and FB appear in an argument list then the name of the subprogram is to be passed to the called segment. (In actual fact, the address of the first executable instruction in the argument subprogram is passed to the called segment.)

In a subprogram, those parameters which correspond to arguments which appear in EXTERNAL statements are "dummy" subprogram names. In the example, for instance, the name FUN took the place of the subprogram name which was passed to MAXMIN at execution time. Note that the called subprogram (MAXMIN in the example) must know the number and type of arguments required to call an unknown subprogram.

The rules of usage of an EXTERNAL statement are few. The general structure of a segment containing one or more EXTERNAL statements is the following.

```
        EXTERNAL namel, name2, ...
        .
        .
        ... name(..namel,...,name2,...)
        .
        END
```

where: "namel", "name2", etc. are names of subprograms or
         built-in functions which, in the case of FUNCTIONs,
         may require their type to be specified.

         "name" is the name of a subprogram to which any
         element of the EXTERNAL list can be passed as an
         argument.

   An EXTERNAL statement appears only in a calling segment.
In the called segment, parameters corresponding to arguments
which appear in an EXTERNAL list are "dummy" subprogram
names. The called segment is written knowing that the dummy
name will be replaced at execution time. The argument list
used with the dummy name is not changed at execution time
and therefore it must be appropriate for the external
subprogram.

Exercise 9.3   (Multiple Entries, Returns and EXTERNAL)

1. For each of the following, state the last value
   assigned to each variable used in the program.

```
    a)   A=B=2                   SUBROUTINE X(P,Q,R)
         CALL X(A,B,C)           R=P/Q*Q
         CALL Y(A,B,C)           ENTRY Y(A,B,C)
         STOP                    Z=AMAX1(R,C,P)
         END                     RETURN
                                 END

    b)   REAL I                  REAL FUNCTION I(J)
         INTEGER J/3/            I=J*2/8
         K=I(J)                  RETURN
         K=L(K)                  ENTRY L(M)
         STOP                    L=J+M
         END                     RETURN
                                 END

    c)   INTEGER A/2/            SUBROUTINE B(/C/)
         CALL B(A)               INTEGER C
         A=A/3                   C=C*2
         CALL D(A)               RETURN
         STOP                    ENTRY D(J)
         END                     J=J**3/C
                                 RETURN
                                 END
```

   d) In (c), let "C" be called by location.

```
    e)      INTEGER I/2/,J/3/        SUBROUTINE X(L,M,N,*)
            CALL X(I,J,K,&2)         N=MAX0(L/M,M/L,M,L)
            K=MAX0(K,J)              IF(N.GT.L) RETURN 1
         2 STOP                      RETURN
            END                      END

    f)      REAL A(3)/3.,2.,1./      SUBROUTINE T(*,X)
         1 CALL T(&2,A)              REAL X(3)
            STOP                     IF(X(1)*X(3).LT.X(2))X(2)=3
         2 A(3)=3                    IF(-X(2)+X(3))1,2,2
            CALL T(&1,A)          1 N=X(3)
            STOP                     RETURN N
            END                   2 RETURN
                                     END

    g)      INTEGER F,J/5/,A         INTEGER FUNCTION A(K,L)
            EXTERNAL F               A=K(L)/2
            J=A(F,J)/2               RETURN
            STOP                     END
            END                      INTEGER FUNCTION F(M)
                                     F=2*M/3
                                     RETURN
                                     END
```

2. Identify the error(s) in each of the following.

```
    a)      CALL A(2.,3.,Z)          SUBROUTINE A(X,Y,Z)
            CALL B                   Z=X+Y
            STOP                     ENTRY B
            END                      B=2*Z
                                     RETURN
                                     END

    b)      J=ISQ(2)                 FUNCTION ISQ(M)
         1 PRINT,J                   IF(M.EQ.0) RETURN
            STOP                     RETURN 1
            END                      END

    c)      B=ZIP(10.,SQRT)          FUNCTION ZIP(A,F)
            PRINT,B                  EXTERNAL F
            STOP                     ZIP=F(A)
            END                      RETURN
                                     END
```

9.11 Summary

1. The basic unit of memory is called a byte. It consists of
   eight bits (ones ond zeros) and has an address.   Other
   units of   memory are a half-word (two bytes), full word
   (four bytes), and double word (eight bytes).   A REAL
   value   and   an INTEGER value each occupy one word of
   memory.

2. For each program segment, the compiler uses a set of consecutive memory locations to store the instructions, simple variables, constants and expressions used in the segment. All arrays, Common Blocks and Equivalenced variables are stored in a common area of memory.

3. A subprogram parameter can be called by value or called by location. If called by value, the value of the subprogram parameter is stored in memory locations which are part of those reserved by the compiler for that segment. If called by location, references to the parameter variable are references to the storage locations in which the calling segment value (argument) is stored.

4. The assignment of storage locations to variables in two-dimensional arrays (matrices) is done column-by-column. For higher dimensioned arrays, the rightmost subscript varies least rapidly when making the assignment of variables to storage locations.

5. Since parameter arrays are called by location, it is possible to specify the dimensions of a parameter array at execution time. If the parameter array is a subset of the argument array, the overall dimensions of the argument array as well as the dimensions of the subset should be passed to the subprogram. This will insure proper correspondences between variables and storage locations.

6. Program segments can communicate with one another by causing variables in different segments to share the same storage locations. This is done by defining one or more Common Blocks of memory. Variables in blocks which are labelled (have a name) can only be given initial values by using a BLOCK DATA subprogram.

7. Variables in the same segment of a program can be made to share the same storage locations by using an EQUIVALENCE statement.

8. Control may pass to a statement in a SUBROUTINE or FUNCTION subprogram to other than the first executable statement. This is done by specifying that certain statements are valid ENTRY points of the subprogram.

9. A SUBROUTINE subprogram may return control to a statement other than one following the CALL statement. This is done by making the statement numbers of the return points arguments in the call to the subprogram.

10. The name of a subprogram may be passed to a called segment. An EXTERNAL statement specifies those subprogram names which may be used as arguments.

Programming Problems

In the following problems, make up a suitable mainline segment to test the subprogram whenever a specific mainline is not requested.

9.1   Write a SUBROUTINE subprogram which has two parameters: N, a positive INTEGER value; K a set of N INTEGER values. The subprogram should replace the value of K(I) with K(I+1) - K(I) for I equal one thru N-1. The value of K(N) should be set equal to K(1)-K(N). Write a mainline segment which reads a value of N (no larger than 20) and N more values which are stored in a mainline vector. Use the subprogram to replace the values read with the differences described above. Print the contents of the mainline vector before and after the call to the subprogram.

9.2   Write a SUBROUTINE subprogram to assign a set of M*N REAL values stored in a vector to the first M rows and N columns of a matrix. Assume M and N are less than ten. The mainline segment should read values of M and N, then MN more values. The subprogram should assign the first N values to row one of the parameter matrix, the next N values to row two, etc.. The subprogram will have six elements in the parameter list: the overall dimensions of the matrix; the values of M and N; the vector containing the MN values; the matrix in which the values are to be stored.

9.3   Write a SUBROUTINE subprogram called MERGE to "merge" two sets of ordered INTEGER values. The number of values in each set should be passed to the subprogram. If the names of the two sets of values are "S1" and "S2" and have M and N elements respectively, the SUBROUTINE should create a third set of M+N values made up of the union of the values in S1 and S2. The values in the third set should also be in order of increasing magnitude. For example, suppose M=5 and S1=(2, 3, 7, 8, 9); N=4 and S2=(3, 5, 7, 10). The merged set is then (2, 3, 3, 5, 7, 7, 8, 9, 10). The merging process can be done efficiently by processing elements in S1 and S2 in order and selecting the lower value of the two being considered as the next value to be put in the merged set. In the mainline, assume M and N are less than ten.

9.4 Use the subprogram written to solve the previous problem to merge K sets of values. Assume K is five or less. This can be done by having the mainline segment: read the value of K; read the first two sets of values; merge them using the subprogram; read the next set of values; merge it with the previous merged sets; read the next set; etc. The second, third, etc. data cards should each contain the number of values in the set followed by the

266

actual values in the set. (The first data card contains the number of sets.)

9.5   Write a FUNCTION subprogram called CENTIL having parameters X, N and K where X is a set of N REAL values in order of increasing magnitude and K is one of 10, 20, 30, ..., 90. The value of CENTIL calculated in the subprogram should be the Kth percentile of the values in X. The Kth percentile is a value such that K percent of the values are less than it and 100-K percent of the values are greater. Use CENTIL to calulate the tenth thru ninetieth percentiles of a set of fifteen typical marks out of one-hundred.

9.6   The Arithmetic Mean (AM), Geometric Mean (GM) and Harmonic Mean (HM) of a set of N values X1, X2, X3, ..., Xn are defined as follows.

$$AM = \frac{X1 + X2 + X3 + \ldots + Xn}{N}$$

$$GM = \sqrt[n]{X1 \; X2 \; X3 \; \ldots \; Xn}$$

$$HM = \frac{N}{\frac{1}{X1} + \frac{1}{X2} + \frac{1}{X3} + \ldots + \frac{1}{Xn}}$$

Write a **single** program segment called AM in which GM and HM are ENTRY points in the segment. Each of AM, GM, and HM is to be a FUNCTION subprogram to calculate the corresponding mean of a set of N REAL values.

9.7   The N coefficients of an (N-1)th degree polynomial f(x) can be chosen so that the curve will pass thru any N points in the XY plane. Suppose (X1,Y1), (X2,Y2), ..., (Xn,Yn) are N points in the XY plane. The value of f(x) which passes thru all N points is given by

$$f(x) = \frac{\sum_{i=1}^{N} (A_i \, y_i)/(x-x_i)}{\sum_{i=1}^{N} \frac{A_i}{x-x_i}}$$

where $A_i = \dfrac{1}{\prod_{j \neq i} (x_i - x_j)}$

Write a REAL valued FUNCTION subprogram called INTERP which has two elements in the parameter list -- the value of N and the value of X for which the function value is to be calculated. In the subprogram and in the calling segment, define a Common Block containing a

267

table of two rows and fifty columns. The row one values
are the values of the X coordinates, those in row two,
the corresponding Y coordinates. To test the subprogram,
use eight data points generated in the following way. In
row one store values of 0, 45, 90, 135, ..., 315. In row
two store values of the sine of the corresponding angle
in row one. Assume the row one values are in degrees.
Use the subprogram INTERP to calculate estimates of the
sine of angles of 15, 60, 105, 150, 195, 240. 285 and
330 degrees. For each of these print the estimated sine
value, the true sine value, and the percent error
resulating from using the approximating function.

9.8   A programming project. In physics, there are five
commonly used equations which describe the relationships
between distance (s), acceleration (a), final velocity
(v), time (t) and initial velocity (u) of a moving body.
Each of the five equations can be identified by the
variable which does not appear in the equation. For this
reason, they are sometimes known as the "SAVTU"
equations. The equations are as follows.

"S" equation: $a = (v-u)/t$

"A" equation: $v = t(u+v)/2$

"V" equation: $s = ut + (at^2)/2$

"T" equation: $v^2 = u^2 + 2as$

"U" equation: $s = vt - (at^2)/2$

Write a SUBROUTINE subprogram called SAVTU which has the
parameters DATA and CODES defined by:

REAL DATA(5)
INTEGER CODES(5)

Let the values in DATA be the values of distance,
acceleration, final velocity, time and intial velocity.
The values in CODES indicate which values are known and
which are to be calculated. If CODES(I) is zero it means
the value of DATA(I) is to be calculated by the
subprogram and stored in DATA(I). If CODES(I) is 1, it
means DATA(I) can be used in the calculation of the
unknown values. Note that in any call to the subprogram,
that at least three values in CODES must equal one. Use
any method you like in the subprogram to calculate the
unknown values. Test your subprogram on at least the ten
different ways that three values of the five can be
specified as known. If you wish, include in your
subprogram a multiple return feature which will return
to an error routine in the calling segment if fewer than
three of the CODES values are 1.

PART II

OTHER TYPES OF VALUES

CHAPTER 10   OTHER TYPES OF VARIABLES -- THE CONCEPTS

Questions Answered In This Chapter

1. What types of variables (other than REAL and INTEGER)
   can be used in WATFIV and what is the purpose of each?

2. What programming principles and concepts are common to
   these other types of variables?

10.1 Other Types Of Variables.

Part I of this book has described the rules for writing
WATFIV programs which use REAL and INTEGER values. Almost
all problems which are solved with the aid of a computer can
be programmed using only these two types of values. In
WATFIV, however, there are three other types of values which
can be defined and manipulated using the statements
described in Part I of this book. The names given to these
other types are CHARACTER, LOGICAL and COMPLEX. Before
describing the purpose of each, you should know that WATFIV
also permits you to use two slightly different forms of REAL
and INTEGER values. These alternate forms are called
INTEGER*2 and Extended Precision Real values. These last two
types of values are described in Chapters 11 and 12
respectively.

CHARACTER Values

Suppose the sentence "ECOLOGY CONCERNS THE
INTERRELATIONSHIP OF MAN AND NATURE" has been punched on a
card. You are asked to write a program to determine the
number of words in the sentence. Could you do it using only
REAL and INTEGER variables? Probably not. It could be done
but the program would be very artificial. The solution of
this problem requires us to analyze a string of symbols. In
WATFIV, strings of symbols are called CHARACTER values. By
using CHARACTER variables, the algorithm for solving the
problem can be easily programmed. This is one example of a
problem in which the use of CHARACTER variables is almost a
necessity. Other uses and examples of CHARACTER variables
can be found in Chapters 15 and 20.

LOGICAL Values

Many problems deal with ideas and relationships which
are true or false. For example, "A.LE.B" can only have a
value of "true" or "false". Quantities which can only have
one of these two values are called LOGICAL quantities in

WATFIV. By using LOGICAL variables, a programmer can manipulate true-false values with relative ease. Note that the INTEGER values of one and zero can also be used to represent true-false quantities. By using LOGICAL variables and constants however, the program is usually more readable and easier to "debug".

COMPLEX Values

Many problems in mathematics and engineering require the use of the square root of negative one in the solution of the problem. Pairs of real numbers in which the second number of the pair is assumed to be multiplied by the square root of negative one are called COMPLEX numbers. The operations of addition, subtraction, multiplication, division and exponentiation of COMPLEX numbers are performed according to well-defined rules. WATFIV permits programmers to create and manipulate COMPLEX numbers easily. Any program using COMPLEX numbers and variables, however, could also be programmed using REAL numbers and variables. By using COMPLEX numbers in a program, the compiler, and not the programmer, does the work in setting up the appropriate machine language instructions to perform COMPLEX arithmetic.

10.2 The Concept of "Length".

In Chapter 2, the point was made that each REAL or INTEGER value is represented in the memory of the computer as a string of thirty-two ones and zeros. Thus we might say that a REAL or INTEGER value has a "memory length" of thirty-two bits. A more common unit of memory length is the "byte". A byte is defined as eight consecutive bits. Thus we can equivalently say that REAL and INTEGER values have a length of four bytes. Throughout the remainder of the book, when we speak of the length of a value, we shall mean the number of bytes of memory used to store the value. For example, assuming X is REAL, the values 2, X, and -3.567E02 each have a length of four.

CHARACTER values in WATFIV can have lengths which vary from one to 255. This means that strings of symbols having anywhere from one to 255 characters can be manipulated in WATFIV. LOGICAL values have a standard length of four. COMPLEX values, which are, in effect, pairs of REAL values, have a length of eight bytes (twice the length of a REAL value).

The fact that any value stored in the computer memory has a finite length means that there are a finite number of unique values which can be taken on by a value. This is the reason that INTEGER values are restricted to the range plus or minus 2.1 billion (roughly) and that REAL values have seven significant digits.

There are two circumstances in which a programmer might wish to change the standard length of a value. First, he might wish to increase the length of a value in order to extend the range of values permitted by that particular type. This can be done for REAL and COMPLEX values. Secondly, he might wish to decrease the length of a value in order to reduce the amount of memory space required to store the values used in the program. This can be done for INTEGER and LOGICAL values. The method for changing the standard length of each of the five types of values (REAL, INTEGER, CHARACTER, LOGICAL, COMPLEX) is described in the appropriate chapter.

Each of the next five chapters discusses a different type of value. Chapters 11 and 12 describe, respectively, INTEGER variables of length two and REAL values of length eight. Chapters 13, 14, and 15 are somewhat more extensive and deal with COMPLEX, LOGICAL and CHARACTER values in that order.

In each of these chapters, the following questions are answered.

How are the constants and variables defined?

How are the variables used in the statements available in WATFIV?

What happens when values of different types are combined in the same statement?

What built-in functions are availble for processing the values?

How are the values input and output in format-free and formatted operations?

Chapter 16 discusses the use of non-REAL and/or non-INTEGER variables in several statements which are not used in most WATFIV programs. These are: EXTERNAL, IMPLICIT, ENTRY, COMMON, BLOCK DATA, DIMENSION, DATA and Statement Functions. Since the same principles apply in using these statements regardless of the type of values appearing in the statement, this discussion is presented in a single chapter for the reader who requires information on this topic.

Exercise 10.1

1 What are the five types of values which can be defined and manipulated in WATFIV programs? What is the purpose of each?

2. What is meant by the "length" of a value or variable?

3. What are the reasons for permitting a programmer to change the standard length of a variable?

10.3 Summary

1. Knowledge of REAL and INTEGER values and the rules for using them is sufficient to translate almost all algorithms into WATFIV. To make the programming of problems which involve strings of symbols, true-false quantities, and complex values much easier, CHARACTER, LOGICAL, and COMPLEX variables and constants are permitted in WATFIV.

2. A length is associated with each value stored in the computer's memory. The length of a value is the number of bytes used to store the value.

3. A programmer may modify the standard length of a variable in order to increase the precision of REAL or COMPLEX values and/or to reduce the memory required for storing INTEGER or LOGICAL values.

CHAPTER 11   INTEGER VARIABLES OF LENGTH TWO

Questions Answered In This Chapter

    1. What are INTEGER*2 variables?

    2. How are INTEGER*2 variables defined and used in
       WATFIV programs?

    Before studying the material of this chapter, the reader
should be familiar with the ideas in Chapter 10.

11.1 Purpose

    INTEGER variables have a standard length of four bytes.
This permits INTEGER values to range between -2147483648 and
+2147483647. If one or more INTEGER variables used in
program are known to have values within the range -32768,
+32767, a saving in memory space can often be achieved by
declaring that these variables are to have a length of two.
INTEGER variables of length two are called Half-Word INTEGER
variables or INTEGER*2 variables. The latter term
(INTEGER*2) will be used in this book.

11.2 Defining INTEGER*2 Variables.

    The pair of statements below are equivalent. Each
specifies that JACK and JILL are to be INTEGER*2 variables
and each assigns a value of 1 to JACK and -17 to JILL.

        INTEGER*2 JACK/1/,JILL/-17/

        INTEGER JACK*2/1/,JILL*2/-17/

Note that the length modifier may follow either the word
INTEGER or the variable name to which it applies.

    The statements below are equivalent. Each defines TABLE
to be a table of INTEGER*2 variables having 100 rows and 90
columns. The initial values in the table are all zero. Each
statement also specifies that AVG is to be an INTEGER
variable having the standard length of four.

        INTEGER*2 TABLE(100,90)/9000*0/,AVG*4

        INTEGER TABLE*2(100,90)/9000*0/,AVG

        INTEGER*4 TABLE*2(100,90)/9000*0/,AVG

The point being illustrated in this example is that if a length specification follows the word INTEGER, then that length is applied to all variables in the list unless a length specification follows a variable or array name. Note also that INTEGER and INTEGER*4 are equivalent.

INTEGER*2 variables can also be declared by using an IMPLICIT statement. This topic is discussed in Chapter 16.

11.3 Constants, Expressions, and Assignment Statements.

Constants

All INTEGER constants in WATFIV have a length of four. Only variables may be given the optional length of two.

Expressions

When evaluating expressions which involve INTEGER*2 variables, the value of the variable is expanded to the equivalent INTEGER value of length four before the operation is performed. This means that when INTEGER*2 variables are used in mixed-mode expressions, the type of result obtained is identical to the type and value of the result obtained had the variable been of length four.

Assignment Statements

When an INTEGER*2 variable appears on the left hand side of an Assignment statement, the value of the expression on the right is converted to an INTEGER*4 value (if it is not already in this form). Next, the digits represented by the bit pattern of the rightmost two bytes of this value are assigned to the INTEGER*2 variable. This means that if the value of the expression on the right lies within the range minus 32768 to +32767, then the "correct" value will be assigned to the INTEGER*2 variable. If the expression value lies outside this range, the value assigned to the variable will be incorrect. Since no warning message is printed, a programmer should satisfy himself that values assigned to INTEGER*2 variables in a program are within the permitted range.

The example program below illustrates the facts described above.

```
INTEGER*2 H1/20/,H2/4/,H3/240000/,H4,H5
H4=H1**H2
H5=H1**H2/100
PRINT,H3,H4,H5
STOP
END
```

When executed, the values printed for H3, H4, and H5 are:

H3 = -22144   H4= 28928   H5= 1600

The reasons are as follows. The value of H3 (namely 240000) lies outside the permitted range of INTEGER*2 values. However the bit pattern of the rightmost two bytes of the INTEGER value 240000 represents an INTEGER*2 value of negative 22144. (Appendix C provides the details on why this is the case). Consider H4. The value of 20**4 lies is greater than 32768. The value printed for H4 represents the INTEGER*2 value of the bit pattern of the rightmost two bytes of the result. Finally, in calculating the value of H5 (which equals H1**H2/100) the calculations are done using the INTEGER*4 equivalents of the values of H1 and H2. The value of the expression is 1600 which does lie within the permitted range. Even though H1**H2 is greater than 32768, the value of this part of the expression is left as an INTEGER*4 value.

11.4 Built-In Functions.

There is only one built-in function for processing INTEGER*2 values. The function HFIX can be used to convert a REAL value to an INTEGER*2 value. For example, the statement "HW=HFIX(3.14)" causes HW to be assigned the value 3. The variable HW in this example is assumed to have been declared as an INTEGER*2 variable. If the function HFIX is used, the function name HFIX must appear in an INTEGER*2 declaration statement. This is necessary so that the compiler will reserve the correct number of bytes of memory (two) for storing the value of the function.

11.5 Input-Output Of Integer*2 Variables.

An I-mask is used to input or output INTEGER*2 variables under format control.

In format-free operations, the default mask is I12 for each INTEGER*2 variable appearing in an output list. In format-free input operations, the programmer should be careful that values assigned to INTEGER*2 variables lie within the permitted range.

11.6 Valid And Invalid Uses Of INTEGER*2 Variables.

INTEGER*2 variables may be used anywhere INTEGER variables are permitted with two exceptions. An INTEGER*2 variable may not be used as the index of an Assigned GO TO. For example, if HALF is an INTEGER*2 variable, then the statements "ASSIGN 6 TO HALF" or "GOTO HALF,(6)" are invalid. Secondly, an INTEGER*2 variable cannot be used in a READ or WRITE statement to store the device number. The following pair of statements, for example, is invalid.

```
INTEGER*2 DEVICE
READ(DEVICE,900) X
```

Exercise 11.1.

1. What is the chief reason for using INTEGER*2 variables?
   What is the most significant restriction on their use?

2. What is the error in the following?

```
INTEGER*2 RESULT
READ,A
RESULT=HFIX(SQRT(A))
PRINT,RESULT
STOP
END
```

11.7 Summary

If memory space is at a premium and if a large number of INTEGER variables are used in a program, a significant reduction in memory requirements can be realized by using INTEGER*2 variables instead of INTEGER variables. The only disadvantages which result are: the values assigned to these variables must lie in the range -32768 thru +32767; INTEGER functions such as MAX0 cannot be used; there may be an increase in execution time. All INTEGER constants have a length of four. Only variables may be given the optional length of two.

Programming Problems

11.1   What triples of integer values (x, y, z) have the property that $x^2+y^2=z^2$? A rigorous way of generating such values is to choose any pair of values m and n such that: m and n are relatively prime (one is not a multiple of the other); m is even and n is odd or m is odd and n is even. If m and n satisfy these conditions then set

$$x = 2mn, \quad y = m^2- n^2 \ , \text{ and } z = m^2+ n^2$$

For example, set m=2 and n=1. The values of x, y, and z are x=4, y=3 and z=5. Note that $3^2 +4^2 =5^2$. Write a program using INTEGER*2 variables for m, n, x, y and z and generate all possible triples using values of m and n of five or less which satisfy the given conditions.

11.2   A programming project. Using INTEGER*2 variables can significantly reduce the memory requirements of any program containing large arrays of INTEGER values. Suppose a fifty-by-fifty matrix contains elements whose

278

values are zero or one. Suppose less than twenty percent of the elements have a value of one and all the rest are zeros. Design any scheme you like for reducing the memory required to store the array values. Make sure your technique will work for an arbitrary set of values and does not depend on the array values having a particular pattern.

11.3   Suppose the value of element (i,j) in a five-by-five matrix called DIST represents the distance between city "i" and city "j". Assume DIST(I,J) = DIST(J,I). Suppose also that DIST(I,I)=0 for any value of I. Suppose you start at city 1 and follow a route which takes you to each of the other cities once and then back to city 1. Write a program to find the route you should take in order to minimize the total distance travelled. In mathematics this problem is known as the "Travelling Salesman Problem". Although there are several methods available for solving small problems such as this efficiently, develop your own algorithm to solve the problem and then write the program.

CHAPTER 12   EXTENDED PRECISION

Questions Answered In This Chapter

   1. What are the three important reasons for using
      numbers having as many as 16 significant digits?

   2. How are these "extended precision" values defined
      and used in WATFIV programs?

Before studying the material of this chapter, the reader
should be familiar with the ideas in Chapter 10.

12.1 Extended Precision Values

    Seven significant digits are stored for each REAL value
used in a WATFIV program. By doubling the amount of memory
used to store a REAL number, numbers with sixteen
significant digits can be stored in the computer memory.
Such numbers are called Extended Precision numbers. The
terms DOUBLE PRECISION and REAL*8 are synonyms for Extended
Precision. The significance of the "*8" is that each such
value occupies eight bytes of memory. In this book, the
words Extended Precision will be used and will be
abbreviated to "E.P." in this chapter.

    What are the reasons for requiring numbers having as
many as sixteen significant digits? Three reasons are:

         i)   To manipulate values which represent large
               sums of money. For example, the figure
               $10,473,126.52 has ten significant digits.

         ii)   To manipulate integer values which lie
               outside the permitted range of INTEGER
               values, eg: -3247565217.

         iii) To reduce the degree of error associated with
               operations involving numbers in which the
               fractional portion of the number is a non-
               terminating string of binary digits. For
               example, .2 in base two is .00110011001... .

12.2 E.P. Constants, Variables and Expressions.

Constants

    E.P. constants may be defined with or without an
exponent. Examples of valid E.P. constants are:

280

123451234512345.1

-17.2D06   i.e: -17.2×10^{6}

0.001425683415D-2   i.e: $.001425683415 \times 10^{-2}$

Examples of invalid E.P. constants are:

123,456,789.012   (commas not permitted)

1.0D-200   (exponent too large)

123451234512345123.   (more than 16 digits)

123.45   (a REAL constant but not an E.P. constant.
The equivalent value as an E.P. constant
would be 123.45D00 or 123.45000.)

Note that a "D" precedes the exponent value when an E.P.
constant is written with an exponent. The D is used with
E.P. numbers in precisely the same way that the E is used
in writing REAL constants. The range of exponents permitted
for E.P. values is the same as that for REAL values, namely
the range between -78 and +76. A discussion of the bit
pattern used to represent E.P. values can be found in
Appendix C.

Variables

Each E.P. value occupies eight bytes of memory instead
of the four bytes used for storing a REAL value. If
variables used in a program are to be assigned E.P. values,
the WATFIV compiler must be informed of this fact in order
that it can reserve sufficient memory space for each such
variable or function value. The two statements below each
inform the compiler that the variables A,B, and C are to be
assigned E.P. values.

REAL*8 A,B,C

DOUBLE PRECISION A,B,C

The statements above are equivalent. In the first, the
length modifier of "*8" is added to the end of the word
REAL.   In the second, the words DOUBLE PRECISION are used to
inform the compiler that the variables A, B, and C are to
have E.P. values. In this chapter, the REAL*8 form of the
declaration statement will always be used since it is
somewhat more flexible as the examples below will show.

Each of the following statements defines a two-by-five
table of E.P. variables which is initialized to zeros. MAX
is declared as a REAL variable with an initial value of 7.

281

REAL*8 TABLE(2,5)/10*0.D00/,MAX*4/7./

REAL TABLE*8(2,5)/10*0.D00/,MAX/7./

REAL*4 TABLE*8(2,5)/10*0.D00/,MAX/7./

The ideas illustrated by these statements are:

i) A length modifier of "*8" or "*4" may follow the word REAL. If omitted, "*4" is assumed.

ii) A length modifier of "*8" or "*4" may follow a variable or array name. If omitted, the length of the variable or array element is that associated with the word REAL.

iii) E.P. variables may be initialized at compile time. The initializing values must agree in number and type with the variables being initialized. The statements "REAL*8 A/1./" and "REAL*8 B/12.E04/" for example, are invalid.

The DIMENSION statement (Chapter 7, Section 9) can also be used to define sets of E.P. variables. The DATA statement (Chapter 7, Section 8) is an alternate method of specifying initial values for E.P. variables. These topics are discussed in Chapter 16.

Expressions

Expresssions which involve E.P. values are of two types: those which involve only E.P. values; and those which involve one or more other types of values as well as E.P. values.

When E.P. values are combined using any of the arithmetic operators + - * / **, the result is an E.P. value. Some examples are:

Expression	Result
2.0D00+3.25D00	5.25D00
-2.D00**3.D00	-8.0D00
(-2.D00)**3.D00	ERROR (negative base used with a REAL type exponent)
1.D25-1.D25+1.D00	1.D00
1.D00+1.D25-1.D25	0.D00 (only 16 digits are kept at each step when evaluating the expression)

In evaluating mixed-type expressions, the general rule is that if an operation involves an INTEGER and an E.P. value or a REAL and an E.P. value, the non-E.P. value is converted to an E.P. value before the operation is performed. The result is an E.P. value. Some examples are:

Expression	Result
2.0D00 + 3.	5.0D00
6.0D00/3	2.0D00
(-.5D00)**(-3)	-8.0D00 (the exception to the rule -- an INTEGER exponent is left unchanged)
5/2*1.D00	2.D00 (the division is done first)
1.D00*5/2	2.5D00 (the multiplication is done first)

Are the values of the three expressions below the same?

    .2D00+.2D00   .2D00+.2E00   .2E00+.2E00

The answer is "No, they are all different.". Why? The reason is primarily due to the fact that a value of two-tenths has a non-terminating string of binary digits to the right of the decimal point when written in the base two number system. This means that the values of .2D00 and .2E00 which are stored in the computer's memory are only approximations to the value .2. Furthermore, since E.P. values have more significant digits, the value of .2D00 is a better approximation than the value .2E00. If we label the values of .2E00 and .2D00 as "good" and "better" respectively, then the "quality" of the result in the three cases is shown below.

.2D00 + .2D00	better + better	i.e: .400000000000
.2D00 + .2E00	better + good	i.e: .399999988079
.2E00 + .2E00	good + good	i.e: .399999976158

As you can see, the most accurate result is obtained by using the two E.P. values and the least accurate by using the two REAL values. The result obtained by using one of each type lies somewhere in between.

The foregoing discussion emphasizes the reason for using E.P. values in situations where numbers have fractional values and a high degree of accuracy is very important.

One further point. The relationship in the statement

IF (.2D00 .EQ. .2E00) ...

is false. The reason is as discussed above. That is, a comparison is being made between a good approximation and a better approximation - but not the same approximation. The relationship (2.D00 .EQ. 2.E00) will always be true however, since the representation of whole numbers (and many fractional values) is exact. Thus, if two E.P. values A and B, say, must be tested for equality, it is wise to compare the absolute value of their difference to some very small value. The built-in function DABS can be used for this purpose. (This and other E.P. built-in functions are described in Section 4.) That is, the statement

IF(DABS(A-B).LE.1.D-1) ...

should be used intead of "IF(A.EQ.B) ...".

12.3 E.P. Assignment Statements.

An E.P. Assignment statement has one of the following forms.

i) E.P. variable = E.P. expression

ii) E.P. variable = non-E.P. expression

iii) non-E.P. variable = E.P. expression

Case (i) is straightforward in that the value of the expression is simply assigned to the variable. In Case (ii), the value of the REAL or INTEGER expression is converted to an E.P. value before the assignment takes place. For example, if A is an E.P. variable, the statement "A=3" results in A being assigned the value 3.D00. The only situation in which unexpected results may occur is illustrated in the following example.

```
REAL*8 B/.2D00/
A=B
IF(A.EQ.B) PRINT,A,B
STOP
END
```

For the reasons discussed in the previous section, the values of A and B are different since they have been assigned different approximations of the value one-fifth.

In Case (iii), a non-E.P. variable is assigned the value of an E.P. expression. When this happens, the value of the expression is converted to the type required by the variable on the left of the equal sign before the assignment takes

place. For example, "I=-2.7D00" results in I having a value
of -2 . "X=.2D00" results in X having a value of .2E00.

Exercise 12.1

1. What is the value assigned to each variable in the
   following sets of statements?

    a)
```
          REAL*8 A,B,C,D/1.D00/
          A=20.*D/1.D1
          B=3.0D00**A
          C=-A**3
```

    b)
```
          REAL*8 W(3)/3.D00,4.D00,5.D00/
          INTEGER XX,YY,ZZ
          YY=ZZ=10.D00/10.E3*W(1)
          DO 1 XX=1,3
        1 W(XX)=W(XX)-W(MOD(XX+1,3)+1.D00)+YY/ZZ
```

    c)
```
          REAL X*8/49.D00/,REAL/4./
          INTEGER ASK/2/
          ASK=ASK/(2*ASK)+X
          REAL=REAL+SQRT(SQRT(FLOAT(ASK))+SQRT(REAL))
```

2. What is the error in each of the following?

    a) REAL*8 A/2.E10/
    b) REAL*4 B(5,8)/40*2.D3/
    c) REAL XYZ*8(3)/1.0D05,-10.346D-8/
    d) REAL A*8,B(2)*8

3. Answer true or false to each of the following.

    a) The number of memory locations used to store a
   REAL*8 value is twice that used for a REAL*4 value.
    b) E.P. representations of whole numbers are exact.
    c) E.P. representations of many fractional values are
   exact.
    d) E.P. representations of all fractional values are
   exact.
    e) E.P. representations of some fractional values are
   better approximations to the value than the REAL*4
   representation of the same value.
    f) Same as (e) but replace "some" with "all".
    g) The number .1 is an E.P. constant.
    h) The number .000000001 is an E.P. constant.
    i) In any operation involving an E.P. value and a non-
   E.P. value, the non-E.P. value is always converted
   to an E.P. value before the operation is performed.
    j) The Assignment statements "A=.2D00" and "A=.2E00"
   are equivalent (i) when A is a REAL variable, and
   (ii) when A is an E.P. variable.

4. Given that the value .1 is a non-terminating binary fraction in the base two number system, determine the values printed by the following sequence of statements.

```
          REAL*4 A*8,EP*8,X
          INTEGER B/2/
          A=.1D00
          IF(.1.EQ.A)PRINT,B
          X=A
          IF(X.EQ..1D00)PRINT,2*B
          B=10.*X+.1
          GO TO (2,3),B
        4 STOP
        2 IF(A.NE..1D00)PRINT,X
        3 IF(A-X+B)4,4,5
        5 PRINT,B
          STOP
```

12.4 Extended Precision Built-In Functions.

The WATFIV language includes a large number of built-in functions for processing E.P. Values. The table below lists those which are commonly used. A complete list can be found in Appendix I. In the table, the symbol "r8" denotes an E.P. argument, the symbol "r4" denotes a REAL argument and "i" denotes an INTEGER argument.

TABLE OF E.P. BUILT-IN FUNCTIONS

Purpose	Name And Arguments	Definition	Result
Square Root	DSQRT(r8)	$\sqrt{}$	E.P.
Trigonometric Functions (angles in radians)	DSIN(r8) DCOS(r8) DTAN(r8) DCOTAN(r8)	sine cosine tangent cotangent	E.P. E.P. E.P. E.P.
Inverse trig Functions (result in radians)	DARSIN(r8) DARCOS(r8) DATAN(r8)	arcsine arccosine arctangent	E.P. E.P. E.P.
Logarithms	DLOG(r8) DLOG10(r8)	log (base e) log (base 10)	E.P. E.P.
Exponential	DEXP(r8)	e**argument	E.P.
Absolute value	DABS(r8)	|argument|	E.P.

286

Transfer of sign	DSIGN(r8,r8)	$\|arg1\| \times sign(arg2)$ where, $sign = \begin{cases} +1 \text{ if } \geqslant 0 \\ 1 \text{ if } =0 \\ -1 \text{ if } <0 \end{cases}$	E.P.
Truncation	IDINT(r8)	integer part of the argument	INTEGER
Modular Arithmetic	DMOD(r8,r8)	remainder of arg1/arg2	E.P.
Maximum & Minimum	DMAX1(r8,r8..) DMIN1(r8,r8..)	largest arg. smallest arg.	E.P. E.P.
Type Conversion	DFLOAT(i)	E.P. value of arg.	E.P.
	SNGL(r8)	REAL value of arg.	REAL
	DBLE(r4)	Adds zeros to REAL value to form an E.P. value	E.P.

There are several important points concerning the use of E.P. built-in functions.

 i) Any function which has an E.P. value and is used in a program must have the function name declared as having an E.P. value. This is necessary in order that the compiler reserve sufficient memory (8 bytes) for storing the value of the function. For example, if the functions DSQRT, DLOG and DABS are used in a program, a statement such as:

    REAL*8 DSQRT,DLOG,DABS

 must be included in the program. If omitted, an error message will occur at execution time.

 ii) The reasons for having the type conversion functions are:

     a) Several Fortran compilers do not permit mixed-type expressions. Thus in order to cause all terms in an expression to have the same mode, the functions DFLOAT,SNGL and DBLE may be required.

     b) Function arguments must be of the type specified in the table. For example to obtain the square root of an INTEGER variable I correct to sixteen significant digits, one could write DSQRT(DBLE(FLOAT(I))).

12.5 Input-Output Of E.P. Values.

Formatted Input-Output

A D-mask or F-mask is used to input or output E.P. values under format control. The operation of a D-mask is similar to that of an E-mask with the exception that as many as 16 significant digits can be printed using a D-mask. The general form of the D-mask is Dw.d where "w" denotes the number of card columns or print positions covered by the mask and "d" denotes the number of digits to the right of the decimal point. A few examples will illustrate its use.

Suppose the symbols "1.23456789D02" are punched in 13 card columns covered by a D-mask. The value assigned to a variable is shown for three different masks.

Mask	Value Assigned
D13.8	1.23456789D02
D13.3	1.23456789D02 (value of d is ignored)
F13.8	error ("D" is an invalid character when read under an F-mask)

Suppose the E.P. value of .123456789 is to be printed. The symbols printed for several masks are shown below.

Mask	Symbols Printed
D16.9	b0.123456789Db00 (b denotes a blank)
D15.9	0.123456789Db00
D13.6	b0.123457Db00
D14.9	*************
F11.9	0.123456789
F10.9	**********
F10.6	bb0.123457

Format-Free Input-Output

On input, values to be assigned to E.P. variables may be punched either with or without an exponent. If an exponent is used, a "D" should precede the exponent value.

On output, the mask used for printing E.P. values is D28.16.

12.6 FUNCTION and SUBROUTINE Subprograms.

The example program of this section illustrates the important points in writing subprograms which utilize E.P. values. The program determines the largest root of the equation $ax^2 + bx + c = 0$. The values of a, b and c are read from a card. The assumption is made that $b^2 - 4ac$ is positive. The FUNCTION subprogram BIGRUT is used to obtain the result.

```
C EXAMPLE 12.1 FIND LARGEST ROOT
      REAL*8 A,B,C,BIGRUT
      READ,A,B,C
      PRINT 1,BIGRUT(A,B,C)
    1 FORMAT('1LARGEST ROOT IS',D23.16)
      STOP
      END

      REAL FUNCTION BIGRUT*8(A,B,C)
      REAL*8 DABS,DSQRT,DMAX1,A,B,C,X,Y,DISC
      DISC=B*B-4.*A*C
      X=(-B+DSQRT(DISC))/(2.*A)
      Y=(-B-DSQRT(DISC))/(2.*A)
      BIGRUT=DMAX1(DABS(X),DABS(Y))
      RETURN
      END
$ENTRY
```

Remarks

i) All E.P. arguments and parameters must be declared
as such in the appropriate segment. Arguments and
parameters should agree in number and type.

ii) The name of an E.P. valued FUNCTION must appear in
a suitable type declaration statement in the
calling segment. (BIGRUT is declared as being
REAL*8.)

iii) The first statement in the FUNCTION subprogram can
only be one of the following:

REAL FUNCTION name*8 (parameter list)

DOUBLE PRECISION FUNCTION name (parameter list)

Note that in the first case, the length
specification "*8" must follow the FUNCTION name.
It cannot appear after the word REAL.

In SUBROUTINE subprograms, no value is assigned to the
SUBROUTINE name. This means that rules (ii) and (iii) above
do not apply to SUBROUTINE subprograms.

12.7 Other Statements Involving E.P. Values.

1. Extended Precision variables may be used in the
following WATFIV statements: IMPLICIT, EQUIVALENCE,
and COMMON. Details can be found in Chapter 16.

2 E.P. Statement Functions can be defined and used in
a program segment. The name of the function and any
E.P. variables used in its definition must be
declared as having E.P. values.

3. E.P. varaibles in COMMON Blocks may be initialized in BLOCK DATA subprograms.

4. E.P. FUNCTION subprograms may appear in EXTERNAL and ENTRY statements. This topic is discussed in Chapter 16, Section 10.

5. E.P. expressions may be used as subscripts. The subscript value is obtained by using the integer part of the value of the expression. For example, if X is an array, then X(1.999) 9D00) is equivalent to X(1).

6. A G-mask can be used to input or output E.P. values under format control. Its effect is similar to that obtained with REAL values.

7. A P-code can be used to modify E.P. values which are: input under an F-mask; output under a D-mask or F-mask.

12.8 Summary

1. Extended Precision values can be used in WATFIV programs. Each E.P. value occupies eight bytes (two words) of memory. The equivalent of sixteen decimal digits are stored for each E.P. value used.

2. The use of E.P. values should be considered when a program manipulates fractional values and high degree of accuracy is important.

Programming Problems

In all of the problems which follow, use Extended Precision variables whenever appropriate.

12.1 In 1624 Peter Minuit bought Manhattan Island from the Indians for $24.00. Suppose the Indians had invested the money at 4% compounded annually. How much would their investment have been worth in 1969? Display the values of the investment at fifteen year intervals starting with 1624 and ending with 1969 as shown below. Use a mask of F20.2 to display each dollar amount.

YEAR	AMOUNT	YEAR	AMOUNT	YEAR	AMOUNT
1624 $	_____	1639 $	_____	1654 $	_____
1669 $	_____	1684 $	_____	1699 $	_____
etc.		etc.		etc.	

12.2 Repeat problem 5.5 using E.P. variables and constants. Stop further execution when the change in the two estimates is less than 1.D-12.

12.3   The value of the inverse sine of a value x is given
by the following expression.

$$\sin^{-1}x = x + \frac{x^3}{2\cdot3} + \frac{1\cdot3}{2\cdot4\cdot5}\,x^5 + \frac{1\cdot3\cdot5}{2\cdot4\cdot6\cdot7}\,x^7 + \ldots$$

Write a FUNCTION subprogram which calculates the inverse
sine of a value of .25. (What angle is such that its
sine equals .25?) Calculate your answer correct to
fourteen decimal places. Compare your result with that
obtained from the built-in function DARSIN.

12.4   A ladder of length L leans against a wall. The top
of the ladder is initially a distance H above the floor.
The top of the ladder starts to slip down the wall.
Calculate the position of the mid-point of the ladder
when the top is .95H, .90H, .85H, ..., .05H above the
floor. Read values of L and H from a data card.

12.5   Large values of factorial N can be approximated using
Stirling's formula which is

N! is approximately $e^{-N}N^N\sqrt{2\pi N}$

Calculate the values of factorial 1, 2, 3, ..., 20 using
the approximation formula. Use E.P. variables, constants and
built-in functions in your program.

12.6   An approximate value of π can be calculated using one
of several formulae. Two of these are:

$$\pi = 4\;\frac{1.1.2.2.3.3.\;\ldots}{1\;3\;3\;5\;5\;7}$$

$$\pi = \sqrt{\frac{6}{1^2} + \frac{6}{2^2} + \frac{6}{3^2} + \frac{6}{4^2} + \ldots}$$

Write two different E.P. FUNCTION subprograms to to
calculate an approximate value of π using the given
formulae. Which formula requires the fewest terms to get
a good approximation to π ?

12.7   Suppose a ball dropped from a height H rebounds to a
height of .9H. (a) Write a program which determines the
number of of bounces which the ball must make before its
maximum height is .1D-10. (b) Add a feature to the
program for (a) to determine the total length of time
the ball is in the air.

12.8   Find the roots of $x^2-325678x-.02=0$ using first, REAL
variables and secondly, E.P. values. Explain the
significant difference in the two results.

CHAPTER 13　　　　　　COMPLEX VALUES

Questions Answered In This Chapter.

    1. What are COMPLEX values?

    2. How are COMPLEX values defined and used in WATFIV programs?

    Before studying the material of this chapter, the reader should be familiar with the ideas of Chapter 10.

13.1 Complex Numbers

    In mathematics and engineering, a complex number can be considered to be a pair of real numbers which obey well defined rules of arithmetic. Suppose (a,b) and (c,d) are two pairs of real numbers. Then, by definition, the operations of addition, subtraction, multiplication and division of the complex numbers (a,b) and (c,d) are:

$$(a,b) + (c,d) = (a+c,b+d)$$

$$(a,b) - (c,d) = (a-c,b-d)$$

$$(a,b) * (c,d) = (ac-bd,ad+bc)$$

$$(a,b) / (c,d) = (\frac{ac+bd}{c^2+d^2} , \frac{-ad+bc}{c^2+d^2})$$

    The complex conjugate of a complex number (a,b) is defined as the number (a,-b). For any complex number (a,b), the first number of the pair is called the real component of the number and the second number of the pair is called the imaginary component of the number.

    Complex numbers are sometimes written in the form "a+ib" where "i" denotes the square root of negative one. In this book, this method of writing complex numbers will not be used since WATFIV uses the the form (a,b) to represent complex numbers.

13.2 COMPLEX Constants, Variables, and Expressions

    WATFIV permits a programmer to define and manipulate complex values. Numbers, variables, functions and expressions which have a complex value are called COMPLEX. In WATFIV, a COMPLEX value is viewed as a pair of REAL numbers. This means each COMPLEX value occupies two words of memory. Operations on COMPLEX values are performed using machine language instructions generated by the WATFIV compiler. The circuits used to perform these calculations are the same as those used to do REAL arithmetic. Of necessity, more machine language instructions are required to add two COMPLEX values, for instance, than to add two REAL values.

Constants

COMPLEX constants are defined by enclosing a pair of REAL constants, separated by a comma, in brackets. Examples of valid COMPLEX constants are:

$$(2.,1.) \quad (-3.257E+06,-5.2) \quad (.0025E-1,.002E-20)$$

Some invalid constants are:

(2.,1)   (imaginary component is an INTEGER)

(3.56E01 -2.1)   (no comma)

(-5.73,X)   (X is not a constant)

(2.*3.,-5.6789)   (real component is an expression)

Since a pair of REAL values is stored for each COMPLEX value used, the real and imaginary components of a COMPLEX number may be only good approximations of the desired value. This will occur in cases where one or both of the components have a non-terminating binary representation.

Variables

COMPLEX variables are defined using a COMPLEX declaration statement. Each such variable occupies eight bytes (two words) of memory. The statement below declares U and V to be COMPLEX variables and defines ARRAY as a three by four table of COMPLEX variables, each having an initial value of zero.

COMPLEX U,V,ARRAY(3,4)/12*(0.,0.)/

The DIMENSION statement can also be used to define sets of COMPLEX variables. The DATA statement is an alternate method of defining initial values. An IMPLICIT statement can be used to specifiy a first-letter rule for COMPLEX variables. These topics are discussed in Chapter 16.

Expressions

Expressions which involve COMPLEX values are of two types: those which involve only COMPLEX values; those which involve only COMPLEX values; those which involve some other type of value as well as one or more COMPLEX values.

Case (i) - All values COMPLEX. When COMPLEX values are combined using any of the four arithmetic operators + - * /, the result is a COMPLEX value. Some examples are:

Expression	Result
(2.,-3.)+(5.,7.)	(7.,4.)
(1.,2.)*(0.,3.)	(-6.,3.)
(1.,0.)/(3.,1.)	(.3,-.1)

The operation of exponentiation is permitted only if the exponent is an INTEGER value. Thus "(1.,2.)**2" is valid whereas "(1.,0.)**2." and "(1.,0.)**(1.,0.)" are invalid.

In a COMPLEX expression, each COMPLEX item must be either a COMPLEX constant or a COMPLEX variable. A COMPLEX value cannot be created simply by putting one or two REAL variables or expressions inside a pair of brackets. For example, if X and Y are REAL variables, the following are invalid COMPLEX values.

$$(X,1.) \qquad (0.2,X) \qquad (X,Y)$$

To create a COMPLEX value from a pair of REAL values, the built-in function CMPLX (discussed in Section 13.4) must be used.

Case (ii) -- Mixed type expressions. Other types of values and variables may be combined with COMPLEX values in an expression. In such cases, the operation is performed by converting the non-COMPLEX value to a COMPLEX value having an imaginary component of zero. The result of the operation is always a COMPLEX value. Some examples are:

Expression	Result
3. + (1.,5.)	(4.,5.)
2 * (-6.,7.)	(-12.,14.)
(1.,-8.)**3.	error - only INTEGER exponents allowed
6/4*(12.,0.)	(12.,0.) (division is done first)
(12.,0.)*6/4	(18.,0.) (multiplication is done first)

13.3 COMPLEX Assignment Statements

A COMPLEX Assignment statement has one of the following forms:

    i) COMPLEX variable = COMPLEX expression

    ii) COMPLEX variable = non-COMPLEX expression

    iii) non-COMPLEX variable = COMPLEX expression

Case (i) is straightforward. The value of the COMPLEX expression is assigned to the variable.

In Case (ii), the value of the expression is assigned to the real component of the variable. The imaginary component is given a value of zero. For example,

```
COMPLEX A
B=2.5
I=3
A=B*I
```

results in A having a value of (7.5,0.)

In Case (iii) (non-COMPLEX variable = COMPLEX expression), the imaginary component of the expression value is ignored and the real component is assigned to the variable on the left. For example,

```
COMPLEX U/(10.125,-3.5)/
J=U
A=U
```

results in J having a value of 10 and in A having a value of 10.125.

13.4 COMPLEX Built-In Functions

Several built-in functions are available for manipulating and creating COMPLEX values. In the following table, "c" denotes a COMPLEX argument and "r" denotes a REAL argument.

TABLE OF COMPLEX BUILT-IN FUNCTIONS

Purpose	Name and Arguments	Definition	Result
Square Root	CSQRT(c)	$\sqrt{}$	COMPLEX
Trigonometric functions	CSIN(c) CCOS(c)	sine cosine	COMPLEX COMPLEX

Exponential & logarithm	CEXP(c) CLOG(c)	e**arg log (base e)	COMPLEX COMPLEX
Absolute value	CABS(c)	$\sqrt{a^2+b^2}$ where c=(a,b)	REAL
Type Conversion	CMPLX(rl,r2)	forms a COMPLEX numbers from rl and r2	COMPLEX
Component Extraction	REAL(c)	the real component of c	REAL
	AIMAG(c)	the imaginary component of c	REAL
Complex Conjugate	CONJG(c)	if c=(a,b), result is (a,-b)	COMPLEX

If a COMPLEX valued built-in function is used in a program segment, the function name must appear in a COMPLEX declaration statement. This is necessary so that the compiler will reserve the required eight bytes of memory to store the function value. The example program below could be used to obtain the roots of the equation $ax^2+bx+c=0$.

```
      C EXAMPLE 13.1 ROOTS OF QUADRATIC
            COMPLEX ROOT1,ROOT2,CMPLX,CONJG
            REAL Y/0./
            READ,A,B,C
            X=-B/(2.*A)
            DISCR=B*B-4.*A*C
            IF(ABS(DISCR).LT.0.000001) GO TO 1
            Y=SQRT(ABS(DISCR))/(2.*A)
            IF(DISCR.LT.0.)GO TO 2
          1 ROOT1=CMPLX(X+Y,0.)
            ROOT2=CMPLX(X-Y,0.)
            PRINT,ROOT1,ROOT2
            STOP
          2 ROOT1=CMPLX(X,Y)
            ROOT2=CONJG(ROOT1)
            PRINT,ROOT1,ROOT2
            STOP
            END
```

13.5 Input-Output Of COMPLEX Values.

Formatted Input-Output

A pair of masks (F-masks, E-masks, or one of each) is used to input or output COMPLEX values under format control. The following program illustrates this point.

```
C EXAMPLE 13.2 FORMATTED I/O OF COMPLEX VALUES
      COMPLEX U,V,W
      READ 1,U,V,W
    1 FORMAT(2F3.1,E6.2,F7.0,2E10.3)
      PRINT 2,U,V,W
    2 FORMAT('1U=(',2F11.2,')',/,' V=(',2E11.3,
     *')',/,' W=(',E11.3,F11.2,')')
      STOP
      END
$ENTRY
2.0-.5.25E04 -1234.  1.000E00 -1.000E00
```

F3.1 F3.1 E6.2 F7.0   E10.3   E10.3

When executed, the following lines are printed.

```
      U=(        2.00       -0.50)
      V=(   0.250E 04 -0.123E 04)
      W=(   0.100E 01       -1.00)
```

Format-Free Input-Output

Each COMPLEX value which is read using a format-free
READ statement must be punched as a valid COMPLEX constant.
This means that the real and imaginary components must be
separated by a comma and enclosed in brackets. A comma
and/or blank column(s) are used to separate successive
values on a card.

When using format-free output, each COMPLEX value
appearing in the output list is printed using the following
set of format codes.

```
    '(',E16.7,' ,',E16.7,')'
```

The following example illustrates these points.

```
C EXAMPLE 13.3 FORMAT-FREE INPUT-OUTPUT
      COMPLEX U,V
      READ,U,V
      PRINT,U
      PRINT,V
      PRINT, +(2.,7.)
      STOP
      END
$ENTRY
   (2.5, 16.E00) , (-7.,3.5)
```

The lines printed are:

```
(   0.2500000E 01 ,   0.1600000E 02)
(  -0.7000000E 01 ,   0.3500000E 01)
(   0.2000000E 01 ,   0.7000000E 01)
```

297

In the statement "PRINT,+(2.,7.)", the "+" sign is necessary. The reason, as you may recall, is that any expression in an output list which begins with a left bracket must be an implied DO-loop.

13.6 FUNCTION And SUBROUTINE Subprograms

The example program of this section illustrates the important points in writing subprograms which utilize COMPLEX values.

If U is a COMPLEX number, the equation $U^N = 1$ has N roots. The N roots are given by the formula below.

$$U = (\cos \frac{2K\pi}{N} , \sin \frac{2K\pi}{N}) , \text{ where } K=0,1,2, \ldots,N-1$$

The mainline segment of the following program reads in a value of N and uses the FUNCTION subprogram CROOT to obtain, in order, the N COMPLEX roots of unity.

```
C ROOTS OF UNITY          COMPLEX FUNCTION CROOT(K,N)
      COMPLEX CROOT,U          COMPLEX CMPLX
      READ,N                   ANG=2.*K*3.14159/N
      DO 1 K=1,N               X=COS(ANG)
      U=CROOT(K,N)             Y=SIN(ANG)
    1 PRINT,U                  CROOT=CMPLX(X,Y)
      STOP                     RETURN
      END                      END
```

Remarks

    i) All COMPLEX arguments and parameters must be declared as such in the appropriate segment. Arguments and parameters should agree in number and type.

    ii) The name of a COMPLEX-valued FUNCTION must appear in a suitable type declaration statement in the calling segment. (CROOT is declared as COMPLEX in the example mainline.)

    iii) The first statement in a FUNCTION subprogram must have the form:

COMPLEX FUNCTION name (parameter list)

In SUBROUTINE subprograms, no value is assigned to the name of the SUBROUTINE. This means that points (ii) and (iii) above do not apply to SUBROUTINE subprograms.

Exercise 13.1

1. What is the value of each of the following expressions?

    a) $(3.,4.)+(2.E00,-8.)$
    b) $(2.,-3.)/(4.,-1.)$
    c) $(2.,1.)**2*(4./(1.,-1.)+(2.,-1.)/(1.,1.))$
    d) $((0.,1.)+(0.,1.)+(0.,1.))/(2-(0.,1.)+(0.,1.))$

2. If $u=(1,1)$, $v=(2,4)$, and $w=(3,-2)$, use the computer to evaluate:

    a) $u+2v-3$
    b) $|2v-3w|$ where $|x|$ denotes the absolute value of x
    c) $(u\bar{v}-v\bar{u})$ where $\bar{u}$ and $\bar{v}$ are the complex conjugates of u and v.

    d) $\dfrac{1}{2}\left(\dfrac{w}{\bar{\bar{w}}}+\dfrac{\bar{w}}{w}\right)$ where $\bar{w}$ is the complex conjugate of w

3. What is the last value assigned to each variable in the following sets of statements?

    a)   COMPLEX U/(1.,2.)/,V(3)/3*(1.,1.)/
                DO 1 I=1,3
          1 V(I)=V(I)+U*I

    b)   COMPLEX A,B,CMPLX,T/(1.,0.)/
                X=2.
                Y=X*2
                A=CMPLX(X+AIMAG(T),Y)
                B=CMPLX(CABS(A),REAL(2*T))
                K=A+B

4. What is the error in each of the following?

    a) COMPLEX J/1/

    b) COMPLEX A,CSQRT
       A=CSQRT(3.,4.)

    c) COMPLEX B/(1.,0.)/
       J=B**2.

    d) COMPLEX AIMAG,U/(6.,8.)/,V,CMPLX
       V=CMPLX(CABS(U),AIMAG(U**2))

    e)   COMPLEX A,B
            READ,A,B

      $ENTRY
        3.,4.   5.,6.

13.7 Extended Precision COMPLEX Values.

In order to understand the material of this section, the reader should be familiar with the ideas in Chapter 12 (Extended Precision).

Since COMPLEX values are stored as a pair of REAL values and since the precision of REAL values can be increased to sixteen significant digits by doubling the amount of memory reserved to store each such value, it is only natural to permit the two components of a COMPLEX value to have Extended Precision (E.P.) values. This is done by declaring each E.P. COMPLEX variable to have a length of sixteen bytes. In this chapter, COMPLEX values in which the real and imaginary components are E.P. values will be called COMPLEX*16 values. The rules for defining, processing, reading and printing the real and imaginary components of a COMPLEX*16 value are those found in Chapter 12. A brief summary of the important points follows.

Constants

Each COMPLEX*16 constant is defined by a pair of E.P. constants enclosed in brackets. Examples are: (1.24D02, .0004D00), (123456789.,+123456.D-8).

Variables

Each of the following statements declares A to be a COMPLEX*16 variable with an initial value of (1.,0.), B as a "regular" COMPLEX variable, and C as a vector of COMPLEX*16 variables each having an initial value of zero.

COMPLEX*16 A/(1.D00,0.D00)/,B*8,C(10)/10*(0.D00,0.D00)/

COMPLEX*8 A*16/(1.D00,0.D00),B,C*16(10)/10*(0.D00,0.D00)/

COMPLEX A*16/(1.D00,0.D00)/,B,C*16(10)/10*(0.D00,0.D00)/

The points illustrated by these examples are:

   i) A length modifier of "*16" or "*8" may follow the word COMPLEX. If omitted, "*8" is assumed.

  ii) A length modifier of "*16" or "*8" may follow a variable or array name. If omitted, the length is taken from the length associated with the word COMPLEX.

 iii) Initial values (if present) must be of the same type as the variable(s) being initialized.

300

Expressions

When a COMPLEX*16 value is combined with other types of values in an arithmetic expression, the result is a COMPLEX*16 value. Some examples are:

Expression	Result
(3.52D00,2.0D00)+(1.,2.)	(4.52D00,4.D00)
(-1.D00,0.D00)-2.D00	(-3.D00,0.D00)
(4.D00,-1.D00)*2	(8.D00,-2.D00)
(20.D00,-1.D00)/2.	(10.D00,-.5D00)

A COMPLEX*16 value is also produced if an operation involves a REAL*8 value and a COMPLEX*8 value. For example, 2.D00*3.,7.) has a value of (6.D00,14.D00).

Assignment Statements

There are two 8ases of interest.

    i) COMPLEX*16 variable = non-COMPLEX*16 value

    ii) non-COMPLEX*16 variable = COMPLEX*16 value

Consider Case (i). If the expression has a COMPLEX value, zeros are added to the right of the real and imaginary components to give each component sixteen significant digits. This value is then assigned to the COMPLEX*16 variable. If the expression is REAL (of either length) or an INTEGER vlaue, the value of the expression is assigned to the real component of the variable and the imaginary component is set equal to zero.

Consider Case (ii). If the variable is COMPLEX, the real and imaginary components of the value are truncated to seven decimal digits. If the variable is REAL (of either length) or INTEGER, the real component of the value is assigned to the variable after any necessary truncation is performed.

Built-In Functions

Several built-in functions are available for processing COMPLEX*16 values. Each function which is used must be declared as having a COMPLEX*16 value in the program segment which uses the function. In the following table, "c16" denotes a COMPLEX*16 value and "r8" denotes an E.P. value.

Table of COMPLEX*16 Built-In Functions

Name and Arguments	Definition	Type of Result
CDSQRT(c16)	Square root	COMPLEX*16
CDSIN(c16)	Sine	COMPLEX*16
CDCOS(c16)	Cosine	COMPLEX*16
CDEXP(c16)	e**argument	COMPLEX*16
CDABS(c16)	Absolute value	REAL*8
DCMPLX(r8,r8)	forms a COMPLEX*16 value from two E.P. values	COMPLEX*16
DCONJG(c16)	complex conjugate	COMPLEX*16

Note that there are no built-in functions for extracting the real and imaginary components of a COMPLEX*16 value. If this is required, an EQUIVALENCE statement must be used to equate the COMPLEX*16 value with a pair of REAL*8 variables. An example is given in Chapter 16 (see EQUIVALENCE).

Input-Output

Formatted

A pair of D-masks, F-masks, or one of each can be used to input or output C*16 values under format control.

Format-Free

On input, each COMPLEX*16 value should be punched as a pair of E.P. constants, separated by a comma and enclosed in brackets. On output, the sequence of format codes used to print each COMPLEX*16 value is

'(',D28.16,' ,',D28.16,')'

Subprograms

Arguments and parameters may have COMPLEX*16 values. If a FUNCTION has a COMPLEX*16 value, then

    i) The first statement of the FUNCTION subprogram must be

        COMPLEX FUNCTION name*16 (parameter list)

    ii) The FUNCTION name must appear in a COMPLEX*16 declaration statement in the calling segment.

13.8 Other Statements Involving COMPLEX Values.

1. COMPLEX variables may be used in statements such as COMMON, EQUIVALENCE, DIMENSION, etc. See Chapter 16 for details.

2. Subscript values may be COMPLEX. If so, the subscript value used is obtained by truncating the fractional part of the real component of the value.

3. G-masks can be used to input or output COMPLEX values. P-codes can be used to modify COMPLEX values which are input or output under one or more E-masks (D-masks if COMPLEX*16 values).

13.9 Summary

COMPLEX values can be used in WATFIV programs. Each COMPLEX value is stored as a pair of REAL values. Although the processing of complex numbers could be done using only REAL numbers and variables, the programming effort required is reduced if the COMPLEX values are used.

Programming Problems

The following ideas may be helpful in solving the problems which follow. A complex number (x,y) can represent a directed line segment (a vector) from the origin to the point (x,y) in the xy plane. Two vectors having the same length and direction but different initial points are considered equal. Thus, in the diagram below, the vectors OP and AB are considered equal.

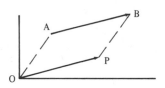

13.1 One of the most famous equations ever discovered is

$$e^{i\pi} + 1 = 0$$

It involves five of the most fundamental quantities in all of mathematics. Write a program to calculate the value on the left hand side of the equation.

13.2 If several forces are acting on a body at rest, they can be replaced by a single equivalent force. Suppose each force is represented by a value (x,y) where the magnitude of the force is given by the distance between the origin and the point (x,y). The direction of the force is represented by the angle between the x-axis and the ray thru the origin and the point (x,y). Assume the body upon which the forces are acting is at the origin. The resultant force is simply the sum of the force vectors. Write a program which reads a value of N and then N pairs of REAL numbers representing the magnitude and direction of the forces. Calculate the resultant force and print its magnitude and direction.

13.3 In the following problem, use COMPLEX numbers to represent the positions of the cat and dog. At time zero, Fifi, the cat, is located at point (0,10) in the xy plane. Fido, the dog, is at the origin. Fifi runs parallel to the x-axis at a rate of 0.8 units per second. Fido runs at a rate of 1 unit per second with his head down in the direction of Fifi. At the end of each second he lifts his head up, sees where Fifi is, and runs in that direction during the next second. How long, to the nearest second, does it take Fido to catch Fifi? Print the positions of Fifi and Fido at one second intervals during the chase.

13.4 A wooden equilateral triangle is used to hold balls on a pool table. If the rack is positioned in the corner of the pool table as shown in the following diagram, what is the distance X? Use any method you like to solve the problem.

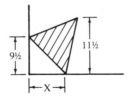

13.5 The angle between a vector represented by the complex number (x,y) and the x-axis can be calculated from the following formula.

$$\cos^{-1}\left(\frac{x}{\sqrt{x^2 + y^2}}\right)$$

Write a FUNCTION subprogram called ANGLE to calculate this value. The subprogram will have only one parameter, a COMPLEX value.

13.6 Write a FUNCTION subprogram to calculate the angle between any two vectors. Use the subprogram written for problem five in the solution to the problem.

13.7 The dot (scalar) product of two complex numbers u and v is denoted by uov and has a value of |u| |v| cos(x) where x is the angle between the vectors. The cross product of u and v has a value of |u| |v| sin(x). Write a pair of FUNCTION subprograms called DOT and CROSS to compute these values. Each will have two COMPLEX parameters. Now, two vectors in the xy plane are parallel if, and only if, their dot product is zero. They are perpendicular if, and only if, their cross product is zero. Write a mainline segment which reads the end coordinates of an unspecified number of pairs of vectors and for each, prints one of "PARALLEL", "PERPENDICULAR", or "OBLIQUE". Use the subprograms DOT and CROSS.

13.8 A man travels 24 miles northwest, 40 miles 35 degrees east of north and then 36 miles 20 degrees south of east. How far and in what direction is he from his starting point?

CHAPTER 14   LOGICAL VALUES

Questions Answered In This Chapter

1. What are LOGICAL values?

2. How are LOGICAL values defined and used in WATFIV programs?

Before studying the material in this chapter the reader should be familiar with the ideas in Chapter 10.

14.1 LOGICAL Values

In general, any statement is either true or false. For example, "Two is less than three." is true; "August comes before July." is false; "The point (3,4) lies outside the circle $x^2 + y^2 = 1$." is true, and so on. If one is writing a program in which some of the variables have true-false values it may be desirable to use LOGICAL variables, constants and operators to represent and manipulate true-false quantities. This chapter describes how.

14.2 LOGICAL Constants, Variables and Expressions

Constants

There are only two LOGICAL constants. They are ".TRUE." and ".FALSE.". Each has a length of four (occupies four bytes of memory). Details of the bit patterns used to represent the values of .TRUE. and .FALSE. can be found in Appendix C.

Variables

LOGICAL variables are those which can be assigned values of .TRUE. and .FALSE.. A LOGICAL statement is used to define LOGICAL variables and (optionally) specify initial values. Consider the following two examples.

i)   LOGICAL U,V/.TRUE./

ii) LOGICAL TF(80)/80*.FALSE./,X/F/,Y/T/

In example (i), the variables U and V are defined as LOGICAL variables and V is given an initial value of .TRUE.. In example (ii), TF is defined as a set of eighty LOGICAL variables each of which has an initial value of .FALSE.. Furthermore, X and Y are simple LOGICAL variables with initial values of .FALSE. and .TRUE. respectively. Note that when specifying initial values for LOGICAL variables, it is sufficient to use "T" or "F" to indicate values of .TRUE. and .FALSE. respectively.

Expressions

The arithmetic operators are meaningless when applied to LOGICAL values. Dividing "true" by "false", for instance, is nonsense. There are three operators which do have meaning, however. They are ".AND.", ".OR.", and ".NOT.". They are called LOGICAL operators. The effect of each is as follows. "U.AND.V" is .TRUE. only if both U and V are individually .TRUE.. "U.OR.V" is .TRUE. if either or both of U and V is individually .TRUE.. Finally, ".NOT.U" is .TRUE. if U is .FALSE. and ".NOT.U" is .FALSE. if U is .TRUE.. That is, the operator .NOT. changes the "truth value" of the value on which it operates.

The priority of the LOGICAL operators (in the absence of brackets) is

.NOT.

.AND.

.OR.

For example,

.TRUE..OR..FALSE..AND..NOT..FALSE.

is evaluated as if written with the following sets of brackets.

.TRUE..OR.(.FALSE..AND.(.NOT..FALSE.))

By working from the innermost brackets outwards the expression is found to have a value of .TRUE.

LOGICAL operations are performed only after all other types of operations have been completed. This means that the complete set of priorities in evaluating WATFIV expressions is as follows.

1. Evaluation of functions

2. Brackets

3. Arithmetic operations (**, *, /, +, -)

4. Relational operations (.LE., .LT., .EQ., etc.)

5. Logical Operations (.NOT., .AND., .OR.)

307

"Truth Tables" can often be used to create a LOGICAL expression having desired properties. A Truth Table can also be used to evaluate a complex LOGICAL expression and perhaps replace it with a simpler but equivalent expression. For example, suppose A and B are LOGICAL variables. What is the value of "(A.OR.B).AND.(.NOT.(A.AND.B))"? The truth table for this expression is shown below.

Truth Table For (A.OR.B).AND.(.NOT.(A.AND.B))

A	B	C=(A.OR.B)	D=(.NOT.(A.AND.B))	C.AND.D
T	T	T	F	F
T	F	T	T	T
F	T	T	T	T
F	F	F	T	F

There are four rows in the table because there are four possible combinations of truth values of A and B. For each combination, columns three and four indicate the truth value of a part of the expression and column five indicates the overall value of the expression for the combination being evaluated. An expression which has the truth values indicated in the foregoing table is often called the "exclusive or" of A and B. That is, it is .TRUE. if exactly one but not both of A and B is .TRUE..

Two identities known as DeMorgan's Laws are frequently useful in writing LOGICAL expressions. These are:

$$.NOT.(A.AND.B) \equiv (.NOT.A).OR.(.NOT.B)$$

$$.NOT.(A.OR.B) \equiv (.NOT.A).AND.(.NOT.B)$$

14.3 Assignment Statements and Comparisons

Assignment Statements

A LOGICAL Assignment statement has the general form:

LOGICAL variable = LOGICAL value

The value on the right may be a LOGICAL constant, variable or expression.

Suppose U and V are LOGICAL variables and X and Y are REAL variables. Examples of LOGICAL Assignment statements are:

$$U = .NOT.V.OR..TRUE.$$

$$V = X.LE.Y$$

Note that the use of a relational operator produces a LOGICAL value.

Comparisons

Relational operators cannot be used to compare LOGICAL quantiles. Instead, the LOGICAL operators are used in conjunction with a Logical IF statement. Consider the following examples. Assume X and Y have LOGICAL values.

Requirement	Solution
Test X for a value of .TRUE.	IF(X) ...
Test X for a value of .FALSE.	IF(.NOT.X) ...
Test X and Y for equality	IF(X.AND.Y)GO TO ... (equal) IF(NOT.(X.OR.Y))GO TO ... (equal)
Test X and Y for being different	IF(X.AND..NOT.Y)GO TO ... (unequal) IF(Y.AND..NOT.X)GO TO ... (unequal)

These examples should make it clear why a Logical IF statement is called a Logical IF statement.

14.4 Built-In Functions

There are no LOGICAL built-in functions. If a particular LOGICAL expression is frequently required, a Statement Function may be useful in reducing programming time. Statement Functions having non-REAL and non-INTEGER values are discssed in Chapter 16. A SUBROUTINE or FUNCTION subprogram may also be useful in performing frequently required LOGICAL operations. Subprograms are discussed in Section 6.

14.5 Input-Output of LOGICAL Values

Formatted

An L-mask is used to input and output LOGICAL values under format control. Its general form is "Lw" where "w" denotes the number of card columns or print positions covered by the L-mask.

On input, the L columns covered by the mask are scanned left to right. The first occurence of a "T" or "F" results in the input variable being assigned a value of .TRUE. or .FALSE. respectively. If no "T" or "F" is found, a value of .FALSE. is assigned to the variable.

On output, values of .TRUE. and .FALSE. are indicated by the appearance of "T" or "F" respectively in the rightmost print position reserved by the L-mask. As with other masks, any unused print positions are left unchanged.

The following program illustrates formatted input-output of LOGICAL values.

```
C FORMATTED I/O OF LOGICAL VALUES
      LOGICAL A,B,C
      READ 900,A,B,C
  900 FORMAT(3L4)
      PRINT 901,A,B,C
  901 FORMAT('1',L3,2L1)
      STOP
      END
$ENTRY
FLATHATSHEAP
```

When this program is executed, The symbols "FTF" appear in print positions four thru six at the top of a page.

Format-Free

When reading LOGICAL values using a format-free READ statement, successive data items are separated by a comma and/or one or more blank card columns. The first "T" or "F" encountered as the data item is scanned left to right results in the input variable being assigned a value of .TRUE. or .FALSE. respectively. If no "T" or "F" is found, a value of .FALSE. is assigned to the variable. The following example illustrates format-free input of LOGICAL values.

```
      LOGICAL U,V,W,X
      READ,U,V,W,X
      ...
      ...
$ENTRY
.TRUE.  HALT, AFTER  NONE
```

When the READ statement is executed, U and V are each assigned a value of .TRUE. and W and X are assigned a value of .FALSE..

In format-free output operations the mask used for each LOGICAL value in the output list is "L8". This means a "T"

310

or "F" is printed in the rightmost print position of the
eight reserved by the mask. The symbols "UUUUUUUU" will be
printed for any LOGICAL variable which has not been assigned
a value.

14.6 Subprograms

LOGICAL values may be used as arguments for a
subprogram. The corresponding parameter will normally be a
LOGICAL variable or an array. If a FUNCTION subprogram is to
have a LOGICAL value, the FUNCTION name must be declared as
being LOGICAL in the calling segment. The first statement of
the subprogram will have the general form

LOCICAL FUNCTION name (parameter list)

The following subprogram could be used to determine if a
point with coordinates (A,B) lies inside the circle $x^2+y^2=1$.

```
LOGICAL CIRCLE,S              LOGICAL FUNCTION CIRCLE(X,Y)
READ,A,B                      Z=SQRT(X*X+Y*Y)
S=CIRCLE(A,B)                 CIRCLE=Z.LE.1.
IF(S)PRINT,'INSIDE'           RETURN
IF(.NOT.S)PRINT,'OUTSIDE'     END
STOP
END
```

14.7 LOGICAL*1 Variables

Each LOGICAL variable has a default length of four. If
a large number of LOGICAL variables are used in a program, a
considerble saving in memory space can be achieved by
specifying that some or all of the LOGICAL variables are to
have a length of one. This is done in the same way that
optional lengths are specified for REAL and INTEGER
variables.

The following three statements are equivalent. Each
specifies that that U and V are LOGICAL variables of length
one and that X is an array of twenty LOGICAL variables of
length four. Initial values are provided for U and X.

   i)   LOGICAL U*1/.TRUE./,V*1,X(20)/20*F/

   ii) LOGICAL*1 U/.TRUE./,V,X*4(20)/20*F/

   iii) LOGICAL*4 U*1/.TRUE./,V*1,X(20)/20*F/

The points illustrated by these statements are:

   i)   A length modifier of "*1" or "*4" may follow the
        word LOGICAL. If omitted, "*4" is assumed.

311

ii) A length modifier of "*1" or "*4" may follow a variable or array name. If omitted, the length of the variable is that associated with the word LOGICAL.

iii) Initial values may be specified for LOGICAL variables. They can be any of: ".TRUE.", ".FALSE.", "T", or "F".

The LOGICAL constants .TRUE. and .FALSE. have a length of four.

LOGICAL*1 variables can be used anywhere that LOGICAL variables are used. If an operation involves a LOGICAL*1 value and a LOGICAL*4 value, the result has a length of four.

Exercise 14.1

1. For each of the following, determine the last value assigned to every variable used in the sequence.

a) LOGICAL U/.TRUE./, V/.FALSE./, T, Z
    T=U.AND..NOT.V
    IF(U.AND.T)Z=V.OR.T

b) LOGICAL U,V,W,X,F/F/
    U=V=F
    W=.NOT.U.OR.V.OR..NOT.F
    IF(.NOT.F.OR.U.AND..NOT.W) X=.TRUE.

c) LOGICAL T/F/,F/T/,TF,Z   LOGICAL FUNCTION TF(T,F)
    I=A=2.7   LOGICAL T,F
    B=I**(-1)   TF=.NOT.T.OR.F
    Z=TF(T,F)   F=T
    IF(A*B.EQ.1)Z=TF(F,T)   T=F
    STOP   RETURN
    END   END

d)   LOGICAL READ,PRINT
        READ,READ
        PRINT,READ
        READ,PRINT
        PRINT,PRINT
        STOP
        END
    $ENTRY
        AFTER THE BALL GAME
        NOT BEFORE

e) LOGICAL TRUE/F/,FALSE/T/,AND,OR,NOT
    AND(OR,NOT)=.NOT.NOT.AND.OR.OR.TRUE.
    OR(NOT)=AND(NOT,NOT).OR.NOT
    FALSE=OR(.NOT.TRUE).AND.AND(FALSE,TRUE)

2. For each of the following LOGICAL expressions, write
   another LOGICAL expression which will have the opposite
   truth value regardless of the values of the variables
   appearing in the expression.

   a)   .NOT.A
   b)   3.GE.X
   c)   B.LT.C.OR.C.GT.D
   d)   .NOT.B.AND.NOT.C
   e)   .NOT.(A.AND.B).AND.A.OR.B
   f)   3..EQ.X.AND..NOT.X.NE.Y.OR.Z

3. a) Construct a truth table for the expression below.

   A.AND.B.AND..NOT.C.OR.B.AND.C.AND..NOT.A

   b) Use the truth table to assist in writing a simpler
   expression which is equivalent to the one given.

4. The truth table below has eight rows. Each row represents
   one of the eight possible different combinations of
   truth values of A, B, and C. The five remaining columns
   are labelled (a), (b), (c), (d), and (e). For each of
   (a) thru (e), write a LOGICAL expression which would
   give the truth values shown in that column for all the
   corresponding combinations of values of A, B, and C.
   Five different expressions are required.

A	B	C	(a)	(b)	(c)	(d)	(e)
T	T	T	F	T	F	F	T
T	T	F	F	F	T	T	F
T	F	T	F	F	F	T	F
T	F	F	F	F	T	F	T
F	T	T	F	T	T	T	T
F	T	F	T	F	T	F	F
F	F	T	F	F	T	F	F
F	F	F	F	F	T	F	F

14.8 Summary

   LOGICAL operations (those involving the manipulation of
true-false quantities) can be performed in a meaningful way
by using LOGICAL constants and variables in a program.
Using LOGICAL values instead of the INTEGER values of zero
and one offers several advantages the most significant of
which is ease of understanding the program logic.

Programming Problems

14.1 Consider the two circles defined by the pair of equations $x^2+y^2=9$ and $(x-2)^2+(y-4)^2=16$. Write a program which reads values of x and y and prints a "T" if the point (x,y) lies inside both circles and "F" otherwise. Test the program on the following points: (1,1), (1,-1), (2,-.5), (0,1), (0,-2.5).

14.2 Suppose each student's answers to a true-false test of ten questions have been punched on cards. On each student card, columns one to six contain the student's ID number; columns seven to ten are blank and columns eleven thru twenty contain "T's" and "F's" indicating the student's answers. Assume twelve students took the test. Preceeding the first student card is a card containing the correct answers. This answer card has an ID number of zeros and the correct answers in columns eleven thru twenty. Write a program which:

    a) Lists each student's answers and calculates the percentage of right answers.

    b) Calculates the average mark on the test.

    c) Prints the percentage of right answers for each question.

    d) Determines how many students answered both of questions 3 and 7 correctly.

    e) Determines those questions for which the students in the bottom half of the class did as well as students in the top half of the class.

The foregoing problem should be solved making the assumption that each student answered all questions. Suppose now that a blank in an answer column means that the student did not answer the question. Explain why this makes the programming problem more difficult. Can you solve the problem with this new assumption?

14.3 The game of Tic-Tac-Toe is well known. Suppose the elements of a three-by-three matrix called BOARD contain values of -1, 1, or 0 where: -1 indicates Player One has chosen the square; +1 indicates Player Two has chosen the square; 0 indicates neither player has chosen the square. Write a program which read values for BOARD and prints one of "PLAYER ONE WINS", "PLAYER TWO WINS", or "UNDECIDED".

14.4 On the island of Ho, there are two races -- the Good Guys who always tell the truth, and the Bad Guys who

always lie. On my last visit to the island, I met three
villagers named Tom, Dick and Zack. I asked each of them
one question.

Q: Tell me Tom, is Dick a Good Guy?
A: Yes.

Q: Dick, do Tom and Zack belong to the same race?
A: No.

Q: Zack, what about Dick, is he a Good Guy?
A: Yes.

Write a program to determine the races of the three
villagers. To solve this problem, generate the eight
possible combinations of race-to-people assignments
using three DO-loops. Check each combination to see if
they would answer the questions in the manner described.
This can be done using as few as three IF statements.
Remember that the computer cannot think or reason and
you must find the implications of each answer under the
assumption that the speaker was first of all, a Good
Guy, and secondly, a Bad Guy. The results of this
analysis will permit you construct the appropriate IF
statements.

14.5   Three men named Able, Baker, and Charlie have
occupations of shipper, pilot and banker. The following
four statements are sufficient to permit you to
determine each man's occupation. (1) If Charlie is the
shipper then Baker is the pilot. (2) If Charlie is the
pilot then Baker is the banker. (3) If Baker is not the
shipper then Able is the pilot. (4) If Able is the
banker then Charlie is the pilot. Write a program to
determine each man's occupation.

CHAPTER 15   CHARACTER VALUES

Questions Answered In This Chapter

    1.   What are CHARACTER values?

    2.   How are CHARACTER values defined and used in WATFIV programs?

    3.   How can one define and use non-standard symbols in WATFIV programs?

    4.   What methods are available for manipulating the patterns of ones and zeros used to represent values of variables used in a WATFIV program?

Before studying the material of this chapter, the reader should be familiar with the ideas presented in Chapter 10.

15.1 CHARACTER Values

Strings of symbols can be defined and manipulated in WATFIV programs. You and I regard "1234" as both a number on which arithmetic operations can be performed and as a string of four symbols. In WATFIV, a distinction is made. If "1234" is to be treated as a number, it will appear in a REAL or INTEGER expression. If the symbols are of interest, it must be defined as a CHARACTER value.

What symbols can be used in CHARACTER values? The standard set of CHARACTER values in WATFIV consists of the following forty-eight symbols.

letters: ABCDEFGHIJKLMNOPQRSTUVWXYZ

digits: 0123456789

special symbols: +-*/,.'()=$ blank

What of the other symbols which appear on a keypunch? Can they be defined, input and/or output under control of a WATFIV program? The answer is yes -- and in fact, many other symbols which do not appear on a keypunch can often be used. Section 15.12 describes how.

15.2 CHARACTER Constants, Variables, and Expressions

Constants

A CHARACTER constant consists of a string of symbols enclosed in single quotes. Examples are: 'FEBRUARY 8,1942', 'K96', and 'AVERAGE='. The length of a CHARACTER constant is simply the number of symbols (including blanks) between the quote signs. The maximum number of symbols permitted in a CHARACTER constant is 255. One byte of memory is used to store each symbol in the constant. Hence the length of a CHARACTER constant is the number of symbols it contains. This means that four symbols can be stored in the amount of memory used to store each REAL or INTEGER value. If a quote sign is one of the symbols in the constant, a pair of successive quote signs is used to indicate this fact to the compiler. For example, the CHARACTER constant "IT'S" is defined as 'IT''S'. The length of 'IT''S' is four, however, since the second quote of any successive pair is not stored in the computer's memory.

Variables

Variables which take on CHARACTER values can be defined and assigned initial values. Unless declared otherwise, each CHARACTER value has a length of one. That is, each CHARACTER variable is capable of storing only one symbol. If more than one symbol must be stored in a CHARACTER variable, the compiler must be informed of this fact as illustrated in the following examples.

   i) CHARACTER A,B*2

   ii) CHARACTER*4 TUF,BAKER*2,LENGTH*6/'LENGTH'/

   iii) CHARACTER MONTH*4(4)/'JAN.','FEB.','MAR.','APR.'/

   iv) CHARACTER*3 X/'A'/,Y/'ABCDE'/

In example (i), the variable A is defined as a CHARACTER variable of length one (one is the default length). Because a length modifier of "*2" follows the variable name B, B is a CHARACTER variable of length two (capable of storing two symbols).

In example (ii), a length modifier of "*4" has been appended to the word CHARACTER. This means that all variables appearing in the list will have a length of four unless declared otherwise. In particular, BAKER has a length of two and LENGTH a length of six with an initial value of 'LENGTH'.

In example (iii), MONTH is declared as being a set of four CHARACTER variables, each of length four. The values of the elements of MONTH are initialized to the abbreviations of the first four months of the year.

In example (iv), X and Y are defined as CHARACTER variables, each of length three. Since the initial value assigned to X has only one symbol, two blanks are added to the right of the constant 'A' to give the initializing constant a length of three. Thus the initial value of X is 'A '. Since the initial value for Y has more than three symbols, two of the symbols must be truncated. O.K. -- which ones? In an assignment operation, the rightmost symbols are truncated. Thus the initial value for Y is 'ABC'.

The points illustrated by these examples are:

i) A length modifier of "*1" thru "*255" may follow the word CHARACTER. If omitted, a length of one is assumed.

ii) A length modifier of "*1" thru "*255" may follow a variable of array name. If omitted, the length of the variable is taken from the length associated with the word CHARACTER.

iii) Initial values may be assigned to CHARACTER variables. Initializing constants which are shorter than the length of the variable are padded on the right with blanks. Initializing constants which have too many symbols are truncated beginning with the rightmost symbol. A warning message is printed in this latter case.

Expressions

There are no operators for manipulating CHARACTER values. It is meaningless, for instance, to multiply 'SEPTEMBER' by 'HAMBURGER'.

15.3 Comparison of CHARACTER Values

In some programs it may be necessary to compare one or more strings of symbols. For example, if X and Y are CHARACTER variables of length ten, the statement

            IF(X.EQ.Y) ...

could be used to test the strings for equality. If two CHARACTER values of different lengths are compared, blanks are added to the right of the shorter value before the comparison is made. This means the values 'A' and 'A ' are considered equal if they are compared using a Logical IF statement.

318

The other five relational operators can also be used to compare CHARACTER values. For example, the following expressions are all true.

'A'.LT.'B'   '2'.LT.'9'

'A'.LE.'B'   '9'.GE.'2'

'C'.NE.'4'   ')'.GT.'('

The "dictionary" order of the standard set of forty-eight WATFIV symbols is as follows.

blank .(+$*)-/,'= A thru Z   0 thru 9

This means that: any letter is "less than" any number; any special character is "less than" any letter and hence "less than" any number, etc. The sequence of symbols above is often called the "collating sequence of CHARACTER values of length one". If strings of length two or longer are compared, the comparison proceeds left to right as you would expect. Thus, since "." is less than "-", '.A93' is less than '-A93'. The constant '*Z)K' is greater than '*A)K', etc.. If the strings being compared have different lengths, the shorter string is padded on the right with blanks before the comparison is made. For example, '/Z3' is greater than '/Z' since '3' is greater than a blank.

15.4 CHARACTER Assignment Statements

A CHARACTER Assignment statement has the form

CHARACTER variable = CHARACTER value

The value on the right may be a CHARACTER constant or a CHARACTER variable. No problem arises if the variable on the left and the value on the right have the same length. If the lengths are different, we need an **apt** reminder of what happens. Here it is.

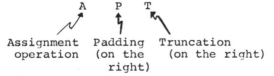

Assignment   Padding   Truncation
operation   (on the   (on the right)
             right)

In the word "APT", the letters "P" (for padding) and "T" (for truncation) appear to the right of the letter "A" (for Assignment).

To illustrate the use of the APT rule, suppose the variable "CHAR" has a length of three. Consider the three statements:

i) CHAR='ABC'   ii) CHAR='A'   iii) CHAR='ABCDEF'

In (i), CHAR is given the value 'ABC'. In (ii), the value of
'A' must be padded with two blanks to give it a length of
three. Using the APT rule, padding occurs on the right.
Thus CHAR is given the value 'A '. In (iii), three symbols
must be truncated. The APT rule says truncate on the right.
Thus CHAR is assigned the value 'ABC'. Note that the APT
rule also describes how initial values are assigned to
CHARACTER variables at compile time.

15.5 Built-In Functions

There are no built-in functions for manipulating
CHARACTER values in WATFIV. Most computing centers however,
have a library of SUBROUTINES for manipulating and analyzing
CHARACTER values. Routines for determining the length of a
string, the positions of a set of symbols within a string,
or creating a long string from a pair of shorter strings,
are often available.

15.6 Input-Output of CHARACTER Values

Formatted Input-Output

An A-mask is used to input or output CHARACTER values
under format control. The general form of an A-mask is "Aw"
where "w" denotes the number of card columns or print
positions covered by the mask. Suppose X is a CHARACTER
variable of length three. The following table shows the
results when different A-masks are used to input a value of
X under format control.

Mask	Symbols In Columns Covered By Mask	Value Assigned To X (length 3)
A3	PQR	'PQR'
A1	P	'P '
A6	PQRSTU	'STU'

How about a tip to help remember where padding and
truncation occur during input operations? Here it is.

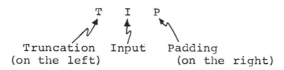

Truncation   Input   Padding
(on the left)   (on the right)

In words, the TIP rule says: "On an input operation, if the
mask covers fewer columns than the length of the variable,
padding occurs (blanks are added) on the right. If the mask

320

covers more columns than the length of the variable, truncation occurs beginning with the leftmost symbol covered by the mask.".

For formatted output operations, the word "POT" should be remembered. That is,

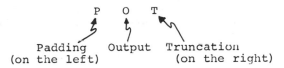

Padding   Output   Truncation
(on the left)   (on the right)

To illustrate the POT rule, consider the following pair of statements.

```
        PRINT 999,'ABC','DEF','GHI'
    999 FORMAT('1',A3,A5,A1)
```

The effect is to print the symbols

ABC DEFG

A3   A5 A1

at the top of a page. Note that on output, padding occurs on the left and truncation occurs on the right. This is just the opposite of the padding-truncation effect on input.

Format-Free Input-Output

CHARACTER variables may appear in an input list used with a format-free READ statement. The data values to be assigned to the variables must be punched as CHARACTER constants and separated by a comma and/or one or more blank columns. When using format-free input for CHARACTER variables, the TIP rule describes where padding and truncation occur.

In format-free output operations, WATFIV assigns a mask of "Aw" to each CHARACTER value in the output list. The value of "w" used is one more than the length of the value being printed. Because of the POT rule, a blank appears to the left of the leftmost symbol in the value. The following example program illustrates format-free input and output of CHARACTER values.

```
            CHARACTER*4 X,Y,Z
            READ,X,Y,Z
            PRINT,X,Y,Z
            STOP
            END
        $ENTRY
        'ABCD',    'EF'    'GHIJKL'
```

321

When the program is executed, the values assigned to the variables, and hence the values printed are: X='ABCD', Y='EF ', Z='IJKL'.

15.7 FUNCTION and SUBROUTINE Subprograms

CHARACTER values may be used as arguments for a subprogram. The corresponding parameter will normally be a CHARACTER variable or array having the same properties. If the argument is an array, the parameter array should be of the same length or shorter than the argument array. Rules of correspondence are the same as those for other types of values.

Suppose a sequence of symbols is read from a card and it is desired to know if the symbols "THE" appear. The following FUNCTION subprogram could be used to indicate the last card column in which the first symbol of "THE" appears. A FUNCTION value of zero means "THE" does not appear.

```
C    EXAMPLE 15.1                 INTEGER FUNCTION TEST(X)
        INTEGER TEST             CHARACTER X(80)
        CHARACTER COL(80)        TEST=0
        READ 99,COL              DO 1 N=1,78
99      FORMAT(80A1)             IF(X(N).NE.'T') GO TO 1
        PRINT,TEST(COL)          IF(X(N+1).NE.'H')GO TO 1
        STOP                     IF(X(N+2).EQ.'E')TEST=N
        END                    1 CONTINUE
                                 RETURN
                                 END
```

Does this program determine which card column contains the last occurence of the beginning of the word "THE"? If you think so, suppose the mainline read a card containing the words "GATHER THERE TO BATHE". What would the output be?

Note that any arguments and parameters which take on CHARACTER values must be defined with an appropriate length in the segment in which they are used.

CHARACTER valued FUNCTION subprograms are not permitted in WATFIV. A statement such as

        CHARACTER FUNCTION INDEX*3(A,B)

will result in a compile time error.

One feature which can be used to great advantage is the following. If an argument is a simple CHARACTER value, the corresponding parameter can be an array provided the total length of the parameter array does not excede the length of the argument value. For example, if X is a CHARACTER variable of length ten then the following program structure is permissible.

```
CHARACTER*10 X              SUBROUTINE LOOK(STRING,N)
READ,X                      CHARACTER STRING(N)
...                         ...
CALL LOOK(X,10)             ...
...                         ...
END                         END
```

The advantage of passing a CHARACTER variable to a parameter array is that the subprogram can be used to analyze the individual symbols stored in the variable.

15.8 Two Example Programs

Example 1

The following program could be used to print whatever is punched in a deck of data cards.

```
C EXAMPLE 15.2 PRINT DATA DECK
      CHARACTER*80 CARD
    1 READ(5,2,END=4) CARD
    2 FORMAT(A80)
      PRINT 3, CARD
    3 FORMAT(' ',A80)
      GO TO 1
    4 STOP
      END
$ENTRY
```

The foregoing program is sometimes called an "80-80 List". That is, eighty columns of each card are read and the symbols in all eighty columns are printed.

Example 2

Suppose a sentence has been punched on a card. The problem is to count the number of words of length 1,2,3,...,15 in the sentence. The method used in the following program is simply to determine the locations of blank card columns. The length of the word between the blanks is then one less than the difference of the positions of the blanks.

```
C EXAMPLE 15.3 WORD LENGTHS
      CHARACTER COLUMN(80),BLANK/' '/
      INTEGER LENGTH(15)/15*0/,POS1/0/,DIFF
      READ 900,COLUMN
  900 FORMAT(80A1)
      DO 20 I=1,80
      IF(COLUMN(I).NE.BLANK) GO TO 20
      DIFF=I-POS1
      IF(DIFF.EQ.1) GO TO 15
      LENGTH(DIFF-1)=LENGTH(DIFF-1)+1
   15 POS1=I
   20 CONTINUE
C CHECK TO SEE IF COLUMN 80 IS BLANK
C   IF SO, TAKE CARE OF LAST WORD
      IF(POS1.EQ.80) GO TO 25
      LENGTH(81-POS1)=LENGTH(81-POS1)+1
   25 PRINT 901,'COUNT OF WORDS OF VARIOUS LENGTHS'
     * ,'LENGTH','COUNT'
  901 FORMAT('1',A32,/,5X,A6,3X,A5)
      PRINT 902,(I,LENGTH(I),I=1,15)
  902 FORMAT('0',I10,5X,I5)
      STOP
      END
```

15.9 Storing Format Codes In CHARACTER Arrays

Aside from a statement number and the word "FORMAT", a FORMAT statement contains a string of codes enclosed in brackets. In WATFIV, the brackets and the codes enclosed by them can be stored in the first element of a CHARACTER array and subsequently referenced by formatted READ, WRITE or PRINT statements. Consider the following example.

```
C EXAMPLE 15.4 FORMAT CODES AS CHARACTER VALUES
      CHARACTER*9 FMT(1)/'(I4,F7.2)'/
      J=301
      X=1.75
      PRINT FMT,J,X
      STOP
      END
```

In this example, the array name "FMT" follows the word "PRINT". This means that the formatting information is to be found in the first element of the array "FMT". Consequently, the PRINT statement in this example produces output which is identical to that which would be obtained using the following pair of statements.

```
      PRINT 999,J,X
  999 FORMAT(I4,F7.2)
```

The statement "WRITE(6,FMT) J,X" could have been used instead of the the PRINT statement shown.

The rules for storing and using format codes assigned to CHARACTER variables are as follows.

i) The format codes stored in a CHARACTER variable must begin with a left bracket and end with a right bracket.

ii) The CHARACTER variable containing the start of the codes to be used must be the first element of an array.

iii) In a formatted input or output statement, the statement number of a FORMAT statement may be replaced by the name of an array containing the codes. The codes are assumed to be found starting in the first element of the array.

Why must the codes be stored in an array element? Why not a simple CHARACTER variable? The reason in that most Fortran languages do not allow CHARACTER variables. Instead, CHARACTER values, and hence format codes, must be stored in an INTEGER, REAL or some other type of array. To be consistent across all types of variables, the rule is that codes must be stored in an array. Further details can be found in Chapter 16, Section 12.

Why store format codes in a CHARACTER array instead of using a FORMAT statement? Because CHARACTER values can be read from a card, this means that different format information can be made available at execution time. For example, the following program structure reads in format information for a report heading which it then passes to a subprogram called report.

```
C EXAMPLE 15.5 EXECUTION TIME FORMAT CODES
      CHARACTER*33 HEADER(1)
      READ 2, HEADER
    2 FORMAT(A33)
      ...
      CALL REPORT(HEADER,...)
      ..
      END

      SUBROUTINE REPORT(LINE1,...)
      ...
      PRINT LINE1
      ...
      END
$ENTRY
('1SPECIAL REPORT FOR J.B.SMITH')
```

A second situation in which storing format codes as CHARACTER values may be useful is found in the following example. Suppose several numbers from one thru six are punched as INTEGER values, one per card. The problem is simply to read in each value and print a "*" in the print position specified by the number on the card. The following program could be used.

```
C EXAMPLE 15.6 FORMAT CODE SELECTION
      CHARACTER*4 FMT(6)/'(A2)','(A3)','(A4)',
     * '(A5)','(A6)','(A7)'/,CODES(1)
    1 READ(5,*,END=2) N
      CODES(1)=FMT(N)
      PRINT CODES,'*'
      GO TO 1
    2 STOP
      END
```

The reason for using the array CODES in the foregoing program is to satisfy the requirement that the start of the format codes must be in the first element of an array.

Suppose now that INTEGER values of one thru one-hundred were permitted for the foregoing problem. Using the approach found in the example would mean that one-hundred different codes of the type '(An)' would have to be defined, simply because we have no way (as yet) of making the value of "w" in a mask such as "Aw" a variable quantity. It would be nice, for instance, to use a sequence of statements such as the following.

```
      READ,N
      PRINT 1,'*'
    1 FORMAT(A(N+1))
```

In order to do something like this, it is necessary to convert the value of N from an INTEGER value to a CHARACTER value. The method for doing this is described in detail in Chapter 20.

Exercise 15.1

1. If the following sequence of statements is executed, what is the last value assigned to each variable?

```
      CHARACTER*3 X/'AC'/,Y/'DE'/,U*2,W*4/'ACDE'/
      U=X
      IF(U.EQ.X)Y=X
      IF(U.EQ.W)W=X
      IF(Y.NE.X)Y=X
```

326

2. Suppose an array T has been defined by

        CHARACTER*3 T(5)

Suppose the symbol "A" is punched in the even numbered columns of a card and the symbol "B" is punched in the odd numbered columns of the same card. What is printed in each of the following cases.

a)   READ 900,T   b)   READ 900,T
   900 FORMAT(5A2)   900 FORMAT(5A2)
       PRINT 901,T   PRINT 902,T
   901 FORMAT('1',5A1)   902 FORMAT('1',5A4)

c)   READ 903,T   d)   READ 903,T
   903 FORMAT(5A4)   903 FORMAT(5A4)
       PRINT 904,T   PRINT 905,T
   904 FORMAT('1',5A1)   905 FORMAT('1',5A4)

3. What is the error in each of the following?

    a)   CHARACTER X*3/ABC/

    b)   CHARACTER SET*256(5)/5*' '/

    c)   CHARACTER U*3/'111'/,V*3/'222'/
          IF(U+V.EQ.'333') STOP

    d)   CHARACTER W(5),S(5)
          READ,W
          S=W
          PRINT,S

    e)   CHARACTER*2 R/'3.3E02'/
          S=3.3E02
          PRINT 9,S,R
        9 FORMAT('0',2E10.3)

    f)   CHARACTER*10 A   SUBROUTINE OHOH(X)
          CALL OHOH(A)   CHARACTER X(10)
          PRINT,A   IF(X.EQ.' ')RETURN
          STOP   RETURN
          END   END

    g)   CHARACTER U,F   CHARACTER FUNCTION F(T)
          READ,U   CHARACTER T
          PRINT,F(U)   IF(T.EQ.'X')F=' '
          STOP   F=T
          END   RETURN
                                     END

4. Where are the APT, TIP and POT rules applied?

5. A synonym for "CHARACTER constant" is "literal". To print a CHARACTER constant, the value of the constant can appear as an item in an output list or as a literal in a FORMAT statement. Does one method have any advantages over the other?

6. Suppose the following sequence of statements appears in a program.

```
      CHARACTER*4 CYEAR
      READ 900,CYEAR,IYEAR,YEAR
  900 FORMAT(A4,T1,I4,T1,F4.0)
```

What is achieved during the input operation?

7. Suppose CHARACTER values are read from a card using a format-free READ statement. (a) What is the maximum number of data values which can be punched on a single card? (b) If each value in the input list has a length of three, what is the maximum number which can be punched on a card?

8. Suppose an unknown number of INTEGER values have been punched on a card. The values are separated by commas. It is necessary to know how many values have been punched on the card. Explain why this problem cannot be solved easily using our present knowledge. (A suitable technique is described in Chapter 20.)

15.10 Hexadecimal Values

Occasionally, a WATFIV programmer wants to "get at the bits". That is, he may want to do one or more of the following.

i) Assign a particular bit pattern to a variable.

ii) Print out the bit pattern of a variable.

iii) Manipulate the individual bits of a value.

Topics (i) and (ii) are described in this section. Topic (iii) is described in Section 15.11.

A byte consists of eight bits. In WATFIV, if one wishes to assign a bit pattern or print a bit pattern stored in one or more bytes of memory, it can be done by working with groups of four bits at a time. A group of four bits is called a hexadecimal value. The term hexadecimal is used since there are sixteen possible patterns of four bits. The sixteen patterns and the hexadecimal symbol used to identify each is found in the following table.

Bit Pattern	Hexadecimal Value	Bit Pattern	Hexadecimal Value
0 0 0 0	0	1 0 0 0	8
0 0 0 1	1	1 0 0 1	9
0 0 1 0	2	1 0 1 0	A
0 0 1 1	3	1 0 1 1	B
0 1 0 0	4	1 1 0 0	C
0 1 0 1	5	1 1 0 1	D
0 1 1 0	6	1 1 1 0	E
0 1 1 1	7	1 1 1 1	F

The following table shows some bit patterns and how to decribe them using hexadecimal symbols.

Bit Pattern	Length (in bytes)	Hexadecimal Representation
00001111	1	0F
10101100	1	AC
0011001100110011	2	3333
1111000111000011	2	F1C3

Note that two hexadecimal digits are required to describe the bit pattern of one byte.

The use of hexadecimal values in WATFIV programs is restricted to the following four situations.

    i) Compile time initialization of variables

   ii) Formatted input operations

  iii) Format-free input operations

   iv) Formatted output operations

Compile Time Initialization

Suppose a CHARACTER variable K of length two is to be assigned the bit pattern shown below.

Bits	0101 1001 1101 0000

Hexadecimal	5 9 D 0

A statement to achieve this result is

```
CHARACTER*2 K/Z59D0/
```

Note that the initializing constant is preceded by the letter "Z". Since two hexadecimal digits are required to represent the bit pattern of one byte, the initializing constant must have four hexadecimal symbols. If fewer symbols are provided than necessary, hexadecimal zeros are added on the left. If the initializing constant contains a surplus of symbols, the leftmost symbols are truncated and a warning message is printed. For example,

```
INTEGER A/ZABCD/,B/Z12345678AB/
```

is equivalent to

```
INTEGER A/Z0000ABCD/,B/Z345678AB/
```

Formatted Input-Output (The Z-mask)

The general form of the Z-mask is "Zw" where "w" denotes the number of card columns (for input) or print positions (for output) covered by the mask. The following example illustrates the use of Z-masks on input and output.

```
C EXAMPLE 15.7 HEXADECIMAL INPUT-OUTPUT
      READ 1,A,B,C
    1 FORMAT(Z8,Z5,Z11)
      PRINT 2,A,A,A
    2 FORMAT('1',Z8,Z5,Z11)
      STOP
      END
$ENTRY
123456789ABCDEF012345678
```

```
   Z8      Z5      Z11
```

Since A, B, and C are REAL variables, each has a length of four bytes. Since each hexadecimal digit represents the bit pattern of one-half byte (four bits), eight hexadecimal symbols are required to define the bit pattern for a REAL (or INTEGER) value. In the example, the READ statement causes A, B and C to have the following hexadecimal values.

A: 12345678,   B: 0009ABCD,   C: 12345678

When the value of A is printed three times, the following line of symbols is printed.

1234567845678bbb12345678

   Z8   Z5   Z11

Format-Free Input

Hexadecimal values can be read using a format-free READ statement. Consider the following example.

```
        READ,A,I,K
        . . .
        . . .
    $ENTRY
        Z12345678, Z12    Z123456789
```

When the data card is read, the hexadecimal values are:

A: 12345678,   I: 00000012,   K: 12345678

The rule for padding and truncation of hexadecimal values is the same for all operations (initialization, input, and output). Padding and truncation occur on the left.

15.11 Bit Assignment And Manipulation

Bit Assignment

By using the hexadecimal features available in WATFIV, any desired bit pattern can be assigned to a variable of any type. In addition, the bit pattern of any value can be displayed on the printer using a Z-mask. What methods are available for manipulating individual bits which represent the value of a variable? Two types of bit manipulation operations will be discussed. These are: (i) single bit manipulation and (ii) bit shifting operations.

Single Bit Manipulation

Since a bit has one of two values -- zero or one, the following operations are meaningful: turning a bit "off" (setting it equal to zero); turning a bit "on" (setting it equal to one); "flipping" a bit (setting it equal to zero if one, and to one if zero); testing a bit to see if it has a particular value. To perform operations of the type suggested above, he built-in functions "AND", "OR", "EOR" and "COMPL" can be used. Each has a REAL value.

There is a close analogy between the purposes of these built-in functions and those of the LOGICAL operators ".AND.", ".OR.", and ".NOT." which were discussed in Chapter 14. The essential difference is that the LOGICAL operators work with the LOGICAL values .TRUE. and .FALSE. whereas the functions AND, OR, COMPL and EOR work with bit patterns of REAL values. The correspondences appear in the following table.

Usual Name Given	LOGICAL Operator	Bit Function (X&Y are 32 bits each)	Value of ith Bit In The Result
and	X.AND.Y	AND(X,Y)	1 if X_i and Y_i are 1
or	X.OR.Y	OR(X,Y)	1 if X_i or Y_i is 1
not	.NOT.X	COMPL(X)	1 if X_i is 0, 0 if X_i is 1
exclusive or	(X.OR.Y).AND. .NOT.(X.AND.Y)	EOR(X,Y)	1 if $X_i \neq Y_i$

Note when using these functions that: (i) any type of argument can be used provided it has a length of four bytes; (ii) The function value is REAL. If it is desired to use any of the functions AND, OR, COMPL, or EOR as an INTEGER value, an EQUIVALENCE statement should be used as is illustrated in the following program.

```
      C EXAMPLE 15.8 USE OF THE FUNCTION "AND"
            EQUIVALENCE (J,X)
            X=AND(243,-571)
            PRINT,J
            STOP
            END
```

The statement "J=AND(243,-571)" could not be used since it would drastically alter the bit pattern of the function value in converting it from a REAL to an INTEGER value.

Examples Of Bit Manipulations

a) Turn the ith bit off. Solution: AND the value with a second value which has a zero in the ith position and ones elsewhere. For example, to turn the leftmost bit off and leave the others unchanged --

```
            REAL OFFLEF/%7FFFFFFF/
            READ,A
            A=AND(A,OFFLEF)
            ...
```

332

b) Turn the ith bit on. Solution: OR the value with a second value which has a one in the ith position and zeros elsewhere. For example, to turn the rightmost bit on and leave the others unchanged --

```
REAL ONRITE/Z00000001/
READ,A
A=OR(A,ONRITE)
...
```

c) Flip (change) the value of the ith bit. Solution: EOR the value with a second value which has a one in the ith position and zeros elsewhere. For example, to flip the value of the second leftmost bit --

```
REAL SECOND/Z40000000/
READ,A
A=EOR(A,SECOND)
...
```

d) Extract the value of the ith bit. Solution: AND the value with a second value having a one in the ith position and zeros elsewhere. For example, to test the second rightmost bit for a value of zero --

```
REAL RIGHT2/Z00000002/,ZERO/Z00000000/
READ,A
B=AND(A,RIGHT2)
IF(B.EQ.ZERO) ...
...
```

e) Flip all bits. Solution: COMPL the value. For example, to flip all bits --

```
READ,A
A=COMPL(A)
```

In performing bit operations it is often desirable to generate two sets of thirty-two values such that the ith variable in the first set has ones everywhere except in the ith leftmost bit position and the ith variable in the second set has zeros everywhere except in the ith leftmost position. In the following program OFF(J) has only the Jth leftmost bit off and ON(J) has only the Jth leftmost bit on. The program takes advantage of the fact that an INTEGER value of $2**N$ for $N=0,1,2,...,30$ has a one in the $(N+1)$th rightmost bit position and zeros elsewhere.

```
C EXAMPLE 15.9 CREATE BIT PATTERNS
      SUBROUTINE CREATE(ON,OFF)
      REAL ON(32),OFF(32),ONLEFT/Z80000000/
      EQUIVALENCE (X,IPOWER)
      INTEGER IPOWER/1/
      ON(32)=X
      OFF(32)=COMPL(X)
      DO 1 K=1,30
      IPOWER=IPOWER*2
      ON(32-K)=X
    1 OFF(32-K)=COMPL(X)
      ON(1)=ONLEFT
      OFF(1)=COMPL(ONLEFT)
      RETURN
      END
```

The reason for the special attention given to ON(1) and OFF(1) is that a one bit in the leftmost position indicates a negative number and not a positive power of two.

The foregoing SUBROUTINE could be used by any program segment in which bit manipulations were required.

Shifting Operations

Occasionally it may be necessary to shift a bit pattern to the right or left. For example, the result of shifting the eight-bit pattern "11011100" two bits to the left is "01110000". The same pattern shifted three positions to the right would look like "00011011". Since multiplication and division of INTEGER values by +2 causes a shift to the left and right of one bit respectively, multiplication and division by powers of two can be employed to shift a bit pattern any desired number of places. Recommended procedures are as follows.

   a) Shift left N positions. Solution: Multiply the value by 2**N. Note that the bit pattern to be shifted must be an INTEGER value.

   b) Shift right N positions. Solution: (i) Divide the value by 2**N; (ii) Set the leftmost N bits to zero using the AND function. The second operation is necessitated by the bit pattern used to represent negative INTEGER values (described in Appendix C).

In the following example, the SUBROUTINE CREATE is that shown in Example program 15.9.

```
C EXAMPLE 15.10 READ VALUES OF A AND B,
C SHIFT A LEFT 5 BITS AND SHIFT B RIGHT 3 BITS
      REAL ON(32),OFF(32)
      EQUIVALENCE (A,M),(B,N)
      CALL CREATE(ON,OFF)
      READ,A,B
      M=M*2**5
      N=N/2**3
      DO 1 I=1,3
    1 B=AND(B,OFF(I))
      PRINT 900,A,B
  900 FORMAT(' A=',Z8,' B=',Z8)
      STOP
      END
$ENTRY
  Z12FD8790 ZFFFFF037
```

Exercise 15.2 (Hexadecimal and Bit Manipulation)

1. For each of the following define an appropriate variable
   and initialize the variable with a hexadecimal constant
   to cause the variable to be assigned the bit pattern.

   a) 0000 0000
   b) 1111 0000 1111 0000 1111 0000 1111 0000
   c) 1011 0011 1000
   d) 0111 1000 0011 1100 0001 1110 0000 1111

2. Write statements to print out the hexadecimal representation of the following constants: '2000', 2000, 2000.0.

3. A programmer wants to "turn on" the rightmost bit of an
   INTEGER value assigned to the variable J and then print
   the resulting INTEGER value. He writes the following
   sequence of statements.

```
      INTEGER K/Z00000001/,J/27436/
      K=AND(J,K)
      PRINT,K
```

   a) Why do these statements not produce the correct
      result?
   b) How can the desired result be obtained?

4. Each of the following asks you to suppose one of the
   built-in functions "AND", "OR", "COMPL" was not available
   but that the other two along with "EOR" was available.
   In each case write a subprogram to achieve the same
   effect as the (supposedly) missing function by using the
   built-in functions suggested.

   a) Use OR and COMPL to achieve the same effect as AND.
   b) Use AND and COMPL to achieve the same effect as OR.
   c) Use AND and OR to achieve the same effect as EOR.

5. Assign the hexadecimal value "A2B3C4D5" to an INTEGER
   variable. Write a sequence of statements to perform each
   the following manipulations in the order shown.

   a) Turn the second leftmost bit off.
   b) Turn the fourth and eighth rightmost bits on.
   c) Test the middle two bits and: if "00" shift the
      pattern left three bits; if "01" shift the pattern
      right three bits; if "10" shift the pattern left
      five bits; if "11" shift the pattern right five
      bits.
   d) Flip the value of every second bit starting with the
      leftmost bit.

15.12 Other Symbols In WATFIV

Occasionally a program must be written in which one or
more of the non-standard WATFIV symbols are required to be
read, defined and/or printed. For example, in a library
application, it may be necessary to use the lower-case
letters of the alphabet. In order to do something like this
(define and display lower-case letters) the printer to be
used must have an appropriate "print train". That is, it
must have a rotating set of metal slugs containing the
symbols which are required. Secondly, since the symbol
printed at any particular position along the print line
depends on the bit pattern which the programmer has assigned
to the print position, it is necessary to know what bit
pattern produces what symbol for the print train being used.
Finally, if the bit pattern for each printed symbol is
known, then we must be able to read or define symbols which
have the appropriate pattern.

In brief, the sequence of events is as follows.

holes in a   ⇨ bit pattern in ⇨ symbol on print
card column   a byte   line

Hole patterns are described by specifying which of the
twelve positions in a column are to be punched. Hole
positions are labelled (beginning from the top) 12, 11, 0,
1, 2, 3, 4, 5, 6, 7, 8, and 9. The pattern 11-4-9 for
instance means holes are punched the second, seventh and
bottom positions of the column starting from the top.
Appendix A describes how to punch any desired hole pattern
in a column. Appendix A also has a chart showing the bit
pattern produced in a byte for any valid hole pattern.
Chapter 22 describes a second method of inputting bit
patterns.

If a bit pattern for a non-standard symbol must be
defined within a program, CHARACTER constants, initialized

336

with the appropriate hexadecimal digits, should be used. For example, the bit patterns for the lower-case letters "b" and "c" can be assigned to the variables BEE and CEE using the following statement.

           CHARACTER BEE/Z82/ , CEE/Z83/

If this is done, a statement pair such as

           PRINT 99,BEE,CEE
        99 FORMAT('0',A1)

would cause the symbols "b" and "c" to be printed on separate lines (provided and appropriate print train was used).

A feature not previously mentioned, available on some printers, is the "Universal Character Set Feature". In effect, it permits you to define the correspondences between bit patterns and the type slugs on any print train. This feature would only be required in very unusual circumstances.

If you have a requirement for using special symbols, check with your computing center to find out what types of print trains are available. Some of the most frequently used print trains and the bit pattern corresponding to each slug on the train are described in Appendix D.

15.13 Other Statements Involving CHARACTER Values

The use of CHARACTER values and variables in statements such as IMPLICIT, COMMON, EQUIVALENCE, Statement Functions, BLOCK DATA subprograms, EXTERNAL, ENTRY, DATA and DIMENSION statements is described in Chapter 16.

CHARACTER values may be used as subscripts. The value of the subscript is that obtained by using the bit pattern in the leftmost byte of the CHARACTER value as a base two number. For example, if VEC is a set of variables then VEC('0') is equivalent to VEC(240) since the value '0' has a bit pattern of "11110000" which, in the base two number system, represents a value of 240. This feature can be useful in translating one set of bit patterns to another.

15.14 Summary

Strings of symbols can be defined and manipulated in WATFIV programs. This is done by using CHARACTER variables and CHARACTER constants. Each symbol in a CHARACTER value occupies one byte of memory.

CHARACTER arrays can be used to store format codes. This permits some degree of flexibility in changing format codes at execution time.

Bit strings can be defined, manipulated and displayed. They are defined by using hexadecimal values. Each hexadecimal value represents a pattern of four bits. By using hexadecimal values, non-standard symbols can be defined, input and output. Bit manipulations can be done by using the built-in functions AND, OR, EOR and COMPL. Shifting operations can be done by multiplying and dividing by powers of two.

CHARACTER variables can also be used to simulate input and output devices. Because of the importance of this application, it is discussed in a separate chapter (Chapter 20).

Programming Problems

15.1 Write a program to count the number of occurences of each letter of the alphabet in a sentence which is punched on a data card.

15.2 Example program 15.3 was used to count the number of words having different lengths in a sentence. Modify the program to take into account that a comma or period as well as a blank can indicate the end of a word.

15.3 Write a program which scans a string of symbols looking for left and right brackets. The program should check that there are equal numbers of each and that at any point during the scan that at least as many left brackets have been encountered as right brackets.

15.4 Write a program which reads in several words punched one per card and determines which are valid variable names.

15.5 Write a program which counts the number of occurences of the word "THE" in a sentence. Test the program on the following sentence. "THE PROBLEM OF FAT THEODORE GOETHE IS THE ACCURATE PRONUNCIATION OF THE WORD THE".

15.6 Write a SUBROUTINE called "CONCAT" which could be used to "concatenate" (join together) two strings of symbols. For example, the concatenation of 'JONES' and '63R' is 'JONES63R'. The values to be concatenated and the result should be stored in separate arrays. The first statement in the SUBROUTINE will be:

          SUBROUTINE CONCAT(A1,L1,A2,L2,R)   where

     A1 is the array containing the first value
     L1 is the number of symbols to be used in the first
        value
     A2 is the array containing the second value
     L2 is the number of symbols to be used in the second
        value
     R is the array containing the concatenated string

15.7 Write a program which reads in twenty words punched one
     per card and prints them in alphabetical order. Write a
     SUBROUTINE to do the sort.

15.8 Suppose a sentence on a card occupies less than fifty
     card columns and contains N words (where N is determined
     by the program).   Write a program which reads in the
     sentence and prints it N times such that on the first
     line the first word starts in print position 60, on the
     second line the second word starts in print position 60,
     etc..   For example, if the sentence is "PROGRAMMING IS
     EASY", the following output would be produced.

                     | T60
                     ↓
                     PROGRAMMING IS EASY
            PROGRAMMING IS EASY
          PROGRAMMING IS EASY

15.9 Modify the program used for problem #8 so that the N
     lines are printed in alphabetical order with respect to
     the words starting in print position 60.

15.10 Modify the program of problem #9 so that all FORMAT
     information is read from cards.

15.11   a) Write a FUNCTION subprogram which will convert an
          array of five CHARACTER constants of length one to
          its equivalent INTEGER value. Assume each symbol is
          one of the digits zero thru nine.

        b) Explain why the reverse operation (INTEGER to
          CHARACTER) is more difficult. (A method of doing
          this easily is described in Chapter 20.)

15.12 Draw a circle. Write the letters of the alphabet and a
     blank around the outside of the circle in a clockwise
     direction.   Write a program which reads in a value of N
     and then a sentence. (a) Translate the sentence into a
     coded message by replacing each symbol in the sentence
     by the symbol which is N positions clockwise around the
     circle. Print the coded message. (b) Print the original
     message by decoding the message produced in part (a).

                              339

15.13 Modify the program of problem 12 in the following way. When a symbol occurs for the first time, translate it into the symbol found N positions clockwise. When it occurs for the second time, translate it into the symbol found (N+1) positions clockwise, etc.. Explain why the coded message produced cannot always be decoded accurately.

15.14 "DOMEWA" is a set of six scrambled letters which spell the word "MEADOW". Write a SUBROUTINE subprogram to print all possible arrangements of a set of N scrambled letters. Assume N is six or less. The SUBROUTINE will have two parameters -- an array containing the scrambled letters and a value of N. Print the arrangements ten per print line. For example, the statement "CALL SCRAM('ATEM',4)" would cause the following lines to be printed.

```
ATEM ATME AEMT AETM AMET AMTE TAEM TAME TEAM TEMA
TMEA TMAE EATM EATM ETMA ETAM EMAT EMTA META MEAT
MTEA MTAE MAET MATE
```

CHAPTER 16   MIXED-TYPE STATEMENTS -- A SUMMARY

Questions Answered In This Chapter

1. What are the statements in which more than one type of variable can appear?

2. What are the rules of use of these "mixed-type" statements?

This chapter summarizes those statements in which more than one type of value or variable may be used. It discusses the use of non-INTEGER and non-REAL values in statements such as COMMON, EQUIVALENCE, DATA, DIMENSION, ENTRY and mixed-type Assignment statements.

16.1 Allowed Types And Lengths of Variables

The table below indicates the standard and optional length(s) of the different types of variables which can be used in WATFIV programs.

Type	Standard Length (bytes)	Optional Length (bytes)	Usual Name(s) Given To Optional Length Variable(s)
INTEGER	4	2	INTEGER*2 or Half-Word INTEGER
REAL	4	8	REAL*8 or Double Precision or Extended Precision
LOGICAL	4	1	LOGICAL*1
COMPLEX	8	16	COMPLEX*16 or Extended Precision COMPLEX or Double Precision COMPLEX
CHARACTER	1	2-255	CHARACTER*n

INTEGER and LOGICAL constants have no optional lengths. Both types of constants have a length of four. REAL, COMPLEX and CHARACTER constants may be given the optional length(s).

16.2 Specification Of Variable Type

There are three ways the type of a variable may be specified. These are:

341

i) Default or first-letter rule. This rule applies unless changed using (ii) or (iii). Variables beginning with any of I, J, K, L, M, or N are INTEGER variables; Those begining with A thru H, O thru Z or a "$" are REAL variables.

ii) IMPLICIT Typing. (See also Chapter 2, Section 5.) An IMPLICIT statement is used to change all or part of the first-letter rule. If present, its specifications apply unless overridden for specific variables by a type declaration statement. Its general form is:

IMPLICIT type*L(x,y,...), type*L(x,y,...)...

where,
"type" is one of INTEGER, REAL, COMPLEX, LOGICAL, CHARACTER or DOUBLE PRECISION
"*L" is a length modifier (optional); It is not allowed if "type" is "DOUBLE PRECISION".
"x", "y" etc. are one of the following
- a letter of the alphabet or a "$"
- a pair of letters separated by a hyphen

Example. The statement

IMPLICIT CHARACTER*10(M,N),REAL*8(A-D,$),
* COMPLEX(Z), LOGICAL(H-J)

specifies that variables beginning with

A thru D are REAL*8
E thru G are REAL (first-letter rule)
H thru J are LOGICAL
K and L are INTEGER (first-letter rule)
M and N are CHARACTER*10
O thru Y are REAL (first-letter rule)
Z are COMPLEX
$ are REAL*8

There are two important rules regarding the IMPLICIT statement. These are that only one IMPLICIT statement is permitted in any segment and, if present, it must be the first statement in the mainline segment or the second statement in a subprogram segment.

iii) Explicit Type Declaration Statement. The type declaration statement is used to override the first-letter rule and/or IMPLICIT statement for specific variables. Its general form is:

type*L name1*L1(D1)/V1/,name2*L2(D2)/V2/,...

342

where,

"type" is one of INTEGER, REAL, COMPLEX, LOGICAL, CHARACTER or DOUBLE PRECISION

"*L" is optional and specifies one of the permitted lengths for the type used. ("*L" is not permitted if "DOUBLE PRECISION" is used to specify the type.) If omitted, the standard length is assumed.

"name1", "name2", etc. are names of variables or arrays.

"*L" following a name is optional and specifies the length of the variable or array elements. If omitted, the length of the variable(s) is (are) that associated with the "type".

"(D1)", "(D2)", etc. are optional and describe the dimensions of an array. Each "Di" represents one to seven unsigned positive INTEGER constants separated by commas.

"/V1/", "/V2/", etc. are optional and specify initial values to be assigned to variables specified by "name*L". The initial values must be constants and must agree in number and type with the variable(s) being initialized. If the "name" refers to an array, values are assigned with the rightmost subscript varying least rapidly. A repeat factor of the form "r*v" in a list of initializing constants indicates that the value "v" is to be repeated "r" times. "r" must be a positive INTEGER constant.

16.3 Defining Arrays

An array can be defined using any one of: an explicit type declaration statement as described in the previous section; a COMMON statement (see Chapter 9, Section 4 and Section 8 of this chapter); a DIMENSION statement (see Chapter 7, Section 9).

If a COMMON statement is used to define an array, the type of variable in the array must have been specified by a previous statement or, if not, its variables must have a length which is the same as that obtained from first-letter rule (or IMPLICIT statement, if used). (See also Section 16.13 on "Ordering Of Statements".)

16.4 Specification Of Initial Values

Values can be assigned to variables of any type at compile time using either an explicit type declaration statement (Section 16.2) or a DATA statement (See Chapter 7,

Section 8.). Occasionally a DATA statement must be used (See Section 16.13 on ordering of statements.)

An example of a DATA statement used to initialize three different types of variables is shown in the following sequence.

```
COMPLEX Z(4,2)
REAL*8 A(3)
LOGICAL LOG
DATA (Z(I,1)I=1,4)/4*(0.,0.)/,A(1),LOG/0.D00,T/
```

16.5 Mixed-Type Expressions And Assignment Statements

Arithmetic Expressions

If two variables or constants of different types are involved in an arithmetic operation, the type of value resulting from the operation is that of the higher of the two types in the following list.

```
COMPLEX*16
COMPLEX
REAL*8
REAL
INTEGER
INTEGER*2
```

For example, "2.5D-6 * 2" equals 5.0D-6 because REAL*8 values appear higher in the list. There are two exceptions to the hierarchy of values appearing in the list. First, an operation involving two INTEGER*2 values produces an INTEGER value of length four. Second, if an operation involves a COMPLEX value and a REAL*8 value, the result is a COMPLEX*16 value. In any operation between a COMPLEX value of either length and a non-COMPLEX value, the non-COMPLEX value is considered to be a complex value with an imaginary component of zero for purposes of performing the operation.

Two facts about exponentiation should be recalled. First, COMPLEX numbers may only be raised to INTEGER powers. Second, if the base and exponent in a "**" operation are REAL, then the base must be positive. For example, the expression "(-2.)**4." is invalid.

Logical Expressions

Logical expressions involve LOGICAL values and/or expressions which use the six relational operators .LE., EQ., etc.. Logical expressions may be combined using the Logical operators .AND., .OR. and .NOT.. The relational operators may only be used to compare

i) Two numeric values, neither of which is COMPLEX

344

ii) Two CHARACTER values of any length

Priorities

A complete summary of priorites of operations and the order in which they are performed is shown in the following list.

1. Functions (right to left)

2. Brackets (innermost first)

3. Arithmetic operations
   a) Exponentiation (right to left)
   b) Multiplication and division (left to right)
   c) Addition and subtraction (left to right)

4. Relational operations
   - All six have equal priority and are processed
     left to right.

5. Logical operations
   a) .NOT. (left to right)
   b) .AND. (left to right)
   c) .OR. (left to right)

Assignment Statements

In an Assignment statement, the permitted combinations of variables on the left and values on the right are:

Type of Variable	Type of Value
numeric	numeric
LOGICAL	LOGICAL
CHARACTER	CHARACTER

All other combinations are invalid. In the foregoing table, "numeric" means INTEGER, REAL or COMPLEX (in each case, of either length).

16.6 Subscript Values

If a subscript value is numeric and non-INTEGER (REAL or COMPLEX of either length), the subcript value used is that obtained by applying IFIX or its equivalent to the REAL value (the real component of a COMPLEX value).

If a subscript is a LOGICAL or CHARACTER value, the subscript value used is that obtained by evaluating the bit pattern of the leftmost byte of the value as a base two number. For example, suppose X is an array of three-hundred variables. Then,

i) X(.TRUE..AND..NOT..FALSE.) is equivalent to X(255) since the leftmost byte used to store ".TRUE. (the expression value) has the bit pattern "11111111" which, in the base two number system, represents a value of 255.

ii) X('A$2Z') is equivalent to X(193) since the bit pattern used to represent 'A' is "11000001" which, in the base two number system has a value of 193.

CHARACTER subscripts can be useful when translating one set of bit patterns to another. The program below translates each of the letters in the alphabet to the one following it. "Z" is translated to "A" and a blank is left unchanged.

```
      C EXAMPLE PROGRAM 16.1 BIT TRANSLATION
            CHARACTER TABLE(255)/255*' '/
            CHARACTER DATA(80)
            READ 1,(TABLE(I),I=193,201),(TABLE(I),I=209,
           * 217),(TABLE(I),I=226,233)
          1 FORMAT(26A1)
            READ 2, DATA
          2 FORMAT(80A1)
            PRINT 3, DATA
          3 FORMAT('1ORIGINAL DATA ',80A1,/)
            DO 4 I=1,80
          4 DATA(I)=TABLE(DATA(I))
            PRINT 5,DATA
          5 FORMAT('1TRANSLATED DATA ',80A1)
            STOP
            END
      $ENTRY
      BCDEFGHIJKLMNOPQRSTUVWXYZA
      THIS MESSAGE WILL BE TRANSLATED
```

Appendix A decribes the bit patterns for CHARACTER values.

16.7 Shared Storage Within A Segment (EQUIVALENCE)

The rules covering the use of an EQUIVALENCE statement and some of its most frequent uses are described in Chapter 9 Section 7. Any type of variable may be used in an EQUIVALENCE statement. Only one additional rule is required. This is that the length of any variable used in an EQUIVALENCE statement must not subsequently (by some later statement) be given a length which is different from that assumed at the time the EQUIVALENCE statement was compiled. The examples below illustrate this rule.

Valid	Invalid
REAL*8 A	EQUIVALENCE (A,B)
EQUIVALENCE (A,B)	REAL*8 A

The following paragraphs describe three situations in which Equivalencing variables of different types may be useful.

First, since there are no built-in functions for extracting the real and imaginary components of a COMPLEX*16 value, the following approach could be used.

```
COMPLEX*16 Z
REAL*8 CMPNT(2),ZREAL,ZIMAG
EQUIVALENCE (Z,CMPNT,ZREAL),(ZIMAG,CMPNT(2))
```

Second, if pairs of numbers must be tested for equality, a saving in execution time may result by Equivalencing the pair to a variable having a length equal to the total length of the pair. For example, suppose you are searching for a particular author-title combination where authors and titles are represented by INTEGER values. The program below reads in pairs of authors and titles and then scans the list to find out if author 2401 and title 3379 appear in the list.

```
C SCAN FOR AUTHOR-TITLE
      INTEGER DATA(2,1000),PAIR(2),NPAIRS/0/
      REAL*8 ATPAIR(1000),ATTEST
      EQUIVALENCE (DATA,ATPAIR),(ATTEST,
     * PAIR(1),AUTHOR),(PAIR(2),TITLE)
      INTEGER AUTHOR/2401/,TITLE/3379/
C READ THE AUTHOR-TITLE PAIRS
      DO 1  I=1,1000
      READ(5,*,END=2) DATA(1,I),DATA(2,I)
    1 NPAIRS=NPAIRS+1
C SEARCH FOR THE PAIR 2401-3379
    2 DO 3 I=1,NPAIRS
      IF(ATTEST.EQ.ATPAIR(I))GO TO 4
    3 CONTINUE
      PRINT,'AUTHOR-TITLE NOT FOUND'
      STOP
    4 PRINT,'AUTHOR-TITLE FOUND'
      STOP
      END
```

In the foregoing program, the array DATA must be defined as having two rows and one-thousand columns and not vice-versa because storage for two-dimensional arrays is reserved column-by-column.

This idea (Equivalencing a pair of INTEGER variables to a REAL*8 variable) could be extended to Equivalencing groups of eight INTEGER*2 variables to a single COMPLEX*16 variable. The procedure is recommended only if a test for equality between groups of values is being made. The use of ".LE.", ".LT.",".GT.", or ".GE." would produce meaningless results except in very unusual circumstances. Keep in mind that this use of EQUIVALENCE is simply to reduce execution time. It is not a necessity.

A third reason for Equivalencing variables of different types would be to use the bit pattern of one variable as the bit pattern, and hence the value, of a different type of variable. This use was illustrated when using the built-in functions AND, OR, EOR and COMPL. Example programs 15.8 thru 15.10 all used the EQUIVALENCE statement for this purpose.

Three additional points about EQUIVALENCE are as follows. First, the total number of bytes used by all variables appearing in or implicated by EQUIVALENCE statements is included in the statistic "ARRAY AREA=XXX BYTES" which is printed following completion of the job. Second, if a LOGICAL variable is Equivalenced to some other type of variable and if, during the execution of the program, a bit pattern which is not a representation of .TRUE. or .FALSE. is stored in the variable, then any format-free printout of the LOGICAL variable will cause "JJJJJJJJ" to be printed instead of "UUUUUUUU". Third, because of the nature of the internal memory structure of computers which process WATFIV jobs, it is much more efficient to Equivalence variables in order of decreasing length. For example,

```
REAL*8 R81,R82,R1*4,R2*4
CHARACTER A,B
EQUIVALENCE (R81,R82),(R1,R2),(A,B)
```

is much better than

```
REAL*8 R81,R82,R1*4,R2*4
CHARACTER A,B
EQUIVALENCE (A,B),(R1,R2),(R81,R82)
```

16.8 Sharing Storage Locations - Different Segments (COMMON)

Different segments can assign variables to the same storage locations by defining a Common Block. By creating one or more Common Blocks, program segments can communicate with one another without using argument and parameter lists. The rules of use of the COMMON statement are described in Chapter 9 as are the rules for BLOCK DATA subprograms (used to initialize variables in labelled Common Blocks). Any type of variable may be put in a Common Block.

The elements in a Common Block should, whenever possible, be specified in order of decreasing length. This will make proper "boundary alignment" of the variables in

348

the Block easy for the compiler to achieve. No errors will
result if this procedure is not followed but execution time
efficiency will likely be greatly reduced. Shown below are
examples of good and bad ordering of items in a Common
Block.

<u>Good</u>   <u>Bad</u>
    REAL*8 A   REAL*8 A
    INTEGER K   INTEGER K
    CHARACTER*1 CHAR   CHARACTER*1 CHAR
    COMMON A,K,CHAR   COMMON CHAR,K,A

One further point. The total number of bytes used by the
Common Blocks in a program is included in the statistic
"ARRAY AREA=XXX BYTES" which is printed following completion
of a job.

16.9 Argument And Parameter Lists

Arguments and parameters may be of any type. Rules of
correspondence are summarized in Section 9.3. Of special
note is that an argument and its corresponding parameter
must be of the same type only if the parameter is a simple
variable. For example, the following structure is valid.

```
C MAINLINE SEGMENT            SUBROUTINE ROUT(Y)
      COMPLEX Z/(1.,2.)/       REAL Y(2)
      CALL ROUT(Z)            ...
      ...                     ...
      END                     END
```

In the foregoing program structure, the SUBROUTINE variables
Y(1) and Y(2) would take on values of the real and imaginary
components of the COMPLEX variable Z.

16.10 FUNCTION Subprograms

The function value in a FUNCTION subprogram may be of
any type except CHARACTER. If the first-letter rule does not
apply, the FUNCTION name must appear in a type declaration
statement in the calling segment and the FUNCTION subprogram
must begin with the statement

        type FUNCTION name*L (parameter list)

where "L" is optional and if used denotes the length of the
FUNCTION value. (If "type" is "DOUBLE PRECISION", the length
modifier must be omitted.)

ENTRY Points (See also Chapter 9 Section 8)

An ENTRY point of a FUNCTION subprogram may have a type
of value other than that specified by the first-letter rule.
To do this, the FUNCTION name at the ENTRY point should

appear in an appropriate type declaration statement both at
the beginning of the subprogram and in the calling segment.
The following program structure illustrates this idea.

```
C MAINLINE                 FUNCTION X(...)
     LOGICAL HERE,NOW       LOGICAL HERE,PARAM
     .                      .
     NOW=HERE(.AND.NOW)     ENTRY HERE(PARAM)
     .                      .
     END                    END
```

EXTERNAL SUBPROGRAMS (See also Chapter 9 Section 10)

Recall that an EXTERNAL statement is used when an
argument is the name of a subprogram or built-in function.
FUNCTION subprograms and built-in functions may be of any
type except CHARACTER. To specify the type of an EXTERNAL
function, the function name must appear in an appropriate
type declaration statement in both the calling and the
called segments. The following program structure illustrates
this idea.

```
C CALLING SEGMENT          SUBROUTINE R(DUMMY)
     EXTERNAL F             INTEGER DUMMY
     INTEGER F              .
     .                      END
     CALL R(F)
     .                      INTEGER FUNCTION F(...)
     .                      .
     .                      F=...
     .                      .
     END                    END
```

16.11 Input-Output

Format-Free Output

The table below summarizes the default mask or codes
used for each type of value appearing in a format-free
output list.

Type Of Value	Mask Or Codes
INTEGER	I12
INTEGER*2	I12
REAL	E16.7
REAL*8	D28.16
COMPLEX	'(',E16.7,' ,',E16.7,')'
COMPLEX*16	'(',D28.16,' ,',D28.16,')'
LOGICAL	L8
LOGICAL*1	L8
CHARACTER*n	A(n+1)

Formatted Input And Output

Normally, I-masks, F-masks or E-masks, pairs of F-masks and/or E-masks, L-masks, and A-masks are used for INTEGER, REAL, COMPLEX, LOGICAL, and CHARACTER type values respectively. However, the following three masks can be used with <u>any</u> type of variable or value: A-masks, Z-masks, and G-masks. Section 12 of this chapter discusses the use of A-masks with non-CHARACTER values.

There are two additional facts concerning the use of P-codes (scale factors). First, the effect of a P-code on a D-mask is similar to that of a P-code on an E-mask. Second, if a P-code is applied to a G-mask its effect depends on whether or not the G-mask becomes equivalent to an F-mask or E-mask. (See Sections 5.16, 5.17, 6.10 and 6.11 for details of the G-mask and P-code.)

16.12 Storing CHARACTER Values In Non-CHARACTER Variables

Any type of variable can be used to store a CHARACTER value. In fact, in most versions of Fortran, this is the only means of storing and manipulating strings of symbols. Recall that each symbol uses one byte of memory. Thus the number of symbols which can be stored in a variable, regardless of its type, is equal to the length of the variable. For example, four symbols can be stored in a REAL or INTEGER variable, sixteen symbols in a COMPLEX*16 variable, etc..

One method of assigning a CHARACTER value to a non-CHARACTER variable is to initialize the variable with the desired string of symbols. The initializing constant may be either a quote-type literal or an H-type literal. The following sequence of statements assigns "ABCD" to the variables J and K and "$ XXX.XX" to the variables A and B. Note that either a type declaration statement or a DATA statement can be used to specify initial values.

```
INTEGER J/'ABCD'/, K/4HABCD/
REAL*8 A/'$ XXX.XX'/,B
DATA B/8H$ XXX.XX/
```

Rules of padding and truncation during compile time initialization are the same as those which apply when CHARACTER values are used. That is, the "APT" rule (Chapter 15, Section 4) applies.

A CHARACTER value can also be assigned to a non-CHARACTER variable by reading the value under control of an A-mask. An A-mask is also used to print strings of symbols stored in non-CHARACTER variables. The following program reads a card and counts the number of blank columns in the card. In this example, INTEGER variables are used to store CHARACTER values.

```
      C EXAMPLE 16.2 COUNT BLANK COLUMNS
            INTEGER BLANK/' '/,COUNT/0/,COL(80)
            INTEGER TITLE(7)/'NUMB','ER O','F BL','ANK ',
          * 'COLU','MNS ','IS'/
            READ 900,COL
      900 FORMAT(80A1)
            DO 1 I=1,80
            IF(COL(I).EQ.BLANK) COUNT=COUNT+1
        1 CONTINUE
            PRINT 901,TITLE,COUNT
      901 FORMAT('1',7A4,I3)
            STOP
            END
      $ENTRY
      BLANKS IN THIS CARD WILL BE COUNTED
```

The foregoing program illustrates how INTEGER variables can be used to read, analyze and print CHARACTER values. Because an INTEGER variable has a length of four, the symbols in the title "NUMBER OF BLANK COLUMNS IS" must be broken up into sets of four each. Therefore seven INTEGER variables are required to store the message. Note that COL is a set of eighty variables and that a mask of A1 is used for each. This causes each symbol in the card to be stored in the leftmost (the TIP rule applies) byte of a unique INTEGER variable. If more than one symbol was stored in a variable, it would be difficult to determine the presence of a blank. The POT (Section 6 of Chapter 15) rule describes truncation-padding operations during output.

If non-CHARACTER variables are used to store CHARACTER values, it is a good policy to consistently use one type of variable for this purpose. Why? Well, for example, in the program statements below, the relationship "X.EQ.K" is not true.

```
      REAL X/'ABCD'/
      INTEGER K/'ABCD'/
      IF(X.EQ.K) ...
```

The reason is simply that when an INTEGER value and a REAL value are compared, the bit pattern of the INTEGER value is converted to its equivalent REAL value before the comparison is made. This means the bit pattern for "ABCD" stored in the variable K is drastically altered before being compared with the bit pattern stored in the variable X. Therefore the relationship is false.

If non-CHARACTER variables are used to store strings of symbols, these variables should not participate in any arithmetic operations. After all, you wouldn't think of adding "ABCD" and "WXYZ" if they were stored in CHARACTER variables. It doesn't make any more sense if they are stored in non-CHARACTER variables.

Section 15.9 explained that format codes could be stored in CHARACTER arrays. Format codes can also be stored in non-CHARACTER arrays using the techniques described in preceding paragraphs. For example,

        REAL*8 FMT(2)/8H('1VALUE,8H IS',I6)/
        PRINT FMT, -71

is equivalent to

        PRINT 900, -71
    900 FORMAT('1VALUE IS',I6)

This section has described techniques which can be used to define and input-output strings of symbols without using CHARACTER variables. In many versions of Fortran it is the only set of techniques available.

6.13 Ordering Of Statements In Program Segments

Because the WATFIV compiler examines each statement only once, non-executable statement must be ordered in such a way that a statement does not contradict any assumption which the compiler had to make in compiling an earlier statement. No problems will arise if statements are ordered in the following sequence.

    SUBROUTINE/FUNCTION/BLOCK DATA

    IMPLICIT

    type declaration statements which do not contain
        any initializing constants

    DIMENSION statements

    COMMON statements

    EQUIVALENCE statements

    DATA statements

    Statement Function definitions

    Executable statements and FORMAT statements

Comments can be placed anywhere. It is not necessary to follow the above ordering. However, there are two errors which are frequently made. First, the initial value for any variable appearing in, or implicated by, a COMMON or EQUIVALENCE statement must follow the COMMON or EQUIVALENCE statement. Second, if a variable is Equivalenced, any subsequent declaration of variable type must not change the length assumed at the time the EQUIVALENCE statement was compiled. The following sequence is in error because at the time the EQUIVALENCE statement was compiled, the variable "A" was assumed to have a length of four.

```
EQUIVALENCE (A,B)
REAL*8 A
```

6.14 Summary

Many statements in the Fortran language which are acceptable to the WATFIV compiler permit more than one type of variable or value to be used in the statement. This chapter has described these "mixed-type" statements and has summarized the rules for, and effects of, using these statements. Several uses of mixed-type statement have been discussed. Some of these are rather sophisticated and are presented for the benefit of the experienced programmer.

PART III

OTHER TYPES OF INPUT/OUTPUT

CHAPTER 17   PUNCHED OUTPUT

Questions Answered In This Chapter

    1. What is punched output?

    2. What statements are used in WATFIV programs to create
       and control punched output?

17.1 Punched Output

    Values used in a program can be punched into cards as
well as displayed on a printer. If punched output is
required, the programmer controls the appearance and
placement of values in much the same way as is done with
printed output. There are two distinct differences however.
First, there are eighty punch positions instead of the one-
hundred-and-thirty-three print positions available with most
printers. Second, the first punch position has no special
use as does print position one. The symbol stored in punch
position one is punched into card column one and is not used
to control the operation of the card punch.

    As with printed output, the formatting of the punched
values can be controlled by the programmer using format
codes or left up to the WATFIV program.

    The most common reason for punching data values into
data cards is to produce a set of values which will be used
as input data for another program. A second use is to
produce duplicate copies of programs or data cards.

    The table below describes the different forms of the
PUNCH and WRITE statements which are used to produce punched
output in WATFIV programs.

	Format-Free	Formatted
Output device assumed to be the card punch	PUNCH,list	PUNCH #,list # FORMAT(codes)
Card punch named as the output device	WRITE(7,*) list	WRITE(7,#) list # FORMAT(codes)

357

In the foregoing table, the symbol "#" refers to the number of the FORMAT statement which describes how the values are to be punched in the cards (the use of the card columns). The symbol "7" is frequently used as the device number of the card punch. If it is different from 7, the appropriate number should be used. The device number can also be assigned to an INTEGER variable. This is frequently a good idea when testing a complex program. During the testing phase a variable such as IOUT can be given a value of six which causes values in a WRITE list to be sent to the printer. Once the program is working properly, IOUT can be given a value of seven. The advantage of this approach should be obvious -- it permits output to be switched from the printer to the punch simply by changing one statement (one data card if the value of IOUT is read from a data card).

17.2 Formatted Punched Output

The FORMAT statement used to punch values into cards may contain masks, literals, and other codes. Since a card has eighty columns, format codes are positioned explicitly or implicitly in punch positions one thru eighty. Any attempt to reference a punch position outside this range is an error. All format codes are valid. Punch position one has no special use as it does with printed output. Each time the right bracket at the end of the format codes is reached, a card is punched which contains the symbols currently stored in the punch positions. After each card is punched, all positions are set to blanks. The following examples should make these ideas clear.

          PUNCH 900,2.,3.
      900 FORMAT(2F3.0)

    Result: the symbols b2.b3. (b denotes a blank)
            are punched in columns 1 thru 6 of a card.

          WRITE(7,901) (J,J=1,4)
      901 FORMAT(/I3,T2,I3,'VALUES'/)

    Result: Six cards are punched. The second and fifth
            cards contain "12" in columns 3 and 4 and
            "VALUES" in columns 5 thru 10. The first,
            third, fourth and six cards are blank.

17.3 Format-Free Punched Output

If values are punched into cards using either of the two format-free statements shown in the table, values are positioned in the cards according to the default mask appropriate to each type of value. Format-free output is generally used when the values will be read back in using a format-free READ statement.

358

The PUNCH statement is considered invalid by most non-WATFIV compilers. For this reason, as well as the flexibility of using other device numbers, the WRITE statement is generally preferred by many programmers.

17.4 An Example Program

The following program could be used to reproduce a deck of data cards. The program also prints the number of cards punched. Such a program is often called an "80-80 Reproduce" because 80 columns are read and 80 columns are punched.

```
C EXAMPLE 17.1 80-80 REPRODUCE
      CHARACTER*80 CARD
      N=0
    1 READ(5,900,END=2) CARD
      N=N+1
      WRITE(7,900) CARD
      GO TO 1
    2 PRINT,'NUMBER OF CARDS PUNCHED=',N
      STOP
  900 FORMAT(A80)
      END
```

Exercise 17.1

1. In each of the following, what symbol is punched in column 6?

   a)   PUNCH 900,2.,3.
         900 FORMAT(F4.2,F4.1)

   b)   PUNCH,-2.4536

   c)   WRITE(7,900) 2,4.235
         900 FORMAT(T5,'HI',T1,I8,T4,F7.2)

2. How many cards are punched by executing each of the following?

   a)   PUNCH 900,A,B,C
         900 FORMAT(E10.2)

   b)   WRITE(7,901) (I,FLOAT(I),I=1,7)
         901 FORMAT(T6,2(3X,I2,/F7.4)/)

   c)   WRITE(7,902)(K+1,(J,J=3,10,3),K-1,K=1,5)
         902 FORMAT((//2I3,4X,T2,2(/I1),3(I2)//))

3. a) Can any set of values which are punched using a
      format-free PUNCH statement be read in using a
      format-free READ statement? Explain.

   b) Suppose the value of the variable AA is punched by
      the statements:

              WRITE(7,900) AA
          900 FORMAT(codes)

      Suppose the card which is punched is read in by the
      statement:
              READ 900,AA

      What restrictions, if any, are there on the codes
      used to punch AA if the READ statement is to cause
      AA to have its previously assigned value?

4. Given the statement

          PUNCH 900,123.123,456.456

   then for each of the following, write a single FORMAT
   statement which will cause a card or cards to have
   the symbols shown. A "b" denotes a blank. Assume the
   symbols start in column one.

   a)   b123.123bb456.bbb456

   b)   b123b456

   c)   123456.123456

   d)   bbb123.123
         456.456

   e)   123.123456.
         456

   f)   123.123456.
             456

   g)   456.456456.456

17.5 <u>Summary</u>

    Output values can be punched in cards as well as
printed. To do this a PUNCH statement or a WRITE statement
specifying the punch is used in a program. Both formatted
and format-free punching is permitted. Unlike output which
is sent to a printer, no special significance is attached to
the symbol stored in punch position one.

Punched output may be useful for creating a set of data cards which will be used as input data for some other program and for creating duplicate copies of program or data decks.

Programming Problems

17.1 Write a program which reads an unknown number of data cards and for each card read, replaces every group of two or more consecutive blanks with a single blank. The compressed data should then be punched into a card.

17.2 Input to the program consists of a set of name and address cards punched according to the following rules. Name cards have a name in columns 1-20. In an address card: line 1 appears in columns 1-20; line 2 in columns 21-40; line 3 in columns 41-60. Write a program which combines each name-address pair and punches it on a single card.

CHAPTER 18   MAGNETIC TAPE INPUT-OUTPUT

Questions Answered In This Chapter

1. What is magnetic tape and what are the
    characteristics of the devices used to record and
    read data stored on magnetic tape?

2. What statements are used to read and write data
    stored on magnetic tape?

18.1 Magnetic Tape And Magnetic Tape Units

     A deck of punched cards is a suitable medium for
recording small volumes of data. If it is necessary to
process large volumes of data, a more suitable medium is a
reel of magnetic tape. The strips of magnetic tape used by
most computer systems are one-half inch wide and come in
standard lengths of 300, 600, 1200 and 2400 feet. Each strip
is wound on a plastic reel. One side of the strip is coated
with a special material which can be magnetized. Data (ones
and zeros) are recorded on the tape by creating little
magnetic spots on its surface. Eight bits of data (one byte)
can be written across the width of the tape. Usually 1600
bytes of data are recorded along one inch of tape.

     In order to mark the two ends of the tape, short strips
of a reflective material are stuck on the ends of the tape.
These reflective markers are detected by photoelectric cells
contained in the magnetic tape unit.

     A Magnetic Tape Unit (MTU) is a device which reads data
from and writes data on magnetic tape. It operates much the
same as a standard tape recorder. That is, the tape
containing the data to be read or on which data is to be
written, comes off one reel, passes under a "read-write
head", and is wound onto a second (take-up) reel. After the
processing is completed, the tape is rewound on to the
original reel.

     If changes are required in data recorded on a magnetic
tape, two separate MTUs should be used. One is used to read
the original data -- the other to write the revised data.
This operation is called "updating". The diagram on the
following page illustrates this idea.

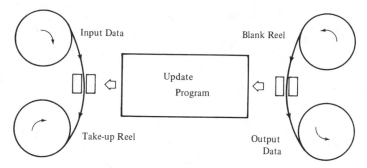

Input Data

Blank Reel

Update
Program

Take-up Reel

Output
Data

18.2 A First Example

Suppose a deck of one-hundred cards each contains ten INTEGER values. We want to read the one-hundred sets of ten numbers and record them on tape. Assume the reel of tape on which the values are to be recorded has been put on a MTU having a device number of two. (Recall the usual device number of a card reader is five.) The following program could be used.

```
C EXAMPLE 18.1 WRITE 100 SETS OF NUMBERS ON TAPE 2
      INTEGER SET(10)
      REWIND 2
      DO 1 I=1,100
      READ,SET
    1 WRITE(2) SET
      ENDFILE 2
      STOP
      END
```

In this example, three statements refer to the MTU. The first, "REWIND 2" causes the reel of tape on device 2 (which we have assumed to be a MTU) to be rewound to the reflective marker at the start of the tape. This insures that we are at the beginning of the tape before starting to write anything on it. The second reference to device 2 is in "WRITE(2) SET". Since there is no reference to a FORMAT statement, values will be written in a format-free mode. Because there are ten elements in the array SET, ten values will be recorded on magnetic tape each time the WRITE statement is executed. Each set of ten values creates a "tape record" on the tape. The statement "ENDFILE 2" causes a special symbol called a tapemark to be written on the tape. The tapemark should be written after all data values have been recorded. Since any data recorded on tape will presumably be read in a some later time, the purpose of the tapemark is simply to indicate the end of data has been reached during the reading operation.

There are five statements which reference Magnetic Tape Units. These are:

REWIND i

BACKSPACE i

ENDFILE i

READ (i, ...)

WRITE (i, ...)

In each statement, the symbol "i" specifies the device number associated with the MTU being used. The value of "i" can be an INTEGER constant or assigned to an INTEGER variable. In some computing centers, device numbers 1, 2, 3, 4 are reserved for Magnetic Tape Units. If you are planning to use magnetic tape, check with your computing center to find out which device numbers can be used. Job Control Statements are available for causing specific MTUs to have a particular device number. See for example, the IBM publication "Fortran H User's Guide.

Suppose device numbers 2 and 3 were MTUs and we wanted to read from 2 and write on 3. The following program structure could be used.

```
C EXAMPLE 18.2 DEVICE ASSIGNMENTS
      INTEGER TAPIN/2/, TAPOUT/3/
      .
      .
      REWIND TAPIN
      REWIND TAPOUT
      .
      .
      READ(TAPIN ...) ...
      WRITE(TAPOUT ...) ...
      .
      .
      ENDFILE TAPOUT
      REWIND TAPIN
      REWIND TAPOUT
      .
      END
```

There are several important questions which must be answered if we are to avoid serious errors in using magnetic tape. With respect to the example problem, these are:

a) Are there spaces on the tape between each set of ten values written on the tape?

b)   Are there spaces on the tape <u>within</u> each set of ten
     values written on the tape?

c)   If I tried to read the data written on the tape,
     would I get the first number recorded, the first
     set recorded, or all 100 values?

There are two very important differences between format-
free and formatted input-output operations with magnetic
tape. In particular, when reading data previously written on
magnetic tape, the same type of statement (format-free or
formatted) should be used almost without exception. The
chart below makes this idea clear.

	Type Of READ Statement Used	
Method Data Was Written	Format-Free	Formatted
Format-Free	O.K.	See note
Formatted	See note	O.K.

Note: You better know what you're doing!

18.3 Format-Free Input-Output

The allowed forms of the format-free READ and WRITE
statement are:

READ(i) list   WRITE(i) list

READ(i,END=n) list

READ(i,ERR=m) list

READ(i,END=n,ERR=m) list

Since data must be written on magnetic tape before it can be
read from magnetic tape, the WRITE statement will be
considered first.

Format-Free WRITE - (WRITE(i))

Each time a format-free WRITE statement is executed

a) Each value in the output list is written on the tape
   <u>exactly</u> <u>as</u> <u>it</u> <u>is</u> <u>stored</u> <u>in</u> <u>the</u> <u>memory</u> <u>of</u> <u>the</u>
   <u>computer</u>.

b) There are no gaps between the values recorded.

c) Together the set of values in the output list form a
   single tape record which is separated from adjacent

tape records by a gap. The gap is necessary to allow the tape motion to be stopped.

d) The length of the tape record (in bytes) is the sum of the lengths of the values in the output list. See Chapter 10 for information on the length of any type of value.

e) By convention, all tape records must be at least sixteen bytes long.

The following example illustrates these ideas. Assume device number one is a MTU.

```
C EXAMPLE 18.3 FORMAT-FREE WRITE
      REAL X(20),Y(50)
      REWIND 1
C READ VALUES FOR X AND Y FROM CARDS
      READ, X, Y
C WRITE VALUES ON TAPE
      WRITE(1) X
      WRITE(1) Y
      WRITE(1) X, Y
      ENDFILE 1
      STOP
      END
```

Recall that the length of a REAL value is 4 bytes. With respect to the preceding program, what ar the answers to the following questions? How many tape records are written? What is the length of each? What value is recorded in bytes 17 thru 20 of the first record?

A picture of what has been recorded on tape is shown below.

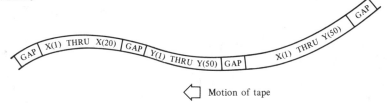

◁ Motion of tape

Answers

a) Four tape records are written. Three data records, one for each WRITE statement, and a tapemark record. The records are separated from each other by a gap.

b) The output list of the first WRITE statement has twenty values. Since each value has a length of four, the first tape record will be 20x4 or eighty

366

bytes long. Similarly, the second and third records will be 50x4 and (20+50)x4 bytes long respectively.

c) The ones and zeros recorded in bytes 17 thru 20 of the first record will be the ones and zeros which represent the value of the variable X(4). Bytes one thru twelve of the first record contain the values of the variables X(1), X(2) and X(3).

It is important to note that when values are written on tape using a format-free WRITE statement, there is no such thing as a default mask. Instead the bit patterns of the values are simply copied onto tape.

Format-Free READ Statements

There are four forms of the format-free READ statement which are valid. They are listed at the beginning of this section. One of them should be used to read data which was written using a format-free WRITE statement. The parameters "END=" and "ERR=" are optional. Either or both may be included.

Executing the statement "READ(i,END=n) list" will cause control to transfer to statement "n" if a tapemark record is read. This is the normal way of dectecting the end of recorded data. The value of "n" must the statement number of an executable statement.

The "ERR=m" feature allows a program to specify that control should be transferred to statement number "m" if it is impossible to execute the READ successfully because of some error condition on the tape or tape unit. Dust on the surface or weak magnetic spots are two possibilities. In example program 18.4, the ERR=m parameter is used.

Each form of the READ statement contains a list of the variables to be assigned values by executing the READ statement. Suppose the lengths of (number of bytes of memory reserved for) the variables in the input list are L1, L2, L3, ... Then, when the statement "READ (i) list" is executed:

a) One tape record is read.

b) The bit pattern in the first L1 bytes of the record is assigned to the first variable in the list. The bit patterns of the next L2, L3, etc. bytes of the record are assigned to the second, third etc. variables in the list.

c) Any unused bytes of data in the record are ignored and cannot be accessed by a subsequent READ statement.

d) Any attempt to access bytes beyond the end of the record is an error and the job will be terminated.

The following program illustrates these ideas. The program reads in six sets of REAL values having a varying number of elements in each set and writes the six sets on tape. Next the tape is rewound and the the sets are re-read (this time from tape and not cards). During the re-read, the average of values in each set is computed. As you may guess, this isn't the most efficient way to solve the problem!

```
C EXAMPLE 18.4 FORMAT-FREE READ
      REAL X(100)
C REWIND 4 AND THEN READ AND STORE VALUES ON TAPE
      REWIND 4
      DO 1 I=1,6
      READ,N,(X(J),J=1,N)
C CHECK FOR FEWER THAN 4 VALUES IN THE SET
      IF(N.LT.4) GO TO 5
    1 WRITE(4) N,(X(J),J=1,N)
      ENDFILE 4
      REWIND 4
C READ TAPE AND COMPUTE AVERAGE OF EACH SET
    2 READ(4,END=3,ERR=4) N,(X(I),I=1,N)
      SUM=NVALS=0
      DO 25 J=1,N
   25 SUM=SUM+X(J)
      NVALS=NVALS+N
      GO TO 2
    3 AVG=SUM/NVALS
      PRINT,'AVERAGE=',AVG
      STOP
    4 PRINT,'ERROR TRYING TO READ TAPE'
      STOP
    5 PRINT,'INSUFFICIENT DATA VALUES TO MAKE A
     * TAPE RECORD OF 16 BYTES'
      STOP
      END
```

The following two points should be noted. The reason for the IF statement "IF(N.LT.4)GO TO 5" is to insure that the length of each tape record written is at least sixteen bytes long (the permitted minimum). If a set contains fewer than four REAL elements, control is transferred to statement 5 which prints an appropriate message. The problem could be overcome by adding sufficient zeros to a short set to make it have four elements. In order to obtain the correct average the number of zeros added would have to be known and written on tape along with the data values. Problem 1 asks you to do this. The second point is simply that when the END= and ERR= parameters are present in a READ statement, it makes no difference in which order they appear.

Bypassing Records (Format-Free Input-Output)

Recall that a gap (an area of blank tape) is present between each pair of records written and between the last data record and the tapemark record. It is possible to cause the tape to move to the next gap in either a forward or a backward direction without reading or writing any data. The following example illustrates how records can be bypassed.

```
C EXAMPLE 18.5 SKIPPING OVER RECORDS
      REAL A(20)/20*0./
      REWIND 3
C WRITE 10 RECORDS ON MTU 3
      DO 1 I=1,10
    1 WRITE(3) A
C MOVE BACK TO THE START OF RECORD 6 AND READ IT
      DO 2 I=1,5
    2 BACKSPACE 3
      READ(3) A
C SKIP RECORDS 7 THRU 10 AND WRITE A TAPEMARK
      DO 3 J=1,4
    3 READ(3)
      ENDFILE 3
C BACKSPACE TO THE BEGINNING OF THE LAST DATA
C    RECORD AND READ IT. NOTE: WE MUST FIRST
C    BACKSPACE PAST THE TAPEMARK
      BACKSPACE 3
      BACKSPACE 3
      READ(3) A
C END OF EXAMPLE
      STOP
      END
```

To summarize. "BACKSPACE" causes the tape to move backward to the gap preceding the last record read. A READ satement with an empty input list cause the tape to move forward to the next gap.

18.4 Formatted Tape Input-Output

Most computer systems provide only one high speed printer for displaying program output. Occasionally, a program could effectively use additional printers to print two or more reports during the execution phase of the job. One solution is to print one report on the available printer and write the other reports on separate magnetic tape units. At the end of the run, the tapes containing the lines in the other reports can be rewound one-at-a-time and the records on them displayed on the printer. This is the most common use of formatted magnetic tape output. Formatted output is not recommended for writing intermediate results which will not be printed directly since formatting is a relatively slow operation. The use of tape files to store "print-line images" is discussed in more detail in Chapter 20. The following information assumes the reader is familiar with format-free output on magnetic tape.

If formatted values are to be written on tape, it is done in the normal way. That is, the WRITE statement has a pointer to format information containing the codes which control the appearance and placement of the values. The general form of the WRITE statement is therefore

WRITE(u,fmt) list

where "u" represents the device number of the tape unit on which records are to be written and "fmt" is a pointer to format information. The following two points are important.

a) Each time the end of the format codes is reached or a slash code is encountered, a tape record is written. The length of the record is determined by the maximum number of bytes used by the format codes processed up to the time the record is written.

b) Each record written must be at least sixteen bytes long. This means: a) Two consecutive slash codes cannot be used, and b) A slash cannot be either the first or the last code in a FORMAT statement.

The following three examples should make these ideas clear. Assume that 4 is the device number of a MTU.

a)   WRITE(4,900) X,Y,Z
   900   FORMAT(3E16.7)

Result: One tape record is written. The length of the record is 48 bytes. Values of X, Y, and Z are each formatted according to the mask E16.7.

b)   WRITE(4,901) X,Y,Z
   901   FORMAT(2E16.7)

Result: Two tape records are written. The first has a length of 32 and contains the formatted values of X and Y. The second has a length of 16 and contains the formatted value of Z.

c)   WRITE(4,902) X, Y, Z
   902   FORMAT(2(E16.7,/),E16.7)

Result: Three tape records are written. Each has a length of 16 and they contain the formatted values of X, Y, and Z respectively. The output is identical to that in (a) above.

d)   WRITE(4,903) V,W,X,Y,Z,P

903   FORMAT(T6,F11.0,/,2(10X,E10.3))

Result: Four tape records are written. Their lengths and
contents are as follows.

record	length	value(s)
1	16	V - positions 6 thru 16
2	40	W, X - positions 11-20, 31-40
3	40	Y, Z - positions 11-20, 31-40
4	20	P - positions 11-20

Formatted Input

If data has been written on tape under format control,
it can and should be read under format control. The
allowable forms of the READ statement are:

```
READ(u,fmt) list
READ(u,fmt,END=n) list
READ(u,fmt,ERR=m) list
READ(u,fmt,END=n,ERR=m) list
```

In the foregoing, "u" is the device number of a magnetic
tape unit; "fmt" is a pointer to format information; "n" and
"m" are statement numbers of executable statements to which
control will be transfered when an end-of-data or error
condition occurs respectively. The END= and ERR= parameters
are used in precisely the same way as with format-free
input.

Bypassing Records (Formatted Input-Output)

When reading records under format control, a slash code
causes the next tape record to be read immediately. This
means slash codes can be used to bypass those records which
are not needed by the program. An unformatted READ with no
input list achieves the same result. Thus, the following
are equivalent. Each causes four records to be skipped.

```
     READ(4,900)          DO 1 I=1,4
900 FORMAT(///)          1 READ(4)
```

Recall that the first left bracket in a FORMAT statement can
be thought of as causing a record to be read.

Regardless of how records have been written "BACKSPACE
u" is used to move back to the beginning of the previous
record.

An example. The following program: writes five records
on tape; writes a tapemark; backspaces to the beginning of
the second record; reads the second and fifth records.

```
C EXAMPLE 18.6 FORMATTED INPUT-OUTPUT
      INTEGER ARRAY(5)/5,4,3,2,1/
      REWIND 2
      WRITE(2,900) ARRAY
  900 FORMAT(I20)
      ENDFILE 2
      DO 1 I=1,5
    1 BACKSPACE 2
      READ(2,901) J,K
  901 FORMAT(I20,///,I20)
      PRINT,J,K
      STOP
      END
```

When the foregoing program is executed, the values printed
are 4 and 1.

18.5 Other Topics

The "*" forms of READ and WRITE statements can be used
with magnetic tape. They are not as efficient as the non-*
forms described in Section 3 of this chapter. The allowed
forms are:

        READ(u,*) list

        READ(u,*,END=n) list

        READ(u,*,ERR=m) list

        READ(u,*,END=n,ERR=m) list

        WRITE(u,*) list

If the "*" form of the WRITE statement is used: (a) Exactly
one record is written. (b) Each value in the output list is
formatted using the default mask appropriate to the type of
value. (c) The length of the record is the sum of the mask
widths used when writing the values.

If one of the "*" forms of the READ statement is used,
sufficient tape records are read to find a value for each
variable in the input list. The data values in the record
must agree in type with the elements of the input list.

Any record written using the "*" form of the WRITE
statement should be read using one of the "*" forms of the
READ statement.

There are several topics related to the use of magnetic
tape which are beyond the scope of this book. Control over
the factors described below is accomplished by control cards
which are not processed by the WATFIV compiler. For the
interested reader, a discussion of these topics can be found

in a reference such as the IBM manual "Fortran H Programmer's Guide".

a) The assignment of device numbers to specific MTUs attached to the system.

b) The creation of "blocked" records to reduce the number of gaps between data records thus increasing the efficiency of tape usage and improving (usually) reading and writing time.

c) The use of a single reel of tape to store more than one data file.

d) The creation of "header" and "trailer" labels to identify, describe and protect a set of tape records.

e) The use of magnetic tape to store programs as well as data.

18.6 Summary

Values may be written on and read from magnetic tape. Each WRITE statement generates one or more tape records which are separated by gaps. Each READ statement reads one or more tape records. Records can only be accessed sequentially in either a forward or backward direction. Data can be written or read with or without format control. Regardless of how the data has been written, it is the programmer's responsibility to know the method, placement, type and number of values recorded in each record. The most significant differences in the two methods are shown below.

	Format-Free	Formatted
Chief use	To store data for use later in the program or by some other program	To create formatted records which will be printed
Appearance of values	The internal represen- tation of the value	The formatted value
Length of Record	Sum of lengths of the values	Depends on format codes
Records written by a WRITE	Exactly one	Depends on format codes
Records read by a READ	Always one	Depends on format codes

373

The statements which control the reading and writing of data on magnetic tape are: READ, WRITE, BACKSPACE, REWIND and ENDFILE.

Exercise 18.1

1. For each of the following, determine the length of the tape record which is written and the values in the record. Assume "A" has been defined by "REAL A(8)/1., 2., 3., 4., 5., 6., 7., 8./" Assume device 1 is a tape unit.

    a) WRITE(1) A
    b) WRITE(1) (A(I),I=1,7,2)
    c) WRITE(1) (J,J+A(J),J=1,8)
    d) WRITE(1) ((A(K),K=I,8),I=1,8)

2. Making the same assumptions as in question 1, suppose the record which is written in (a) thru (d) above is read by the corresponding READ statement below. What values are assigned to the variables in the input list?

    a) READ(1) X,Y,Z
    b) READ(1) (A(I),I=3,8,3),Z
    c) READ(1) (M,A(9-K),K=1,8)
    d) READ(1) ((A(J),J=1,I),I=1,8)

3. Suppose a set of ten data records have been written on MTU 3 and is followed by a tapemark. What is the last record read after executing the following sequence of statements?

                    REWIND 3
                1   READ(3,END=2)
                    GO TO 1
                2   BACKSPACE 3
                    DO 3 I=1,6,2
                    BACKSPACE 3
                    BACKSPACE 3
                3   READ(3,END=4)
                    READ(3)

4. What will cause a program error when
              a) writing records in a format-free mode
              b) reading records in a format-free mode

5. State two important differences between format-free tape output and formatted tape output.

6. How many records are written by each of the following and
   what is the length of each? Assume 3 is a magnetic tape
   unit.

   a)   WRITE(3,900) I,J,K
         900 FORMAT(2I12,/,I20)

   b)   WRITE(3,901) (A,J=1,20)
         901 FORMAT(3X,F7.4,4(T12,2F3.0),/,E16.7)

7. What values are assigned to the variables in the input
   list in each of the following?

   a)   WRITE(2,900) 3.5,7,60.
         900 FORMAT(F8.3,2X,I4,E12.2)
             BACKSPACE 2
             READ(2,900)X,J,B

   b)   WRITE(2,901) .1234567,1234567
         901 FORMAT(T10,F8.6,T1,I7)
             BACKSPACE 2
             READ(2,902) I,A,L
         902 FORMAT (I6,F4.2,4X,I3)

Programming Problems

18.1   Modify example program 18.4 to permit sets of three
         or fewer values to be processed. A method of doing this
         is suggested in the discussion which follows the
         example.

18.2   Write a program which reads a set of twenty INTEGER
         values; sorts them into increasing order of magnitude;
         and writes them in four groups of five values each on a
         MTU. Repeat this process for a second set of values and
         write the output on a different MTU. Using these two
         sets of values as input, perform a merge (explained
         below) of the two sets of values to produce one string
         of forty non-decreasing values. Write the merged set on
         a third MTU in records of four values per record. Print
         the values in the original sets and in the   merged set.
         An example of a merged string of values obtained from
         two strings of five and four values respectively is
         shown below.

                 Direction Of Tape Motion ➡

   String A: 10 9 7 4 3 ⟍   Merged String

                              ⟶ 10 9 8 7 6 4 3 2 1

   String B: 8 6 4 2 1 ⟋

375

18.3   Prepare a deck of twenty-five data cards each of which has the following information.

card columns	item
1-5	student number
6	year of studies (1,2,3 or 4)
7-9	mark in course 1 (format F3.0)
10-12	mark in course 2
13-15	mark in course 3
16-18	mark in course 4
19-21	mark in course 5

a) Arrange the cards in order of increasing student number and write them on tape -- one tape record per student. Call this the student master file.

b) Read the student master file and: (i) print the student number, marks, and average of each student. (ii) While reading the data from tape, accumulate statistics required to print the report shown below. Print the report at the end of the run. One page should be printed for each year. Assume a pass requires a 60% average.

PASS/FAIL REPORT

	YEAR OF STUDIES				OVERALL
	1	2	3	4	
NUMBER OF STUDENTS	XX	XX	XX	XX	XX
% WHO PASSED	XX.X	XX.X	XX.X	XX.X	XX.X
% WHO FAILED	XX.X	XX.X	XX.X	XX.X	XX.X
AVERAGE MARK	XX.X	XX.X	XX.X	XX.X	XX.X

18.4   Prepare several cards of each of the following types. Each of the cards is either an "add" or "delete" card which refers to the student master file created in problem 3 above. Add cards have the same data as the student cards described in problem 3 but in addition, have a "1" in column 80. Delete cards have a student number in columns 1-5 and a "0" in column 80. Arrange the add/delete cards in order of increasing student number. The inputs to the program are the student master file and the set of add/delete cards. The output is a new student master file (written on a tape which is different from the old student master file). The new master file should reflect the changes specified by the add/delete cards. The program should detect and print error messages for the following conditions: an attempt to delete a student record which is not on the old student master file; an attempt to add a student who is already on the old student master file; an add or delete card which is out of sequence -- the student number on the add/delete card is less than the student number on the previous add/delete card. Once the new student master file has been written, rewind the tape and print the same two reports described in problem 3.

CHAPTER 19   DIRECT ACCESS INPUT OUTPUT

Questions Answered In This Chapter

1. What is direct access input output?

2. What statements are available for creating, changing
    and reading from files of direct access data?

19.1 Direct Access Concepts

Large volumes of data can be recorded on direct access
devices. The words "direct access" means that the time
required to locate a particular item or items of data is
largely independent of the position of the data item(s) on
the device. A card reader or a device for processing a reel
of tape is <u>not</u> a direct access device since each record of
data (each card) must be read in sequence. A direct access
card reader, if such a thing existed, would permit a
programmer to use statements such as: "Read card number 50";
"Read card number 417"; etc.. By recording punched card
data on a direct access device so that each card's data is
recorded as a separate record, statements such as: "Read
record 50"; "Read record 417"; can be used to obtain the
data in any desired order.

The most common type of direct access device is called a
magnetic disk unit. Data is recorded on the top and bottom
surfaces of a set of circular disks which together form a
"disk pack". The disk pack is placed on a rapidly rotating
spindle in a disk drive. Reading and writing of data is
accomplished by "read-write heads" located on the tips of a
comb-like mechanism which moves back and forth between the
disk surfaces. A typical disk pack can store as much data
as 300,000 punched cards. The average time to locate an item
of data recorded on the pack is approximately a twentieth of
a second. The chief advantage of direct access is that any
particular collection of data (any data record) can be read
or written simply by specifying a record number along with a
list of variables and, optionally, a pointer to formatting
information.

19.2 Direct Access In WATFIV

The WATFIV compiler recognizes statements which create
and process direct access files of data. A "file" is a
collection of records. A "record" is the amount of data
normally read or written in a single READ or WRITE

statement. For example, there might be one record in a payroll file for each employee. For each direct access file, the compiler must know certain facts such as the file number and the length of each record in the file. All records must have the same length. READ and WRITE statements are used to input and output direct access records. Each READ or WRITE contains at least a file number and a record number. Because there are significant differences between format-free and formatted operations, they will be discussed separately.

19.3 Format-Free Input-Output

Suppose one-hundred cards each contain ten INTEGER values. The values are to be read and stored on a direct access file. The ten values on card one are to constitute record one; those in card two, record two; etc.. Once the cards have been read and the data written in the file, additional cards are to be read each of which contains a single INTEGER value. If the value is K, the total of the values in the Kth and (K+1)th records is to be calculated and printed. The following program solves the problem. It illustrates the most important features of format-free input-output.

```
C EXAMPLE 19.1 FORMAT-FREE I/O
C DEFINE THE DIRECT ACCESS FILE - FILE #8, 100
C    RECORDS OF 10 VALUES EACH USING FORMAT-FREE
C    INPUT-OUTPUT STATEMENTS
      DEFINE FILE 8(100,10,U,NEXT)
      INTEGER SET(10)
C READ AND WRITE THE 100 SETS OF DATA
      DO 1 I=1,100
      READ,SET
      WRITE(8'I) SET
    1 CONTINUE
C READ A CARD TO GET A VALUE OF K
    2 READ(5,*,END=5) K
      ISUM=0
C READ THE KTH AND (K+1)TH DATA RECORDS AND
C    FIND THE TOTAL
      READ(8'K) SET
      DO 3 I=1,10
    3 ISUM=ISUM+SET(I)
      READ(8'NEXT) SET
      DO 4 I=1,10
    4 ISUM=ISUM+SET(I)
      PRINT,'SUM OF VALUES IN SETS',K,'AND',K+1,
    * 'IS',ISUM
      GO TO 2
    5 STOP
      END
```

<u>Remarks</u>

1. The statement which defines the direct access file is

   DEFINE FILE 8 (100,10,U,NEXT)

   In this statement:

   "8" is the "file number". A different file number
   should be used for each direct access file in
   a program. Check with your computing center
   to find out what device numbers refer to
   direct access files.

   "100" is the number of records in the file. Any
   attempt to reference a record beyond 100
   would result in an error.

   "10" is the length of each record. For unformatted
   records, this length must be stated in
   "words". Since each INTEGER value occupies
   one word (4 bytes) of memory, the length of
   each record is ten words.

   "U" indicates that format-free READ and WRITE
   statements will be used to read and write the
   records in the file.

   "NEXT" is called the "associated variable".
   Following execution of any READ or WRITE it
   has a value which is one more than the record
   number of the record used in the READ or
   WRITE statement.

2. The statement "WRITE(8'I)SET" causes the ten values
   in SET to be written in the space reserved for
   record I in file 8. Note that a single quote
   separates the file number and the record number.
   Since there is no pointer to format information,
   the operation is format-free. This means that a
   copy of the bit patterns of the ten INTEGER values
   in SET is written into record I.

3. The statement "READ(8'K)SET" causes a copy of the
   first ten words of the Kth record in file 8 to be
   stored in the ten words of memory reserved for SET.
   Since NEXT is the associated variable, following
   execution of this statement, the value of NEXT will
   automatically be K+1.

4. The statement "READ(8'NEXT)SET" is similar to the
   previous READ statement. It illustrates the use of
   the associated variable. If the program had

attempted to assign a value to NEXT, an error would
have occured.

19.4 Summary Of Format-Free Input-Output

1. The general form of the DEFINE FILE statement is

DEFINE FILE file# (number of , length of , U , assoc.)
                   records   record   var

where: the file# must be in the range 1 thru 99

the length of a record is stated in words

the associated variable is an INTEGER variable

2. The READ statement has the general form

READ (file# ' record#) list

where: "file#" is an INTEGER constant or variable
indicating the file from which data is to be
read

"record#" is an INTEGER constant, variable or
expression indicating which record is to be
read. Its value must be positive and not
greater than the number of records in the
file.

"list" is optional and, if present, indicates the
variables to be assigned a value by executing
the READ statement. The bit patterns found
in the record are assigned sequentially
(byte-by-byte) to the memory locations
reserved for variables in the list. The
total length of the input list must not
excede the record length.

3. The WRITE statement has the general form

WRITE (file# ' record#)list

where: "file#" is as above.

"record#" is as above and indicates which record
is to contain the values in the output list.

"list" describes the values which are to be
written into the record. If the total length
of the values in the output list is less than
the length of the record, the unused portion
of the record is filled with zero bits. If

the length of the values in the output list excedes the
length of the record, an error occurs.

4. A FIND statement (Section 19.8) can be used with format-
free direct access files.

Format-free direct access files should be used for
temporary storage of data values. That is, when the data
will be used as input later in the program or perhaps by
some other program.

19.5 Formatted Input-Output

The rules and use of formatted direct access files will
be presented using two example problems. A summary of the
rules can be found in Section 19.6.

Problem 1

Suppose the XYZ Company maintains records of how much
money is owed by each of its 1700 customers. The information
is currently punched on cards. The problem is to store the
data on a direct access file. Assume that each customer has
a customer number in the range 1 thru 2000. Input to the
program consists of 1700 cards each of which contains the
following information.

columns	mask	data
1-4	I4	customer number
5-24	A20	customer name
25-32	F8.2	amount owing
33-38	I6	date of last change (DDMMYY)

The following program reads the cards and records the
information about customer N in the Nth record of direct
access file 27. Further comments follow the program.

```
C EXAMPLE 19.2 FORMATTED DIRECT ACCESS
C DEFINE A FILE OF 2000 RECORDS OF LENGTH 50
      DEFINE FILE 27(2000,50,E,IVAR)
      INTEGER CUSTNO,DATE
      CHARACTER*34 DATA
C READ EACH CARD AND WRITE THE DATA IN THE FILE
      DO 1 N=1,1700
      READ(5,900) CUSTNO, DATA
  900 FORMAT(I4,A34)
      WRITE(27'CUSTNO,901)DATA
  901 FORMAT(A34)
    1 CONTINUE
      STOP
      END
```

Remarks

1. The statement which defines the direct access file is

   DEFINE FILE 27 (2000 , 50 , E , IVAR)

   In this statement:

   "27" is the file number. A different file number should be used for each direct access file.

   "2000" is the number of records in the file. Since customer numbers can be as large as 2000 and since the data for customer N is to be in the Nth record, the file contains 2000 records even though not all records will be used.

   "50" is the length of each record in bytes. Aside from the customer number, there are 34 bytes of data about each customer. The length was chosen as 50 to allow additional information to be kept if needed in the future.

   "E" indicates that formatted READ and WRITE statements will be used to process the records in the file.

   "IVAR" is the associated variable. Following any READ or WRITE its value is automatically set to the next higher record number. IVAR was not used in this program.

2. Consider the statement pair

   READ(5,900,END=2) CUSTNO,DATA
   900 FORMAT(I4,A34)

When reading the symbols in the cards, the information in columns 1-38 is of interest. Specifically, columns 1-4 contain the customer number and columns 5-38 the information about the customer. Since our purpose is simply to store the data in the file, it is not necessary to separate the name, amount and date information.

3. The statements

   WRITE(27'CUSTNO,901)DATA
   901 FORMAT(A34)

   cause the 34 symbols stored in DATA to be stored in the first 34 positions of record number CUSTNO of direct access file 27. The remaining 16 bytes of the record are automatically set to blanks.

Problem 2

In order to keep its set of customer records up to date, changes are necessary in records of the direct access file created to solve problem one. In particular, suppose change cards have the following information.

columns	mask	item
1-4	I4	customer number
5-12	F8.2	dollar amount
13-18	I6	date (DDMMYY)

Suppose an unspecified number of change cards have been keypunched and are in no particular order with respect to customer number. The problem is simply to read the cards and: add the amount value in the card to the amount value in the customer record (assume a negative amount represents a payment); change the date in the record to the date in the card. The following program could be used.

```
      C EXAMPLE 19.3 UPDATE CUSTOMER FILE
            INTEGER CUSTNO,DATE,CDATE
            CHARACTER*20 NAME
            DEFINE FILE 27(2000,50,E,MMM)
      C READ A CHANGE CARD
          1 READ(5,900,END=2)CUSTNO,CAMNT,CDATE
        900 FORMAT(I4,F8.2,I6)
      C READ THE RECORD FROM THE FILE
            READ(27'CUSTNO,901)NAME,AMT,DATE
        901 FORMAT(A20,F8.2,I6)
            AMT=AMT+CAMNT
            DATE=CDATE
      C WRITE THE REVISED RECORD
            WRITE(27'CUSTNO,901)NAME,AMT,DATE
            GO TO 1
          2 STOP
            END
```

Remarks

1. The DEFINE FILE statement is identical to the one used when the file was created.

2. The statements

```
        READ(27'CUSTNO,901) NAME,AMT,DATE
    901 FORMAT(A20,F8.2,I6)
```

cause NAME, AMT and DATE to be assigned a value using information stored in record number CUSTNO of

384

file 27. Why is NAME an element of the input list? Why not leave it out since no change is being made in the name? The answer has nothing to do with the READ statement but a great deal to do with the WRITE statement. If the value of NAME is not obtained at READ time, it would be impossible to know what to put in the name area of the record at WRITE time. That is, a WRITE statement replaces the entire contents of a record.

3. The statement "WRITE(27'CUSTNO,901)NAME,AMT,DATE" causes the contents of record number CUSTNO to be replaced with the values of NAME, AMT, and DATE according to the format codes in statement 901.

19.6 Summary Of Formatted Input-Output

1. The DEFINE FILE statement has the general form

DEFINE FILE file# (number of , length of , E , assoc.)
                    records   a record   var.

where: "file#" is a constant in the range 1-99

"number of records" is the number of records in the file

"length of a record" is the length of each record in bytes.

"E" indicates that formatted input-output statements will be used to process the records in the file.

"associated variable" is an INTEGER variable which has a value one greater than the number of the record most recently read or written.

2. The READ statement has one of the following forms:

READ(file#'record#, fmt) list

READ(file#'record#, fmt,ERR=m) list

where: "file#" is the number of the direct access file from which data is to be read. An INTEGER variable can be used to store the file# value.

"record#" is an INTEGER constant, variable or expression whose value indicates which record within the file is to be read. The value must be positive and not greater than the number of records in the file.

"fmt" is a reference to the set of format codes
to be used when reading the data.

"ERR=m" indicates that control is to be
transferred to statement number m if an
equipment problem occurs when reading the
record.

"list" is a list of variables to be assigned a
value by executing the READ statement.

3. The WRITE statement has the form

WRITE(file#'record#, fmt) list

where: "file#", "record#" and "fmt" have the same use as
when present in a READ statement.

"list" is optional and contains the values which
are to be stored in the record by executing
the WRITE statement.

A WRITE statement causes the entire contents of a record
to be replaced. All positions skipped over or
unreferenced by the format codes will contain blanks.
All positions covered by masks or literals will contain
the symbols appropriate to the use of the particular
code.

4. Executing a single READ or WRITE statement may cause more
than one record to be read or written. It depends on the
format codes. If it is necessary to recycle format codes
because there are fewer masks than items in the input or
output list, the record number is automatically
increased by one each time the end of the format codes
is reached. A slash code can be used in an input
operation to cause the next record to be read. On
output, a slash code causes: a record to be written
before the end of the format codes is reached; the
record number to be increased by one. Care should be
used in the use of recycling and slash codes on input
operations since any attempt to read a record in which
nothing has previously been written is an error.

5. The symbol "E" in a DEFINE FILE statement also permits
the "*" form of READ and WRITE statements to be used.
The allowed forms are:

READ(file#'rec#,*)...

READ(file#'rec#,*,ERR=m)...

WRITE(file#'rec#,*)...

386

If the "*" form of the WRITE statement is used, each
item in the output list is written according to the
default mask appropriate to the type of value. On
input, WATFIV routines scan successive records beginning
with the one whose record number appears in the READ
statement. Values in the records are assumed to be
separated by a comma or blanks. As many records will be
read as is necessary to find a value for each item in
the input list.

19.7 Direct Access Using A Mix Of Input-Output Statements

When using a direct access file, the same type of
statement (format-free or formatted) is normally used for
all READ and WRITE statements used to process records in a
particular file. If it is necessary to use a mixture of
format-free and formatted input-output statements then:

   i) In the DEFINE FILE statement, an "L" is used
       instead of an "E" or "U" to indicate that a mix of
       statement types may be used.

   ii) The length of each record is stated in bytes.

  iii) All format-free READ and WRITE statements ar
       processed according to the rules in Section 4 of
       this chapter.

   iv) All formatted READ and WRITE statements are
       processed according to the rules in Section 6 of
       this chapter.

A word of caution. It is extremely unlikely that a
format-free WRITE statement and a formatted READ statement
(or vice-versa) would ever be used to process the same
record in a file.

19.8 The FIND Statement

The FIND statement has the general form

                FIND (file# ' record#)

where "file#" and "record#" indicate the direct access
file and record within that file which is to be "found".

There are two delays which occur when locating a record
to read or write. The names given to these delays are "seek
time delay" and "rotational delay". By issuing a FIND for a
record before it is read or written, the first of these two
delay times may be reduced thus speeding up the overall
execution time of the job. The program structure below
illustrates the use of a FIND statement.

```
C EXAMPLE 19.4 USING A FIND STATEMENT
      DEFINE FILE 8(...)
      .
      .
      FIND (8'i)
      .
      .
      READ(8'i,...) ...
      .
      END
```

After the execution of a FIND statement, the associated variable has a value equal to the record number which appeared in the FIND statement.

19.9 Other Topics

Several direct access files can be defined in a single DEFINE FILE statement. The information about each file is separated by a comma. For example:

DEFINE FILE 8 (100,34,E,IVAR1), 9 (60,10,U,IVAR2)

defines two direct access files. File 8 contains 100 formatted records of 34 bytes each and file 9 contains 60 unformatted records of 10 words each. IVAR1 and IVAR2 are the names of the associated variables.

There are several topics related to the use of direct access files and devices which are beyond the scope of this book. Control over the factors outlined below is accomplished by cards which are not processed by the WATFIV compiler. A description of these topics can be found in a publication such as the IBM manual "Fortran H Programmer's Guide".

a) The assignment of file numbers to specific devices and/or direct access storage media.

b) Selection of efficient record lengths and the use of blocked records to avoid wasting large amounts of direct access storage.

c) The creation of labels to identify and protect files of data.

d) The use of direct access files to store programs as well as data.

e) The standard techniques for converting record identification numbers (e.g. social security numbers) to record numbers for use in locating data in a direct access file.

1. For each of the following, write a suitable DEFINE FILE statement to define the file characteristics.

   a) Records in the file will be read and written using format-free READ and WRITE statements. Each record will have 20 INTEGER values. Assume the file number is 20 and the associated variable is NEXT.

   b) Direct access file 12 is to be a set of 137 records some of which may require as many as 200 characters of data. Formatted READ and WRITE statements will be used to process the records. No use is expected to be made of the associated variable.

   c) Records in file 17 may be read with or without format control. ION is to take on the value of the next higher record number following execution of any input-output statement. As many as 10000 records may be needed and the largest records will have to store the values in 12 by 5 matrix of REAL numbers.

2. What is the output of the following program?

```
              DEFINE FILE 25(10,8,U,NEXT)
              INTEGER VEC(8),NUM(4)
              DO 1 I=1,4
              READ,VEC
            1 WRITE(25'VEC(1))(VEC(J),J=2,8,2)
            2 READ,IREC
              READ(25'IREC)NUM
              IF(NUM(3).EQ.0) STOP
              PRINT,NUM
              GO TO 2
              END
      $ENTRY
              3 8 0 2 5 6 1 10
              6 0 3 5 1 0 2 0
              8 9 0 0 6 1 8 0
              1 0 3 5 7 8 4 6
              8
              3
              6
              1
```

3. What is the output of the following program?

```
        DEFINE FILE 16(16,16,E,J)
        REAL A(3)/2.,4.5,7.3/,I(3)/12,2,5/
        WRITE(16'1,900)(A(K),I(K),K=1,3)
900 FORMAT(F3.1/I6)
        READ(16'2,901)X,Y,Z
901 FORMAT(F6.2)
        PRINT,X,Y,Z
        READ(16'J,902)M,N
902 FORMAT(I1,1X,I6)
        PRINT,M,N,J
        STOP
        END
```

19.10 Summary

Data can be recorded on, and read from, direct access devices. All records in a direct access file must have the same length. A DEFINE FILE statement is used to specify the characteristics of a direct access file. A WRITE statement replaces the entire contents of a record.

If format-free READ and WRITE statements are used to process records,

- The length of each record is specified as being a number of words.

- Exactly one record is read by any READ statement.

- Exactly one record is written by any WRITE statement.

If formatted READ and WRITE statements are used to process records,

- The record length is stated in bytes.

- The number of records which are read or written in an input-output operation depends on the format codes which are used.

Proper use of a FIND statement may reduce the time necessary to locate a record on a direct access device.

Programming Problems

19.1 Assume that each of twelve students takes two courses -- math and English. Prepare a deck of twelve cards containing the following data.

cols.	item
1-2	student number (range 01-99)
3-24	student name
25-26	math mark (F2.0)
27-28	English mark (F2.0)

Write a program which reads the twelve cards and records the information on a direct access file so that the information about the student having a student number of K is found in the Kth record of the file. On a second direct access file write a single record containing the twelve valid student numbers in order of increasing magnitude. Display the contents of each card for future reference.

19.2 Using the data files created in problem one, print a report which, for each student, displays the student number, name, math mark, English mark, and average. Rewrite each student's record to include his average in the information kept in the file.

19.3 Using the data created in problem two as input to the program, write a program which prints the names and averages of the twelve students in order of decreasing standing in the class based on the student's average.

19.4 Write a program which will store the elements of a matrix on a direct access file. Each row of values in the matrix should be recorded as a separate record in the file. The file should be large enough to accommodate matrices having as many as 500 rows and 200 columns. Input to the program consists of the number of rows and columns in the matrix followed by the values in the matrix -- row by row. Once the values have been read and stored in the file, use the file information as input to determine: (a) which column of elements contains the longest sequence of decreasing values; (b) the number of non-decreasing sequences of values in each row.

19.5 Create two direct access files each of which contains twenty records of one INTEGER value each. The values in each set should be in order of non-decreasing magnitudes. Using these files as input, determine how many values are present in both sets. Use an algorithm such that each record needs to be read only once. Use format-free input-output.

391

CHAPTER 20   CHARACTER "DEVICES"

Questions Answered In This Chapter

    1. How are CHARACTER variables used as the source of data in a READ statement? What are the reasons for wanting to do this?

    2. How can CHARACTER variables be used to store the output of a WRITE operation? How is this technique useful in creating "print-line images" and modifying FORMAT codes at execution time?

20.1 Concepts And Uses Of CHARACTER Devices

Consider the following simple problem. An unknown number of REAL values have been punched on each of several cards. Each card contains from one to ten values and the values on any card are separated by commas. The problem is to determine the average of the values punched on each card. So you say "What's so hard about that?". O.K. -- write a program to solve the problem! The difficulty results from the following chain of implications. (1) Commas are used to separate the data values and so a format-free READ statement must be used. (2) Given that a format-free READ statement must be used, then the input list in the READ statement must have the same number of variables as there are values punched on the card. (If there are more variables than values, more than one card would be read. If there are fewer variables than values, some numbers would not be read since we can't read the same card twice.) (3) The problem then is we must know how many values are on each card before we read it and yet we can't find this out until we read it.

The solution to the problem is essentially the following. Read each card and store the symbols in the card in a set of eighty CHARACTER variables. Determine the number of values in the card by counting the number of commas in the card. Set up an input list (using an implied DO-loop) in a format-free READ statement which has the appropriate number of variables. "Read" the values using the CHARACTER variable(s) as the source of input. A suitable program can be found later in the Chapter.

A second problem. Suppose INTEGER values in the range one thru one-hundred are being read in, one value per card. For each value read, a line is to be printed which contains a "*" in the print position specified by the number on the card. To solve this problem a brute force approach could be used which would involve writing 100 FORMAT statements and perhaps a Computed GO TO with 100 values in the statement number list. What we would like however, is to be able to use a sequence of statements such as

```
          READ,N
          PRINT 900
      900 FORMAT(' ',TN,'*')
```

Unfortunately, variables and expressions cannot be used in a string of format codes. Since format codes are strings of symbols, the problem would be solved if there was some way of converting an INTEGER value to its equivalent CHARACTER value representation.

The two preceding problems can be easily programmed if there was some way of converting CHARACTER values to non-CHARACTER values and vice-versa. This is the subject of this chapter. When converting CHARACTER values to non-CHARACTER values, the basic idea is to consider a CHARACTER variable or array as being a "dummy card reader" from which data can be read. To convert non-CHARACTER values to CHARACTER values, a CHARACTER variable is treated as though it were a single print line.

20.2 CHARACTER Variables Used As Input Devices

How To Do It

Suppose the variable SYMBLS has been defined by

```
      CHARACTER*4 SYMBLS/'1234'/
```

The problem is to convert the constant '1234' to the INTEGER value 1234 and to the REAL value 1234.. If J and A are the two variables which are to have the converted values, statements such as

```
          J=SYMBLS
          A=SYMBLS
```

will cause errors since a CHARACTER value cannot be assigned to a non-CHARACTER variable. The following statements do the job.

```
      C CONVERT THE SYMBOLS TO AN INTEGER VALUE
            CHARACTER*4 SYMBLS/'1234'/
            READ(SYMBLS,900) J
        900 FORMAT(I4)
      C CONVERT THE SYMBOLS TO A REAL VALUE
            READ(SYMBLS,901) A
        901 FORMAT(F4.0)
```

393

In both READ statements the source of data (the input "device") is the CHARACTER variable SYMBLS. The input list contains the variables which are to be assigned a value as a result of executing the READ statement. The FORMAT statement serves its usual purpose -- to describe the locations within the source of data which are to be scanned when looking for a value to be assigned to each variable in the list.

Why use a READ statement? Why not have a built-in function or library subprogram to perform the conversion? The answer is that by using a READ statement, the programmer can take advantage of the tremendous power of formatting. Consider the following examples.

i)   CHARACTER*4 SYMBLS/'1234'/
       READ(SYMBLS,900) J,A
    900 FORMAT(I4,T1,F4.0)

   Result: J=1234 and A=1234.

ii)   CHARACTER STRING*12/'-2.73E01589.'/
       READ(STRING,901) A,B,K
    901 FORMAT(E8.2,2X,F2.0,T1,I2)

   Result: A=-27.3, B=9., K= -2

iii)   CHARACTER VEC(5)/'1','2','3','4','5'/
       READ(VEC,902) I,J,K,L,M
    902 FORMAT(I1)

   Result: I=1, J=2, K=3, L=4, M=5
   That is, each element of the array is treated
   as a separate "card".

iv)   CHARACTER DATA*8/'1234 678'/
       READ(DATA,*) I,J

   Result: I=1234, J=678

v) Two examples of errors.

   a)   CHARACTER*10 ARRAY(3)/'1', '2', '3'/
        READ(ARRAY,903) J,K,L,M
     903 FORMAT(I10)

      Error: Four input variables and only three vari-
             ables in ARRAY. The "END=" parameter should
             be used.

   b)   CHARACTER*3 DATA/'123'/
        READ(DATA,904) K
     904 FORMAT(I4)

> Error: Length of format codes excedes length of
> variable. (Similar to attempting to read
> beyond column 80 in a card.)

To summarize. A READ statement in which the the input "device" is a CHARACTER variable or CHARACTER array or array element is permitted in WATFIV. All forms of format-free and formatted READ statements are permitted. The source of data (the CHARACTER variable(s)) can be thought of as an internal card reader in which:

a) The number of cards in the card reader equals the number of variables specified by the CHARACTER device. That is: 1 if a simple variable; N if the name of an array having N elements; (N-I+1) if the Ith element of an array of N elements is specified as the source of data.

b) The length of each "card" is length of the CHARACTER variable or array element used as the source of data.

20.3 Use Of CHARACTER Input Devices

A CHARACTER variable or array must be used as an input device when the input data contains information which is essential to properly read the data. The information may indicate what format codes should be used and/or which and how many variables should be in the input list. This means the program must be able to select or construct appropriate format codes and/or an input list by examining the symbols found in the data. Once this has been done, the data can be re-read using the CHARACTER variable(s) as the source of data. The determination of suitable format codes or input list may be a simple or a very complex problem. The following problem is simple.

A First Example

Suppose a data deck contains two types of cards -- name cards and wage cards. Name cards contain an employee number in columns 1-5, the person's name in columns 6-30 and a "1" in column 80. Wage cards contain an employee number in columns 1-5, a wage rate in columns 6-10 (F5.2), the number of hours worked in columns 11-15 (F5.2) and a "2" in column 80. Assume that the cards are arranged in order of increasing employee number and that a wage card follows the name card. Although there is a name card for every employee, there may or may not be a wage card for each employee since some employees did not work during the period for which the payroll is to be calculated. The problem is to read the data cards and print the pay of those employees having a wage card following their name card. The following program solves the problem.

```
C EXAMPLE 20.1 PAYROLL REPORT
      INTEGER CDTYPE,NAMNUM,WAGNUM
      CHARACTER*79 DATA,NAME*25
    1 READ (5,900,END=4) DATA,CDTYPE
  900 FORMAT(A79,I1)
C DETERMINE IF A NAME OR WAGE CARD
      IF(CDTYPE.EQ.2) GO TO 5
      READ(DATA,901) NAMNUM,NAME
  901 FORMAT(I5,A25)
      GO TO 1
C PROCESS WAGE CARD
    5 READ(DATA,902)WAGNUM,RATE,HOURS
  902 FORMAT(I5,2F5.2)
C CHECK FOR MATCH ON EMPLOYEE NUMBER
      IF(WAGNUM.NE.NAMNUM) GO TO 3
      PAY=HOURS*RATE
      PRINT 903,WAGNUM,NAME,PAY
  903 FORMAT('0',I5,2X,A25,F8.2)
      GO TO 1
    3 PRINT,'WAGE AND NAME CARD DO NOT MATCH'
    4 STOP
      END
```

A Second Example

The problem which introduced the material in this chapter was that of calculating the average of an unknown number of REAL values punched in each of several data cards. The values on each card are separated by commas. This means a format-free READ statement is required. Because the READ statement must be format-free, the program must know how many items are on the card in order to set up an appropriate input list. Unfortunately this value can only be determined after the card has been read. In the following program, the symbols in the card are read and stored in a set of eighty CHARACTER variables. Then commas are counted and finally the required number of values are read using the CHARACTER variable as the source of data.

```
C EXAMPLE 20.2 READING FROM A CHARACTER VARIABLE
      CHARACTER SCAN(80),CHDEV*80,COMMA/','/
      REAL VALUE(20)
C READ A CARD AND STORE ITS SYMBOLS AS ONE GROUP
C   OF 80 AND 80 GROUPS OF 1
    1 READ (5,900,END=4) CHDEV,SCAN
  )00 FORMAT(A80,T1,80A1)
C COUNT COMMAS BY EXAMINING ELEMENTS OF SCAN
      NVALS=1
      DO 2 I=2,79
    2 IF(SCAN(I).EQ.COMMA)NVALS=NVALS+1
C READ THE NVALS VALUES USING CHDEV AS THE
C   SOURCE OF DATA
      READ(CHDEV,*) (VALUE(I),I=1,NVALS)
```

396

```
C COMPUTE THE AVERAGE AND PRINT IT
      SUM=0.
      DO 3 I=1,NVALS
    3 SUM = SUM+VALUE(I)
      AVG=SUM/NVALS
      PRINT,'AVERAGE OF',NVALS,'VALUES IS',AVG
      GO TO 1
    4 STOP
      END
```

Some remarks. Note that the symbols are stored in both SCAN and CHDEV. SCAN is necessary so that each symbol in the card can be checked for a comma. CHDEV (length 80) is necessary when the data is read using the CHARACTER variable as the source of the input. The statement "READ(SCAN,*)list" could not be used since it would be treated as an input device of 80 "cards" of one column each instead of one card of 80 columns. Equivalencing SCAN and CHDEV could have been used to achieve the same effect.

Is it really necessary to count commas? No. If one assumes there are twenty or fewer values in any card, the following approach could have been used: (a) Read a card and store its symbols in CHDEV. (b) Set all elements of VALUE to zero. (c) Attempt to assign a value to all elements of VALUE by reading from CHDEV using format-free input and the "END=" parameter. (d) Count backwards from VALUE(20) to find the first non-zero value in VALUE and thus determine the number of values in the card. (e) Calculate the average and continue with the next card. Problem 20.2 asks you to use this algorithm to solve the problem.

Exercise 20.1

1. For each of the following, determine the last value assigned to each variable.

```
a)          CHARACTER*8 STR/'123 56.8'/
            READ(STR,*) I,A
            READ(STR,900) B,C,K
        900 FORMAT(2F3.0,1X,I1)
            READ(STR,901) M,E,L,D
        901 FORMAT(I2,2(F1.1,I1))

b)          CHARACTER*3 STR(6)/2*'1',4*'2'/,STR2*2(6)
            CHARACTER*2 STR3(3)
            INTEGER SET1(6),SET2(6)
            READ(STR,*) STR2
            READ(STR,902) STR3
        902 FORMAT(/A2)
            READ(STR,*) SET1
            READ(STR,903)SET2
        903 FORMAT(I3)
```

2. What is printed by the following program?

```
          CHARACTER*79 CARD
          DO 1 I=1,5
          READ 900, ICODE,CARD
     900  FORMAT(I1,A79)
          IF(ICODE.EQ.1) GO TO 2
          READ(CARD,902)N1,N2
     902  FORMAT(3X,I2,I2)
          PRINT,N1,N2
          GO TO 1
       2  READ(CARD,903) A1,A2
     903  FORMAT(F5.2,F3.1)
          PRINT,A1,A2
       1  CONTINUE
          STOP
          END
   $ENTRY
   123456789
   223456789
   12.456.89
   12.456 89
   2.        .
```

3. Suppose the symbols "1234" are punched in the first four
   columns of a card. These symbols can, of course, be read
   three times in the same READ statement by the following
   statements.

```
          CHARACTER*4 SYMS
          READ 900, SYMS, A,M
     900  FORMAT(A4,T1,F4.0,T1,I4)
```

   Under what circumstances could a T-code not be used to
   re-read card columns? Give an example.

4. Below are four READ statements. In each, the "?" is one
   of the following: a CHARACTER variable; an INTEGER
   constant; an implied DO-loop; an array containing format
   codes; an element of a CHARACTER array. Indicate which
   of the foregoing could be substituted for the question
   mark. Also indicate whether the READ statement is
   formatted or format-free.

```
       a)   READ, ?, list
       b)   READ(?) list
       c)   READ ?, list
       d)   READ, +(?), list
```

20.4 CHARACTER Variables As Output "Devices"

In formatted output operations, a CHARACTER variable or array can be used an an output "device". To do this, a WRITE statement is used in which a CHARACTER variable, array or array element replaces the reference to a printer, card punch, tape unit or direct access file. When the WRITE statement is executed, the symbols stored in the CHARACTER element(s) are those which would normally have been sent to the output device. A simple example is the following.

```
            CHARACTER*8 RECEVE
            WRITE(RECEVE,900) 12345678
        900 FORMAT(I8)
```

Result: The symbols "12345678" are stored in RECEVE

Why use CHARACTER variables as output devices? One important application is to perform "dynamic formatting". Dynamic formatting allows you to change format codes under program control at execution time. This application is described in Section 5 of this chapter. A second important application is in the preparation of "print-line images". This latter application is useful when a program needs to print two or more reports and only one printer is available. This application is discussed in Section 4 of this chapter.

How To Do It

Recall that there are 133 print positions in a line of printing. When values in the output list of a PRINT or WRITE statement are sent to the printer, symbols are stored in the print positions according to format codes or default masks. The same principles apply when a CHARACTER element is used as the output device. That is, each CHARACTER variable used as an output device can be viewed as a print line with a length equal to the length of the variable. However, the first symbol stored in each variable has no special use as it does when output is sent to the printer. Rules of use follow the examples below.

Example 1 - The output device is a simple variable

```
            CHARACTER*14 B
            WRITE(B,900) 'VALUE IS',-9.99
        900 FORMAT(A8,F6.2)
```

Result: The variable B contains "VALUE IS -9.99"

Example 2 - The output device is an array

```
            CHARACTER*5 X(4), Y*3/'ABC'/
            WRITE(X,901) Y,Y,Y,Y
        901 FORMAT(A3)
```

Result: Each of the four elements of X contains the symbols "bbABC" ("b" denotes a blank). Since there is only one one mask, each time the end of the format codes is reached, the codes are recycled and apply to the next variable in the array. The blanks precede rather than follow the "ABC" because of the POT rule.

Example 3 - The output device is an array element

```
    CHARACTER*6 Y(8)/8*'ZZZZZZ'/
    WRITE(Y(3),902) (J,J=1,4)
903 FORMAT(2I3)
```

Result: Y(1) and Y(2) are unchanged
      Y(3) contains "bb1bb2"
      Y(4) contains "bb3bb4"
      Y(5) thru Y(8) are unchanged

The use of an array element allows you to begin the write operation at a variable other than the first element of an array. Otherwise it is the same.

Example 4 - Typical errors

```
a)    CHARACTER*5 X
      WRITE(X,904) 123
904 FORMAT(I8)
```

Reason: The format codes excede the length of the CHARACTER variable.

```
b)    CHARACTER*4 X(3)
      WRITE(X,905) 1, 2, 3, 4
905 FORMAT(I4)
```

Reason: Since there is only one mask, four variables or more are required for the device. X has only three.

Summary of Rules

1. The WRITE statement can be used to store symbols in CHARACTER variables. The allowed forms are:

      WRITE (char, fmt) list

      WRITE (char, *) list

   where: "char" is a CHARACTER variable, array or array element;

"fmt" is any valid format reference. The "*" denotes format-free.

"list" is a set of values which will be converted to symbols and stored in the CHARACTER variable(s) specified by "char". The list is optional.

2. When the WRITE statement is executed:

a) The first variable specified by "char" is is set to blanks.

b) If a formatted WRITE statement is used, the format codes are processed left to right in normal fashion. That is, as each mask is encountered, the next item in the output list is converted to symbols and stored in the CHARACTER variable. Slash codes and recycling can cause successive elements of an array to contain elements from the output list of a single WRITE statement. Before any symbols are stored in a variable, the variable is set to blanks.

c) Variables in "char" which are unaffected by the format codes are left unchanged.

3. The total width of the format codes must not excede the length of the variable to which they apply. The maximum number of recycling operations or slash codes is limited by the number of variables specified by "char".

20.5 Print-Line Images

Suppose two or more printed reports must be produced by the same program. If only one printer is available, one solution would be to run the job twice and print a different report on each run. A much better approach is to print one of the reports on the printer and write "print-line images" of the second report on an intermediate storage device such as magnetic tape or a direct access file. A print-line image is simply a string of 133 symbols (for the typical printer) which are stored in a CHARACTER variable and which contains the symbols which will eventually appear on a printed line. The following problem and subsequent program illustrates the use of print-line images.

Suppose a deck of cards has data in the following format.

columns	data	mask
1-20	name	A20
21-50	address	A30
51	sex (M or F)	A1
52-53	age	I2
54-55	height in inches	I2
56-58	weight in pounds	I3

Two reports are to be printed. Report 1 is simply a name and address list. Report 2 is to show the sex, age, height and weight of each person. The reports are to appear as shown below.

In the following program, the SUBROUTINE TAPRNT is used to print the lines in the Personal Data Report. The print-line images for this report are written on device 3 which is assumed to be a magnetic tape unit.

```
C EXAMPLE 20.3 PRINT-LINE IMAGES
      INTEGER TAPE/3/,AGE, HEIGHT, WEIGHT
      CHARACTER IMAGE*133, NAME*20,ADDRSS*30,SEX
      REWIND TAPE
C PRINT HEADINGS FOR REPORT 1
      PRINT 900
  900 FORMAT('1',10X,'NAME AND ADDRESS REPORT'//)
C WRITE HEADING FOR REPORT 2 INTO IMAGE AND THEN
C              ON TAPE
      WRITE(IMAGE,901)
  901 FORMAT('1',10X,'PERSONAL DATA REPORT')
      WRITE(TAPE)IMAGE
```

(continued on next page)

```
C
C  READ CARDS AND PRINT APPROPRIATE DATA FOR EACH
C  REPORT - PERSONAL DATA GOES ON TAPE
     1 READ(5,902,END=2) NAME,ADDRSS,SEX,AGE,HEIGHT,
       * WEIGHT
     902 FORMAT(A20,A30,A1,2I2,I3)
C  PRINT LINES FOR REPORT ONE
         PRINT 903,NAME,ADDRSS
     903 FORMAT('0',A20,/,5X,A30)
C  CREATE PRINT-LINE IMAGE FOR REPORT 2
         WRITE(IMAGE,904)NAME,SEX,AGE,HEIGHT,WEIGHT
     904 FORMAT('0',A20,A3,3I8)
C  WRITE PRINT-LINE IMAGE ON TAPE
         WRITE(TAPE) IMAGE
         GO TO 1
C  END OF CARD DATA PROCESSING
     2 ENDFILE TAPE
C  CALL SUBROUTINE TO PRINT REPORT 2
         CALL TAPRNT(TAPE)
         STOP
         END

         SUBROUTINE TAPRNT(I)
         CHARACTER*133 LINE
         REWIND I
     1 READ(I,END=2) LINE
         PRINT 900,LINE
         GO TO 1
     900 FORMAT(A133)
     2 RETURN
         END
```

Several comments about the preceding program. In the
mainline segment, each line of Report 2 is written into the
variable IMAGE and then IMAGE is written on tape. Note that
an appropriate vertical control character is stored in the
first symbol of IMAGE. Why not write the lines of Report 2
directly on tape? This certainly could be done. The only
advantage in using the variable IMAGE is that all tape
records written will be the same length. That is, if a
formatted WRITE statement was used to produce the tape
records, the length of each record would depend on the total
length of the format codes used. Since IMAGE is a simple
variable, it means that no slash codes or recycling is
possible when writing into IMAGE. The use of slash codes or
recycling would be O.K. if IMAGE was an array but this would
add unnecessary complexity.

The only information needed in the subprogram is the
device number of the tape on which the print-line images
have been written. Because of this, the subprogram TAPRNT
could be used in different programs or at different points
in the same program. In fact, a mainline as simple as

```
            READ, ITAPE
            CALL TAPRNT(ITAPE)
            STOP
            END
```

could be used to print any report previously written in the
form of print-line images on tape.

The general procedure to create and use a tape (or
direct access file) of print-line images is:

      1. Rewind the tape
      2. For each line, write the print-line symbols into
         a CHARACTER variable of length 133.
      3. Write the variable on tape (format-free).
      4. Write a tapemark record (ENDFILE).

To use the tape:

      1. Rewind the tape.
      2. Read each tape record (format-free) and print it
         using a mask of A133.

The use of print-line images allows
      a) More than one report to be printed in a run.
      b) A copy of a report to be kept for later use.

20.6 Execution Time Formatting

This section illustrates and summarizes the different
methods of using and changing format codes at execution
time.   In this section, a PRINT statement will be used for
output which is sent to the printer. A WRITE statement will
be used for all non-printed output operations.

On   output, format codes are used to control the
appearance and positioning of of program data. During an
input operation, format codes are used to describe the usage
of card columns in the cards read by executing a READ
statement. In formatted statements such as

```
            READ fmt, list
            READ(...,fmt) list
            PRINT fmt, list
            WRITE(..., fmt) list
```

the "fmt" is either the statement number of a FORMAT
statement or the name of an array containing format codes.
The use of CHARACTER arrays to store format codes is
described in Chapter 15 Section 12. The use of non-CHARACTER
arrays to store format codes is described in Chapter 16
Section 9. It is assumed the reader is familiar with this
material. As a brief review, the following pairs of
statements are equivalent.

```
        CHARACTER*10 FMT(1)/'(''0HELLO'')'/
        PRINT FMT

        PRINT 900
   900  FORMAT('0HELLO')
```

Recall that two successive quotes are necessary to define a
single quote as part of a Quote-type literal.

Method 1 - Reading Format Data From An Input Device

   a) Reading An Entire Set Of Codes

If format codes need to be changed for different runs of
the same program, the entire set of codes can be read from
an input device. The following example illustrates this
technique.

```
        CHARACTER*20 FMT(1)
        READ 900, FMT
   900  FORMAT(A17)
        .
        .
        PRINT FMT, X, I
        .
        .
   $ENTRY
   ('1',F11.5,2X,I3)
```

Recall that format codes must be stored in an array and that
the array name is used in the READ, PRINT or WRITE statement
in place of a statement number of a FORMAT statement.

   b) Reading Only Literal Data

If a literal of either type (Quote or H-type) appears in
a set of format codes used by a READ statement, the symbols
in the card columns covered by the literal replace the
symbols in the literal. For example, the following program
prints "FEBRUARY 8,1975" at the top of a page.

```
        READ 900
        PRINT 900
   900  FORMAT('THIS IS CHANGED ')
        STOP
        END
   $ENTRY
   1FEBRUARY 8,1975
```

This method of changing a literal in a set of format codes
is infrequently used because it implies the same set of
format codes would be used for both input and output -- a
situation which does not frequently occur.

Method 2 - Changes Made By Statements Within The Program

Each symbol in a set of format codes is stored as a CHARACTER value. Thus the problem of modifying format codes is that of modifying the appropriate symbols. The most powerful technique is to "write" the approprate symbols into the CHARACTER variable(s) used to store the codes. For example, in the following, the codes

(nX , I8)

are used. The "n" denotes a value which is assigned to an INTEGER variable N in the program.

```
      C EXAMPLE 20.4 EXECUTION TIME FORMATTING
            CHARACTER*8 FMT(1)
            DO 1 N=1,5
            WRITE(FMT,900) N
        900 FORMAT('( ',I1,'X,I8)')
          1 PRINT FMT,N
            STOP
            END
```

In this example, the WRITE statement is used to put the appropriate value of "n" in the format codes. The PRINT statement simply displays the value of N using the format codes set up by the WRITE statement. In words, the statement "WRITE(FMT,900)N" says "Store the value of N in the CHARACTER array FMT according to the format codes in statement 900.". The format codes in the statement

900 FORMAT('(', I1, 'X,I8)')

consist of two literals and one I-mask. Note that "I8" is not a mask but simply two of the symbols in the literal "'X,I8)'". This means that when N has a value of 3 for example, that the eight symbols stored in FMT(1) are:

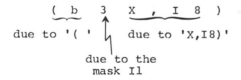

The result of executing the program is to display the values one thru five on five lines with successive values appearing in print positions 9 thru 13 respectively.

An alternate way of achieving the same result would be to put the two literals in the output list of a WRITE statement and use A-masks to position them within FMT(1). This is done in the statements below.

406

```
      WRITE(FMT,901) '(', N, 'X,I8)'
  901 FORMAT(A1,I1,A5)
```

This second approach is not as frequently used as the first. The remaining examples will use the first approach.

A second example. Suppose we want to print the letter "V" using asterisks in the print positions shown below.

```
print      ⎧ 1        2
positions  ⎨ 123456789012

         **          **
          **        **
           **      **
            **    **
             ****
              **
```

To solve the problem, we need a set of format codes of the type

$$(\; Tm \; , \; '**' \; , \; Tn \; , \; '**' \;)$$

where "m" and "n" change by +1 and -1 respectively each time a line is printed. The following program could be used.

```
C EXAMPLE 20.5 THE BIG "V"
      CHARACTER*21 CODES(1)
      M=10
      N=22
      DO 1 I=1,6
      M=M+1
      N=N-1
      WRITE(CODES,901) M, N
  901 FORMAT('(T',I2,',''**'',T',I2,',''**'')')
    1 PRINT CODES
      STOP
      END
```

Note that there are five format codes in statement 901. These include three literals which define the non-varying symbols used to print each line and an I-mask for each of the values M and N.

Example 3 - Plotting

A graph of the function $y = (x-4)**2$ for integer values of x in the range 1 thru 14 is to be printed. As a first step, we can calculate and store the x-y coordinates of the fourteen points to be plotted in a table called POINT. If a "*" symbol is used to indicate a point on the graph, our first reaction might be to have the output appear as shown below.

407

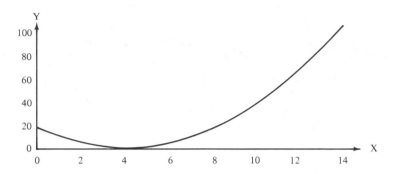

There are two disadvantages to this approach. First, on some printed lines more than "*" will have to be printed. This means changes would have to be made in both the position and number of format codes required by the PRINT statement. Second, since the graph is printed from the top down, the set of data points would have to be sorted in order of decreasing magnitude of function values. These two disadvantages can be overcome by turning the graph on its side as shown in the following diagram.

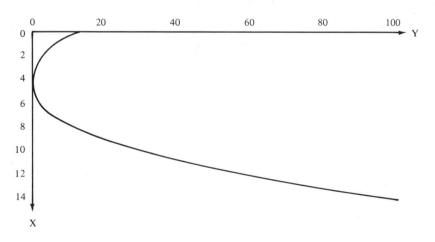

The following program solves the problem. It also prints axes for the graph.

```
      C EXAMPLE 20.6 PLOT OF Y=(X-4)**2 FOR X=1,2,...,14
            INTEGER POINT(14,2)
            CHARACTER*18 FCODES(1)
      C CALCULATE X-Y COORDINATES OF THE DATA POINTS
            DO 1 I=1,14
            POINT(I,1)=I
          1 POINT(I,2)=(I-4)**2
      C DISPLAY HEADING AND POINTS TO BE PLOTTED
            PRINT 900,POINT
        900 FORMAT('1GRAPH OF THE POINTS'//' X VALUES-',
           * 14I4,' Y VALUES-',14I4,//)
      C DRAW Y-AXIS WITH LABELS
            PRINT 901,(I-1,I=1,106,5)
        901 FORMAT(' ',22I5)
            PRINT 902,'   0',('*',I=1,106),' Y'
        902 FORMAT(A3,106A1,A2)
      C
      C DRAW GRAPH USING VALUES IN POINT
      C
            DO 2 I=1,14
      C PUT VALUE OF N IN "(I3,' *',TN,'*')" WHERE
      C THE FIRST "*" IS FOR THE X-AXIS AND THE SECOND
      C   FOR THE DATA POINT
            WRITE(FCODES,903) POINT(I,2)+5
        903 FORMAT('(I3,''*'',T',I3,',''*'')')
          2 PRINT FCODES, I
      C PRINT "X" TO LABEL X-AXIS AND SKIP TO NEW PAGE
            PRINT 904
        904 FORMAT(T5,'*'/T5,'X'/'1')
            STOP
            END
```

In this example, the asterisks which represent the X-axis are located in print position five. This is the reason that five is added to each function value in order to determine the position of the data point in each line.

Execution Time Formatting - A Summary Of The Method

1. Define a CHARACTER array to store the format codes. The length of the array element(s) should be sufficient to contain all the symbols in the set of codes which will be used at print time.

2. WRITE the value(s) of the INTEGER(s) which vary from one line to the next into the array under control of a FORMAT statement. The FORMAT statement will contain literals (for those symbols which do not change) and an I-mask for each value which does change.

3. Print the required line using the format codes stored in the array.

Exercise 20.2 CHARACTER Variables As Output Devices

1. Assume VAR has been defined by "CHARACTER*20 VAR". Describe the symbols stored in VAR or explain why an error occurs.

    a)   WRITE(VAR,900) 245
            900 FORMAT(I20)

    b)   WRITE(VAR,901)(FLOAT(J)+.5,J=1,4)
            901 FORMAT(4F5.2)

    c)   WRITE(VAR,902)('$12',I=3,16,3)
) 02 FORMAT(T4,3A3,2A2)

    d)   WRITE(VAR,903) 3, 7, 2
            903 FORMAT('(I',I1,',''X'',T',I1,',',I2,'A3)')

    e)   WRITE(VAR,904) -2.35E-17,3.
            904 FORMAT(E16.7)

    f)   WRITE(VAR,905)((I+J,J=1,4),I=1,3)
            905 FORMAT(3I3,T2,4I4,T4,5I5)

2. Assume CODES has been defined by "CHARACTER*20 CODES(1)" Describe the printed output.

    a)   WRITE(CODES,900) 3
            900 FORMAT('(I',I1,')')
                PRINT CODES, 8

    b)   DO 1 N=1,5
                WRITE(CODES(1),901) N
            901 FORMAT('(''0'',',I1,'I3)')
              1 PRINT CODES, (J,J=1,N)

    c)   DO 2 I=1,4
                WRITE(CODES,902) 20-4*I, I
            902 FORMAT('(T',I2,',',I2,'I4)')
              2 PRINT CODES, (I,J=1,I)

3. Suppose X is a CHARACTER array containing a single variable. For each of the following, assign X some initial value so that the statement shown can be executed without an error.

    a)   PRINT X, X
    b)   WRITE(X,X)
    c)   WRITE(X,X) X

4. State the use of "X" in the four statements shown below. In each case, select from the following list those things which are permitted for X: CHARACTER constant; CHARACTER variable; CHARACTER array; CHARACTER array element; non-CHARACTER variable, constant or expression; implied DO-loop.

   a) PRINT X, list
   b) PRINT, X, list
   c) PRINT,'X', list
   d) PRINT,(X), list

20.7 Summary

1. One or more CHARACTER variables may be used as an internal "card reader" in which: the number of "cards" equals the number of variables specified as the input device; the length of each "card" is the length of the variable(s) specified as the device. The use of CHARACTER variables as input devices means that it is possible to read and process "self-descriptive" data. That is, the data itself contains information which is essential to properly read the values present in the card.

2. One or more CHARACTER variables may be used as an internal "printer". The length of the print-line equals the length of the variable being used as the output device. The number of print-lines available equals the number of variables used as the output device. The two most important uses of CHARACTER output devices are:

  a) To create print-line images

  b) To create appropriate sets of format codes at execution time.

3. Both formatted and format-free input-output operations are allowed when CHARACTER variables are specified as the device in a READ, PRINT or WRITE statement.

Programming Problems

20.1 Each data card which is read by the program contains either one REAL value or one INTEGER value. The program should read the cards and print the sum of the REAL values and the sum of the INTEGER values. Note: a REAL value will have a decimal point as one of the symbols in the value.

20.2 Modify example program 20.2 so that the card need not be scanned for commas. A suggested algorithm is found in Remark (ii) following the program. Under what circumstances would putting a zero in each element of VAL (step 2 of the algorithm) cause the average to be incorrect? How could this problem be overcome?

20.3 Write a FUNCTION subprogram called ICNVRT which converts a CHARACTER value whose symbols are digits to an equivalent INTEGER value. Test the subprogram using the following mainline.

```
CHARACTER*80 X/'123456'/
I=ICNVRT(X)
PRINT,I
STOP
END
```

20.4 Add a second parameter called ICODE to the subprogram ICNVRT of Problem 3. The subprogram should assign ICODE a value of zero if the symbols in the CHARACTER value represent a valid INTEGER constant. If invalid, set ICODE equal to one. Test the subprogram using a mainline which prints each CHARACTER value along with the word "VALID" or "INVALID".

20.5 Modify example program 20.1 to permit an employee to have multiple wage cards.

20.6 Write a program which reads in an INTEGER value representing a number of cents. Calculate the smallest number of coins required to pay this amount using quarters, dimes, nickels and cents. Display the output as shown in the following example.

46 CENTS REQUIRES 1 QUARTER, 2 DIMES, 0 NICKELS, 1 CENT

Use only one FORMAT statement in your program. Note: the program must use the plural or singular (e.g. DIMES or DIME) depending on the number of coins required.

20.7 Modify program 20.6 so that zero values are supressed. For example, the output for 46 cents would appear as

46 CENTS REQUIRES 1 QUARTER, 2 DIMES, 1 CENT

20.8 Write a SUBROUTINE to display the status of a Tic-Tac-Toe playing surface at any stage of the game. The SUBROUTINE will have a single parameter -- a three-by-three matrix of INTEGER values. The value of the (i,j)th element of the matrix will be : "-1" if Player One has selected that position; "0" if neither player has selected the position; "+1" if Player Two has selected that position. Display the playing surface using an "X" to indicate Player One's moves and an "O" to indicate Player Two's moves. Unused squares should be left blank.

Use only one FORMAT statement to print the lines containing the X's and O's.

20.9 Write a program which reads a set of twenty-five INTEGER values of varying magnitudes and prints them using as few lines as possible. Do not print any symbols to the right of print position thirty.

20.10 Use execution time formatting to produce the following four patterns.

```
****        ****        *               *
 ***         ***        **              **
  **          **        ***            ***
   *           *        ****          ****
```

20.11 Write a program which reads a value of N and then N more INTEGER values. Print the N values as shown below.

X(1)= ___   X(2)= ___   ...   X(n)= ___

20.12 Suppose each of several data cards contains one of five INTEGER values, five REAL values, or five CHARACTER values. The values are found in columns 11 to 80 of a card. Beginning in column one is a set of format codes which describe how the values have been punched in columns 11-80. Examples are: "5I5"; "5F10.3"; "2A14,3A12", etc.. Use the information in columns one thru ten to read the values. Print the values in each card read.

20.13 Write a SUBROUTINE to do dynamic formatting. A call to the SUBROUTINE will have four arguments. The first three are: a CHARACTER value representing the set of codes which also indicate which values in the codes are to be given a value; a vector of INTEGER values containing the values to be put in the codes; an INTEGER value indicating the number of values to be put in the codes. In the codes, assume any occurence of the letter "N" which is not part of a literal indicates a value which is to be inserted by executing the SUBROUTINE. The fourth argument should be used to store the result. For example, if IVEC(1) and IVEC(2) have values of 3 and 8 respectively, then

CALL DYNFMT('(2X,FN.0,NI4)',IVEC,2,RESULT)

would cause RESULT to have the value "(2X,F3.0,8I4)".

Questions Answered In This Chapter

    1.   What is NAMELIST input-output?

    2.   How and why is the DUMPLIST statement used in WATFIV programs?

21.1 NAMELIST Output

    Format-free output statements are not allowed in most members of the Fortran family of languages. Instead, the NAMELIST statement is used to provide format-free-like output. Consider the following simple example.

```
C EXAMPLE 21.1 NAMELIST OUTPUT
        INTEGER NUM(3)/1,2,3/, NEG20/-20/
        REAL A/31.5/,BSET(2)/-5.,-7./
        COMPLEX Z/(1.,2.)/
        NAMELIST /LIST1/NUM,NEG20,A,BSET,Z
        WRITE(6,LIST1)
        PRINT LIST1
        STOP
        END
$ENTRY
```

Result: Two sets of the two lines below are printed.

```
    &LIST1
    NUM= 1, 2, 3, NEG20= -20,A= 0.3150000E 02,
    (continued) BSET= -0.5000000E 01, -0.7000000E 01,
    (continued) Z=( 0.1000000E 01, 0.2000000E 01), &END
```

The following points should be noted.

    a) In the NAMELIST statement, a name enclosed in slashes is used to identify a list of variables or array names which are to be output using the NAMELIST feature. In the example, "LIST1" was the name given to the list. Any valid WATFIV name can be used.

    b) The WRITE or PRINT statement used to display the values of variables and array elements contains a NAMELIST name instead of a reference to formatting information.

    c)   The printed output consists of two or more lines for each list printed. Each begins in print position two. The first line contains the list name preceeded by a "&". The second and subsequent lines consist of the names in the list followed by the value(s) currently assigned to the variable(s). Values of array elements appear in storage order (rightmost subscript varying least rapidly). Values are printed using the normal default mask for the particular type of value. The symbols "&END" follow the last value.

General Form And Rules Of NAMELIST Output

a) The general form of a NAMELIST statement is

        NAMELIST /name1/ list1 /name2/ list2   etc.

   where: "name1", "name2", etc. are any valid WATFIV names and are used to identify the list which follows the name; "list1", "list2", etc. are lists of simple variables or array names which are separated by commas. A variable or array name can appear in more than one list.

b) A NAMELIST statement is a non-executable statement. It should follow any declaration statements which are required to define the type or dimensions of elements in a list. Subprogram parameters may not appear in a NAMELIST list.

c) To create NAMELIST output one of the following two statements should be used.

        WRITE(device,name)
        PRINT name

   where: "device" specifies the output device on which the data is to be written (e.g. "6" for the printer); "name" is a NAMELIST name.

d) The statements

        NAMELIST /name/var1,var2,var3,...
        PRINT name

   produce the same output as

     PRINT,'&name'
     PRINT,'var1=',var1,',var2=',var2, ...,',&END'

e) More than one NAMELIST statement is permitted in a segment. For example,

415

```
             NAMELIST /LIST1/X,Y /LIST2/T,U,X

     is equivalent to
             NAMELIST /LIST1/ X,Y
             NAMELIST /LIST2/ T,U,X
```

21.2 <u>NAMELIST Input</u>

For non-NAMELIST input operations, the question "What variables are to be assigned a value?" is answered by including an input list in the READ statement. In NAMELIST input operations, the variables which are to be assigned a value as well the values themselves are found on the data cards. There are definite rules for kepunching the name-value pairs. Any variable which is permitted to be assigned a value in this way must belong to a NAMELIST list. Consider the following example.

```
             C EXAMPLE 21.2 NAMELIST INPUT
                   INTEGER NUM(3), K
                   REAL A(5), B
                   NAMELIST /INLIST/ NUM, K, A, B
                   READ(5, INLIST)
             C NOTE: "READ INLIST" COULD ALSO HAVE BEEN USED
                   STOP
                   END
             $ENTRY
              &INLIST NUM(2)=3, B=-7.24E03, A=1., 2., 3*-400.
```

Results: NUM(2) has a value of 3; NUM(1) and (NUM(3) are left unchanged.
B has a value of -7240.
A(1)=1; A(2)=2; A(3) thru A(5) each equal -400.
The value of K is left unchanged.

<u>General Form And Rules Of NAMELIST Input</u>

a) One or more NAMELIST statements are used to specify lists of non-subscripted variables and arrays whose values may be assigned in a NAMELIST input operation. Rules of the NAMELIST statement are those found in the preceding section (NAMELIST Output).

b) A READ statement used for NAMELIST input has one of the following forms.

```
                   READ name
                   READ(device, name)
                   READ(device, name, END=n)
                   READ(device, name, ERR=m)
                   READ(device, name, END=n, ERR=m)
```

where: "name" is a NAMELIST name and "device" is a
reference to the input device on which the input
data is located (e.g. "5" for the card reader).

c) Keypunching NAMELIST Data

i) Column 1 of each data card read by a NAMELIST READ
statement must be blank.

ii) The first data card read by a NAMELIST READ should
have a "&" in column 2 and the NAMELIST name
beginning in column 3. The NAMELIST name must
be followed by at least one blank column.

iii) Each variable-value pair is punched as follows:
variable name followed by "=" followed by the
value. In the case of an array having more
than one element, the sequence is array name
followed by "=" followed by the values which
are separated by a comma. The constants must
agree in type with the variables to which
they are assigned. Commas are used to
separate variable-value pairs and array-
values data items. A comma follows the last
data item and is followed by "&END".

iv) If the data is punched on more than one card,
variable names, array names and constants
cannot be split onto two cards. That is, the
first symbol following column 1 (which must
be blank) must be the beginning of a variable
name, array name or constant.

v) LOGICAL constants may be punched as "T", ".TRUE.",
"F" or ".FALSE.".

4. The value of any element of a NAMELIST input list
which is not assigned a value by the data cards is
unchanged by the execution of a NAMELIST input
operation.

5. Variable-value pairs on the data-cards can appear in
any order. Each variable or array however, must be
an element of the NAMELIST list specified in the
READ statement.

6. If "&name" is not found starting in column 2 of the
first card read, successive cards are read until it
is found or until the end of data is reached.

7. NAMELIST input is not restricted to data stored on
punched cards. Any valid input device can be used.

21.3 DUMPLIST Output

Occasionally, one would like to have NAMELIST-type output only if a program terminates abnormally. This is the purpose of the DUMPLIST statement. For this reason, the DUMPLIST statement is often useful for debugging programs. Values of the variables in all DUMPLIST statements are printed automatically if a program terminates because of an execution time error. Consider the following simple example.

```
C EXAMPLE 21.3 DUMPLIST OUTPUT
      INTEGER I/2/, J/0/
      DUMPLIST /LIST/I,J,K
      K=I/J
      STOP
      END
```

When the program is executed, the messages "Limit Exceeded For Fixed Point Division By Zero" and "Program Was Executing Line 3 When Termination Occurred" are followed by the lines

```
&LIST
I=      2, J=      0, K= UUUUUUU, &END
```

Note that the name of each variable in the DUMPLIST list is printed followed by its value at the time the job was terminated. Any type of variable or array can be put in a DUMPLIST list. The rules of DUMPLIST usage are identical to those of NAMELIST output with the following four exceptions.

i) The word "DUMPLIST" replaces the word "NAMELIST".

ii) A DUMPLIST list name does not appear in a WRITE or PRINT statement.

iii) A DUMPLIST statement has no effect if the program executes normally.

iv) If a program terminates abnormally, the contents of all DUMPLIST lists are printed in the order in which they appear in the program.

21.4 Summary

NAMELIST output provides many of the features of format-free output with the bonus that the variable names are automatically printed ahead of the values which they have. NAMELIST output however, is not as "natural" to use as format-free output.

NAMELIST input permits the input data to answer (to a limited extent) the question "What variables are to be assigned values?". Its use is seldom required.

DUMPLIST output can be handy for debugging programs. It is easy to use and has no effect if the program runs without errors.

Programming Problems

21.1 Suppose students in a class take one or more of the following subjects: English, French, Math, Science, History. One card has been punched for each student in the class. Each card contains one or more subject abbreviation-mark pairs. For example, a typical card might contain

ENG=79, HIST=92, MATH=58

Write a program which will read and process data cards of this type and print a report showing: (a) the number of students taking each subject; (b) the average mark of students taking each subject; (c) the class average. Use NAMELIST input in your program. Use one or more DUMPLIST statements to help during the debugging phase of the problem.

CHAPTER 22   BINARY INPUT-OUTPUT

Questions Answered In This Chapter

    1. What is Binary Input-Output?

    2. How any why is it used?

22.1 Binary Input-Output

    Binary input-output involves the direct transmission of
bit patterns to and from devices attached to the computer.
Unlike format-free or formatted input-output, the bit
patterns are not tested, examined or altered in any way.

    There are essentially three different types of input-
output operations -- formatted, format-free, and binary.
With binary, the number of bytes of data which is
transferred during an input-output operation depends only on
the total length of the items in the input or output list.
The type of item (INTEGER, REAL, etc.) is of no consequence.

    The allowed forms of binary READ and WRITE statements
are:
          READ(u) list   WRITE(u) list

          READ(u,END=n) list

          READ(u,ERR=m) list

          READ(u,END=n,ERR=m) list

In these statements, "u" is any valid reference to a device
and "list" is optional.

    Binary READ and WRITE statements were used in Chapters
18 and 19. In those chapters they were called "format-free"
instead of binary. Consider the following example. Assume
"5" refers to the card reader and "6" refers to the printer.

                READ(5) K,X
                WRITE(6) K,X
                PRINT,K,X
                STOP
                END
          $ENTRY
           234 67.

420

When this program is executed, two lines are printed. The first line contains " 234 67.". (The first blank is in print position 1.) The second line contains "1089598195" followed by "0.9647109E 00"! Why? The statement "READ(5)K,X" is a binary READ statement. There are two items in the input list each of length four. This means the first four bytes of data sent from the card reader (the bit pattern produced by the symbols punched in columns one thru four) will be stored in the four bytes of memory reserved for the variable K. The four bytes of data produced by the hole patterns in columns five thru eight will be stored in the four bytes of memory reserved for X. The bit patterns produced by columns one thru eight and therefore those stored in the memory locations for K and X are:

cols.1-4 " 234"   01000000 11110010 11110011 11110100

cols.5-8 " 67."   01000000 11110110 11110111 01001011

Appendix A describes the bit pattern produced for any of the 256 valid hole patterns. It is important to note that the type of variable in the input list doesn't matter at all. Any symbols could be "assigned" to an INTEGER variable using a binary READ. The statement "WRITE(6)K,X" causes eight bytes of data to be stored in print positions one thru eight. The symbols represented by these eight bytes are then printed. The statement "PRINT,K,X" is a format-free output statement. It means "Interpret the bit patterns found in the memory locations for K and X as those of an INTEGER and REAL value respectively. Display those values on the printer using the (default) masks of I12 and E16.7.". Appendix C describes the correspondences between bit patterns and values.

Some Other Facts About Binary Input-Output

1. The effect of binary input-output is identical to that of formatted operations in which an A-mask is used for each item in the list. However, the width of each mask must be the same as the length of the variable to which it applies.   For example, the two sets of statements below are equivalent.

    READ(5) A,B,C

    READ(5,900) A,B,C
900 FORMAT(A4,A4,A4)

   Binary input-output is faster than the the equivalent formatted input-output.

2. If the total length of the input list excedes the length of a record on the input device (80 bytes for card input), an error occurs.

3. If the total length of values in an output list excedes the length of a record on the output device (133 for a printer), an error occurs.

4. Binary input-output may be useful for:

   a) Assigning a specific bit pattern to a variable.

   b) Reducing the space required to store values on tape, direct access files, and punched cards.

   c) Reducing the execution time of input-output operations.

5. Binary input-output cannot be used when CHARACTER variables are used as the device in a READ or WRITE statement.

Exercise 22.1

1. Write a suitable READ statement and show the data card which would be read to cause the bit pattern

   11110000 01100000 11111001 11110110

   to be assigned to an INTEGER variable N using

   a) A binary READ statement
   b) A formatted READ statement with an A-mask
   c) A formatted READ statement with a Z-mask
   d) A format-free READ statement.

   Verify your answers by using a binary WRITE statement to print the results -- all four methods should produce the same output.

22.2 Summary

In a binary READ operation, the number of bytes of data transferred from the input device equals the total length of items in the input list. The bytes of data are stored sequentially in the memory locations reserved for items in the list.

In a binary WRITE operation, the number of bytes of data transferred to the output device equals the total length of items in the output list. The bytes of data are sent sequentially from the memory locations reserved for items in the list.

Programming Problems

Solve any of the programming problems from Chapter15 which require A-mask input. Where possible, use binary READ and WRITE statements.

PART IV

APPENDICES   with WATFIV S

The standard punched card is 7.375 inches long and 3.25 inches wide. There are 960 positions in which holes can be punched in a card. These hole positions are arranged in a table of eighty vertical columns and 12 horizontal rows. The columns are numbered one thru eighty and the rows are called, beginning from the top, "row 12, row 11, row 0, row 1, row 2, row 3, ..., row 8, row 9. Although there are 4096 unique patterns of holes which could be punched in any column, only 256 of these patterns are acceptable to the card reader. Each valid hole pattern represents a different symbol and causes a unique pattern of eight bits (eight ones and zeros) to be stored in the computer memory. In the following table the hole patterns are numbered from zero thru 255. The hexadecimal (base 16) representation of the bit pattern, the bit pattern, and the keypunch symbol associated with the bit pattern is shown for each of the valid hole patterns. Those hole patterns for which no symbol is shown can be punched using the "multiple punch" key on the keyboard. Many references describe the operation of a keypunch. See for example the IBM publication "IBM 29 Card Punch".

Dec	Hex	Hole Pattern	Bits	Sym
0	00	12-0-9-8-1	0000 0000	
1	01	12-9-1	0000 0001	
2	02	12-9-2	0000 0010	
3	03	12-9-3	0000 0011	
4	04	12-9-4	0000 0100	
5	05	12-9-5	0000 0101	
6	06	12-9-6	0000 0110	
7	07	12-9-7	0000 0111	
8	08	12-9-8	0000 1000	
9	09	12-9-8-1	0000 1001	
10	0A	12-9-8-2	0000 1010	
11	0B	12-9-8-3	0000 1011	
12	0C	12-9-8-4	0000 1100	
13	0D	12-9-8-5	0000 1101	
14	0E	12-9-8-6	0000 1110	
15	0F	12-9-8-7	0000 1111	
16	10	12-11-9-8-1	0001 0000	
17	11	11-9-1	0001 0001	
18	12	11-9-2	0001 0010	
19	13	11-9-3	0001 0011	
20	14	11-9-4	0001 0100	
21	15	11-9-5	0001 0101	
22	16	11-9-6	0001 0110	
23	17	11-9-7	0001 0111	
24	18	11-9-8	0001 1000	
25	19	11-9-8-1	0001 1001	
26	1A	11-9-8-2	0001 1010	
27	1B	11-9-8-3	0001 1011	
28	1C	11-9-8-4	0001 1100	
29	1D	11-9-8-5	0001 1101	
30	1E	11-9-8-6	0001 1110	
31	1F	11-9-8-7	0001 1111	

Dec	Hex	Hole Pattern	Bits	Sym
32	20	11-0-9-8-1	0010 0000	
33	21	0-9-1	0010 0001	
34	22	0-9-2	0010 0010	
35	23	0-9-3	0010 0011	
36	24	0-9-4	0010 0100	
37	25	0-9-5	0010 0101	
38	26	0-9-6	0010 0110	
39	27	0-9-7	0010 0111	
40	28	0-9-8	0010 1000	
41	29	0-9-8-1	0010 1001	
42	2A	0-9-8-2	0010 1010	
43	2B	0-9-8-3	0010 1011	
44	2C	0-9-8-4	0010 1100	
45	2D	0-9-8-5	0010 1101	
46	2E	0-9-8-6	0010 1110	
47	2F	0-9-8-7	0010 1111	
48	30	12-11-0-9-8-1	0011 0000	
49	31	9-1	0011 0001	
50	32	9-2	0011 0010	
51	33	9-3	0011 0011	
52	34	9-4	0011 0100	
53	35	9-5	0011 0101	
54	36	9-6	0011 0110	
55	37	9-7	0011 0111	
56	38	9-8	0011 1000	
57	39	9-8-1	0011 1001	
58	3A	9-8-2	0011 1010	
59	3B	9-8-3	0011 1011	
60	3C	9-8-4	0011 1100	
61	3D	9-8-5	0011 1101	
62	3E	9-8-6	0011 1110	
63	3F	9-8-7	0011 1111	

Dec	Hex	Hole Pattern	Bits		Sym
64	40	no punches	0100	0000	
65	41	12-0-9-1	0100	0001	
66	42	12-0-9-2	0100	0010	
67	43	12-0-9-3	0100	0011	
68	44	12-0-9-4	0100	0100	
69	45	12-0-9-5	0100	0101	
70	46	12-0-9-6	0100	0110	
71	47	12-0-9-7	0100	0111	
72	48	12-0-9-8	0100	1000	
73	49	12-8-1	0100	1001	
74	4A	12-8-2	0100	1010	¢
75	4B	12-8-3	0100	1011	.
76	4C	12-8-4	0100	1100	<
77	4D	12-8-5	0100	1101	(
78	4E	12-8-6	0100	1110	+
79	4F	12-8-7	0100	1111	|
80	50	12	0101	0000	&
81	51	12-11-9-1	0101	0001	
82	52	12-11-9-2	0101	0010	
83	53	12-11-9-3	0101	0011	
84	54	12-11-9-4	0101	0100	
85	55	12-11-9-5	0101	0101	
86	56	12-11-9-6	0101	0110	
87	57	12-11-9-7	0101	0111	
88	58	12-11-9-8	0101	1000	
89	59	11-8-1	0101	1001	
90	5A	11-8-2	0101	1010	!
91	5B	11-8-3	0101	1011	$
92	5C	11-8-4	0101	1100	*
93	5D	11-8-5	0101	1101	)
94	5E	11-8-6	0101	1110	;
95	5F	11-8-7	0101	1111	¬

Dec	Hex	Hole Pattern	Bits	Sym
96	60	11	0110 0000	-
97	61	0-1	0110 0001	/
98	62	11-0-9-2	0110 0010	
99	63	11-0-9-3	0110 0011	
100	64	11-0-9-4	0110 0100	
101	65	11-0-9-5	0110 0101	
102	66	11-0-9-6	0110 0110	
103	67	11-0-9-7	0110 0111	
104	68	11-0-9-8	0110 1000	
105	69	0-8-1	0110 1001	
106	6A	12-11	0110 1010	
107	6B	0-8-3	0110 1011	,
108	6C	0-8-4	0110 1100	%
109	6D	0-8-5	0110 1101		
110	6E	0-8-6	0110 1110	>
111	6F	0-8-7	0110 1111	?
112	70	12-11-0	0111 0000	
113	71	12-11-0-9-1	0111 0001	
114	72	12-11-0-9-2	0111 0010	
115	73	12-11-0-9-3	0111 0011	
116	74	12-11-0-9-4	0111 0100	
117	75	12-11-0-9-5	0111 0101	
118	76	12-11-0-9-6	0111 0110	
119	77	12-11-0-9-7	0111 0111	
120	78	12-11-0-9-8	0111 1000	
121	79	8-1	0111 1001	
122	7A	8-2	0111 1010	:
123	7B	8-3	0111 1011	#
124	7C	8-4	0111 1100	@
125	7D	8-5	0111 1101	'
126	7E	8-6	0111 1110	=
127	7F	8-7	0111 1111	"

Dec	Hex	Hole Pattern	Bits	Sym
128	80	12-0-8-1	1000 0000	
129	81	12-0-1	1000 0001	a
130	82	12-0-2	1000 0010	b
131	83	12-0-3	1000 0011	c
132	84	12-0-4	1000 0100	d
133	85	12-0-5	1000 0101	e
134	86	12-0-6	1000 0110	f
135	87	12-0-7	1000 0111	g
136	88	12-0-8	1000 1000	h
137	89	12-0-9	1000 1001	i
138	8A	12-0-8-2	1000 1010	
139	8B	12-0-8-3	1000 1011	
140	8C	12-0-8-4	1000 1100	
141	8D	12-0-8-5	1000 1101	
142	8E	12-0-8-6	1000 1110	
143	8F	12-0-8-7	1000 1111	
144	90	12-11-8-1	1001 0000	
145	91	12-11-1	1001 0001	j
146	92	12-11-2	1001 0010	k
147	93	12-11-3	1001 0011	l
148	94	12-11-4	1001 0100	m
149	95	12-11-5	1001 0101	n
150	96	12-11-6	1001 0110	o
151	97	12-11-7	1001 0111	p
152	98	12-11-8	1001 1000	q
153	99	12-11-9	1001 1001	r
154	9A	12-11-8-2	1001 1010	
155	9B	12-11-8-3	1001 1011	
156	9C	12-11-8-4	1001 1100	
157	9D	12-11-8-5	1001 1101	
158	9E	12-11-8-6	1001 1110	
159	9F	12-11-8-7	1001 1111	

Dec	Hex	Hole Pattern	Bits	Sym
160	A0	11-0-8-1	1010 0000	
161	A1	11-0-1	1010 0001	
162	A2	11-0-2	1010 0010	s
163	A3	11-0-3	1010 0011	t
164	A4	11-0-4	1010 0100	u
165	A5	11-0-5	1010 0101	v
166	A6	11-0-6	1010 0110	w
167	A7	11-0-7	1010 0111	x
168	A8	11-0-8	1010 1000	y
169	A9	11-0-9	1010 1001	z
170	AA	11-0-8-2	1010 1010	
171	AB	11-0-8-3	1010 1011	
172	AC	11-0-8-4	1010 1100	
173	AD	11-0-8-5	1010 1101	
174	AE	11-0-8-6	1010 1110	
175	AF	11-0-8-7	1010 1111	
176	B0	12-11-0-8-1	1011 0000	
177	B1	12-11-0-1	1011 0001	
178	B2	12-11-0-2	1011 0010	
179	B3	12-11-0-3	1011 0011	
180	B4	12-11-0-4	1011 0100	
181	B5	12-11-0-5	1011 0101	
182	B6	12-11-0-6	1011 0110	
183	B7	12-11-0-7	1011 0111	
184	B8	12-11-0-8	1011 1000	
185	B9	12-11-0-9	1011 1001	
186	BA	12-11-0-8-2	1011 1010	
187	BB	12-11-0-8-3	1011 1011	
188	BC	12-11-0-8-4	1011 1100	
189	BD	12-11-0-8-5	1011 1101	
190	BE	12-11-0-8-6	1011 1110	
191	BF	12-11-0-8-7	1011 1111	

Dec	Hex	Hole Pattern	Bits	Sym
192	C0	12-0	1100 0000	
193	C1	12-1	1100 0001	A
194	C2	12-2	1100 0010	B
195	C3	12-3	1100 0011	C
196	C4	12-4	1100 0100	D
197	C5	12-5	1100 0101	E
198	C6	12-6	1100 0110	F
199	C7	12-7	1100 0111	G
200	C8	12-8	1100 1000	H
201	C9	12-9	1100 1001	I
202	CA	12-0-9-8-2	1100 1010	
203	CB	12-0-9-8-3	1100 1011	
204	CC	12-0-9-8-4	1100 1100	
205	CD	12-0-9-8-5	1100 1101	
206	CE	12-0-9-8-6	1100 1110	
207	CF	12-0-9-8-7	1100 1111	
208	D0	11-0	1101 0000	
209	D1	11-1	1101 0001	J
210	D2	11-2	1101 0010	K
211	D3	11-3	1101 0011	L
212	D4	11-4	1101 0100	M
213	D5	11-5	1101 0101	N
214	D6	11-6	1101 0110	O
215	D7	11-7	1101 0111	P
216	D8	11-8	1101 1000	Q
217	D9	11-9	1101 1001	R
218	DA	12-11-9-8-2	1101 1010	
219	DB	12-11-9-8-3	1101 1011	
220	DC	12-11-9-8-4	1101 1100	
221	DD	12-11-9-8-5	1101 1101	
222	DE	12-11-9-8-6	1101 1110	
223	DF	12-11-9-8-7	1101 1111	

Dec	Hex	Hole Pattern	Bits	Sym
224	E0	0-8-2	1110 0000	
225	E1	11-0-9-1	1110 0001	
226	E2	0-2	1110 0010	S
227	E3	0-3	1110 0011	T
228	E4	0-4	1110 0100	U
229	E5	0-5	1110 0101	V
230	E6	0-6	1110 0110	W
231	E7	0-7	1110 0111	X
232	E8	0-8	1110 1000	Y
233	E9	0-9	1110 1001	Z
234	EA	11-0-9-8-2	1110 1010	
235	EB	11-0-9-8-3	1110 1011	
236	EC	11-0-9-8-4	1110 1100	
237	ED	11-0-9-8-5	1110 1101	
238	EE	11-0-9-8-6	1110 1110	
239	EF	11-0-9-8-7	1110 1111	
240	F0	0	1111 0000	0
241	F1	1	1111 0001	1
242	F2	2	1111 0010	2
243	F3	3	1111 0011	3
244	F4	4	1111 0100	4
245	F5	5	1111 0101	5
246	F6	6	1111 0110	6
247	F7	7	1111 0111	7
248	F8	8	1111 1000	8
249	F9	9	1111 1001	9
250	FA	12-11-0-9-8-2	1111 1010	
251	FB	12-11-0-9-8-3	1111 1011	
252	FC	12-11-0-9-8-4	1111 1100	
253	FD	12-11-0-9-8-5	1111 1101	
254	FE	12-11-0-9-8-6	1111 1110	
255	FF	12-11-0-9-8-7	1111 1111	

FLOWCHARTING

A program flowchart is a diagram of the steps which are followed in solving a problem. There is a standard set of symbols and connectors to represent different kinds of operations (input-output, computation, decision, etc.). These are listed below along with the type of statement which is usually a translation of the logic represented by the symbol.

Flowchart Symbol	Name	Statement(s)
	Terminal Operation	START, STOP, ENTRY, RETURN
	Input-Output	READ, WRITE, PUNCH, PRINT, BACKSPACE, ENDFILE, FIND, REWIND
	Compute	Assignment i.e: "="
	Decision	IF, Computed or Assigned GO TO
	Program Modification	Action which could cause a change in the order of execution. e.g: ASSIGN
	Predefined Process	To indicate a FUNCTION or SUBROUTINE is being used
	Comment	

Flowchart symbols are joined by straight lines. Arrowheads should be used on the connecting lines if the direction of flow is unclear. Flow is ususally assumed to be down and to the right. Connecting lines which cross have no logical interrelationship unless the arrowhead(s) indicate the nature of the relationship. Two types of connector symbols can be used to reduce the number of flowlines in a flowchart.

Onpage Connector

Used to identify an entry to, or an exit from, a point in the flowchart on the same page.

Offpage Connector

Used to identify an entry to, or an exit from, a point in the flowchart on a different page.

Special DO Symbol

If the logic shown in a flowchart will be converted to a Fortran-like program, a special symbol is frequently used to represent the logic of a DO statement. It has the following appearance.

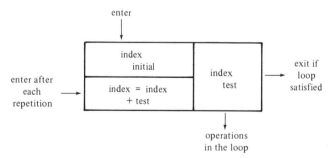

An Example

Shown below is a flowchart which incorporates most of the symbols used in flowcharting. The program describes a procedure to calculate the sum of as many as N values of f(x) where only positive values of x are used. The procedure stops if the sum is negative before N values of x have been processed. A program which is a translation of the flowchart logic is shown on the right.

B.2

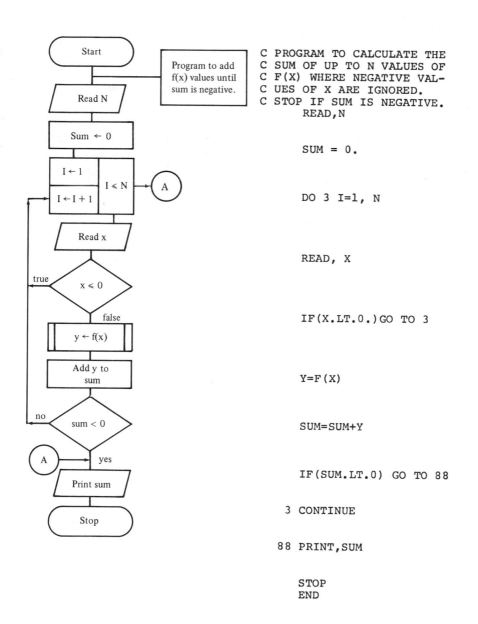

```
C PROGRAM TO CALCULATE THE
C SUM OF UP TO N VALUES OF
C F(X) WHERE NEGATIVE VAL-
C UES OF X ARE IGNORED.
C STOP IF SUM IS NEGATIVE.
      READ,N

      SUM = 0.

      DO 3 I=1, N

      READ, X

      IF(X.LT.0.)GO TO 3

      Y=F(X)

      SUM=SUM+Y

      IF(SUM.LT.0) GO TO 88

   3  CONTINUE

  88  PRINT,SUM

      STOP
      END
```

437

APPENDIX C   NUMBER SYSTEMS AND INTERNAL REPRESENTATION
OF VALUES

1. Number Systems

In the decimal (base ten) number system, a value of three-hundred-and-forty-seven-and-a-quarter is written as "347.25". The value of each symbol is based on its position relative to the decimal point and the fact that we are using base ten. The value of 347.25 is arrived at as shown below.

$$3 \qquad 4 \qquad 7 \quad . \quad 2 \qquad 5$$

$$3 \times 10^2 + 4 \times 10^1 + 7 \times 10^0 + 2 \times 10^{-1} + 5 \times 10^{-2}$$

That is, to construct the value of the number, each digit beginning from the left, is multiplied by successively decreasing powers of ten (the base) and the values are added. The decimal point is a reference point which divides the non-negative and negative powers of ten. If the base were changed to eight, say, the value of 347.25 would be

$$3 \times 8^2 + 4 \times 8^1 + 7 \times 8^0 + 2 \times 8^{-1} + 5 \times 8^{-2} = 231.308125 \text{ (base 10)}$$

Frequently this equality is stated in the form shown below.

$$(347.25)_8 = (231.308125)_{10}$$

where the "8" and the "10" denote the bases used in determining the value of the number.

Note that N symbols are needed to represent all possible numbers in the base N number system. This allows the interval between two successive negative powers of the base to be split into N equally spaced subintervals simply by putting another symbol on the rightmost end of the number.

Most computer systems use the base two (binary) number system to represent all REAL and INTEGER values. The value of 347.25 in base two is $(101011001.01)_2$.

INTEGER Values

Each INTEGER value occupies one word (4 bytes or 32 bits) of the computer memory. The 32 bits are numbered, beginning from the left, 0, 1, 2, ..., 31. Bit zero indicates the sign of the number -- zero for positive, one for negative. Let Vi denote the value of bit i. Each Vi equals zero or one. The value of a positive INTEGER value is then:

$$V1 \times 2^{30} + V2 \times 2^{29} + V3 \times 2^{28} + \ldots + V31 \times 2^{0}$$

This means that positive INTEGER values can range from $(0111\ldots111)_2$ thru $(000\ldots0001)_2$. That is from 2147483647 down to one. (An INTEGER value of zero has all 32 bits equal to zero.)

A negative INTEGER value is stored as the "two's complement form" of the positive value. To get the two's complement form of any base two number: (a) write down the bit pattern of the positive value; (b) Change each zero to a one, each one to a zero; (c) Add one to the resulting number. For example, the internal representation of -156 can be obtained as follows:

a) +156 is   00000000000000000000000010011100
b) flip the bits   11111111111111111111111101100011
c) add one to get   11111111111111111111111101100100

Many references are available which describe how to do base two arithmetic. Any introductory book on computers would suffice.

For example: $(011)_2 + (1)_2 = (100)_2$. i.e: $3 + 1 = 4$

Why are negative INTEGER values stored in two's complement form? The reason is simply that subtracting any base two value is the same as adding its two's complement. Consequently, only addition circuits are required to do INTEGER arithmetic.

If an operation involving two INTEGER values would produce a result which would require more than thirty-two bits to represent the value, only the rightmost thirty-two bits are used as the result. Because a "1" in the leftmost bit position indicates a zero and because negative numbers are stored in two's complement form, totally unexpected results may be obtained if you are not careful when working with large INTEGER values.

INTEGER*2 Values

Recall that all INTEGER constants are of length four. Only variables may be given the optional length of two. For each INTEGER*2 variable, a half-word of memory is used. The use of the sixteen bits is identical to that for length four INTEGER values. That is, the leftmost bit idicates the sign of the value; the other bits represent the value of the

number in base two. Two's complement form is used for
negative values. Because only fifteen bits are used for the
value, INTEGER*2 values range from -2**15 thru (2**15-1).
That is between -32768 and +32767. This reduced range means
overflow (out-of-range) conditions can be generated more
easily.

REAL Values

One word (4 bytes or 32 bits) of memory is used to store
each REAL value. The bits are numbered, beginning from the
left, 0, 1, 2, ..., 31. The use of the bits is shown in the
following diagram.

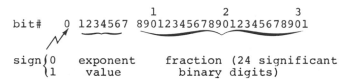

```
                     1          2         3
bit#    0 1234567 890123456789012345678901

sign┌0    exponent    fraction (24 significant
    └1    value                binary digits)
```

The decimal point precedes the first digit in the fraction.
If Vi denotes the value (one or zero) of bit i in a REAL
value, the value of the REAL number is

$$(V8 \times 2^{-1} + V9 \times 2^{-2} + V10 \times 2^{-3} + \ldots + V31 \times 2^{-24}) \times 2^{4(y-64)}$$

where: $y = V1 \times 2^{6} + V2 \times 2^{5} + \ldots + V7 \times 2^{0}$.

The number is positive if V0 is zero and negative if V0 is
one. The largest value of y is 127 and the smallest is of
course zero. This means that exponent values can range from
2**252 thru 2**(-256) or equivalently between 16**63 and
16**(-64)

This method of representing REAL numbers means that the
magnitude of the largest and smallest REAL values are:

Largest	Smallest
$(.11111\ldots111) \times 2^{252}$	$(.00000\ldots001) \times 2^{-256}$
i.e: $(.7237005) \times 10^{76}$	i.e: $(.0000051) \times 10^{-79}$

For reasons which are beyond the scope of this book,
fractional values are always "normalized". Normalized values
are such that at least one of the four leftmost bits in the
fractional value is one. This means that the magnitude of
the smallest   REAL value which a programmer can define
in a WATFIV program without doing bit manipulation in the
program is approximately .5397605*10**(-78).

If an arithmetic operation or a definition of a REAL constant requires an exponent value outside the permitted range, an error condition is generated. The terms "exponent overflow" and "exponent underflow" refer, respectively, to the conditions where the exponent value is too large or too small. Three subprograms are normally supplied with the WATFIV compiler which may be useful in handling overflow and underflow conditions. The names of these subprograms are "TRAPS", "ALLOW" and "OVERFL". In addition, there is an "ON ERROR GO TO s" statement which will transfer control to statement "s" if _any_ type of error occurs. Information about the three subprograms can likely be obtained from your computing center.

Extended Precision (REAL*8) Values

The reader should be familiar with the information about REAL values before reading this section.

Each Extended Precision value occupies a double-word (8 bytes or 64 bits of memory). The use of the sixty-four bits is shown in the following diagram.

```
                        1         2        6
  bit#     0  1234567  89012345678901 ...  0123
         ↗
  sign⎰0     exponent    fraction (56 significant
      ⎱1      value        binary digits)
```

The only difference between Extended Precision and REAL values is that Extended Precision values have 56 significant binary digits instead of 24 for REAL values. The range of exponent values is the same. Overflow and underflow conditions may occur and can be handled in the same way as for REAL values.

COMPLEX Values

A COMPLEX value occupies two consecutive words (8 bytes or 64 bits) of memory. Each of the words contains a REAL value. The value in the first word is the value of the real component of the complex number, that in the second, the value of the imaginary component of the complex number.

Extended Precision COMPLEX values (COMPLEX*16) each occupy two consecutive double-words of memory. The Extended Precision value in the first and second double words represents respectively, the value of the real and imaginary component of the value.

LOGICAL Values

LOGICAL values occupy one word (4 bytes or 32 bits) of memory. Only the leftmost byte is used to represent the value. If the leftmost byte contains "11111111" the value represented is .TRUE.. Eight zero bits in the leftmost byte represent a value of .FALSE.. Although four bytes are reserved for a LOGICAL value, only the leftmost byte of the four is affected by operations on the variable.

LOGICAL*1 variables each occupy one byte of memory. .TRUE. is represented by a string of eight one bits, .FALSE. by a string of eight zero bits.

CHARACTER Values

A CHARACTER value of length N occupies N consecutive bytes of memory. Since a byte has 256 possible bit patterns, there are 256 different "symbols" which any byte can represent. Appendix A contains a table showing the hole pattern which produces each possible bit pattern.

When a byte is sent to a printer, the symbol printed depends on the print "train" which is on the printer. Appedix D shows the symbol produced by a bit pattern for four of the more commonly used print trains.

Undefined Values

When a WATFIV program is compiled, any variable which is not assigned an initial value has bit pattern of "10000000" put in each byte of memory reserved for the value of the variable. When a statement references the value, a comparison is made to see if this bit pattern is still present. This is the method of detecting undefined variables. Using the "$NOCHECK" feature described in Appendix E eliminates the test for the special bit pattern. Occasionally, the results of computation may accidentally generate the pattern. (The pattern represents an INTEGER value of -2139062144 and a REAL value of -0.4335017E-77.) If this is the case, the $NOCHECK feature must be used to circumvent the problem.

SYMBOLS FOUND ON COMMONLY USED
PRINT TRAINS

The tables which follow show the symbols printed by four commonly used print trains. The bit pattern which produces each symbol is specified as two hexadecimal digits. The first digit is the row label and the second, the column label. For example, on the LN Train the letter "c" is produced by the bit pattern "10000011" (hexadecimal "83").

LN Train

	0	1	2	3	4	5	6	7	8	9	A	B	C	D	E	F
0		..	.						∩	⊃			∪		/	
1										~		\	∪			
2	¿	¡														
3																
4									¢	.	<	(	+	|		
5		&	'	"					!	$	*	)	;	¬		
6		-	/	1					£	,	%	>	?			
7				†		"	{		:	#	@	⊤	=	"		
8		a	b	c	d	e	f	g	h	i	}	⩽	(	+	‡	
9	—	j	k	l	m	n	o	p	q	r	{	□	)	±	■	
A		●	s	t	u	v	w	x	y	z	L	⌐	[	⩾	.	
B											⌟	¬	�	≠	—	
C		A	B	C	D	E	F	G	H	I						
D		J	K	L	M	N	O	P	Q	R						
E			S	T	U	V	W	X	Y	Z						
F	0	1	2	3	4	5	6	7	8	9						

HN Train

	0	1	2	3	4	5	6	7	8	9	A	B	C	D	E	F
0																
1																
2																
3																
4									.	)	(	+				
5		&							$	*	)					
6		-	/						,	(						
7									=	'	'	=				
8																
9																
A																
B																
C		A	B	C	D	E	F	G	H	I						
D		J	K	L	M	N	O	P	Q	R						
E			S	T	U	V	W	X	Y	Z						
F	0	1	2	3	4	5	6	7	8	9						

PN Train

	0	1	2	3	4	5	6	7	8	9	A	B	C	D	E	F
0																
1																
2																
3																
4												.	<	(	+	|
5	&											$	*	)	;	¬
6	-	/										,	%		>	?
7											:	#	@	⊤	=	"
8																
9																
A																
B																
C		A	B	C	D	E	F	G	H	I						
D		J	K	L	M	N	O	P	Q	R						
E			S	T	U	V	W	X	Y	Z						
F	0	1	2	3	4	5	6	7	8	9						

TN Train

	0	1	2	3	4	5	6	7	8	9	A	B	C	D	E	F
0																
1																
2																
3																
4											¢	.	<	(	+	|
5	&										!	$	*	)	;	¬
6	-	/										,	%		>	?
7											:	#	@	⊤	=	"
8		a	b	c	d	e	f	g	h	i	}	≤	(	+	†	
9	_	j	k	l	m	n	o	p	q	r	}	□	)	±	■	
A	•	s	t		u	v	w	x	y	z	⌐	⌐	[	≥	•	
B											⌐	⌐	⌐	≠	—	
C		A	B	C	D	E	F	G	H	I						
D		J	K	L	M	N	O	P	Q	R						
E			S	T	U	V	W	X	Y	Z						
F	0	1	2	3	4	5	6	7	8	9						

APPENDIX E   JOB CONTROL STATEMENTS AND MULTIPLE
             STATEMENTS PER CARD

1. Control Cards

Any card containing a "$" in column 1 is considered to be a job control card. Two job control cards must be present in every job. These are the "$JOB" and "$ENTRY" cards. The options which can be included on the $JOB card are described in this section. Other job control cards are described in Section 2.

The JOB card has "$JOB" in columns 1-4, "WATFIV" in columns 8-13, an account number beginning in column 16. Job options may follow the account number. If options are present, a comma follows the account number. A comma is used to separate each pair of options. Symbols following the first blank column after column 16 are considered to be a comment. Any or all of the following ten options may be used.

In the table below, the underlined option is usually the the default value. Check with your computing center to find which values are the default options. Items in braces indicate the available choices.

Application	Options	Description
Keypunch Model	KP=$\begin{Bmatrix} 29 \\ \underline{26} \end{Bmatrix}$	The number indicating the model used to punch the program.
Limit On Execution Time	TIME=n or T=n	n has one of the following forms: "m"; "(m,s)", or "(,s)"; where "m" denotes minutes and "s" seconds
Limit On Pages Of Of Execution Time Printed Output	PAGES=p or P=p	p denotes the maximum number of pages permitted before the job is stopped
Lines Printed Per Page	LINES=n	n denotes the number of lines printed per page
Processing With Error Conditions	RUN=$\begin{Bmatrix} \underline{CHECK} \\ NOCHECK \\ FREE \end{Bmatrix}$	See Section 2 for the use of the options. "RUN=" is optional.

Listing Of Source Deck	$\left\{ \begin{array}{l} \underline{LIST} \\ \overline{NOLIST} \end{array} \right\}$	controls listing of source statements
Listing Of Library Subprograms	$\left\{ \begin{array}{l} LIBLIST \\ \underline{NOLIBLIST} \end{array} \right\}$	controls listing of statements in library subprogs.
Warning Messages	$\left\{ \begin{array}{l} \underline{WARN} \\ NOWARN \end{array} \right\}$	used to allow or suppress WARNING messages
Extension Messages	$\left\{ \begin{array}{l} \underline{EXTEN} \\ NOEXTEN \end{array} \right\}$	used to allow or suppress EXTENSION messages
Library mainline	PGM=xxxxxx	"xxxxxx" is the name of a library program to be used as the mainline segment

Note

1. All 80 columns may be used. Options can be punched in any order. The first blank column encountered to the right of column 16 indicates that what follows is a comment.

b) If an option is invalid, it and all options which follow it are ignored.

c) If an option appears more than once, the last specification is the one used when running the job.

2. Other WATFIV Control Cards

All WATFIV jobs must have a $JOB card and a $ENTRY card. The following control cards may also be used. If present, they override the option (default or specified) associated with the $JOB card unless a subsequent control card negates the option. The effect of each of these control cards applies only to those statements and comments which follow the card. In each of these cards, the "$" must be in column one.

Group One - Control Of The Compile Time Listing

$PRINTON - source statements and comments which follow will be listed by the compiler.

$PRINTOFF - source statements and comments which follow will not be listed by the compiler.

$EJECT - the next line of compiler output will be at the top of a new page.

$SPACE - a blank line will appear before the next statement or comment.

$WARN - WARNING messages will be printed.

$NOWARN - WARNING messages will not be printed.

$EXTEN - EXTENSION messages will be printed.

$NOEXTEN - EXTENSION messages will not be printed.

Group Two - Control Of Job Termination Due To Errors

$CHECK - an execution time check is to be made to insure that each variable has been assigned a value before being used in a computation.

$NOCHECK - no error will be generated if an undefined variable is used in a computation.

A third option is available. It is to use either "RUN=FREE" or simply "FREE" as an option on the $JOB card. If this option is used, program execution will be attempted even though there may be compile time errors.

Group Three - Tracing Execution Of Statements

$ISNON - turns the trace on. This causes statement numbers to be listed in the order in which they are executed. At least one executable statement must precede the $ISNON control card.

$ISNOFF - turns the trace off.

3. Multiple Statements Per Card

More than one WATFIV statement can be punched on a card. Use of this feature is especially advantageous if source decks are stored on an auxilliary storage medium such as tape or disk since fewer storage locations are used and fewer read operations are required to access the program.

When punching more than one statement on a card, the following rules must be followed.

a)   A semicolon is used to indicate the end of a statement.

b)   Statements are punched in columns 7 thru 72.

c)   Column six is used in the normal way -- to indicate a continuation of the statement on the previous card.

d) Statement numbers may be punched in columns 1 thru 5. If a statement number is required in columns 7 thru 72, a colon must follow the statement number. A statement number cannot be split onto two cards.

e)   Comment cards and FORMAT statements should be punched in the usual way.

f) A comment may appear on a statement card. To do this, a
    "zigamorph" is punched following the end of the
    statement and the comment follows the zigamorph. The
    hole pattern for a zigamorph is 12-11-0-7-8-9. The
    symbols following a zigamorph and preceding either a
    semicolon or column 73 are considered to be a comment.
    The comment is printed on the compiler listing. No
    symbol is printed for the zigamorph.

APPENDIX F   MAJOR DIFFERENCES BETWEEN WATFIV AND
                        IBM FORTRAN

There   are   many   varieties   of   Fortran.   Because   the
alternative to using WATFIV in many computing centers is to
use IBM's Fortran G or Fortran H, the comparisons in this
Appendix will be limited to these languages. Detailed
specifications of the IBM Fortrans can be found in IBM
publications.

The   material   is   divided into four sections. The first
describes features in WATFIV which are not acceptable to the
Fortran   G   and   H   compilers.   These   features   could be
considered extensions of the Fortran language.   The second
section   describes   incompatabilities between WATFIV and IBM
Fortran. That   is,   situations   in which the same source
statements may produce different results.   The third section
describes features in "Extended Fortran H" which are not
acceptable to the WATFIV compiler. Finally some suggestions
are made for when each of the three languages should be
used.   No claim is made that the information in this
appendix is complete.   Only important differences   are
described.

Fortran "Extensions" Present In WATFIV

1.   CHARACTER Values. See Chapter 16, Section 12 for methods
     of proccessing strings of symbols without using
     CHARACTER variables.

2.   Multiple Assignment statements.

3.   Expressions in output lists. Note that expressions may
     not begin with a left bracket. "PRINT,(A+B)/C" is
     invalid whereas "PRINT,+(A+B)/C" is valid.

4.   Variables in an unlabelled Common Block may be
     initialized in a type declaration statement or a DATA
     statement. Variables in a labelled Common Block can only
     be initialized in a BLOCK DATA subprogram. The name of a
     Common Block cannot also be used as a variable name.

5.   Implied DO-loops may be used to create a list of
     variables in a DATA statement.

6.   Subscripted variables may be used in Statement Function
     definitions.

7. Subscripts may be LOGICAL, COMPLEX or CHARACTER values.

8. If the object of a DO is a Logical IF statement, the trailer can be any executable statement other than a DO or another Logical IF.

9. Multiple statements per card. (See Appendix E.)

10. Comments following a statement are permitted in WATFIV.

11. Because WATFIV is a "one-pass" compiler, there are certain restrictions on the ordering of statements which are not restrictions in IBM Fortran.

12. DO-loops may be nested to any depth. Not more than 255 DO-loops are permitted in any one segment.

13. Format-free input-output is not allowed for card input and/or printed and punched output in IBM Fortran.

Incompatabilities (No compile time differences but may cause execution time differences)

1. Input-Output
   a) In WATFIV, REAL*4 values are printed with seven significant digits. If the format code specifies that more than seven decimal places are to be displayed, zeros are added on the right.

   b) When using any of the format codes I, F, E, D, G or A, only non-blank symbols are stored in the print positions covered by the code. This may cause differences in the appearance of output if T-codes are used to overprint data previously stored in print positions.

   c) In WATFIV, commas are not required between format codes if their omission does not cause any ambiguity.

   d) In WATFIV there is no numeric limit on the number of continuation cards which can be used for a single FORMAT statement.

   e) WATFIV does not allow group counts and/or repetition factors to be zero.

   f) The symbol "+" on both the Model 26 and the Model 29 keypunch is an acceptable vertical control character in WATFIV.

2. Only the leftmost byte of a LOGICAL*4 value is moved in an assignment operation. Thus if U and V are LOGICAL

variables, the statement "U=V" causes one byte to be moved.

3. Comment cards may precede a continuation card in WATFIV. Any number of comment cards can be used.

4. In WATFIV, a Function having a type of value other than that which can be assumed from the first-letter rule must have its type declared in an appropriate declaration statement.

5. In WATFIV, many REAL-valued built-in functions are evaluated in Extended Precision and the result truncated to a REAL value of length four.

6. In WATFIV, control of the number of lines printed per page depends on the "LINES=" parameter found on the $JOB card.

7. In WATFIV, "FORMAT(" cannot be the first seven characters of a statement. "FORMAT(I)=2.5" is invalid whereas "X=FORMAT(I)" is acceptable.

8. In WATFIV a "$" cannot be punched in column one of a data card. It will be interpreted as being a WATFIV control card.

Extended Fortran H Features Not Supported In WATFIV

1. REAL*16 and COMPLEX*32. A Q-mask is used for these types of values.

2. A "&" preceding a function name in an EXTERNAL statement means the user-supplied routine is to be used instead of any library function having the same name.

3. Asynchronous input-output statements. A feature exists which permits input-output operations and computations to proceed simultaneously.

4. By using a GENERIC statement, it is not necessary to use a unique name for the built-in functions which differ only in the type of value produced. For example, "SIN" includes DSIN, CSIN and CDSIN.

Use Of WATFIV And Fortran G and H

The following suggestions are based on the ideas found in the following table. They are not intended to be rules.

	WATFIV	Fortran G	Fortran H
Compile speed	best	better	good
Execute speed	good	better	best
Compile must precede execution	yes	no	no
Diagnostic messages	best	good	good

1. Small, one-shot programs should be written, debugged and executed using WATFIV.

2. Small programs which will be run many times should be written and debugged in WATFIV and run using a Fortran H object deck.

3. Large programs, especially those that will be run several times should be written and debugged in WATFIV; debugged in Fortran G to remove incompatabilities; executed using a Fortran H object deck.

APPENDIX G   DEBUGGING HINTS AND PROGRAM EFFICIENCY

Debugging Hints

1. Echo your input data. That is, print the input values
    from cards as soon as they are read.

2. Use meaningful variable names.

3. Use statement numbers which increase or decrease from
    start to finish.

4. Use lots of comments.

5. Use the DUMPLIST statement. (See Chapter 21.)

6. Use "ON ERROR GO TO __" (See Appendix C.)

7. Print intermediate results until you are sure that the
    program logic is correct.

8. Use a LOGICAL variable called "DEBUG" and statements of
    the type "IF(DEBUG) PRINT,..." .

9. Carefully check your program logic after the program has
    been written and before it is keypunched. Carefully
    check your keypunching before the job is submitted.

10. Use $ISNON and $ISNOFF to trace through very complex
    sequences of statements. See Appendix E for details.

11. If you make a change in program logic, satisfy yourself
    that it will not affect other parts of the program.

12. During the debug phase, print any values which will
    eventually be sent to some other output device to insure
    that the correct values are being generated.

13. What not to do. Don't plan. Assume your logic is
    correct. Assume your input data is correct. If an
    error occurs, don't make any changes -- put the deck in
    again -- it must have been the computer's mistake.

Program Efficiency

    What is meant by an efficient program? Efficiencies can
be achieved in the following areas: memory requirements;
compile time; execution time; programming and keypunching

time. Usually however, there is a tradeoff. That is, efficiency in one area means inefficiencies result in another area. The following list is not suggested as being complete. The suggestions in the list will generally decrease the execution time of a WATFIV program. Compile time is not usually a significant factor in running WATFIV jobs. In other types of Fortran, it may be very significant.

1. DO-loops

    a) Implied DO-loops are inefficient.

    b) A subscripted variable which is used more than once in the range of a loop should be assigned to a simple variable.

    c)
```
    DO 1 I=1,999,2                        DO 1 I=1,1000
    X(I)=0.         is better than    1 X(I)=0.
  1 X(I+1)=0.
```

    c) If possible, nested loops should have the innermost loops with the most repetitions. For example:

```
    DO 1 I=1,10                        DO 1 J=1,100
    DO 1 J=1,100   is better than     DO 1 I=1,10
  1 CONTINUE                        1 CONTINUE
```

2. Subscripted Variables

    a) Avoid using arrays having many dimensions.

    b) Assign subscripted variables used more than once in a DO-loop to a simple variable.

3. Branching (Conditional Control)

    a) In a Logical IF statement, choose a relational operator which makes the most likely result .FALSE..

    b) Use Logical IFs instead of Arithmetic IFs.

    c) Use a Computed GO TO instead of a sequence of Logical IFs.

    d) Use an Assigned GO TO instead of a Computed GO TO.

    e) Use a LOGICAL*1 variable for any "on-off" program switch.

4. Expressions

    a) Use INTEGER exponents instead of REAL exponents.

b) Avoid mixing two types of values. "X+2." is better than "X+2".

c) Addition is usually faster than multiplication. "X+X" is better than "2.*X".

d) Use SQRT(X) instead of "X**.5".

e) To evaluate a polynomial such as $Ax^3 + Bx^2 + Cx + D$, write it as (D+X*(C+X*(B+X*A))).

5. Boundary Alignment

a) Order type declaration statements so that the variables having the longest length(s) are defined before those of lesser length(s).

b) In Common Blocks, arrange the variables in the list in order of decreasing length.

c) When Equivalencing two or more variables, put the variable with the longest length first.

6. Input-Output

a) A single READ is better than two separate READs.

b) Temporary tape and direct access files should use format-free READ and WRITE statements.

c) Implied DO-loops are inefficient. For example:

Bad

```
INTEGER SET(100)
READ,N
READ,(SET(I),I=1,N)
STOP
END
```

Best

```
INTEGER SET(100)
COMMON N
READ,N
CALL READ(SET)
STOP
END

SUBROUTINE READ(SET)
COMMON N
INTEGER SET(N)
READ,SET
RETURN
END
```

d) Read and write "blocks" of records when using tape and direct access files. For example:

Bad	Better
INTEGER SET(20)	INTEGER SET1(20),SET2(20)
DO 1 I=1,100	DO 1 I=1,99,2
READ,SET	READ,SET1,SET2
1 WRITE(2) SET	1 WRITE(2) SET1,SET2

    e) Formatting is slow. Use format-free if it doesn't matter much.

7. Subprograms

    a) Use COMMON instead of parameter lists.

    b) Avoid subprograms for small repeated tasks.

    c) Use Statement Functions if a function value can be calculated in a single expression.

8. Memory Requirements

    a) Use INTEGER*2 and LOGICAL*1 variables.

    b) Use $NOCHECK for debugged parts of a program.

    c) Use call by location instead of call by value.

    d) Use EQUIVALENCE if variables are not required at the same time.

    e) Use "WATFIVS" if available.

9. Miscellaneous

    a) Avoid DATA statements. Use type declaration statements to specify initial values.

    b) Use $PRINTOFF to save paper and reduce print time.

Generalization Hints

A generalized program is one which can be used to solve a wide variety of problems without making changes in the program. This is usually done by reading in information from cards which define the characteristics of the problem to be solved. Not only will a generalized program solve many problems but it will also permit someone with no programming knowledge to use the program simply by preparing an appropriate set of input data. Some generalization hints are:

1. Check for error conditions which although not present in the problem for which the program was written, could be present using a different set of data.

2. Use execution time dimensioning of parameter arrays.

3. Use execution time formatting.

4. Use statements which are acceptable to almost all Fortran compilers.

5. Use INTEGER variables for device assignments. For example, "INPUT=5; READ(INPUT,...)...".

6. Read the number of problems to be solved from a data card.

7. Read DO-loop parameter values.

Other Hints

1. Large programs should have a tree-like structure as shown in the following diagram.

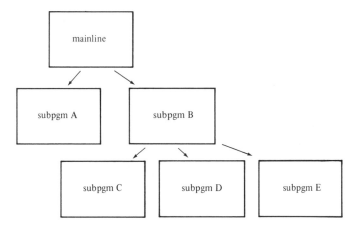

Don't make program segments too large. About 30 to 70 statements per segment is a reasonable range.

2. Documentation. The beginning of the program and/or each segment should have comment cards which describe: the purpose of the segment; error conditions; inputs and outputs; computation methods used; meaning of variable names; etc..

3. Style. Use meaningful variable names. Arrange the program logic in blocks. Don't jump back and forth all over the place. Use sequential statement numbers with a definite step size. Be consistent in the use of statement numbers and the placement of FORMAT statements.

Beginning on this page is a list of the messages which may be produced at compile time or execution time when running WATFIV jobs.

'ASSEMBLER LANGUAGE SUBPROGRAMMES'
AL-0   'MISSING END CARD ON ASSEMBLY LANGUAGE OBJECT DECK'
AL-1   'ENTRY-POINT OR CSECT NAME IN AN OBJECT DECK WAS PREVIOUSLY
       DEFINED.FIRST DEFINITION USED'

'BLOCK DATA STATEMENTS'
BD-0   'EXECUTABLE STATEMENTS ARE ILLEGAL IN BLOCK DATA SUBPROGRAMS'
BD-1   'IMPROPER BLOCK DATA STATEMENT'

'CARD FORMAT AND CONTENTS'
CC-0   'COLUMNS 1-5 OF CONTINUATION CARD ARE NOT BLANK.
       PROBABLE CAUSE:STATEMENT PUNCHED TO LEFT OF COLUMN 7'
CC-1   'LIMIT OF 5 CONTINUATION CARDS EXCEEDED'
CC-2   'INVALID CHARACTER IN FORTRAN STATEMENT.
       A '$' WAS INSERTED IN THE SOURCE LISTING'
CC-3   'FIRST CARD OF A PROGRAM IS A CONTINUATION CARD.
       PROBABLE CAUSE:STATEMENT PUNCHED TO LEFT OF COLUMN 7'
CC-4   'STATEMENT TOO LONG TO COMPILE (SCAN-STACK OVERFLOW)'
CC-5   'A BLANK CARD WAS ENCOUNTERED'
CC-6   'KEYPUNCH USED DIFFERS FROM KEYPUNCH SPECIFIED ON JOB CARD'
CC-7   'THE FIRST CHARACTER OF THE STATEMENT WAS NOT ALPHABETIC'
CC-8   'INVALID CHARACTER(S) ARE CONCATENATED WITH THE FORTRAN KEYWORD'
CC-9   'INVALID CHARACTERS IN COLUMNS 1-5.STATEMENT NUMBER IGNORED.
       PROBABLE CAUSE:STATEMENT PUNCHED TO LEFT OF COLUMN 7'
CC-A   'CONTROL CARDS MAY NOT BE CONTINUED'

'COMMON'
CM-0   'THE VARIABLE IS ALREADY IN COMMON'
CM-1   'OTHER COMPILERS MAY NOT ALLOW COMMONED VARIABLES TO BE INITIALIZED IN
       OTHER THAN A BLOCK DATA SUBPROGRAM'
CM-2   'ILLEGAL USE OF A COMMON BLOCK OR NAMELIST NAME'

'FORTRAN TYPE CONSTANTS'
CN-0   'MIXED REAL*4,REAL*8 IN COMPLEX CONSTANT;REAL*8 ASSUMED FOR BOTH'
CN-1   'AN INTEGER CONSTANT MAY NOT BE GREATER THAN 2,147,483,647 (2**31-1)'
CN-2   'EXPONENT ON A REAL CONSTANT IS GREATER THAN 2 DIGITS'

CN-3 'A REAL CONSTANT HAS MORE THAN 16 DIGITS.IT WAS TRUNCATED TO 16'
CN-4 'INVALID HEXADECIMAL CONSTANT'
CN-5 'ILLEGAL USE OF A DECIMAL POINT'
CN-6 'CONSTANT WITH MORE THAN 7 DIGITS BUT E-TYPE EXPONENT,ASSUMED TO BE REAL*4'
CN-7 'CONSTANT OR STATEMENT NUMBER GREATER THAN 99999'
CN-8 'AN EXPONENT OVERFLOW OR UNDERFLOW OCCURRED WHILE CONVERTING A CONSTANT IN A SOURCE STATEMENT'

'COMPILER ERRORS'
CP-0 'COMPILER ERROR - LANDR/ARITH'
CP-1 'COMPILER ERROR.LIKELY CAUSE:MORE THAN 255 DO STATEMENTS'
CP-4 'COMPILER ERROR - INTERRUPT AT COMPILE TIME,RETURN TO SYSTEM'

'CHARACTER VARIABLE'
CV-0 'A CHARACTER VARIABLE IS USED WITH A RELATIONAL OPERATOR'
CV-1 'LENGTH OF A CHARACTER VALUE ON RIGHT OF EQUAL SIGN EXCEEDS THAT ON LEFT. TRUNCATION WILL OCCUR'
CV-2 'UNFORMATTED CORE-TO-CORE I/O NOT IMPLEMENTED'

'DATA STATEMENT'
DA-0 'REPLICATION FACTOR IS ZERO OR GREATER THAN 32767. IT IS ASSUMED TO BE 32767'
DA-1 'MORE VARIABLES THAN CONSTANTS'
DA-2 'ATTEMPT TO INITIALIZE A SUBPROGRAM PARAMETER IN A DATA STATEMENT'
DA-3 'OTHER COMPILERS MAY NOT ALLOW NON-CONSTANT SUBSCRIPTS IN DATA STATEMENTS'
DA-4 'TYPE OF VARIABLE AND CONSTANT DO NOT AGREE. (MESSAGE ISSUED ONCE FOR AN ARRAY)'
DA-5 'MORE CONSTANTS THAN VARIABLES'
DA-6 'A VARIABLE WAS PREVIOUSLY INITIALIZED.THE LATEST VALUE IS USED. CHECK COMMONED AND EQUIVALENCED VARIABLES'
DA-7 'OTHER COMPILERS MAY NOT ALLOW INITIALIZATION OF BLANK COMMON'
DA-8 'A LITERAL CONSTANT HAS BEEN TRUNCATED'
DA-9 'OTHER COMPILERS MAY NOT ALLOW IMPLIED DO-LOOPS IN DATA STATEMENTS'

'DEFINE FILE STATEMENTS'
DF-0 'THE UNIT NUMBER IS MISSING'
DF-1 'INVALID FORMAT TYPE'
DF-2 'THE ASSOCIATED VARIABLE IS NOT A SIMPLE INTEGER VARIABLE'
DF-3 'NUMBER OF RECORDS OR RECORD SIZE IS ZERO OR GREATER THAN 32767'

'DIMENSION STATEMENTS'
DM-0 'NO DIMENSIONS ARE SPECIFIED FOR A VARIABLE IN A DIMENSION STATEMENT'
DM-1 'THE VARIABLE HAS ALREADY BEEN DIMENSIONED'
DM-2 'CALL-BY-LOCATION PARAMETERS MAY NOT BE DIMENSIONED'
DM-3 'THE DECLARED SIZE OF ARRAY EXCEEDS SPACE PROVIDED BY CALLING ARGUMENT'

'DO LOOPS'
DO-0 'THIS STATEMENT CANNOT BE THE OBJECT OF A DO-LOOP'
DO-1 'ILLEGAL TRANSFER INTO THE RANGE OF A DO-LOOP'
DO-2 'THE OBJECT OF THIS DO-LOOP HAS ALREADY APPEARED'
DO-3 'IMPROPERLY NESTED DO-LOOPS'
DO-4 'ATTEMPT TO REDEFINE A DO-LOOP PARAMETER WITHIN THE RANGE OF THE LOOP'
DO-5 'INVALID DO-LOOP PARAMETER'
DO-6 'ILLEGAL TRANSFER TO A STATEMENT WHICH IS INSIDE THE RANGE OF A DO-LOOP'
DO-7 'A DO-LOOP PARAMETER IS UNDEFINED OR OUT OF RANGE'
DO-8 'BECAUSE OF ONE OF THE PARAMETERS, THIS DO-LOOP WILL TERMINATE AFTER THE
      FIRST TIME THROUGH'
DO-9 'A DO-LOOP PARAMETER MAY NOT BE REDEFINED IN AN INPUT LIST'
DO-A 'OTHER COMPILERS MAY NOT ALLOW THIS STATEMENT TO END A DO-LOOP'

'EQUIVALENCE AND/OR COMMON'
EC-0 'EQUIVALENCED VARIABLE APPEARS IN A COMMON STATEMENT'
EC-1 'A COMMON BLOCK HAS A DIFFERENT LENGTH THAN IN A PREVIOUS
      SUBPROGRAM:GREATER LENGTH USED'
EC-2 'COMMON AND/OR EQUIVALENCE CAUSES INVALID ALIGNMENT.
      EXECUTION SLOWED.REMEDY:ORDER VARIABLES BY DECREASING LENGTH'
EC-3 'EQUIVALENCE EXTENDS COMMON DOWNWARDS'
EC-4 'A SUBPROGRAM PARAMETER APPEARS IN A COMMON OR EQUIVALENCE STATEMENT'
EC-5 'A VARIABLE WAS USED WITH SUBSCRIPTS IN AN EQUIVALENCE STATEMENT BUT HAS
      NOT BEEN PROPERLY DIMENSIONED'

461

'END STATEMENTS'
EN-0 'MISSING END STATEMENT:END STATEMENT GENERATED'
EN-1 'AN END STATEMENT WAS USED TO TERMINATE EXECUTION'
EN-2 'AN END STATEMENT CANNOT HAVE A STATEMENT NUMBER. STATEMENT NUMBER
     IGNORED'
EN-3 'END STATEMENT NOT PRECEDED BY A TRANSFER'

'EQUAL SIGNS'
EQ-0 'ILLEGAL QUANTITY ON LEFT OF EQUALS SIGN'
EQ-1 'ILLEGAL USE OF EQUAL SIGN'
EQ-2 'OTHER COMPILERS MAY NOT ALLOW MULTIPLE ASSIGNMENT STATEMENTS'
EQ-3 'MULTIPLE ASSIGNMENT IS NOT IMPLEMENTED FOR CHARACTER VARIABLES'

'EQUIVALENCE STATEMENTS'
EV-0 'ATTEMPT TO EQUIVALENCE A VARIABLE TO ITSELF'
EV-2 'A MULTI-SUBSCRIPTED EQUIVALENCED VARIABLE HAS BEEN INCORRECTLY
     RE-EQUIVALENCED.REMEDY:DIMENSION THE VARIABLE FIRST'

'POWERS AND EXPONENTIATION'
EX-0 'ILLEGAL COMPLEX EXPONENTIATION'
EX-1 'I**J WHERE I=J=0'
EX-2 'I**J WHERE I=0, J.LT.0'
EX-3 '0.0**Y WHERE Y.LE.0.0'
EX-4 '0.0**J WHERE J=0'
EX-5 '0.0**J WHERE J.LT.0'
EX-6 'X**Y WHERE X.LT.0.0, Y.NE.0.0'

'ENTRY STATEMENT'
EY-0 'ENTRY-POINT NAME WAS PREVIOUSLY DEFINED'
EY-1 'PREVIOUS DEFINITION OF FUNCTION NAME IN AN ENTRY IS INCORRECT'
EY-2 'THE USAGE OF A SUBPROGRAM PARAMETER IS INCONSISTENT WITH A PREVIOUS
     ENTRY-POINT'
EY-3 'A PARAMETER HAS APPEARED IN A EXECUTABLE STATEMENT BUT IS NOT A
     SUBPROGRAM PARAMETER'
EY-4 'ENTRY STATEMENTS ARE INVALID IN THE MAIN PROGRAM'

462

EY-5   'ENTRY STATEMENT INVALID INSIDE A DO-LOOP'

'FORMAT'

SOME   FORMAT ERROR MESSAGES GIVE CHARACTERS IN WHICH ERROR WAS DETECTED
FM-0   'IMPROPER CHARACTER SEQUENCE OR INVALID CHARACTER IN INPUT DATA'
FM-1   'NO STATEMENT NUMBER ON A FORMAT STATEMENT'
FM-2   'FORMAT CODE AND DATA TYPE DO NOT MATCH'
FM-4   'FORMAT PROVIDES NO CONVERSION SPECIFICATION FOR A VALUE IN I/O LIST'
FM-5   'AN INTEGER IN THE INPUT DATA IS TOO LARGE.
         (MAXIMUM=2,147,483,647=2**31-1)'
FM-6   'A REAL NUMBER IN THE INPUT DATA IS OUT OF MACHINE RANGE (1.E-78,1.E+75)'
FM-7   'UNREFERENCED FORMAT STATEMENT'
FT-0   'FIRST CHARACTER OF VARIABLE FORMAT IS NOT A LEFT PARENTHESIS'
FT-1   'INVALID CHARACTER ENCOUNTERED IN FORMAT'
FT-2   'INVALID FORM FOLLOWING A FORMAT CODE'
FT-3   'INVALID FIELD OR GROUP COUNT'
FT-4   'A FIELD OR GROUP COUNT GREATER THAN 255'
FT-5   'NO CLOSING PARENTHESIS ON VARIABLE FORMAT'
FT-6   'NO CLOSING QUOTE IN A HOLLERITH FIELD'
FT-7   'INVALID USE OF COMMA'
FT-8   'FORMAT STATEMENT TOO LONG TO COMPILE (SCAN-STACK OVERFLOW)'
FT-9   'INVALID USE OF P FORMAT CODE'
FT-A   'INVALID USE OF PERIOD(.)'
FT-B   'MORE THAN THREE LEVELS OF PARENTHESES'
FT-C   'INVALID CHARACTER BEFORE A RIGHT PARENTHESIS'
FT-D   'MISSING OR ZERO LENGTH HOLLERITH ENCOUNTERED'
FT-E   'NO CLOSING RIGHT PARENTHESIS'
FT-F   'CHARACTERS FOLLOW CLOSING RIGHT PARENTHESIS'
FT-G   'WRONG QUOTE USED FOR KEY-PUNCH SPECIFIED'
FT-H   'LENGTH OF HOLLERITH EXCEEDS 255'
FT-I   'EXPECTING COMMA BETWEEN FORMAT ITEMS'

'FUNCTIONS AND SUBROUTINES'
FN-1   'A PARAMETER APPEARS MORE THAN ONCE IN A SUBPROGRAM OR STATEMENT
         FUNCTION DEFINITION'
FN-2   'SUBSCRIPTS ON RIGHT-HAND SIDE OF STATEMENT FUNCTION.

PROBABLE CAUSE:VARIABLE TO LEFT OF EQUAL SIGN NOT DIMENSIONED'
FN-3   'MULTIPLE RETURNS ARE INVALID IN FUNCTION SUBPROGRAMS'
FN-4   'ILLEGAL LENGTH MODIFIER'
FN-5   'INVALID PARAMETER'
FN-6   'A PARAMETER HAS THE SAME NAME AS THE SUBPROGRAM'

'GO TO STATEMENTS'
GO-0   'THIS STATEMENT COULD TRANSFER TO ITSELF'
GO-1   'THIS STATEMENT TRANSFERS TO A NON-EXECUTABLE STATEMENT'
GO-2   'ATTEMPT TO DEFINE ASSIGNED GOTO INDEX IN AN ARITHMETIC STATEMENT'
GO-3   'ASSIGNED GOTO INDEX MAY BE USED ONLY IN ASSIGNED GOTO AND ASSIGN STATEMENTS'
GO-4   'THE INDEX OF AN ASSIGNED GOTO IS UNDEFINED OR OUT OF RANGE,OR INDEX OF COMPUTED GOTO IS UNDEFINED'
GO-5   'ASSIGNED GOTO INDEX MAY NOT BE AN INTEGER*2 VARIABLE'

'HOLLERITH CONSTANTS'
HO-0   'ZERO LENGTH SPECIFIED FOR H-TYPE HOLLERITH'
HO-1   'ZERO LENGTH QUOTE-TYPE HOLLERITH'
HO-2   'NO CLOSING QUOTE OR NEXT CARD NOT A CONTINUATION CARD'
HO-3   'UNEXPECTED HOLLERITH OR STATEMENT NUMBER CONSTANT'

'IF STATEMENTS (ARITHMETIC AND LOGICAL)'
IF-0   'AN INVALID STATEMENT FOLLOWS THE LOGICAL IF'
IF-1   'ARITHMETIC OR INVALID EXPRESSION IN LOGICAL IF'
IF-2   'LOGICAL,COMPLEX OR INVALID EXPRESSION IN ARITHMETIC IF'

'IMPLICIT STATEMENT'
IM-0   'INVALID DATA TYPE'
IM-1   'INVALID OPTIONAL LENGTH'
IM-3   'IMPROPER ALPHABETIC SEQUENCE IN CHARACTER RANGE'
IM-4   'A SPECIFICATION IS NOT A SINGLE CHARACTER.THE FIRST CHARACTER IS USED'
IM-5   'IMPLICIT STATEMENT DOES NOT PRECEDE OTHER SPECIFICATION STATEMENTS'
IM-6   'ATTEMPT TO DECLARE THE TYPE OF A CHARACTER MORE THAN ONCE'
IM-7   'ONLY ONE IMPLICIT STATEMENT PER PROGRAM SEGMENT ALLOWED. THIS ONE IGNORED'

'INPUT/OUTPUT'
IO-0 'I/O STATEMENT REFERENCES A STATEMENT WHICH IS NOT A FORMAT STATEMENT'
IO-1 'A VARIABLE FORMAT MUST BE AN ARRAY NAME'
IO-2 'INVALID ELEMENT IN INPUT LIST OR DATA LIST'
IO-3 'OTHER COMPILERS MAY NOT ALLOW EXPRESSIONS IN OUTPUT LISTS'
IO-4 'ILLEGAL USE OF END= OR ERR= PARAMETERS'
IO-5 'INVALID UNIT NUMBER'
IO-6 'INVALID FORMAT'
IO-7 'ONLY CONSTANTS,SIMPLE INTEGER*4 VARIABLES,AND CHARACTER VARIABLES ARE
       ALLOWED AS UNIT'
IO-8 'ATTEMPT TO PERFORM I/O IN A FUNCTION WHICH IS CALLED IN AN OUTPUT
       STATEMENT'
IO-9 'UNFORMATTED WRITE STATEMENT MUST HAVE A LIST'

'JOB CONTROL CARDS'
JB-0 'CONTROL CARD ENCOUNTERED DURING COMPILATION;
       PROBABLE CAUSE:MISSING C$ENTRY CARD'
JB-1 'MIS-PUNCHED JOB OPTION'

'JOB TERMINATION'
KO-0 'SOURCE ERROR ENCOUNTERED WHILE EXECUTING WITH RUN=FREE'
KO-1 'LIMIT EXCEEDED FOR FIXED-POINT DIVISION BY ZERO'
KO-2 'LIMIT EXCEEDED FOR FLOATING-POINT DIVISION BY ZERO'
KO-3 'EXPONENT OVERFLOW LIMIT EXCEEDED'
KO-4 'EXPONENT UNDERFLOW LIMIT EXCEEDED'
KO-5 'FIXED-POINT OVERFLOW LIMIT EXCEEDED'
KO-6 'JOB-TIME EXCEEDED'
KO-7 'COMPILER ERROR - EXECUTION TIME:RETURN TO SYSTEM'
KO-8 'TRACEBACK ERROR. TRACEBACK TERMINATED'
KO-9 'CANNOT OPEN WATFIV.ERRTEXTS. RUN TERMINATED'
KO-A 'I/O ERROR ON TEXT FILE'

'LOGICAL OPERATIONS'
LG-0 '.NOT. WAS USED AS A BINARY OPERATOR'

465

'LIBRARY ROUTINES'
LI-0 'ARGUMENT OUT OF RANGE DGAMMA OR GAMMA. (1.382E-76 .LT. X .LT. 57.57)'
LI-1 'ABS(X) .GE. 175.366 FOR SINH,COSH,DSINH OR DCOSH OF X'
LI-2 'SENSE LIGHT OTHER THAN 0,1,2,3,4 FOR SLITE OR 1,2,3,4 FOR SLITET'
LI-3 'REAL PORTION OF ARGUMENT .GT. 174.673, CEXP OR CDEXP'
LI-4 'ABS(AIMAG(Z)) .GT. 174.673 FOR CSIN, CCOS, CDSIN OR CDCOS OF Z'
LI-5 'ABS(REAL(Z)) .GE. 3.537E15 FOR CSIN, CCOS, CDSIN OR CDCOS OF Z'
LI-6 'ABS(AIMAG(Z)) .GE. 3.537E15 FOR CEXP OR CDEXP OF Z'
LI-7 'ARGUMENT .GT. 174.673, EXP OR DEXP'
LI-8 'ARGUMENT OF CLOG OR CDLOG IS ZERO'
LI-9 'ARGUMENT IS NEGATIVE OR ZERO, ALOG, ALOG10, DLOG OR DLOG10'
LI-A 'ABS(X) .GE. 3.537E15 FOR SIN, COS, DSIN OR DCOS OF X'
LI-B 'ABSOLUTE VALUE OF ARGUMENT .GT. 1, FOR ARSIN, ARCOS, DARSIN OR DARCOS'
LI-C 'ARGUMENT IS NEGATIVE, SQRT OR DSQRT'
LI-D 'BOTH ARGUMENTS OF DATAN2 OR ATAN2 ARE ZERO'
LI-E 'ARGUMENT TOO CLOSE TO A SINGULARITY, TAN, COTAN, DTAN OR DCOTAN'
LI-F 'ARGUMENT OUT OF RANGE DLGAMA OR ALGAMA. (0.0 .LT. X .LT. 4.29E73)'
LI-G 'ABSOLUTE VALUE OF ARGUMENT .GE. 3.537E15, TAN, COTAN, DTAN, DCOTAN'

'MIXED MODE'
MD-0 'RELATIONAL OPERATOR HAS LOGICAL OPERAND'
MD-1 'RELATIONAL OPERATOR HAS COMPLEX OPERAND'
MD-2 'MIXED MODE - LOGICAL OR CHARACTER WITH ARITHMETIC'
MD-3 'OTHER COMPILERS MAY NOT ALLOW SUBSCRIPTS OF TYPE COMPLEX,LOGICAL OR
       CHARACTER'

'MEMORY OVERFLOW'
MO-0 'INSUFFICIENT MEMORY TO COMPILE THIS PROGRAM.REMAINDER WILL BE ERROR
       CHECKED ONLY'
MO-1 'INSUFFICIENT MEMORY TO ASSIGN ARRAY STORAGE. JOB ABANDONED'
MO-2 'SYMBOL TABLE EXCEEDS AVAILABLE SPACE,JOB ABANDONED'
MO-3 'DATA AREA OF SUBPROGRAM EXCEEDS 24K -- SEGMENT SUBPROGRAM'
MO-4 'INSUFFICIENT MEMORY TO ALLOCATE COMPILER WORK AREA OR WATLIB BUFFER'

'NAMELIST STATEMENTS'
NL-0 'NAMELIST ENTRY MUST BE A VARIABLE,NOT A SUBPROGRAM PARAMETER'

NL-1   'NAMELIST NAME PREVIOUSLY DEFINED'
NL-2   'VARIABLE NAME TOO LONG'
NL-3   'VARIABLE NAME NOT FOUND IN NAMELIST'
NL-4   'INVALID SYNTAX IN NAMELIST INPUT'
NL-6   'VARIABLE INCORRECTLY SUBSCRIPTED'
NL-7   'SUBSCRIPT OUT OF RANGE'

'PARENTHESES'
PC-0   'UNMATCHED PARENTHESIS'
PC-1   'INVALID PARENTHESIS NESTING IN I/O LIST'

'PAUSE, STOP STATEMENTS'
PS-0   'OPERATOR MESSAGES NOT ALLOWED:SIMPLE STOP ASSUMED FOR STOP,
      CONTINUE ASSUMED FOR PAUSE'

'RETURN STATEMENT'
RE-1   'RETURN I, WHERE I IS OUT OF RANGE OR UNDEFINED'
RE-2   'MULTIPLE RETURN NOT VALID IN FUNCTION SUBPROGRAM'
RE-3   'VARIABLE IS NOT A SIMPLE INTEGER'
RE-4   'A MULTIPLE RETURN IS NOT VALID IN THE MAIN PROGRAM'

'ARITHMETIC AND LOGICAL STATEMENT FUNCTIONS'
    PROBABLE CAUSE OF SF ERRORS - VARIABLE ON LEFT OF = WAS NOT DIMENSIONED
SF-1   'A PREVIOUSLY REFERENCED STATEMENT NUMBER APPEARS ON A STATEMENT
      FUNCTION DEFINITION'
SF-2   'STATEMENT FUNCTION IS THE OBJECT OF A LOGICAL IF STATEMENT'
SF-3   'RECURSIVE STATEMENT FUNCTION DEFINITION:NAME APPEARS ON BOTH SIDES OF
      EQUAL SIGN.LIKELY CAUSE:VARIABLE NOT DIMENSIONED'
SF-4   'A STATEMENT FUNCTION DEFINITION APPEARS AFTER THE FIRST EXECUTABLE
      STATEMENT'
SF-5   'ILLEGAL USE OF A STATEMENT FUNCTION NAME'

'SUBPROGRAMS'
SR-0   'MISSING SUBPROGRAM'
SR-1   'SUBPROGRAM REDEFINES A CONSTANT,EXPRESSION,DO-PARAMETER OR ASSIGNED
      GOTO INDEX'

467

SR-2   'THE SUBPROGRAM WAS ASSIGNED DIFFERENT TYPES IN DIFFERENT PROGRAM
       SEGMENTS'
SR-3   'ATTEMPT TO USE A SUBPROGRAM RECURSIVELY'
SR-4   'INVALID TYPE OF ARGUMENT IN REFERENCE TO A SUBPROGRAM'
SR-5   'WRONG NUMBER OF ARGUMENTS IN A REFERENCE TO A SUBPROGRAM'
SR-6   'A SUBPROGRAM WAS PREVIOUSLY DEFINED. THE FIRST DEFINITION IS USED'
SR-7   'NO MAIN PROGRAM'
SR-8   'ILLEGAL OR MISSING SUBPROGRAM NAME'
SR-9   'LIBRARY PROGRAM WAS NOT ASSIGNED THE CORRECT TYPE'
SR-A   'METHOD FOR ENTERING SUBPROGRAM PRODUCES UNDEFINED VALUE FOR
       CALL-BY-LOCATION PARAMETER'

'SUBSCRIPTS'
SS-0   'ZERO SUBSCRIPT OR DIMENSION NOT ALLOWED'
SS-1   'ARRAY SUBSCRIPT EXCEEDS DIMENSION'
SS-2   'INVALID SUBSCRIPT FORM'
SS-3   'SUBSCRIPT IS OUT OF RANGE'

'STATEMENTS AND STATEMENT NUMBERS'
ST-0   'MISSING STATEMENT NUMBER'
ST-1   'STATEMENT NUMBER GREATER THAN 99999'
ST-2   'STATEMENT NUMBER HAS ALREADY BEEN DEFINED'
ST-3   'UNDECODEABLE STATEMENT'
ST-4   'UNNUMBERED EXECUTABLE STATEMENT FOLLOWS A TRANSFER'
ST-5   'STATEMENT NUMBER IN A TRANSFER IS A NON-EXECUTABLE STATEMENT'
ST-6   'ONLY CALL STATEMENTS MAY CONTAIN STATEMENT NUMBER ARGUMENTS'
ST-7   'STATEMENT SPECIFIED IN A TRANSFER STATEMENT IS A FORMAT STATEMENT'
ST-8   'MISSING FORMAT STATEMENT'
ST-9   'SPECIFICATION STATEMENT DOES NOT PRECEDE STATEMENT FUNCTION DEFINITIONS
       OR EXECUTABLE STATEMENTS'
ST-A   'UNREFERENCED STATEMENT FOLLOWS A TRANSFER'
ST-B   'STATEMENT NUMBER MUST END WITH COLON. STATEMENT NUMBER WAS IGNORED'

'SUBSCRIPTED VARIABLES'
SV-0   'THE WRONG NUMBER OF SUBSCRIPTS WERE SPECIFIED FOR A VARIABLE'
SV-1   'AN ARRAY OR SUBPROGRAM NAME IS USED INCORRECTLY WITHOUT A LIST'

SV-2 'MORE THAN 7 DIMENSIONS ARE NOT ALLOWED'
SV-3 'DIMENSION OR SUBSCRIPT TOO LARGE (MAXIMUM 10**8-1)'
SV-4 'A VARIABLE USED WITH VARIABLE DIMENSIONS IS NOT A SUBPROGRAM PARAMETER'
SV-5 'A VARIABLE DIMENSION IS NOT ONE OF SIMPLE INTEGER VARIABLE,SUBPROGRAM
       PARAMETER,IN COMMON'

'SYNTAX ERRORS'
SX-0 'MISSING OPERATOR'
SX-1 'EXPECTING OPERATOR'
SX-2 'EXPECTING SYMBOL'
SX-3 'EXPECTING SYMBOL OR OPERATOR'
SX-4 'EXPECTING CONSTANT'
SX-5 'EXPECTING SYMBOL OR CONSTANT'
SX-6 'EXPECTING STATEMENT NUMBER'
SX-7 'EXPECTING SIMPLE INTEGER VARIABLE'
SX-8 'EXPECTING SIMPLE INTEGER VARIABLE OR CONSTANT'
SX-9 'ILLEGAL SEQUENCE OF OPERATORS IN EXPRESSION'
SX-A 'EXPECTING END-OF-STATEMENT'

'TYPE STATEMENTS'
TY-0 'THE VARIABLE HAS ALREADY BEEN EXPLICITLY TYPED'
TY-1 'THE LENGTH OF THE EQUIVALENCED VARIABLE MAY NOT BE CHANGED.
       REMEDY: INTERCHANGE TYPE AND EQUIVALENCE STATEMENTS'

'I/O OPERATIONS'
UN-0 'CONTROL CARD ENCOUNTERED ON UNIT 5 AT EXECUTION.
       PROBABLE CAUSE:MISSING DATA OR INCORRECT FORMAT'
UN-1 'END OF FILE ENCOUNTERED (IBM CODE IHC217)'
UN-2 'I/O ERROR (IBM CODE IHC218)'
UN-3 'NO DD STATEMENT WAS SUPPLIED (IBM CODE IHC219)'
UN-4 'REWIND,ENDFILE,BACKSPACE REFERENCES UNIT 5, 6 OR 7'
UN-5 'ATTEMPT TO READ ON UNIT 5 AFTER IT HAS HAD END-OF-FILE'
UN-6 'AN INVALID VARIABLE UNIT NUMBER WAS DETECTED (IBM CODE IHC220)'
UN-7 'PAGE-LIMIT EXCEEDED'
UN-8 'ATTEMPT TO DO DIRECT ACCESS I/O ON A SEQUENTIAL FILE OR VICE VERSA.
       POSSIBLE MISSING DEFINE FILE STATEMENT (IBM CODE IHC231)'

UN-9 'WRITE REFERENCES 5 OR READ REFERENCES 6 OR 7'
UN-A 'DEFINE FILE REFERENCES A UNIT PREVIOUSLY USED FOR SEQUENTIAL I/O (IBM
       CODE IHC235)'
UN-B 'RECORD SIZE FOR UNIT EXCEEDS 32767,OR DIFFERS FROM DD STATEMENT
       SPECIFICATION (IBM CODES IHC233,IHC237)'
UN-C 'FOR DIRECT ACCESS I/O THE RELATIVE RECORD POSITION IS NEGATIVE,ZERO,OR
       TOO LARGE (IBM CODE IHC232)'
UN-D 'AN ATTEMPT WAS MADE TO READ MORE INFORMATION THAN LOGICAL RECORD
       CONTAINS (IBM CODE IHC236)'
UN-E 'FORMATTED LINE EXCEEDS BUFFER LENGTH (IBM CODE IHC212)'
UN-F 'I/O ERROR – SEARCHING LIBRARY DIRECTORY'
UN-G 'I/O ERROR – READING LIBRARY'
UN-H 'ATTEMPT TO DEFINE THE OBJECT ERROR FILE AS A DIRECT ACCESS FILE
       (IBM CODE IHC234)'
UN-I 'RECFM IS NOT V(B)S FOR I/O WITHOUT FORMAT CONTROL " (IBM CODE IHC214)'
UN-J 'MISSING DD CARD FOR WATLIB.NO LIBRARY ASSUMED'
UN-K 'ATTEMPT TO READ OR WRITE PAST THE END OF CHARACTER VARIABLE BUFFER'
UN-L 'ATTEMPT TO READ ON AN UNCREATED DIRECT ACCESS FILE (IHC236)'

'UNDEFINED VARIABLES'
UV-0 'VARIABLE IS UNDEFINED'
UV-3 'SUBSCRIPT IS UNDEFINED'
UV-4 'SUBPROGRAM IS UNDEFINED'
UV-5 'ARGUMENT IS UNDEFINED'
UV-6 'UNDECODABLE CHARACTERS IN VARIABLE FORMAT'

'VARIABLE NAMES'
VA-0 'A NAME IS TOO LONG.IT HAS BEEN TRUNCATED TO SIX CHARACTERS'
VA-1 'ATTEMPT TO USE AN ASSIGNED OR INITIALIZED VARIABLE OR DO-PARAMETER IN A
       SPECIFICATION STATEMENT'
VA-2 'ILLEGAL USE OF A SUBROUTINE NAME'
VA-3 'ILLEGAL USE OF A VARIABLE NAME'
VA-4 'ATTEMPT TO USE THE PREVIOUSLY DEFINED NAME AS A FUNCTION OR AN ARRAY'
VA-5 'ATTEMPT TO USE A PREVIOUSLY DEFINED NAME AS A SUBROUTINE'
VA-6 'ATTEMPT TO USE A PREVIOUSLY DEFINED NAME AS A SUBPROGRAM'
VA-7 'ATTEMPT TO USE A PREVIOUSLY DEFINED NAME AS A COMMON BLOCK'

VA-8   'ATTEMPT TO USE A FUNCTION NAME AS A VARIABLE'
VA-9   'ATTEMPT TO USE A PREVIOUSLY DEFINED NAME AS A VARIABLE'
VA-A   'ILLEGAL USE OF A PREVIOUSLY DEFINED NAME'

'EXTERNAL STATEMENT'
XT-0   'A VARIABLE HAS ALREADY APPEARED IN AN EXTERNAL STATEMENT'

471

APPENDIX I   BUILT-IN FUNCTIONS

This appendix contains a list of built-in functions which can be used in source programs compiled by the WATFIV compiler. In the table:

    i2 denotes any INTEGER*2 expression

    i4 denotes any INTEGER*4 expression

    r4 denotes any REAL*4 expression

    r8 denotes any REAL*8 expression

    c8 denotes any COMPLEX*8 expression

    c16 denotes any COMPLEX*16 expression

These symbols also denote the type of function value produced.

If the function has only one argument, "a" represents its value. If a function has two arguments, "a1", and "a2" denote their values. If a function can have more than two arguments, dots ("...") indicate this fact.

TABLE OF BUILT-IN FUNCTIONS

PURPOSE	NAME AND ARGUMENTS	DEFINITION	TYPE OF RESULT
Square Root	SQRT(r4) DSQRT(r8) CSQRT(c8) CDSQRT(c16)	$\sqrt{a}$	r4 r8 c8 c16
Sine	SIN(r4) DSIN(r8) CSIN(c8) CDSIN(c16)	sin a (a in radians)	r4 r8 c8 c16
Cosine	COS(r4) DCOS(r8) CCOS(c8) CDCOS(c16)	cos a (a in radians)	r4 r8 c8 c16
Tangent	TAN(r4) DTAN(r8)	tan a (a in radians)	r4 r8

472

Cotangent	COTAN(r4) DCOTAN(r8)	cot a (a in radians)	r4 r8
Arcsine	ARSIN(r4) DARSIN(r8)	x= arcsin a $-\pi/2 \leqslant x \leqslant \pi/2$	r4 r8
Arccosine	ARCOS(r4) DARCOS(r8)	x=arccos a $-\pi/2 \leqslant x \leqslant \pi/2$	r4 r8
Arctangent	ATAN(r4) DATAN(r8)	x=arctan a $-\pi/2 \leqslant x \leqslant \pi/2$	r4 r8
	ATAN2(r4,r4) DATAN2(r8,r8)	x=arctan(a1/a2) $-\pi/2 \leqslant x \leqslant \pi/2$	r4 r0
Exponential	EXP(r4) DEXP(r8) CEXP(c8) CDEXP(c16)	e**a	r4 r8 c8 c16
Natural Logarithm	ALOG(r4) DLOG(r8) CLOG(c8) CDLOG(c16)	log a (base e)	r4 r8 c8 c16
Common Logarithm	ALOG10(r4) DLOG10(r8)	log a (base 10)	r4 r8
Hyperbolic Sine	SINH(r4) DSINH(r8)	sinh a	r4 r8
Hyperbolic Cosine	COSH(r4) DCOSH(r8)	cosh a	r4 r8
Hyperbolic Tangent	TANH(r4) DTANH(r8)	tanh a	r4 r8
Error Function	ERF(r4) DERF(r8)	$erf(a) = \dfrac{2}{\sqrt{\pi}} \int_0 e^{-t^2} dt$	r4 r8
	ERFC(r4) DERFC(r8)	1 - erf(a)	r4 r8
Gamma Function	GAMMA(r4) DGAMMA(r8)	$\Gamma(a) = \int_0^\infty t^{a-1} e^{-t} dt$	r4 r8
	ALGAMA(r4) DLGAMA(r8)	log(gamma(a)) (base e)	r4 r8

Absolute Value	IABS(i4) ABS(r4) DABS(r8)	$\lvert a \rvert$	i4 r4 r8
	CABS(c8) CDABS(cl6)	$\sqrt{x^2+y^2}$ for $\quad$ a=(x,y)	r4 r8
Complex Conjugate	CONJG(c8) DCONJG(cl6)	(x,-y) for a=(x,y)	c8 cl6
Transfer Of Sign	ISIGN(14,14) SIGN(r4,r4) DSIGN(r8,r8)	$\lvert a1 \rvert$ *sign(a2), where $sign(x)=\begin{cases} 1 & \text{if } x>0 \\ 1 & \text{if } x=0 \\ -1 & \text{if } x<0 \end{cases}$	i4 r4 r8
Truncation	INT(r4) AINT(r4) DINT(r8)	x*sign(a) where x is the largest integer $\leq \lvert a \rvert$	i4 r4 r8
Modular Arithmetic	MOD(i4,i4) AMOD(r4,r4) DMOD(r8,r8)	a1-a2*int(a1/a2)	i4 r4 r8
Largest Value	MAX0(i4,i4,...) MAX1(r4,r4,...) AMAX0(i4,i4,...) AMAX1(r4,r4,...) DMAX1(r8,r8,...)	max(a1,a2,...)	i4 i4 r4 r4 r8
Smallest Value	MIN0(i4,i4,...) MIN1(r4,r4,...) AMIN0(i4,i4,...) AMIN1(r4,r4,...) DMIN1(r8,r8,...)	min(a1,a2,...)	i4 i4 r4 r4 r8
Positive Difference	IDIM(i4,i4) DIM(r4,r4)	a1 - min(a1,a2)	i4 r4
Type Conversion	IFIX(r4) HFIX(r4)	convert from REAL to INTEGER	i4 i2
	FLOAT(i4) DFLOAT(i4)	convert from INTEGER to REAL	r4 r8
	SNGL(r8)	truncate REAL*8 to REAL*4	r4
	DBLE(r4)	pad REAL*4 value to make REAL*8 value	r8
	CMPLX(r4,r4) DCMPLX(r8,r8)	create COMPLEX value from 2 REAL values	c8 cl6

REAL(c8)	real component of a COMPLEX value	r4
AIMAG(c8)	imaginary component of a COMPLEX value	r4

APPENDIX J   WATFIV-S

WATFIV-S is a programming language which includes and extends the features of WATFIV. The "S" in WATFIV-S stands for "structured". The new features are designed to make it easier to write well-structured programs. This improvement is achieved by adding several powerful control statements and block structures to the WATFIV language. Use of these statements and blocks will usually decrease the number of statements needed to transfer control from one point of the program to another. This reduces the amount of "jumping around" in a program and makes the program logic appear more sequential.

Because the features of WATFIV-S are not available with other compilers, a translator program has been written which will analyze the extended control features in a WATFIV-S program and produce an equivalent program using standard Fortran IV statements. It is anticipated that new features will be added to WATFIV-S from time-to-time. The latest information concerning statement formats, keywords, specifications and the translator program can be obtained by writing to the WATFIV-S Group at the University of Waterloo Computing Centre, Waterloo, Ontario, Canada.

The WATFIV-S features described in this appendix include the EXECUTE and WHILE-EXECUTE statements and the following five block structures:

        IF-THEN-ELSE : END IF

        WHILE-DO : END WHILE

        DO CASE : END CASE

        REMOTE BLOCK : END BLOCK

        AT END DO : END AT END

A block structure (or, more simply, a block) is a group of consecutive statements which begins with a special statement and ends with a special END statement. These blocks, like DO-loops, may be wholly contained within another block but cannot overlap in other ways.

IF-THEN-ELSE : END IF

This block provides an extension of the capabilities of the Logical IF statement by permitting more than one statement to be executed if the condition being tested is true. Recall that the trailer in the Logical IF statement is limited to one statement.

General Form

```
                    IF (logical-expression) THEN DO
                       .
                       .        statement(s)
range of               .
   the              ELSE DO
   block               .
                       .        statement(s)
                       .
                    END IF
```

Rules

1. If the logical-expression is true, statements following the IF and preceding the the ELSE DO statement are executed. Control then transfers to the statement following the END IF statement.
   If the expression is false, statements following the ELSE DO statement and preceding the the END IF statement are executed. Control then transfers to the statement following the END IF statement.

2. The ELSE DO statement is optional. If omitted, control transfers to the statement following the END IF statement whenever the logical-expression is false.

3. The IF statement in an IF-THEN-ELSE block cannot be the trailer statement in a Logical IF statement or the object statement in a DO-loop.

4. The END IF and ELSE DO statements are non-executable statements.

5. Transfers of Control.
   Control may be transferred to a statement outside the range from a statement inside the range.
   Control may be transferred to a statement inside the range from a statement outside the range. In this case, the ELSE DO statement, if present, is ignored.

477

```
          READ,I
          IF(I/2*2.EQ.I) THEN DO
              PRINT,'I IS AN EVEN NUMBER'
          ELSE DO
              PRINT,'I IS AN ODD NUMBER'
          END IF
          STOP
```

Result: An appropriate message indicating whether I has an even or odd value will be printed.

WHILE-DO : END WHILE

The WHILE-DO block allows a set of statements to be repeatedly executed until a specified condition is found to be true. A DO-loop on the other hand must specify a maximum number of repetitions.

General Form

```
                    WHILE (logical-expression) DO
          range of      .
          the           .      statement(s)
          block         .
                    END WHILE
```

Rules

1. If the logical-expression is true, statements following the WHILE-DO statement and preceding the END WHILE statement are executed. Control then returns to the WHILE DO statement.
   If the statement is false, control is transferred to the statement following the END WHILE statement.

2. The WHILE-DO statement cannot be the trailer statement in a Logical IF statement or the object statement in a DO-loop.

3. The END WHILE statement is a non-executable statement.

4. Transfers of control.
   Control may be transferred to a statement outside the range from a statement inside the range.
   Control may be transferred to statement inside the range from a statement outside the range. When this happens, upon reaching the END WHILE statement, control transfers to the WHILE-DO statement.

```
J=1
READ,N
WHILE(N.GT.J**2) DO
  PRINT,'N IS GREATER THAN',J**2
  J=J+1
END WHILE
STOP
```

Result: Depending on the value of N, one or more lines
of the type N IS GREATER THAN 1,4,9, etc.
may be printed.

DO CASE : END CASE

The DO CASE block provides capabilities similar to
those resulting from the use of a Computed GO TO statement.

General Form

```
                 DO CASE index
                 CASE
                   .
                   .   statement(s)
                   .
                 CASE
                   .
                   .   statement(s)
    range of       .
       the
       block       .
                   .   (additional cases)
                   .

                 IF NONE DO
                   .
                   .   statement(s)
                   .
                 END CASE
```

Rules

1. "index" must be an INTEGER variable of length four.

2. If the value of the index is:
    a) Negative, zero, or greater than the number of
        CASE statements, statements following the
        IF NONE DO statement and preceding the END
        CASE statement are executed. Control then
        transfers to the statement following the
        END CASE statement.

b) N, where N is in the range one up to the number of CASE statements, statements between the Nth and (N+1)th CASE statements are executed. Control then transfers to the statement following the END CASE statement.

3. The DO CASE statement may not be the trailer statement in a Logical IF statement or the object statement in a DO-loop.

4. Transfers of control.
    Control may be transferred to a statement outside the range from a statement inside the range.
    Control may be transferred to a statement inside the range from a statement outside the range. When this happens, the IF NONE DO, END CASE, and any CASE statements encountered are ignored.

5. The CASE statement following the DO CASE statement is optional. If omitted, the logic described in rule 2 applies as though it were present.

6. The IF NONE DO statement is optional. If omitted, control transfers to the statement following the END CASE statement whenever the index is negative, zero, or greater than the number of cases.

7. The IF NONE DO statement, if present, must follow the statements associated with the last case. Only one IF NONE DO statement is permitted in a DO CASE block.

8. A CASE statement may be immediately followed by another CASE statement. This permits one or more values of the index to be effectively ignored by causing control to be transferred to the statement following the END CASE statement.

9. The CASE, IF NONE DO, and END CASE statements are non-executable statements.

10. A comment may follow the word CASE on a CASE statement. Warning! If an "=" symbol appears in the comment, it may result in the statement being compiled as an Assignment statement.

```
                    READ,I
                    DO CASE I
                      CASE
                        PRINT,'I HAS THE VALUE 1'
                      CASE
                        PRINT,'I HAS THE VALUE 2'
                      IF NONE DO
                        PRINT,'I IS NEITHER 1 NOR 2'
                    END CASE
                    STOP
```

Result: Depending on the value of I, the appropriate
        message is printed. This same result could
        of course be programmed more efficiently.

EXECUTE Statement

The EXECUTE statement causes a REMOTE BLOCK to be
executed. (REMOTE BLOCKs are described later.)

General Form

                    EXECUTE name

Rules

1. "name" is the name of a REMOTE BLOCK defined within
   the segment in which the EXECUTE statement
   appears.

2. Following execution of the REMOTE BLOCK named in the
   EXECUTE statement, control returns to the
   statement following the EXECUTE statement.

3. An EXECUTE statement may be used as the trailer
   statement in a Logical IF statement or as the
   object statement in a DO-loop.

Example

                    EXECUTE CALCS

Result: The REMOTE BLOCK named CALCS is executed and
        control returns to the statement following
        the EXECUTE statement.

REMOTE BLOCK : END BLOCK

A REMOTE BLOCK in a program segment is a group of consecutive statements preceded by a REMOTE BLOCK statement and terminated by an END BLOCK statement. The block can only be executed by using an EXECUTE statement. The use of REMOTE BLOCKs provides subprogram-like capabilities within a segment.

General Form

```
                    REMOTE BLOCK name
        range of    .
          the       .    statement(s)
        block       .
                    END BLOCK
```

Rules

1. The name of the REMOTE BLOCK may be any valid WATFIV name. Each REMOTE BLOCK must have a unique name. The name may be the same as the name of a variable or subprogram used in the segment. No ambiguity results from this duplication of names.

2. A maximum of 255 REMOTE BLOCKS may be defined in a program segment.

3. The statements in the range of the block may be any valid WATFIV or WATFIV-S statements or block structures subject to the following two restrictions:
   a) Another REMOTE BLOCK may not be defined within the range of a REMOTE BLOCK.
   b) No statement may transfer control to a point outside the block except as noted in Rule 5 below. An attempt to do this will result in a compile-time error.

4. A block may only be entered by means of an EXECUTE statement. Block execution is terminated by executing the statement preceding the END BLOCK statement. Attempts to transfer control to a statement within the block from a statement outside the block will result in an execution-time error.

5. Subprograms may be called from within a block. A block may contain an EXECUTE statement causing another REMOTE BLOCK to be executed. Any chain of blocks executed in this way must not form a loop. (A block may not EXECUTE itself either directly or indirectly.)

6. Blocks may be defined anywhere in a program segment. Any executable statement preceding a REMOTE BLOCK statement should cause a transfer of control. Similarly, the first executable statement not belonging another REMOTE BLOCK which follows an END BLOCK statement should have a statement number. Otherwise it can never be executed.

7. The REMOTE BLOCK and END BLOCK statements are non-executable statements. Comments may follow the words "END BLOCK". Warning! If the comment contains an "=" symbol, the statement may be compiled as an Assignment statement.

Example

```
        Z=3.
        EXECUTE A
        PRINT,B
        Z=11.
        EXECUTE A
        PRINT,B
        STOP
        REMOTE BLOCK A
        B=(3.*Z+1)/2.
        END BLOCK
        END
```

Result: The values 5. and 17. are printed. Note that variables used outside the block are "known" within the block and vice-versa.

WHILE-EXECUTE Statement

The WHILE-EXECUTE statement causes a REMOTE BLOCK to be EXECUTEd repeatedly until a specified condition is true.

General Form

        WHILE (logical expression) EXECUTE name

Rules

1. If the logical-expression is true, the REMOTE BLOCK is executed and control retrurns to the WHILE statement.
   If the expression is false, execution continues with the next executable statement.

2. A WHILE-EXECUTE statement may not be the trailer statement in a Logical IF statement or the object statement in a DO-loop.

Example

WHILE (N.LE.100) EXECUTE BOOPS

Result: The REMOTE BLOCK named BOOPS will be executed
over and over until N has a value greater than
100. If BOOPS does not assign a value to N which
is greater than 100, the program could loop
indefinitely.

AT END DO : END AT END

This block can be used to specify the processing to be
done when an end-of-file condition is detected during a READ
operation.

General Form

```
                    (READ statement)
                    AT END DO
    range of            .
       the              .    statement(s)
      block             .
                    END AT END
```

Rules

1. The AT END DO statement must immediately follow the
    READ statement to which it applies.

2. If an end-of file condition is not detected during
    the READ operation, control is transferred to the
    statement following the END AT END statement.
    If the end-of-file condition is detected, statements
    following the AT END DO and preceding the END AT
    END statement are executed. Control then
    transfers to the statement following the END AT
    END statement.

3. The READ statement associated with an AT END DO
    block cannot be:
    a) the trailer in a Logical IF statement.
    b) the object statement in a DO-loop.
    c) used with direct access files or core-to-core
        READ operations
    d) used when the "END=" parameter is used in the
        READ statement preceding the AT END DO
        statement.

4. Control may be transferred to a statement outside
    the range from a statement inside the range.
    Control may be transferred to a statement inside

the range from a statement outside the range. When this happens, the END AT END statement is ignored.

5. The AT END DO and END AT END are non-executable statements.

Example

```
READ,N
AT END DO
PRINT,'END-OF-DATA'
END AT END
```

Result: When the end-of-data condition is detected, an appropriate message will be printed before continuing further execution of the program.

INDEX

487

489

491